M. M. BOBER, Professor of Economics at Lawrence College for many years and now retired, was born in Russia in 1891. He received his Ph.D. from Harvard University in 1920 and holds an LL.D. from Grinnell College. He has taught economics at Harvard University, the University of Illinois, and other American universities. During World War II he served with the Office of Price Administration in Washington, D. C. A Fellow of the Royal Economic Society and a past president of the Midwest Economic Association, he has contributed to professional journals and is the author of *Karl Marx's Interpretation of History*, which was awarded the David A. Wells Prize in its first edition, and *Intermediate Price and Income Theory*, published by W. W. Norton & Company, Inc.

# Karl Marx's Interpretation of History

SECOND EDITION, REVISED

BY

M. M. BOBER

The Norton Library

W · W · NORTON & COMPANY · INC ·

NEW YORK

# TO OLGA

## HARVARD ECONOMIC STUDIES

### VOLUME XXXI

AWARDED THE DAVID A. WELLS PRIZE FOR
THE YEAR 1925–26 AND PUBLISHED FROM
THE INCOME OF THE DAVID A. WELLS FUND

THE STUDIES IN THIS SERIES ARE PUBLISHED BY THE DEPART-
MENT OF ECONOMICS OF HARVARD UNIVERSITY, WHICH, HOW-
EVER, ASSUMES NO RESPONSIBILITY FOR THE VIEWS EXPRESSED

PRINTED IN THE UNITED STATES OF AMERICA

1 2 3 4 5 6 7 8 9 0

# CONTENTS

## PART I. THE MATERIAL BASIS OF HISTORY

## PART II. THE HUMAN ELEMENT IN HISTORY

## PART III. THE IDEOLOGICAL ELEMENT IN HISTORY

## PART IV. THE TREND OF HISTORY

## PART V. CRITICAL OBSERVATIONS ON MARX'S THEORY

# PREFACE TO THE FIRST EDITION

In this essay Marx and Engels are treated like one personality. The two friends thought and worked together, and it would be impossible to dissever the thoughts of one from those of the other. Even if the task were possible, it is doubtful whether it would yield fruitful results.

Nor is frequent reference made to whatever ideas on the subject the two writers entertained prior to 1847, for their conception of history began to mature only after that date. My aim in the pages which follow is not to examine the growth of Marx's mind; my object is rather to present a more or less comprehensive analysis of a famous and much-discussed doctrine.

This study has been suggested by Professor A. A. Young, and the work has been carried on under his general guidance. For his kindliness, his inspiration, and his valuable suggestions I am deeply grateful. I am also indebted to Professors F. W. Taussig, A. P. Usher, C. H. McIlwain, and A. M. Schlesinger for advice on various points; and to Professor E. S. Mason and Mr. R. Opie for having read the manuscript and made corrections. All these scholars are at Harvard University.

It is a duty and a pleasure to record that my wife rendered invaluable assistance at each stage of the work, and bore with patience and fortitude the trials of an impecunious aspirant for the doctorate.

# PREFACE TO THE SECOND EDITION

This revision was governed by the desire to expand the exposition of certain topics, to change the emphasis or the attitude in dealing with certain issues, and to consider additional questions — in the perspective of new writings by Marx and Engels that have come to light, of discussions directly bearing on Marx by new personalities, of the newer theories and viewpoints in economics, and of the greater prominence assumed of late by certain problems, e.g., the business cycle and economic calculation. Over two thirds of the former book has been rewritten, and hardly a page of the remainder has escaped revision; new material has been added, ranging from paragraphs to chapters.

I wish to express my gratitude to the Social Science Research Council for a grant-in-aid which lightened the financial problem of spending summers in libraries. For advice and encouragement, I am indebted to Professors W. Leontief, E. S. Mason, and A. P. Usher, of Harvard University, and to my colleague, Professor A. W. McConagha. Thanks are also due to the *American Economic Review* for permission to reprint Chapter XIV.

M. M. Bober

Lawrence College
Appleton, Wisconsin

# PART I
# THE MATERIAL BASIS OF HISTORY

# CHAPTER I

## TECHNIQUE AND THE MODE OF PRODUCTION

Twelve years before the *Origin of Species* was given to the world a book appeared in which was formulated an evolutionary theory of history at once comprehensive and challenging. It claimed to account for the past and it confidently predicted the future; no phase of social life escaped its notice. Several months later the same author, in collaboration with his friend, issued a pamphlet which applied this theory concretely, sketching the transition from feudalism to capitalism, and pointing to the forces which are gradually undermining the existing order and paving the way to socialism. The book was Karl Marx's *Poverty of Philosophy* and the pamphlet was the *Communist Manifesto*. This idea of history and society goes under various names: historical materialism, the materialist conception of history, the economic interpretation of history, economic determinism; there are objections to each name. In general formulation or specific application this theory runs through all the writings of Marx and Engels, beginning especially with their joint work, *Die Deutsche Ideologie*, written in 1845 but published almost ninety years later. This view has exercised a penetrating influence on thinking in every phase of social science and has stirred continual controversy over many decades. In practical politics, it symbolizes to some the hope of human regeneration, and to others the menace of a dark upheaval.

Marx files a protest against the conceptions that the foundations and prime motors of human affairs are to be sought in the ways of Providence, in great personages inspired by mighty ideas at fitful moments, in the metaphysical unfolding of the Absolute Idea of Hegel's imagination, or in the dynastic ambitions and political stratagems of kings and nobles. He urges that human history is not an accidental aggregate of events, not a confused and arbitrary ebb and flow of circumstance, but a unified realm of phenomena marked by regularity of occurrences like the regularity of the occurrences in nature, and following a determined path of evolutionary processes. There are ascertainable objective forces which govern civilization. They are responsible for the relationship of man to man, and they play a major part in shaping man's motives and ideas, in building institutions, and in directing the flow of events to predictable goals. These forces are to be investigated in a scientific manner and are to be derived from history itself.

The foundations of social life, Marx teaches, are not to be found in elevated spheres but in earthly facts. To procure a livelihood, people organize their productive activities in a certain manner. This is the sovereign datum of the community's culture. Production, the way in which society earns its living, is, "in the last instance," the overmastering cause, and all the rest is little more than a consequent: group interests, institutions, ideas, progress. This is what Engels had in mind when he stated in his biographical sketch of Marx: "History for the first time was placed on its real foundation; the obvious fact, hitherto totally neglected, that first of all men must eat, drink, have shelter and clothing, and therefore must work, before they can struggle for supremacy and devote themselves to politics, religion, philosophy, etc., — this obvious fact at last found historical recognition." [1]

It is the object of this book to analyse the main elements of this intricate conception of history. In order to see the element under consideration in perspective and in its relation to the whole, it is desirable to present at the outset a brief summary of the outstanding features of the theory. Marx's often-cited formulation, given in the introduction to his *Critique of Political Economy*, will serve best: [2]

(1) In the social production which men carry on they enter into definite relations that are indispensable and independent of their will; these

[1] Reprinted in W. Liebknecht, *Karl Marx, Biographical Memoirs*, p. 49. When no edition is specified in a footnote, the edition given in the bibliography is assumed.        [2] Pages 11–13.

relations of production correspond to a definite stage of development of their material powers of production.

(2) The sum total of these relations of production constitutes the economic structure of society — the real foundation on which rise legal and political superstructures and to which correspond definite forms of social consciousness.

(3) The mode of production in material life determines (*bedingt*) the general character of the social, political, and spiritual (*geistigen*) processes of life.

(4) It is not the consciousness of men that determines their existence, but, on the contrary, their social existence determines (*bestimmt*) their consciousness.

(5) At a certain stage of their development, the material forces of production in society come in conflict with the existing relations of production, or — what is but a legal expression for the same thing — with the property relations within which they had been at work before.

(6) From forms of development of the forces of production these relations turn into their fetters.

(7) Then comes the period of social revolution.

(8) With the change of the economic foundation the entire immense superstructure is more or less rapidly transformed.

(9) In considering such transformations the distinction should always be made between the material transformation of the economic conditions of production which can be determined with the precision of natural science, and the legal, political, religious, aesthetic, or philosophic — in short, ideological forms in which men become conscious of this conflict and fight it out.

(10) Just as our opinion of an individual is not based on what he thinks of himself, so can we not judge of such a period of transformation by its own consciousness; on the contrary, this consciousness must rather be explained from the contradictions of material life, from the existing conflict between the social forces of production and the relations of production.

(11) No social order ever disappears before all the productive forces, for which there is room in it, have been developed; and new higher relations of production never appear before the material conditions of their existence have matured in the womb of the old society.

(12) Therefore, mankind always takes up only such problems as it can solve; since, looking at the matter more closely, we will always find that the problem itself arises only when the material conditions necessary for its solution already exist or are at least in the process of formation.

(13) In broad outlines we can designate the Asiatic, the ancient, the feudal, and the modern bourgeois methods of production as so many epochs in the progress of the economic formation of society.

(14) The bourgeois relations of production are the last antagonistic form of the social process of production — antagonistic not in the sense of individual antagonism, but of one arising from conditions surrounding the life of individuals in society; at the same time the productive forces

developing in the womb of bourgeois society create the material conditions for the solution of that antagonism.

(15) This social formation constitutes, therefore, the closing chapter of the prehistoric stage of human society.

## TECHNIQUE

The aim of this chapter is to look into the nature of Marx's basis of history; that is, into his idea of production. Here we come upon a situation which will appear more than once as we proceed. Marx was not often in the habit of taking sufficient pains to give clear expression to the concepts he employed and careful elaboration to the theories he advanced. Hence the many obscurities and inconsistencies which perplex the careful reader. There is disagreement among students of Marx on the point under consideration. Some believe that in Marx's view the basis of social organization lies in technological advances; others insist that he has in mind something more comprehensive. What is the evidence?

There are a number of passages in Marx which impute, more or less definitely, considerable importance to the rôle of instruments in social development. In the *Deutsche Ideologie* the statement runs that "to-day bread is produced by steam-mills, earlier by windmills and water-mills, still earlier by handmills; that these different modes of production . . ."[3] It seems that he here identifies production with technique. More telling is the pronouncement: "In acquiring new productive forces men change their mode of production, and in changing their mode of production, their manner of gaining a living, they change all their social relations. The windmill gives you society with the feudal lord; the steam-mill society with the industrial capitalist."[4] In the *Communist Manifesto* (page 16) there is the well-known assertion: "The bourgeoisie cannot exist without constantly revolutionizing the instruments of production, and thereby the relations of production, and with them the whole relations of society."

There are likewise some passages in *Capital*, volume I, which give technology much prominence. Marx says:

[3] Pages 501–502.     [4] *The Poverty of Philosophy*, p. 119.

Relics of by-gone instruments of labor possess the same importance for the investigation of extinct economic forms of society as do fossil bones for the determination of extinct species of animals. It is not the articles made, but how they are made, and by what instruments, that enables us to distinguish different economic epochs. Instruments of labor not only supply a standard of the degree of development to which human labor has attained, but they are also indicators of the social conditions under which that labor is carried on.[5]

Any attempt to whittle down the significance of this utterance should be discouraged by the following declaration which Marx attaches as a footnote to it:

However little our written histories up to this time notice the development of material production, which is the basis of all social life, and therefore of all real history, yet prehistoric times have been classified in accordance with the results, not of so-called historical, but of materialistic investigations. These periods have been divided to correspond with the materials from which their implements and weapons are made, namely, into the stone, the bronze, and the iron ages.

An even more explicit declaration is found in another footnote:

Darwin has interested us in the history of Nature's Technology, that is, in the formation of the organs of plants and animals, which organs serve as instruments of production for sustaining life. Does not the history of the productive organs of man, of organs that are the material basis of all social organization, deserve equal attention? . . . Technology discloses man's mode of dealing with Nature, the process of production by which he sustains his life, and thereby also lays bare the mode of formation of his social relations, and of the mental conceptions that flow from them.[6]

Then there is, in other affirmations in this volume, a seeming willingness to equate technique and the mode of production. Marx observes, for example: "At first capital subordinates labor on the basis of the technical conditions in which it historically finds it. It does not, therefore, change immediately the mode of production." [7] A few pages later he indicates that if surplus-value is to be enlarged, not by prolonging the working day, but by raising the productivity of labor, "the technical and social conditions of the process, and consequently the very mode of production must be revolutionized." [8]

[5] Page 200.
[6] *Capital*, I, 406n.
[7] *Capital*, I, 339.     [8] *Capital*, I, 345. Note that he adds "and social."

It is important to register that the first of these two propositions is in flat contradiction to Marx's view that capitalism does introduce a revolution in the mode of production and that the revolution consists in a change in the organization and in the status of labor. An acute thinker, Marx was a careless writer.[9]

Among the writers on Marx there is an occasional attempt to urge reservations respecting some of the foregoing citations. Consider, for example, the citation from *Poverty of Philosophy*, given above on page 6, ending with the statement, "The windmill gives you society with the feudal lord; the steam-mill society with the industrial capitalist." Dr. Heinrich Cunow, past editor of the orthodox socialist organ *Die Neue Zeit*, contends that Marx merely intended to assert that a stage of economic development at which the windmill flourishes corresponds to feudalism, and a stage of society at which the steam-mill prevails corresponds to capitalism. He argues that Marx did not mean in this pronouncement to maintain that technique determines the form of society, since in the next sentence Marx teaches: "The same men who establish social relations conformably with their material productivity produce also the principles, the ideas, the categories conformably with their social relations."[10] This sentence, Dr. Cunow continues, conveys the idea that the mode of production,[11] and not technique, conditions the changes in social relations.[12]

Dr. Cunow's position will hardly bear examination. Marx says that the windmill "gives you" a feudal society and the steam-mill a capitalist society. The implication is not that a society using a windmill is at a stage corresponding to feudalism, and similarly with the steam-mill and capitalism. "Gives you" implies that the windmill brings about, fosters, induces a feudal order, and likewise with the steam-mill and capital-

---

[9] See below, pp. 15, 57, 60ff., and Chapter IX.

[10] *Poverty of Philosophy*, p. 119.

[11] "Mode of production" is inaccurate. The English translation has "material productivity," and the original, written by Marx in French, has *productivité matérielle*.

[12] *Die Neue Zeit*, XXIX, no. 2 (1911), 856n.

ism. Too, in the sentence preceding the statement about the windmill and steam-mill, Marx affirms clearly that with a change in the productive forces the mode of production changes, and with it the social relations. Then he gives the windmill and the steam-mill as examples of changes in productive forces. In other words, technique is a productive force, and a change in technique entails a change in the social order and its institutions. Technology is obviously assigned here a preëminent rank. The only reservation that can be inserted in this connection is that, as will be seen shortly, technique is not the exclusive productive force in Marx's scheme, and changes in social relations and institutions may be induced by changes in productive forces other than technique.

Despite possible reservations that may be made more or less legitimately at one point or another, the foregoing citations tend to demonstrate, as a whole, that at times Marx puts the accent on technological developments, and those who give this narrow construction to his idea of the motive forces of history are not without substantial support for their case. Wilhelm Liebknecht tells us that Marx noticed an electric locomotive on exhibition on Regent Street in London, and, excited with visions of an impending revolution, he exclaimed: "Now the problem is solved — the consequences are indefinable. In the wake of the economic revolution the political must necessarily follow, for the latter is only the expression of the former." [13]

As far as Engels is concerned, it is probably safe to say that one cannot find in him an outright declaration that instruments constitute the primal force in society. The nearest approach is perhaps found in a letter written by him in 1894. There he states that economic conditions denote the way in which society produces its livelihood and include the technique of production; that this technique determines exchange and distribution as well as the other phases of social life. Economic conditions, he continues, also include the geographical environment. A paragraph or two later he declares: "We regard economic conditions as the factor which ultimately deter-

[13] *Karl Marx, Biographical Memoirs*, p. 57.

mines historical development. But race is itself an economic factor." [14] From these and other opinions in this letter one can see that while he considers technique of outstanding moment, he is eager to include nontechnical elements in the "economic conditions" which, in his view, govern history.

He also seems to attach much prominence to implements when summarizing, in his *Origin of the Family, Private Property, and the State*, Lewis Morgan's stages of primitive society. The middle stage of savagery is introduced, he indicates, by the use of fish and fire, and the higher stage by the invention of the bow and arrow, while the three stages of barbarism are marked, respectively, by the art of pottery, by agriculture and the domestication of animals, and by the knowledge of how to melt iron. [15] However, we must keep in mind that in the preface to this book Engels announces that primitive society is based primarily on the organization of the family and not on the development of production. [16] Too, the various stages of savagery and barbarism are not regarded by Marx and Engels as so many distinct modes of production; on the contrary, all these stages combined represent one productive system, called by them the gens or primitive communism. Engels makes several statements to this effect in this book. [17] As will be seen below in Chapter III, Marx finds four modes of production in history up to his day, and the first mode is the gens (followed by ancient slavery), and not this or that period of savagery or barbarism. Still, as is seen in the following paragraph, the invention of fire is regarded as a phenomenon of surpassing effect.

There is lastly the notable paragraph in *Anti–Dühring*. [18] In

[14] Marx and Engels, *Selected Correspondence*, p. 517.

[15] Pages 27–34.

[16] Pages 8–9.

[17] "A growth of the middle stage and a product of further development during the upper stage of savagery, the gens reached its prime . . . in the lower stage of barbarism" (p. 191).

[18] *Herr Eugen Dühring's Revolution in Science* (*Anti–Dühring*), pp. 125–126. Hereafter this work will be referred to as *Anti–Dühring*. It is important to record that the views expressed in this work are essentially Marx's. Engels acknowledges (see *Anti–Dühring*, p. 13) that the book embodies mainly Marx's ideas, and on this account the manuscript was read to Marx before publication.

common with Marx (and Hegel), Engels voices the idea that the essence of progress in civilization rests on progress in human freedom. At the dawn of history, he says, the invention of fire by friction was at once a powerful aid in freeing man from bondage to nature and a towering achievement which marked the separation of man from the other animals. In modern times, the outstanding freedom-giving agency is typified by the translation of heat into mechanical force, by the steam engine, which, however, despite "the gigantic and liberating revolution" which it wrought in society, is of less penetrating consequences than the invention of fire. Engels concludes the paragraph with the significant observation that "all past history can be characterized as the history of the epoch from the practical discovery of the transformation of mechanical motion into heat [i.e., fire] up to that of the transformation of heat into mechanical motion." While technique is not explicitly represented here as the incubator of institutions and ideas, it evidently appears to Engels' mind as a factor of enormous significance in historical processes.

### The Mode of Production

In the typical formulations of their theory of history, Marx and Engels stress the mode of production or the productive forces as the prime movers. We saw this, for instance, in the long excerpt from Marx's introduction to his *Critique of Political Economy*, given on a previous page. Following is a typical utterance by Engels:

> The materialist conception of history starts from the proposition that the production of the means to support human life and, next to production, the exchange of things produced, is [*sic*] the basis of all social structure . . . From this point of view the final causes of all social changes and political revolutions are to be sought . . . in changes in the modes of production and exchange.[19]

Some writers on Marx take it for granted that the mode of production or the productive forces refer exclusively to technique. Werner Sombart quotes from Marx's preface to the

[19] *Socialism, Utopian and Scientific*, p. 45.

*Critique of Political Economy*, where, as we saw, the emphasis falls on the "mode of production" and "productive forces"
and where there is no mention of instruments and technology,
and declares: "If these sentences are to have, in general, any
meaning, it can only be this: given a definite basis of technical
development — for what 'productive forces' can be if not
technical potentialities is hard to comprehend. This technique
determines the formation of economic life . . . this formation
determines all other culture." [20] Professor Paul Barth declares
that Marx treats all social phenomena as the fruit of technological progress, only instead of technique Marx uses such expressions as "productive forces" or "the mode of production
of material life." To demonstrate that Marx envisages all collective thought, action, and suffering as direct or indirect derivatives from the development of material productive forces, in
themselves primary phenomena without independent causes,
Barth exhibits an array of quotations from Marx, italicizing
such terms as "production," "modes of production and exchange," "material productive forces," and "processes of production of life." He concludes: "There is therefore according
to Marx this causal series: a determined state of technique
— determined industrial form — determined property system . . . — determined political structure — determined social forms of consciousness, which are characterized as religious, artistic, or philosophical." [21]

However, when we do not take for granted the meaning of
the concepts, mode of production and productive forces, but
probe into their nature, we readily perceive that equating
them to technique is an unwarranted step. Let us consider
first the mode of production. Marx analyzes the production
process in the first volume of *Capital.*[22] At all times, he says,
"The elementary factors of the labor-process are 1, the personal activity of man, *i.e.*, work itself; 2, the object (*Gegen-*

[20] *Archiv für Sozialwissenschaft und Sozialpolitik*, XXXIII (1911), 316.
[21] *Philosophie der Geschichte als Soziologie*, pp. 629, 633–635. See also Professor A. H. Hansen, *Quarterly Journal of Economics*, XXXVI (1921–22),
73–76.
[22] Pages 197–206.

*stand*) of the work; and 3, its instrument." [23] This reminds one of the "trinitarian formula," land, labor, and capital; but Marx gives his factors of production somewhat different meanings.

That Marx holds labor a vital factor of production is well known. Nothing has value unless "fermented" with labor. "Bathed in the fire of labor, appropriated as part and parcel of labor's organism," natural resources become use-values or means of further production. The laborer starts and regulates the material reactions between himself and nature. Unlike the spider, he is not governed at his work by instincts, but plans his procedures and foresees the result in his imagination; and he uses reason and cunning in his contest with nature. [24]

Labor directs its energies on the second factor, the object of labor. This denotes natural resources — water, timber, ore. Here also belong raw materials, or resources to which some labor has been applied, like seeds, cotton, yarn; and "auxiliaries," like fuel, or substances used to modify the principal raw material, as chlorine or dyestuffs. The third factor, instruments, stands for the things "which the laborer interposes between himself and the object of his labor . . . He makes use of the mechanical, physical, and chemical properties of some substances in order to make other substances." Here belongs the earth as the instrument in agriculture and as the *locus standi* for other types of production; also domestic animals, workshops, canals, furnaces. Finally, the last two factors, the object of labor and the instruments, constitute what Marx calls the objective factor, the "means of production," handled by the other factor, labor. [25]

It seems that, including as it does "mechanical, physical and chemical properties of some substances," and animals, land, buildings, and roads, the third factor, instruments, is

[23] Page 198. The translation has "subject" for *Gegenstand.* "Object" is better. The French translation has *"l'objet"*: see G. Deville's edition of *Capital* (Paris, 1897), p. 117.

[24] Pages 198, 204.

[25] Pages 199–203, 682.

meant to stand for a broad concept.[26] Point is given to this suggestion by the fact that to Marx technique on the one hand and discoveries, inventions, and science on the other hand are intimately related, especially under capitalism. Already at the dawn of capitalism the rising bourgeoisie appreciated the indispensability of science and joined science in its struggle against the restrictions of the Catholic Church.[27] The alliance has become stronger since the Industrial Revolution. When in England, Marx tells us, the growing market expanded the demand for goods beyond the capacity of hand labor to satisfy it, the need for machinery arose, and the intensive use of science began. The machine, he observes, eliminates the rule of thumb and introduces the use of science at each step. The problems of modern production are problems posed and analyzed by the "whole range of natural sciences," and the mode of production combines the coöperative physical labor with the "universal labor of the human mind," that is, "scientific labor, such as discoveries and inventions." [28]

The fourth factor, the entrepreneur, the "capitalist," Marx is inclined to slight although he is aware of his functions. The complexities of modern production and the massing of aggregations of capital and multitudes of workers within a single enterprise require a presiding mind to organize all the elements involved, to adjust and apportion the multiple tasks, and to secure the coördination and efficiency of a smoothly running business unit. It is also necessary to supervise the daily work of purchasing and selling, of hiring and firing, and of watching the vagaries of the market. All this, Marx says, the capitalist claims to perform, but he is bluffing. It is the hired managers who do all the work while the pretentious capitalist idles away his time.[29]

It appears, then, that the mode of production is not defined by technique alone, but is also a function of the other two fac-

---

[26] ". . . natural wealth in the instruments of labor, such as waterfalls, navigable rivers, wood, metal, coal, etc." (*Capital*, I, 562).

[27] Engels, *Socialism, Utopian and Scientific*, p. xx.

[28] *Poverty of Philosophy*, p. 152; *Capital*, I, 415, 421, 422, 504, 684; III, 124.

[29] See below, p. 281.

tors. There is no want of corroborative assertions, in the pages of *Capital* and elsewhere, that the peculiarities of these two factors contribute to the character and content of production. Thus the grouping of the workers in a scheme of division and coöperation of labor, and the social status of the laborer, may assume a key position in describing and distinguishing a system of production. As will be seen in Chapter III, the skilled laborer is the basis of production in the manufacturing period, or the first phase, of capitalism, lasting two hundred years, before the second phase, or "modern industry," came with the Industrial Revolution.[30] "Even without an alteration in the system of working," says Marx, "the simultaneous employment of a large number of laborers effects a revolution in the material conditions of the labor–process"; [31] and he records that the guilds tried to prevent the guild-master from turning capitalist by restricting the number of workers he could employ: we recall the dialectic principle that "merely quantitative differences beyond a certain point pass into qualitative changes." [32] Of great importance, too, is the status of labor. Discussing the unique features of capitalism, he says: ". . . the form of labor, as wage labor, determines the shape of the entire process and the specific mode of production itself." [33]

The second factor, the object of labor, is of coördinate effect in shaping a productive order. The earth is man's larder and "original tool house." It furnishes the materials that man gradually learns to utilize.[34] Her resources determine the scope and character of the productive process, and her waywardness, like her bounties, stimulates research in technique and science. The lack of rivers with "a good fall on them," coupled with an overabundance of water in other regards, "compelled

[30] *Capital*, I, 403. "In manufacture the revolution in the mode of production begins with the labor-power" (*ibid.*, p. 405). "Manufacturing thoroughly revolutionizes" the "mode of working" by introducing detailed division of labor (*ibid.*, p. 396) ; Marx and Engels, *Selected Correspondence*, p. 142. See below, p. 61.

[31] *Capital*, I, 355.

[32] *Capital*, I, 337–338, 362.

[33] *Capital*, III, 1028. See below, Chapter IX.

[34] *Capital*, I, 199, 204; III, 961.

the Dutch to resort to wind as a motive power." In England, since the wind was "uncontrollable," water power was used, but because this too presented difficulties, there was a stimulus to investigate the "scientific and technical elements" of production.[35] "Different communities," he teaches, "find different means of production [that is, objects of labor and instruments] and different means of subsistence in their natural environment. Hence their mode of production and of living and their products are different." [36] It may be presumed that Marx meant to apply such ideas to backward times and countries, since modern means of communication, international trade, and the progress of science generally render less close the dependence of production on the immediate natural surroundings.

It should be observed, however, that it would be misleading to ascribe to Marx the view that the mode of production is preeminently a function of the three factors, so that as one factor or more is changed the mode of production is automatically recast. Marx was a believer in relativity. A given event, without fitting into a complexity of relevant circumstances, cannot by itself make transformations. Antecedent conditions, a permissive environment, and a context of evolutionary ripeness are all imperative. Thus division of labor is the outstanding characteristic of the mode of production in the early phase of capitalism, but division of labor could not have been established in the first place had it not been for a chain of historical development which led to the emergence of capitalism.[37] The part which nature plays is equally contingent upon circumstances. It is true that if nature is niggardly and does not allow the laborer a degree of productiveness which will leave a surplus above his needs, there can be no such phenomenon as surplus-labor, "and therefore no capitalists, no slave-owners, no feudal lords, in one word, no class of large proprietors. Thus we may say that surplus-value rests on a natural basis." Not at all. Nature can furnish the "possibility, never the

---

[35] *Capital*, I, 409n., 411–412.
[36] *Capital*, I, 386.
[37] See below, pp. 57ff.

reality, of surplus-labor, nor, consequently, of surplus-value and a surplus product." Capital and its attending human relations, symbolized by surplus-value, is the fruit of a complex evolution, and "the productiveness of labor that serves as its foundation and starting point is a gift, not of nature, but of a history embracing thousands of centuries." [38]

Similarly, a new technique cannot intrude into a society and refashion its productive organization as a matter of course. The presence of favorable conditions and preparatory steps is indispensable. "The inventions," Marx tells us, "of Vaucanson, Arkwright, Watt, and others were, however, practicable only because those inventors found, ready to hand, a considerable number of skilled mechanical workmen, placed at their disposal by the manufacturing period." [39] A machine is not intrinsically capital, regardless of the social milieu. "A negro is a negro. In certain conditions he is transformed into a slave. A spinning jenny is a machine for spinning cotton. Only under certain circumstances does it become capital. Outside these circumstances it is no more capital than gold is intrinsically money, or sugar is the price of sugar." [40] Nor does the use of machinery and other modern techniques certify the presence of the capitalist mode of production. If these elements of production are owned by the workers collectively, we have a communist mode of production; if by the exploiters of labor, a capitalist mode: the distinction is determined, among other things, by the different status of labor in these two cases. In the union of labor with the means of production for the purpose of providing the necessities of life, the status of labor, Marx tells us, plays a commanding part in distinguishing the productive system.[41]

## PRODUCTIVE FORCES

The mode of production and the productive forces are the same thing viewed in different lights. The mode of produc-

[38] *Capital*, I, 561–564.
[39] *Capital*, I, 417.
[40] *Wage–Labor and Capital*, p. 28.  Cf. *Capital*, III, 948.
[41] *Capital*, II, 44.  Cf. *ibid.*, I, 839–840, III, 207.

tion is the collective term embracing the elements engaged in the productive process, and productive forces refer specifically to these elements. The productive forces, the "forces of production," the "productive powers," give flesh, blood, and physiognomy to a system of production. If the prevailing productive forces are elementary, the form of production is elementary. Discussing surplus-labor under serfdom, Marx observes that, since "it rests upon the imperfect development of all productive powers of society," it offers less surplus-labor "than under developed modes of production." [42] As the productive forces change in character a new organization of production develops, and with it a new social order. This is how capitalism came, and this is how it will go. The scientific analysis of capitalism, Marx teaches, demonstrates that "it, like any other definite mode of production, is conditioned . . . upon the historically developed form of the forces of production." [43] The development of the productive forces "is the historical task and privilege of capital. It is precisely in this way that it unconsciously creates the material requirements of a higher mode of production." In this task, to which many agencies contribute, credit is an accelerating factor and competition is an active force.[44]

It is not difficult to trace what, specifically, the productive forces are. Criticizing Proudhon, Marx comments: "In so far as Prometheus only informs us of the division of labor, the application of machinery, the exploitation of natural forces and scientific power, multiplying the productive forces of men. . . ." [45] The *Communist Manifesto* gives a more extended enumeration:

The bourgeoisie, during its rule of scarce one hundred years, has created more massive and more colossal productive forces than have all preceding

---

[42] *Capital*, III, 921–922.      [43] *Capital*, III, 1023.
[44] *Capital*, III, 304, 522; *Poverty of Philosophy*, pp. 163–164. Writers on Marx recognize the place of productive forces in his scheme. P. Barth gives to his discussion of Marx's interpretation of history the title: "Die Geschichte gelenkt durch die Produktionskräfte" (*Philosophie der Geschichte als Soziologie*, p. 627). M. I. Tugan-Baranowsky, in considering Marx's basis of history, limits his analysis to the productive forces. See his *Theoretische Grundlagen des Marxismus*.      [45] *Poverty of Philosophy*, p. 107.

generations together. Subjection of Nature's forces to man, machinery, application of chemistry to industry and agriculture, steam navigation, railways, electric telegraphs, clearing of whole continents for cultivation, canalization of rivers, whole populations conjured out of the ground — what earlier century had even a presentiment that such productive forces slumbered in the lap of social labor? [46]

If we classify these productive forces, we come once more on the broader conception of the three factors of production and not merely on technique. There are not a few scattered utterances corroborating this theme. Elaborating on the condition of the laborer under capitalism, Marx declares: "His existence has no other value than that of a simple productive force, and the capitalist treats him accordingly." [47] Similarly with natural resources and instruments, termed collectively means of production. Marx indicates that one of the main attributes of capitalist production is "concentration of means of production in a few hands, whereby they cease to appear as the property of the immediate laborers and transform themselves into social powers of production." [48] And Engels observes: "But the bourgeoisie . . . could not transform these puny means of production into mighty productive forces." [49] Likewise with the third factor, technique, and its close associate, science. "Machinery is only a productive force," says Marx.[50] Discussing the alienation of intelligence from the laborer as a requirement in the work-process, he states: "It is completed in modern industry, which makes science a productive force distinct from labor and presses it into the service of capital." [51]

The Russian economist Tugan-Baranowsky, who was probably the first to emphasize the place of productive forces in Marx's theory and to attempt the analysis of their nature, is of the opinion that Marx could have meant to designate by

---

[46] Page 18. For other enumerations, see, e.g., Marx, *Capital*, I, 839; *Theorien über den Mehrwert*, II, No. 2, 301, 310.
[47] *Free Trade*, reprinted as an appendix to *Poverty of Philosophy*, p. 224.
[48] *Capital*, III, 312.
[49] *Socialism, Utopian and Scientific*, pp. 49, 67.
[50] *Poverty of Philosophy*, p. 145.
[51] *Capital*, I, 397.

this term only material agencies participating in the processes of production, beginning with the raw materials from the earth and ending with the finished product. He insists that science and race should not be included, although he is well aware that both Marx and Engels ranked them, particularly science, as of commanding influence in production.[52] He argues that science is a spiritual, cultural force and, according to Marx, is not independent but, like every other form of consciousness, is derivative from the economic situation. If science is to be regarded as a productive force, the other ideologies, like philosophy, religion, and law, with equal logic may be included also. Likewise with race, he argues. According to the materialistic interpretation of history, race is the product of economic circumstances and cannot accordingly be ranked among the productive forces. To incorporate science and race is to render the materialistic interpretation neither monistic nor materialistic, and to obliterate any distinction between Marx's conception of history and the idealistic pronouncements of his predecessors and contemporaries which he vehemently repudiates.[53]

Tugan's reasoning seems valid, but not his conclusion. He who propounds a materialistic philosophy of history cannot include science as a primary factor; he must limit himself to material agents and consider other agents as secondary and derivative. But one must question Tugan's conclusion that, to give consistency to Marx, we ought to ignore what Marx says about science and conclude that by productive forces he must have meant only material elements of production. Marx and Engels treat science as a productive force, and stress times without number the indissoluble connection between technique and technical development on the one hand and science and scientific progress on the other. To Marx mod-

---

[52] Tugan is hardly correct in holding that Marx and Engels include race as a factor of production. They accord to racial peculiarities only a subordinate place in production or in history generally. See Marx, *Capital*, I, 562, III, 919, 922; and Marx and Engels, *Selected Correspondence*, p. 517.

[53] M. I. Tugan–Baranowsky, *Theoretische Grundlagen des Marxismus*, pp. 4ff.

ern industry is scientific industry. With him science plays an enormous part in the exploitation of labor, in the accumulation of capital, in the changes of the composition of the constant and variable components of capital, and in the concentration of industry — circumstances which, according to his theory, exercise a disruptive effect on capitalism and lead it to final destruction. Kautsky interprets Marx well when he says:

> The development of natural science goes hand in hand with the development of technique, in the widest sense of the term. By the technical development of a given period we ought not to understand merely instruments and machines. Modern methods of chemical research and modern mathematics form integral parts of the existing technique. Just try to build a steamship or a railroad bridge without mathematics! Without present-day mathematics capitalist society would be impossible. The present state of mathematics belongs to the economic conditions of existing society as much as the present state of machine technique or of world commerce. They are all most intimately connected with one another.[54]

It is better for an interpreter of Marx and Engels to present the facts as he finds them and not to undertake to adjust their ideas to a standard of consistency and reasonableness. Marx intends to offer a materialistic conception of history. Yet he frequently stresses the power of science as a component of modern technique and production. The incorporation of science in the foundation of his theory is no more defensible than the inclusion of all other nonmaterial phenomena. But for this inadequacy Marx is responsible, and the interpreter is to point out the weakness, but he is not to remove it. A measure of adjusting is at times unavoidable, for Marx is not noted for clarity and consistency; but reiterated statements of his cannot be ignored. Once the interpreter assumes the task of remodeling Marx's ideas, he will hardly know where to stop. Tugan maintains that Marx *must* have meant by productive forces only material factors involved in production. Would Tugan call division of labor, coöperation of labor, the skills of labor, the organization of labor in general, and the status of labor, material factors? Yet in Marx's scheme it is precisely these factors that signal the arrival of capitalism and characterize the system of production during the first capitalistic phase — as Tugan himself points out when he takes a stand against the view which attributes to Marx a technological theory of history.[55]

## ECONOMIC STAGES

There is a third source which may throw light on our problem. From the writings of Marx and Engels one can construct an account of the succession of productive orders which, in their view, have prevailed since the dawn of history to the present day. Their treatment of the circumstances responsible for the transformation of one system of production into another may provide one more indication of what these two writers have in mind when they point to production as the keystone of social organization and social change.

An outline of this account is given below, in Chapter III; we may briefly summarize here, by way of anticipation, the pertinent inferences that can be drawn from it. Only in one case is the discovery of a new way of producing articles made to explain, and then only partially, the transition from one form of production to another. The reference is to the disintegration of primitive communism and the introduction of the slave order in classical antiquity. From that time on until today productive orders appear to have succeeded one another without the intervention of a new technique as the governing cause. Nowhere, so far as I know, do Marx and Engels propound the theory that the feudal productive order differed from its predecessor, the slave system, by virtue of divergent technical procedures in making goods. Likewise, feudalism went under and capitalist production appeared by a chain of developments in which technique played no part. Only after over two hundred years of capitalism, when its "second phase" arrived in the eighteenth century, machinery began to play an overwhelming rôle, without, however, introducing a new historical mode of production.

[55] *Theoretische Grundlagen des Marxismus*, pp. 8–9.

It will be no different with the coming of socialism, which is the early phase of communism, according to Marx. The *Communist Manifesto* (pages 41–42) enumerates the measures which are "unavoidable as a means of entirely revolutionizing the mode of production." Ten measures are listed, but there is no mention of technique; the emphasis falls on changes in the status of labor, in the credit system, and in the distribution of wealth. Engels teaches that under socialism "The old mode of production must therefore be revolutionized from top to bottom, and in particular the former division of labor must disappear." In his elaboration of this theme, he merely expounds his views of a new division of labor.[56] The battle cry of socialism is not new instruments of production, but the abolition of private property and a new status for the laborer. Far from abandoning capitalist techniques, the boast of socialism is the intended full utilization of all the productive forces potential under capitalism. In *Klassenkämpfe in Frankreich* Marx gives what Engels calls, in the preface to this work, the formula for the "economic reorganization" under socialism. The "formula" reads: ". . . appropriation of the means of production, their subjection to the associated working class, therefore the abrogation of wage-labor, of capital, and of their reciprocal relations."[57] The call is once more for a change in the position of the laborer.

## CONCLUSION

Such is the evidence. On the one hand, certain statements by Marx and Engels and to some extent their discussion of the transition from the gens order to ancient slavery indicate that they consider technology of predominant influence in social organization. On the other hand, an examination of their concepts of production and productive forces, as well as a study

[56] *Anti–Dühring*, pp. 320–325. There are other declarations that socialism will introduce a revolutionized form of production, but nowhere is there mention of mechanical changes. E.g., Marx, *Capital*, III, 713; Engels, *Feuerbach*, p. 112; *Anti–Dühring*, pp. 166, 174.

[57] Pages 10, 51. Cf. Engels, *Socialism, Utopian and Scientific*, pp. 72, 86; *Anti–Dühring*, p. 167.

of their account of the evolution of productive systems, place the root causes of history in a larger light. Of these two views which one is to be chosen?

It would be better to keep both in mind. There is no reason to ignore what Marx and his colleague state repeatedly and clearly. But if a choice has to be made, it seems that the evidence and the spirit of their writings combine to justify a preference for the broader interpretation. It seems that when they advance the mode of production as the controlling factor in history, "in the last instance," they refer to an organic whole uniquely characterized by the following components: (1) the organization of labor in a scheme of division and coöperation, the skills of labor, and the status of labor in the social context with respect to degrees of freedom or servitude; (2) the geographical environment and the knowledge of the use of resources and materials; and (3) technical means and processes and the state of science generally. It is the manner of making a living, so conceived, that determines the class divisions of society and the corollary dominant interests which play an overshadowing part in the building of institutions and ideas, in arousing conflicts, and in giving coherence to the flow of events.

That this theory is open to objections will be indicated in future chapters. Here, in pursuit of the theme of this chapter, two concluding remarks are pertinent. First, in prehistoric epochs the foundations of group living lie not so much in the development of production as in the organization of the family. In the *Deutsche Ideologie* (page 18), Marx and Engels record that before the time arrives when increasing needs create new social relations, the family is important in "historical development," but when needs multiply the family surrenders its place to production in historical significance. This idea is repeated by Engels in the preface to his *Origin of the Family* (pages 9–10).

Second, Marx and Engels are in the habit of according conspicuous prominence to exchange (*Verkehr*) alongside production. Their treatment of exchange appears in an unfinished essay by Marx and in scattered statements. The essay, obscure in presentation but rich in suggestiveness, deals with general observations on economics, its content and its methodology, and part of it touches on the connections between production on the one hand and consumption, distribution, and exchange on the other.[58] In as much as this part throws light on the overtones of production and its association with closely related aspects, it may be of interest to sketch briefly the thread of the argument instead of excising the portion which deals directly with exchange.

He begins with the assertion that in some respects there is an interaction between production and consumption. Wants are the impulse behind production, while production, providing the market with multifarious articles, develops the tastes and the demands of the consumers.[59] After discussing a few similar points, he hastens, however, to deny consumption any influence on production, and declares that "it is the simplest matter with a Hegelian to treat production and consumption as identical," but in reality they appear as one process "in which production forms the actual starting-point and is, therefore, the predominating factor. Consumption, as a natural necessity, as a want, constitutes an internal factor of productive activity, but the latter is the starting-point of realization and, therefore, its predominating factor. . . . Consumption thus appears as a factor of production." [60]

In much the same manner distribution is treated as a creature of production. First, only the fruits of production can be distributed. Second, a definite organization of production, a definite pattern of grouping the participating agencies in the productive enterprise, implicitly define the unique framework for the distribution of the resulting product.[61] In his criticism of the Gotha program he charges it with the error of emphasiz-

---

[58] Reprinted as an appendix to *Critique of Political Economy*, pp. 265–312
[59] *Critique of Political Economy*, p. 280.
[60] *Critique of Political Economy*, pp. 282–283.
[61] *Critique of Political Economy*, p. 286.

ing distribution: "The distribution of the means of consumption at any period," he teaches, "is merely the consequence of
the distribution of the conditions of production themselves." [62]
It may appear, he continues in the essay, that in some instances
a scheme of distribution precedes and therefore determines
production. A conquering invader may turn the vanquished
into slaves and establish a mode of production based on slavery. But, says Marx, this merely implies that the invaders do
not introduce a new type of distribution but rather a new order
of production. Moreover, the mode of production in vogue with
the conquerors must have been of a character to which slave
labor is proper; else the innovation will be spurious and will
not endure.

Similarly a revolution may break up large estates into small
parcels, or a law may introduce small holdings, and by the
redistribution of wealth impose a new organization of production. But, Marx contends, the scheme will be of no avail, and
the concentration of land holdings will soon reëstablish itself,
unless indeed the parceling of land is compatible with the existing productive system. In the previous case as well as in this
one, we do not witness a new distribution of wealth instituting
new modes of production, but rather a new structure of production, with a new alignment of the agents of the productive
processes, necessitating corresponding changes in distribution.[63] Likewise, while Marx believes that as a precondition
of capitalist production there had to take place an expropriation of laborers on the one hand and a concentration of wealth
on the other, he maintains in the third volume of *Capital* (pages
1024ff.) that this is not distribution in the same sense in which
he commonly employs the term, and he proceeds to elaborate
the point on a few nebulous pages there.

The treatment of exchange in the essay is no different, at
first. Exchange in the narrow or broad sense, that is, between
producers within a city, between town and country, or between
distant commercial markets, has no transforming reaction on

[62] *Critique of the Gotha Programme*, p. 32.
[63] *Critique of Political Economy*, pp. 287–289.

production. Exchange is governed by production, "and is itself a species of productive activity. . . . Exchange thus appears in all its aspects to be directly included in or determined by production." [64]

These views are presented in a halting and somewhat contradictory manner. We are dealing with a tentative draft, posthumously published, and not with a polished essay. However, Marx seems to speak his mind definitely when he summarizes the argument. His tone changes, and he clearly invests exchange, distribution, and consumption with a measure of effectiveness. He concludes on a firm note:

> The result we arrive at is not that production, distribution, exchange, and consumption are identical, but that they are all members of one entity, different sides of one unit. Production predominates . . . over the other elements . . . Of course production . . . is in its turn influenced by the other elements; for example, with the expansion of the market — that is of the sphere of exchange — production grows in volume and is subdivided to a greater extent. With a change in distribution, production undergoes a change; as, for example, in the case of concentration of capital . . . [65] Finally, the demands of consumption also influence production. A mutual interaction takes place between the various elements. Such is the case with every organic body.[66]

Whatever the status of exchange in this essay, in his writings in general he invariably gives exchange a commanding position. Exchange, commerce, the market, exercise an enormous influence on division of labor, act as an accelerating impulse in the dissolution of old systems of production, and bear a considerable degree of responsibility even in the rise of capitalism, in its manufacturing and industrial phases alike.[67] In 1850 he writes that the bourgeois class will attain its fullest power only in the country which had conquered for its industry a world market, since the national boundaries are insufficient to permit the complete course of capitalist development.[68] In their joint works the two friends couple exchange with production when

---

[64] *Critique of Political Economy*, pp. 290–291.
[65] Cf. Engels, *Anti–Dühring*, p. 165.
[66] *Critique of Political Economy*, pp. 291–292.
[67] *Poverty of Philosophy*, p. 139; *Capital*, I, 388; III, 389–391.
[68] *Klassenkämpfe in Frankreich*, pp. 31–32.

pointing to the factor of overshadowing power in social affairs.[69]
In the condensed formulations of his, and his colleague's, conception of history, Engels seldom fails to cite exchange next to production.[70]

[69] *Die Deutsche Ideologie*, pp. 15, 17, 19, 27; *Communist Manifesto*, p. 14 and *passim*.

[70] *Anti-Dühring*, p. 32; *Socialism, Utopian and Scientific*, pp. xviii, 41, 45; preface of 1888 to *Communist Manifesto*.

# CHAPTER II

## THE DIALECTIC

SINCE the unfolding of the many phases of civilization is vitally correlated with changes in the modes of production, it is important to examine Marx's ideas on the nature of economic evolution. This question is connected with Marx's theory of the dialectic development of reality, in nature and society. The subject matter of this chapter and Chapter VI constitutes what Marxians call dialectic materialism. This chapter deals with Marx's idea of dynamics, and Chapter VI with his theory of cognition, or the acquisition of ideas.

The conception of the dialectic Marx borrows from Hegel, his master. But there is a difference between the teacher and the pupil. To Hegel, the total of ultimate reality in the universe is embodied in the Absolute Idea, in the Universal Reason, growing and unfolding by a process of its own; our minds and ideas are alike participants in the Idea, and they alone represent reality, in so far as reality is accessible to us at all. Sticks and stones are real only by virtue of our ideas of them. Reality proceeds from, and is identical with, the Idea.[1]

Not so with Marx and Engels. To them reality equals the total of objects and facts, existing independently of minds and ideas, regardless of whether anybody is ever present to perceive them or not, and regardless of whether such a thing as mind ever existed or not. Reality is the realm of phenomena and objects which we can reach with our senses or instruments.[2] With Hegel the dialectic movement is achieved by the Idea; with our two writers, by the real phenomena. To Marx and his friend ideas are merely reflections of the real world. As

[1] Engels, *Feuerbach*, p. 94; *Anti-Dühring*, p. 30; *Dialectics of Nature*, p. 26. But see B. Croce, *Historical Materialism*, pp. 6–7.
[2] Cf. Marx, Introduction to *Critique of Political Economy*, p. 12; Marx and Engels, *Deutsche Ideologie*, p. 33.

Marx teaches, his "dialectic method is not only different from the Hegelian, but is its direct opposite. . . . With him it is standing on its head. It must be turned right side up again, if you would discover the rational kernel within the physical shell." [3]

FLUX

The philosophy of the dialectic is not without intricacy and unintelligibility, but only some of the elementary aspects will be outlined here, as Marx and Engels see them. The dialectic method seeks to ascertain the laws governing phenomena and their evolution; it attempts to prove the necessity of a given social order as well as the necessity of its successor; it treats social movements "as a process of natural history," not only independent of human will but determining human will; it stresses material facts as prior and ideas as derivative; it holds that every epoch is subject to its own laws; and in exploring a social order it is essentially "critical and revolutionary." [4] The dialectic approach regards facts as interrelated and in motion. Phenomena are not conceived as finished entities, suddenly sprung into existence, isolated and lasting, with clearly demarked attributes, and set in a context of mechanical and linear cause and effect relations. Things are in a flux, in an agitation of becoming and changing, are parts of a larger picture, and are in endless interlacings, so that demarcations and classes, divisions and contrasts, while in evidence, are yet relative and blurred. Opposites are as inseparable as they are antagonistic; and in a larger or in a different framework, cause and effect may exchange places. [5]

These principles, Marx and Engels claim, find exemplification in the physical, biological, and social worlds. Kant abol-

[3] *Capital*, I, 25; Engels, *Feuerbach*, p. 95. But see Croce, *Historical Materialism*, p. 6.

[4] Marx, *Capital*, 22–26.

[5] *Anti-Dühring*, pp. 17–19, 26–28; Engels, *Dialectics of Nature*, pp. 38–39, 173, 205–208. Cf. *Der Briefwechsel zwischen Friedrich Engels und Karl Marx*, IV, 344. The treatment of the dialectic is found mainly in *Anti-Dühring* and *Dialectics of Nature*, both by Engels. As was already indicated, the ideas in *Anti-Dühring* are largely Marx's; *Dialectics of Nature* is an elaboration.

ished the idea of a stable solar system and introduced the
hypothesis that the earth and other planets originated gradually, by the "historical process," from a rotating mass of
nebulae. This theory was subsequently formulated mathemat-
ically by Laplace; still later the spectroscope disclosed the
presence in space of glowing masses of gas in different stages
of condensation.[6] Gases can be liquefied, and bodies can be
put in positions in which liquid and gas stages can scarcely be
differentiated. Energy can be translated into kinetic energy,
into electricity, heat, light, and chemical energy, and so "the
last vestige of a creator external to the world is obliterated."[7]

In the biological world it is similarly hard to maintain
sharply defined frontiers inasmuch as intermediate specimens
are periodically discovered. The individuality of the animal is
now difficult to delineate because of the discovery of the
amoeba in the blood corpuscles of higher animals.[8] At times
it is no easy matter to decide whether an animal is alive or
not, and it is equally difficult to tell the precise moment when
death sets in, because "physiology has established that death
is not a sudden, instantaneous event, but a very protracted
process."[9]

What is true of nature "is true also of the history of society
in all its branches," and of all sciences dealing with things
human and divine.[10] Marx teaches: "There is a continual
movement of growth in productive forces, of destruction in the
social relations, of formation in ideas; there is nothing immutable but the abstraction of the movement — *mors immor-
talis*."[11] It is for this reason, explains Engels, that Marx never
offers fixed and universally applicable definitions in *Capital*.
Marx, he says, viewed phenomena and their mutual interrelations as incessantly changing, and the mental images of them,

[6] *Anti-Dühring*, p. 29; *Dialectics of Nature*, pp. 8–9.
[7] *Anti-Dühring*, pp. 17–19; *Feuerbach*, p. 99; *Dialectics of Nature*, pp. 15, 46, 177.
[8] *Anti-Dühring*, p. 18; *Dialectics of Nature*, p. 12.
[9] *Anti-Dühring*, p. 28.
[10] Engels, *Feuerbach*, p. 102.
[11] *Poverty of Philosophy*, p. 119. Cf. *Capital*, I, 16.

the ideas concerning them, as correspondingly fluid; therefore, they could not be "sealed up in rigid definitions." [12]

## THE CORE OF THE DIALECTIC

The core of the dialectic lies in the conception of the process by which change takes place. The conception embraces the celebrated triad of thesis, antithesis, and synthesis (or the formula of affirmation, negation, and negation of negation), and the law of the transformation of quantity into quality, both borrowed from Hegel.[13] Implicit in all phenomena, natural or social, and accordingly in all ideas, is the indwelling power of motion by contradictions and of development to higher stages by the struggle of opposites. Contradiction is the mother of change; and the dialectic is the cult of contradiction. This propensity for self-improvement, especially when applied to nature — and it is so applied by Marx and Engels — seems to be charged with animism.[14]

As to the triad. A given object, phenomenon, or idea is a complex of opposite elements, and is impregnated with an inner hostility against itself. Herein lies the source of its internal dynamics. The inherent contradictions create the motion and the development, and change is thus auto-dynamic and dialectical and not mechanical; that is, change is not wrought by an impulse from without. This idea is stamped by Marxians as the law of the union of opposites. It relates to the thesis and antithesis. What generates the contradiction is the thesis; what represents the contradiction is the antithesis.

Examples are provided in *Anti-Dühring*. Motion is a contradiction, implying as it does that a body is "at one and the same moment . . . in one place and in another place." Life means that the living creature is at one time itself and some-

---

[12] *Capital*, III, Engels' preface, p. 24.

[13] Marx, *Poverty of Philosophy*, pp. 114–118; *Capital*, I, 338. In Hegel the dialectic is presented under three laws: the law of the transformation of quantity into quality, the law of the union of opposites, and the law of the negation of the negation. While Marx and Engels were familiar with this (see, e.g., Engels, *Dialectics of Nature*, p. 26), their discussions of the dialectic were not presented in this pattern. I follow their pattern and not Hegel's.

[14] See below, p. 44.

thing different, and "as soon as the contradiction ceases, life too comes to an end." In general, a thing is itself and not itself, because it is interpenetrated with its opposite and is changing at each moment, so that instead of saying "it is" it is more valid to say "it is becoming." In its treatment of variable magnitudes mathematics too is immersed in dialectics, and "it was a dialectical philosopher, Descartes, who first introduced this advance in mathematics." It is a contradiction that a root of a quantity should be a power of it; yet $\sqrt{a}=a^{\frac{1}{2}}$. Differential calculus "assumes that under certain circumstances straight lines and curves are nevertheless identical." [15]

The synthesis represents the negation of the negation, or the reconstitution of aspects of the thesis with aspects of the antithesis into a higher composite. A grain of barley falls to the ground and begins to germinate. The grain disappears, it is negated; but in its place appears a plant, the negation of the grain. This plant grows, ripens, and dies. By virtue of this negation of the negation a progeny of 10, 20, or 30 grains of barley are left where one grain was before. This is as it should be, for the new synthesis is always of a higher order than the old thesis. Similarly, the insects leave the egg through a negation of the egg; at maturity they copulate, die after copulation, but leave behind them more eggs. All geology is a series of negated negations, inasmuch as the old layers are destroyed to become the foundations for new layers.[16]

In mathematics, negate quantity $a$, and we get $-a$; negate this negation, i.e., multiply it by itself, and the result is $a^2$: behold the original quantity but in a higher synthesis. So thoroughly is the negation negated in $a^2$, says Engels, that it always has two roots, $a$ and $-a$. Differentiate $x$ and $y$ functionally related. We get $\dfrac{dx}{dy}=\dfrac{o}{o}$ [?]; that is, $x$ and $y$ have vanished, continues Engels, have been negated. Proceed further, treating $dx$ and $dy$ as quantities "subject to certain

[15] Engels, *Anti–Dühring*, pp. 132–134; *Dialectics of Nature*, pp. 162–164, 198–200.
[16] *Anti–Dühring*, pp. 148–150.

exceptional laws," and negate the negation, or integrate. We have then $\int dx = x$ and $\int dy = y$ [?]. We arrive at no synthesis of a higher level, but Engels is not dismayed. He consoles himself saying: "But by using this method I have solved the problem on which ordinary geometry and algebra might perhaps have broken their teeth in vain." As a matter of fact, the mathematics of variable quantities "is in essence nothing other than the application of dialectics to mathematical relations." [17]

It may be objected, Engels observes, that we also negate a grain when we grind it, and an insect when we crush it. But this objection, he affirms, is worthy only of the metaphysical manner of thinking. Dialectically speaking, to negate does not mean to destroy; we must "so construct the first negation" as to make a second negation possible, and the procedure will vary with the requirements of the case. If Dühring desires to expel the dialectic from the processes of thought he will have to invent, Engels threatens, a system of mathematics in which $-a$ multiplied by itself does not give $a^2$, and in which differential and integral calculus is forbidden by law.[18]

A prominent component of the dialectic is Hegel's law of the transformation of quantity into quality. When, by negation or by negation of negation, or by some other process, quantitative changes of a given attribute continue to accumulate, a critical point is reached at which there emerges, by a sudden leap, a different attribute, a qualitative change. Marx indicates that the possession of money barely sufficient to hire a few laborers does not make one a capitalist. Only when the possession reaches a certain larger magnitude does the employer turn capitalist; and the decisive minimum varies with the state of the arts and the branch of industry.[19] As the temperature of water rises or falls a point is reached at which the water suddenly becomes steam or ice. Both Marx and Engels cite the molecular theory of modern chemistry as resting on this law:

[17] *Anti–Dühring*, pp. 147–148, 150–151.
[18] *Anti–Dühring*, pp. 155–156.
[19] *Capital*, I, 336–338.

different bodies are obtained with the progressive addition of certain molecules.[20] Indeed, physical and chemical transformations are "leaps," including the chemical leap which signaled the origin of life, "the transition from ordinary chemical action to the chemistry of albumen which we call life."[21]

The dialectic is evidently considered by our two friends a sufficient theory of evolution in animate or inanimate nature and in society. Phenomena persist in a given state, as far as their large outlines are concerned, until contradictions accumulate. These contradictions provide the inner principle of progressive self-development, without benefit of an outside force. In inanimate nature, it seems, this universal attribute of indwelling contradictions sprouts by a sort of cosmic fiat. In the animal and plant kingdoms the contradictions may be bred by a changing environment or by a mutation within the plant or animal. In society, human beings in a given economic and social setting act in such a manner that strains and stresses, dissatisfaction and suffering develop in cumulative proportions. Then comes the negation or the negation of negation. There is an accumulation of quantitative changes which at a certain climactic stage emerge as new forms and crystallize new qualities. The negation of negation is impersonal where nature, animate or inanimate, is concerned. But in social life it expresses human conservatism and progressivism, the antagonistic alignment of interests and classes, clashes and revolutions, all motivated and fostered by the mode of production. In society, each aspect of the evolutionary process is saturated with production, ideas, purposes, and activity; only production is the alma mater of all the rest. More will be said on this in the pages to follow.

Marx and Engels are familiar with Darwin's theory of evolution, and they mention him with high praise, something uncommon in these two critical and hard-bitten intellectuals. For

---

[20] *Capital*, I, 338n.; Engels, *Anti-Dühring*, pp. 139–141; Engels, letter to Marx in 1858, in *Marx-Engels, Historisch-kritische Gesamtausgabe*, Part III, vol. 2, pp. 326–327. Hereafter this work will be referred to briefly as *Gesamtausgabe*.

[21] Engels, *Anti-Dühring*, pp. 75, 82; *Dialectics of Nature*, pp. 27ff.

his great contribution they refer to England as a "classical country." They expound his theories, briefly but repeatedly, and they warmly defend him against Dühring. But they do not demonstrate how Darwin can be brought into explicit accord with the dialectic. They take it for granted that the two theories are of one cloth and that Darwin's procedures and conceptions are understandable applications of the dialectic.[22] The struggle for existence is equated with the dialectic "contradiction." [23] In a letter to Engels Marx writes about *The Origin of Species* as "the book which contains the basis in natural history for our view," and in a letter to Lassalle he asserts that "Darwin's book is very important and serves me as a basis in natural science for the class struggle in history." [24] He likens division of labor and competition to the war of all against all in the animal kingdom, which "more or less preserves the conditions of existence of every species." [25]

But their approval of Darwin is not unalloyed. Darwin bit of the Malthusian apple, and Marx and Engels dislike "parson" Malthus and his ideas. Darwin acknowledges that he found stimulus to his studies of the struggle for existence in Malthus' theory of population. He regarded Malthus' theory a valid one for society, and he generalized it for the plant and animal world. Marx and Engels perceive two weaknesses in Darwin. First, they deprecate the transfer, or retransfer, of the theory from nature and the jungle to the affairs of society. Natural history, Engels objects, and society are things apart. Animals, he says, collect such food as they find, while man produces his food, provides for himself what nature does not provide, and develops methods of production. Moreover, under capitalism, he continues, it is not scarcity of food that creates difficulties, but, on the contrary, it is the overabundance of goods that eventuates in periodic crises.[26] The two writers are vehemently opposed to giving the sanction of a law of

[22] Engels, *Anti-Dühring*, pp. 76–83.

[23] *Anti-Dühring*, p. 78.

[24] Marx and Engels, *Selected Correspondence*, pp. 126, 125.

[25] *Capital*, I, 391.

[26] *Dialectics of Nature*, pp. 208–209.

nature to capitalist individualism, competition, and extravagant pursuit of material interests. The successive modes of production, the transformations of social structures, and the class struggles as the motors of history are not to be viewed without specific probing into their unique content, and are not to be treated as mere exemplifications of the natural law of variation and selection compounded with Malthusianism.[27]

The point is that to Marx and Engels the goal of human history and the essence of human destiny rise above the ways of the animal (even if these ways are so amply exemplified in capitalist society) and find their ultimate expression in the coöperative society of the future, with consciously planned production and with a distribution of the product informed by the highest reaches of ethics. To them the atomism of modern society is rapidly becoming an unfortunate anachronism which will be thrown into the historical ash can by the communist form of production. The elevation of the enormities of capitalism, which they never tire of denouncing, to the level of a normal law of nature is in their eyes a sad perversion. It may be observed, too, that much as they scorn the iniquities which are to them capitalism incarnate, and however much of the jungle they see in capitalist processes, the equation which puts capitalism on par with the animal world is scarcely pleasing to them. Viewed in the historical perspective, primitive society was already a conspicuous departure from the ways of the animal kingdom, and each succeeding form of production was a milestone of human progress. Capitalism, the creator of enormous productive forces, the necessary predecessor of communism, and the gateway to it in terms of the unfolding material elements, is to them, in the historical sense, a phenomenon towering far above the animal processes. There is probably a mixture of approval, disapproval, and sarcasm in the following assertions. "It is noteworthy," says Marx, "that Darwin rediscovers among plants and animals his English society with its division of labor, competition, opening up of new markets, 'inventions,' and the Malthusian struggle for

[27] See Marx's letter to Kugelmann, June 27, 1870.

existence. It is Hobbes' *bellum omnium contra omnes*." [28] Engels writes in the same vein: "Darwin did not know what a bitter satire he wrote on mankind, and especially on his countrymen, when he showed that free competition, the struggle for existence, which the economists celebrate as the highest historical achievement, is the normal state of the *animal kingdom*." [29]

Second, in the conception of our two writers, Darwin commits the error of placing insufficient emphasis on some of the elements in his formula. There is inadequate recognition of the interaction, of the harmony and coöperation, among natural bodies dead and living, so that it is "absolutely childish" to epitomize the complexity of evolution by the phrase "struggle for existence." But much more important is Darwin's failure, according to Engels, to draw an emphatic distinction between the struggle for existence, on the one hand, and adaptation, on the other, in the development of new species. Selection by the struggle for existence finds its focus in overpopulation of plant or animal, exclusive of man (since Marx and Engels repudiate Malthusianism in society). But selection by adaptation to a changed environment may have little or nothing to do with Malthusianism. Animals and plants may migrate to new regions with new conditions of life, and some may while others may not adapt themselves to the new situations. Or there may be a gradual change in the geographical surroundings, in climate, food, soil, moisture, and the like. Engels sums up "Darwin's mistake" by saying that Darwin lumps together "in 'natural selection' or the 'survival of the fittest' two absolutely separate things," namely, selection by struggle and selection by adaptation.[30] It is obvious that what Marx and Engels eminently approve of in Darwin's "epoch-making work" is his scientific method, his empiricism, realism, and indisposition to metaphysical speculation; his powerful contribution to the dethronement of the old ideas of fixity and rigidity; and his

[28] Letter, June 18, 1862, in Marx and Engels, *Gesamtausgabe*, Part III, vol. 3, pp. 77–78.    [29] *Dialectics of Nature*, p. 19. Engels' italics.
[30] *Dialectics of Nature*, pp. 208, 235–236.

transforming conceptions. But they see blemishes in his presentation, and, above all, they do not favor his social views nor the non-Marxian implications of his ideas.

## ECONOMIC DYNAMICS

This theory of evolution permeates Marx's treatment of changes in the modes of production as a preliminary to changes in the other departments of social phenomena. "Dialectics is nothing more than the science of the general laws of motion and development of Nature, human society and thought." [31] In correlation with a given system of production there develops a determinate complex of property relations among the participants in production and a definite aggregate of institutions. The productive forces continue to grow and with them the mode of production and the institutional superstructure. But this harmony does not endure. Sooner or later the productive system and the corresponding personal relations and institutional composite assume a mature and hardened complexion, while the productive forces move in unarrested development.[32] The solidified order no longer possesses the elasticity needed to accommodate the dynamic productive forces. "Irreconcilable contradictions" becloud the horizon. The new productive forces demand a new context in which to thrive, but the irresponsive environment blocks their development. The existing order, the thesis, becomes a barrier to progress in production and must be negated by the antithesis, the new productive forces.

A revolution finally bursts out which resolves the contradiction by disrupting the old order and by instituting a new productive system which embodies alike the new productive forces and some phases of the old form of production. A new synthesis is achieved, and corresponding institutions begin to emerge. The class struggle plays a prominent part in the drama, but of that later. Marx teaches: "At a certain stage of their development the material forces of production in society come in conflict with the existing relations of produc-

[31] Engels Anti-Dühring, p. 155.      [32] Marx, Capital, III, 921.

tion. . . . From forms of development of the forces of production these relations turn into their fetters. Then comes the period of social revolution." [33]

The curtain will fall in time on capitalism, and the communist synthesis, the only solvent of the disruptive contradictions of our present order, will introduce a new society. These contradictions are variously defined as those between the ever-growing productive forces, on the one hand, and the capitalist property relations, or productive relations, or distribution, or mode of production, on the other hand.[34] But often enough the apocalyptic event is painted on a larger dialectical canvas. In the penultimate chapter of *Capital*, volume I, Marx treats the individual property of the petty industry and agriculture in the late Middle Ages as the thesis. The negation of this thesis comes with the expropriation of these small producers and the introduction of large capitalist property. At present "capitalist production begets, with the inexorability of a law of Nature, its own negation. It is the negation of negation." In the fullness of time, "The knell of private property sounds. The expropriators are expropriated." [35] In another place another triad is sketched. All primitive peoples begin with communal property. At a certain stage the negation develops in the form of private property. The next step, the negation of this negation into common property again, may be confidently expected.[36]

There is necessity, and no arbitrariness, in this process of social change. The eventually contradictory productive forces and their distinctive character in a given society provide the impulse to the changes in the mode of production, govern the timing of the changes, and give coherence to the succession of developments. A system of production will persist until all the productive forces of which it is capable are unfolded, and no

[33] Introduction to *Critique of Political Economy*, p. 12; *Capital*, III, 1030; Marx and Engels, *Communist Manifesto*, pp. 18-19; Engels, *Anti-Dühring*, pp. 167, 174; *Socialism, Utopian and Scientific*, pp. 47, 80.

[34] Same references as in the previous note.

[35] *Capital*, I, 835-837. Cf. *Die Heilige Familie*, pp. 205-206.

[36] Engels, *Anti-Dühring*, p. 151.

new order is born before its material conditions have matured within the old order.[37] There are close links between the old and the new, and external influences cannot derange the sequence of productive systems but may only act as a retarding or catalytic agent. Commerce possesses the power of dissolving an elementary system of production into which it is projected, but the type of the new system is not contingent on commerce but rather on the old system. In antiquity commerce "always results in a slave economy"; in modern times in a capitalist economy.[38]

MARX ON RUSSIA

As will be seen in the next and other chapters, there is, to Marx, a definite series of forms of production: primitive communism, ancient slavery, medieval feudalism, modern capitalism, and future communism. That he is aware of exceptions to this sequence will be noted in Chapter XVI. Here, however, it is worth recording one particular exception, concerning Russia's transition to communism. In a letter in 1877 Marx writes that since 1861, the year of the emancipation of her serfs, Russia had been in a position to avoid the "catastrophe" of capitalism and to make a direct change to communism; but once she took the road of capitalism (and, as Marx indicates, she had gone far in that direction by 1877), she would have to run the full course of capitalist development before evolving into communism. In this letter Marx protests against generalizing his sketch of the origin of capitalism in Western Europe into "a historico-philosophical theory of the general path imposed by fate on all peoples regardless of their historical circumstances." He cites the failure of Rome to adopt capitalism despite the favoring conditions of a large accumulation of capital and a large dispossessed proletariat, and he suggests that each development ought to be studied separately.[39]

[37] Marx, Introduction to *Critique of Political Economy*, p. 12.
[38] Marx, *Capital*, III, 390–391.
[39] "Lettre sur le développement économique de la Russie" (*Le mouvement socialiste*, VII, 968–972). See Marx and Engels, *Selected Correspondence*, pp. 352–355. Marx wrote this letter in French.

In 1881, two years before Marx's death, a Russian revolutionary asked him whether it was inevitable that capitalism run its full course in Russia, rendering all revolutionary activity there premature and futile. In his somewhat noncommittal reply, Marx stated that his account of the inauguration of capitalism as given in *Capital*, volume I, applied only to England and Western Europe generally, and that the Russian rural commune, the *mir*, might well be the basis of "the social regeneration of Russia," provided, however, that all the hostile influences threatening the *mir* were first eliminated.[40]

But more revealing than this letter are three of the four discarded drafts of his intended reply, which came to light in 1927.[41] These drafts are pessimistic about Russia's avoiding the full sweep of capitalism, and with minor variations and omissions they repeat, among other things, the following theme. All countries began with primitive communism and lost it for the terrors of capitalism, but Russia may escape this fate, and for two reasons. First, Russia is the contemporary of and in contact with capitalistic countries, and she may borrow from them favorable economic features just as she borrowed from them the machine, the steamboat, banks, etc., without the painful period of independent incubation.[42] Second, the Russian commune, the *mir*, survived intact for long centuries, while capitalism in Europe and America finds itself in a mortal crisis which will give birth to communism there in the near future. The implication is clear that Russia would be in a position to borrow this superior form of social construction without the antecedent pains of full-blown capitalism.[43]

Nevertheless, despite its vitality, Marx is pessimistic, in these drafts, about the fate of the "archaic" Russian commune. Crushed by state exactions, exploited by industrialists and landlords, oppressed by merchants and usurers, and torn by internal conflicts, the *mir* may disintegrate, he fears. More-

[40] D. Rjazanov, ed., *Marx–Engels, Archiv*, I, 341–342.
[41] *Archiv*, I, 318–340.
[42] *Archiv*, I, 319, 323, 332, 338.
[43] *Archiv*, I, 319–320, 324, 326, 331.

over, the Russian state and the Russian capitalists, induced by the wretched condition of Russian agriculture to regard the *mir* as an anachronistic vehicle of exploitation, prefer the proletarianization of the peasant. Accordingly, to save the Russian commune from its enemies and to make it a direct bridge to modern communism, he considers a Russian revolution in the nearest future an indispensable condition.[44]

As is readily seen, Marx's analysis went wrong. Communism did not come to Western Europe and America; the Russian *mir*, far from being dissolved by its enemies, continued to exist; and during the Bolshevik revolution as well as for years afterwards, it was the peasant, tutored in the rural commune, who clamored for private property in land. Nor did Marx's condition of a revolution soon after 1881 to save the *mir* see fulfillment.

In 1882 Marx and Engels record in their preface to the Russian edition of the *Communist Manifesto* that by virtue of her experience with the village commune Russia can avoid capitalism and make a direct transition to communism in land property, provided that the revolution in Russia is followed by a workers' revolution in the West, "so that one supplements the other." [45] Not long before his death Engels touches on this problem in a letter to a Russian revolutionary. The commune and the artel, he says, contained possibilities which in suitable circumstances could develop enough virility to save Russia "the torments" of the full career of capitalism. But, in Marx's and in his own opinion, "the first condition required to bring this about was the *impulse from without*," the breakdown of capitalism in Western Europe.[46] He repeats this theme, with some new remarks, in a letter to the same person several months later.[47]

[44] *Archiv*, I, 326–329, 334.

[45] Marx and Engels, *Selected Correspondence*, p. 355.

[46] *Selected Correspondence*, pp. 508–509. Engels' italics. In old Russia the artel, an example of producers' coöperatives, was a group of artisans associated for the purpose of undertaking certain jobs, like house or road building, and dividing the profits.

[47] *Selected Correspondence*, pp. 513–515.

## CONCLUDING REMARKS

It is not easy to escape the impression that there is an element of mysticism in the dialectic. Wrought into matter is the property of breeding contradictions which are meant to function as the matrix of the evolutionary progression. Rocks, ores, water, air are at a given time what they are, and then they are not, because they are permeated with an inner "hostility" against themselves and are in a ceaseless state of "becoming." Likewise the plants and animals, in their cell structure and behavior, live the life of contradictions implicit in their natures. Human history is the panorama of man's activity in a social context, but here too there is the ubiquitous inwrought principle. There is the progressive march to freedom as the quintessence of unfolding history. Communism, the final mode of production within the orbit of Marx's contemplation, is invested with the quality of a synthesis projected against the tribal communism as the original thesis, and is linked in kinship with the gens through the chain of the contradictory stages of slavery, feudalism, and capitalism. History, that is, is striving to make full circle. There is talk of "progressive or retrogressive changes" in the universe, and there is mention that nature has "its history in time," with the "recurrent cycles . . . assuming infinitely vaster dimensions." [48] There are assertions like the following: "The old teleology has gone to the devil, but the certainty now stands firm that *matter* in its eternal cycle *moves* according to laws which at a definite stage — now here, now there — *necessarily* give rise to the thinking *mind* in organic beings." [49] It seems that Marx and Engels turned, as they claimed, Hegel's dialectic upside down, but not inside (the mysterious inside) out.

In a broad sense, the dialectic embraces Marx's conceptions of matter, human nature and conduct, the methods of acquiring knowledge, the interaction of phenomena, and evolution.

---

[48] Engels, *Anti-Dühring*, pp. 29, 31.

[49] Engels, *Dialectics of Nature*, p. 187. My italics. Says Marx: ". . . the laws of appropriation or of private property . . . become by their own inner and inexorable dialectic changed into their very opposite" (*Capital*, I, 639).

When used as such an overarching principle in viewing the surrounding scene of man, society, nature, and the universe, this approach can be called dialectical materialism. When focused on man alone as he reveals himself in social action through the ages, this approach is referred to as historical dialectics or historical materialism.

Marx and Engels have a high regard for the dialectic. For years it had been their "best tool" and "sharpest weapon." [50] They proclaim: "An exact representation of the universe, of its evolution and that of mankind, as well as of the reflection of this evolution in the human mind, can therefore only be built up in a dialectical way." It is "the highest form of thinking." When each science clarifies its "position in the great totality of things," philosophy will die as a superfluous discipline, but formal logic and the dialectic will endure. Of these two the dialectic is superior as a method of advancing from the known to the unknown, "because in forcing its way beyond the narrow horizon of formal logic it contains the germ of a more comprehensive view of the world." What is true of the results obtained by the dialectic may appear false when tested by logic, for logic dares not scale the heights which the dialectic can reach. All procedures of investigation and reasoning are common to man and the higher animals, and differ only in degree; but "dialectical thought — precisely because it presupposes investigation of the concepts — is only possible for man." [51]

The two friends are grieved to see that only a few appreciate the value of the dialectic. In Marx's opinion, "There is at present much need in the finer world (I mean naturally the 'intellectual' part of it) of mastering the dialectic"; and Engels laments that the number of those capable of thinking dialectically "are still few and far between." [52]

[50] Engels, *Feuerbach*, p. 96.
[51] Engels, *Anti-Dühring*, pp. 29, 26, 31, 148; *Dialectics of Nature*, p. 203.
[52] *Der Briefwechsel zwischen Friedrich Engels und Karl Marx*, III, 424; *Anti-Dühring*, p. 29.

# CHAPTER III

## THE BASES OF HISTORY UP TO THE PRESENT

UP to the present the dialectic has evolved four distinct productive régimes, and Marx divides past history into four epochs. "In broad outlines we can designate the Asiatic, the ancient, the feudal, and the modern bourgeois modes of production" as progressive epochs in the economic formation of society. All these are "prehistoric" eras, mere preludes to the future epoch, the socialistic.[1]

### PRIMITIVE COMMUNISM

The first economic order, the Asiatic, prevails in the infancy of human development, and the best examples of it available at the time Marx was writing *Capital* are the Slavic villages, especially the Russian, and the "Asiatic communities," notably in India.[2] This mode of production is characterized by communal property and "directly associated labor." Agriculture and crafts are the chief occupations. The land is held and tilled in common by the members of the tribe, and the yield is divided among the producers, for consumption.[3] The other needs are supplied by each family through handicraft labor. The patriarchal industries of the peasant household or certain Indian communities furnish the illustration: spinning, weaving, cattle raising, and the preparation of clothing, are functions performed by the whole family; division of labor within this unit is based on differences of age and sex, and on natural conditions varying with the seasons. Side by side with the masses thus occupied, there is a handful of people charged

[1] *Critique of Political Economy*, p. 13.
[2] *Capital*, I, 89 and n.; III, 1023; D. Rjazanov, ed., *Marx-Engels, Archiv*, I, 320–322, 335–336.
[3] Cf. Engels, *Anti-Dühring*, p. 294.

with duties of public interest, and maintained at the expense of the community; like the smith, the carpenter, watchmen, and judges. Goods are produced mainly for consumption; trading is carried on to a limited extent, and chiefly between neighboring tribes, who make different articles according to the natural resources. This is the origin of exchange.[4]

Marx's general comment on this epoch is as follows:

> Those ancient social organisms of production are, as compared with bourgeois society, extremely simple and transparent. But they are founded either on the immature development of man individually, who has not yet severed the umbilical cord that unites him with his fellow men in a primitive tribal community, or upon direct relations of subjection. They can arise and exist only when the development of the productive power of labor has not risen beyond a low stage, and when, therefore, the social relations within the sphere of material life, between man and man, and between man and Nature, are correspondingly narrow.[5]

Marx states that this economic stage dominates "at the dawn of history of all civilized races."[6] A more or less detailed discussion of this period among the peoples of classical antiquity is furnished by Engels in his *Origin of the Family*.[7] He does not refer to it, however, as the Asiatic stage, but prefers to term it the "gens" organization of society, following the terminology of Lewis Morgan in *Ancient Society*.

The gens is Engels' favorite, and he cannot lavish enough praise on it.[8] In its truest form he finds it only among the Iroquois Indians of North America, at the lower stage of barbarism; and he discusses at length their social organization, emphasizing coöperative production, common ownership of land, and the general absence of private property. At the dawn of Athens' history, we see her at the upper level of barbarism, or two stages beyond the Iroquois. It is the heroic era described in the epics of Homer. "Gentilism" is fully alive, although not in its pure archaic form. However, soon an ominous phenomenon appears that ultimately deals a death blow

---

[4] Marx, *Capital*, I, 90ff., 100, 392ff., 386.
[5] *Capital*, I, 91.
[6] *Critique of Political Economy*, p. 29.
[7] See also Marx and Engels, *Communist Manifesto*, p. 12n.
[8] See Engels, *Origin of the Family*, p. 117.

to the communal order. It is private property. Maternal law is gradually superseded by paternal rule, leading to the inheritance of wealth by the children, to the rise of the family as the unit, and to the accumulation of riches. "Rising private property had thus made its first opening in the gentile constitution," and "the fundament of the gentile law was shattered" (pages 120, 129).

Engels realizes that it was private property that swept away this economic stage and unloosened the many evils upon mankind. "The advent of private property in herds of cattle and articles of luxury led to an exchange between individuals, to a transformation of products into commodities. Here is the root of the entire revolution that followed" (page 135). But to the crucial question why private property sprang into existence at all, and why the "splendid men and women" developed by the gens did not zealously guard their communal constitution, "so wonderful . . . in all its natural simplicity" (page 117), and allowed the sinister institution of the "formerly so despised private property" (page 130) to fasten itself upon them — to this Engels gives no answer. Already in the middle stage of barbarism, he indicates, private property in cattle makes its appearance in Asia, but "How and when the herds were transferred from the collective ownership of the tribe or gens to the proprietorship of the heads of the families, is not known to us" (page 195). He is content with the naïve remark that "the herds drifted into the hands of private individuals" (page 194).[9]

In the general summary at the end of the book Engels records that at the upper stage of barbarism iron becomes the servant of man. "It is the last and most important of all raw products that play a revolutionary rôle in history; the last — if we except the potato" (page 197). Iron furnishes adequate tools in agriculture and crafts; but it does this gradually, because "the first iron was often softer than bronze" and there-

---

[9] In another work he makes a general statement, no more illuminating, to the effect that wherever private property arises, it appears as a result of a change in the methods of production and exchange, in the interests of the increase of production and the development of commerce (*Anti-Dühring*, p. 180).

fore it had not displaced stone axes even as late as the battle at Hastings in 1066 (page 197). When discussing the developments in Athens, he completely fails to mention the discovery of iron. The influence he ascribes to the new technical methods made possible by this metal is, therefore, somewhat obscure.

At any rate, during the last period of upper barbarism, progress is "irresistible, less interrupted, and more rapid." Agriculture develops and yields new products, like oil and wine. Handicraft industry becomes increasingly diversified, especially in textiles and metals. The town and the artisan are more and more divided off from the country and the agricultural laborer. Wealth is sought after. Production for exchange increases, and commerce advances. The sea trade "drifts" rapidly out of the power of the Phoenicians and into the hands of the Athenians. Tribes surrender their peaceful pursuits, and devote themselves to plunder on land and piracy on sea. Production improves to such a degree that a worker can produce more than he requires to maintain himself. As a consequence, labor power becomes desirable, and since the communal system affords no source of surplus laborers except prisoners of war, the captives are killed no longer but are retained as slaves. Before, slavery was only a sporadic phenomenon; now it becomes an institution. The gens régime is dying, and the second economic stage, the era of classical slavery, arrives.[10]

From this account we see that Engels finds several causes of the disintegration of primitive communism. One consists in the change of the family organization; for group marriage begins to lose ground, and paternal lineage supplants maternal law. This is in agreement with Marx's and Engels' thesis that in primitive times the structure of the family, and not the mode of production, is of supreme importance in promoting a transition from one stage of development to another. A second cause is the appearance of private property, which leads to

[10] Engels, *Origin of the Family*, pp. 130ff., 197ff.; also *Anti-Dühring*, pp. 178, 199–200. Note that on p. 199 (*Anti-Dühring*) he contends that slavery is the dominant form of production among all people who had developed beyond the tribal communal stage.

the inheritance of wealth, to exchange, and therefore to the transformation of products into commodities, that is, merchandise; and which breaks up the community of interests and introduces the antagonism between rich and poor.[11] A third is the discovery of iron. How much significance Engels attaches to this factor is hard to say, for he omits this fact entirely in his main treatment of the extinction of the gens. At best, then, we may surmise that the transition from tribal communism to the next order is partly due to new technical developments in the methods of production.

## ANCIENT SLAVERY

We are now at the point where upper barbarism is gone, and civilization is dawning. We come to an era of slaves, "whose forced labor formed the basis on which the whole superstructure of society was reared" (page 203). They are recruited not only from prisoners of war, but also from "tribal and gentile associates" (page 129). In the period of her bloom there are in Athens 90,000 free citizens and 365,000 slaves (page 143); Corinth and Aegina possess about half a million slaves, ten times the number of free citizens (page 203, footnote). Slaves swarm in the shops and factories.[12] Labor by a free citizen is despised; nevertheless there are many free artisans who earn a living, in competition with slave labor (page 143). Engels esteems this régime as of enormous historical value. It was a distinct step ahead. It gave to the world Greece, the glory of ancient civilization, the watershed from which flowed the streams of modern thought and institutions. "Without slavery, no Greek state, no Greek art and science; without slavery, no Roman Empire . . . no modern Europe . . . no modern socialism."[13]

The surplus produced by the slaves stimulates trade, commerce, and navigation still further. A new figure appears in a

---

[11] *Origin of the Family*, p. 200. Cf. *Anti-Dühring*, p. 180.

[12] "The great number of slaves is explained by the fact that many of them worked together in large factories under supervision" (p. 143). See also *Anti-Dühring*, p. 179.

[13] *Anti-Dühring*, p. 200.

new division of labor, the merchant. The division between town and country is one among producers; but this "class of parasites, genuine social ichneumons," [14] does not engage in production, it merely connects producers and extends markets. The merchant becomes, however, the central figure in society. He exploits the direct producers, amasses wealth, gains prestige, and struggles with the old nobility for supremacy. He employs a new powerful weapon, "before which the whole of society must bow down," money, which comes into use to facilitate exchange (page 136). Engels fears money, for it possesses the power of dissolving social orders with its "corrugating acid" (page 133). Wherever this agent appears, social systems disintegrate. [15]

In the hands of the merchant and the nobility money begins to work havoc in Greece also. The old communal ties that protected the farmer against the loss of land had been loosened with the appearance of private property. He contracts now monetary debts, mortgages his land, and, unable to pay the usurious rates, forfeits his property and is sold into slavery. "Such was the pleasant dawn of civilization among the people of Attica." [16] "You have clamored for free, full, saleable land. Well, then, there you have it — *tu l'as voulu, Georges Dandin;* it was your own wish, George Dandin" (page 203). This strife between the rich and the poor results in a series of constitutions by Theseus, Solon, and Cleisthenes, which mitigate the evils, but only temporarily. Soon exploitation shifts from one between rich and poor to one between master and slave, and continues through the rest of the history of Athens. The Athenian state is an instrument of the rich against the poor and of the master against the slave (pages 142, 207).

No such troubles, Engels reflects, could have come upon a gens order, where the unchanging mode of production is primitive, but man has control over his product. Private property leads to exchange, and exchange implies that the producer no

---

[14] *Origin of the Family*, p. 201.
[15] *Anti-Dühring*, pp. 332, 339, 164.
[16] *Origin of the Family*, p. 134.

longer controls his product. The product turns against the producer and oppresses him. "No society can, therefore, retain for any length of time the control of its own production and of the social effects of the mode of production, unless it abolishes exchange between individuals" (pages 135–136).

Greece meets her fate. "Not democracy caused the downfall of Athens . . . but slavery ostracizing the labor of the free citizen" (page 143). For the transition to the third epoch, or feudalism, we have to turn tó Rome.

Like Greece, Rome steps into history with the gens institution, and, as in Greece, tribal communism cedes its place to slavery. At its zenith we find the empire extended all around the Mediterranean, dominating a multitude of nations by the iron power of the State (page 178). Rome as well as the provinces are oppressed and impoverished by grinding taxes, by imposts and tithes, by constant bleeding through wars, and by "blackmailing practices" of the officials (page 179). Commerce and industry are never a strong point with the Romans (page 179); yet about these rudimentary pursuits is woven a magnificent code of law which, Engels acknowledges, could suit the capitalist conditions in various countries many centuries later.[17] Usury reaches the highest scale of development ever attained in antiquity. Instead of helping the war-ruined plebeians directly with the prerequisites of production like grain, horses, and cattle, the patricians lend them the copper looted in the wars that the same plebeians were forced to fight, exact from them exorbitant interest payments, and turn the defaulting victims into their debtor slaves. "The mere death of a cow may render the small producer unable to renew his reproduction on the former scale. Then he falls into the clutches of the usurer, and once he is in the usurer's power, he never extricates himself."[18]

The poverty of the masses contributes to the decline in traffic and the decay of the towns. The shrinking markets restrict production. As the immense estates, the *latifundiae*, where

[17] *Socialism, Utopian and Scientific*, p. xxvii; *Feuerbach*, p. 115.
[18] *Origin of the Family*, pp. 179–180; Marx, *Capital*, III, 697, 703–704.

slaves engage in large scale agriculture, are no longer remunerative, they are parceled out to hereditary tenants for a fixed rent, but mainly to colonists, who pay a fixed sum annually, and who can be "transferred by sale together with their lots." Colonists are not freemen; they are "the prototypes of the medieval serfs." Nor does manufacture, based on slave labor, yield profitable returns. Slavery is finally abolished here too, and small scale production is instituted everywhere. However, free artisans are not prevalent, for labor is despised as slavish. Rome is in a "closed alley." "There was no other help but a complete revolution." [19] The provinces fare no better. To escape the oppression of the officials, the judges, and the usurers, the independent farmers place themselves under the protection of a man of power. The patron takes advantage of their plight, and imposes on them the harsh condition of a transfer to him of their title to the land. Servitude is the outcome of the oppressive policy of Rome.[20]

The settlement of the barbarian invaders on Roman soil does not alter conditions. Ever since their contact with the Romans their communal order had begun to crumble. When they triumph over Rome, overrun its territories, and take the reins of government, they find the gens constitution too primitive and too inadequate an instrument to solve the new problems.[21] Roman methods are adopted; and in the ninth century we face the same social and economic conditions that we saw in Rome four hundred years before. Serfdom spreads on an increasing scale.

However, the barbarians make some contributions. They are but slightly contaminated with the institution of slavery, and they do not despise free labor. Again, they bequeath to feudalism several traces of the gens elements of property ownership; this legacy serves, at least in France, Germany, and England, as a tower of strength to the oppressed serfs, later in the Middle Ages.[22]

[19] *Origin of the Family*, pp. 180–182.
[20] *Origin of the Family*, p. 182. Cf. Marx, *Capital*, III, 703.
[21] *Origin of the Family*, pp. 184–185.
[22] *Origin of the Family*, p. 189.

As in the case of the transition from the gens to slavery, it is not exactly clear how the dialectic manages to achieve a transformation of the slave mode of production into a feudal mode. What are the productive forces liberated by slavery that unavoidably create a higher order? Wherein consists the contradiction between these productive forces and the old mode of production? Feudalism is ushered in by agencies not inherently bred by a slave régime. It is rather the decadence of the markets that renders slavery unprofitable. It is rather the insecurity of the independent farmer, caused by wars and an oppressive government, that compels him to seek protection. It is rather the force of external historical events that injects into decrepit Rome the fresh vigor of the Germans, who "introduce the mild form of servitude which they had been practising at home." [23] The crucial question is: does a slave mode of production inevitably produce circumstances which must result in feudalism? To this question we find no answer.

## MEDIEVAL FEUDALISM

Under feudalism, "Peasant agriculture on a small scale, and the carrying on of independent handicrafts . . . together form the basis of the . . . mode of production." [24] In the country, the serf possesses the land by hereditary right or by some other understanding, although absolute ownership is vested in the lord.[25] In addition to farming, the peasant and his family are engaged in domestic industry in order to provide for the other needs. In both pursuits the worker owns the means of production, produces chiefly for his consumption or for a very narrow market, and enjoys full control over the product.[26] But he is a serf. He has to perform forced labor for the state, as *corvée*, and he must pay a rent to the lord. The rent may be in the form of labor done on the lord's estate: this is a clear, unmistakable form of surplus-value. Later, the rent in kind appears,

---

[23] *Origin of the Family*, p. 189.

[24] Marx, *Capital*, I, 367n.

[25] *Capital*, III, 921.

[26] *Capital*, III, 918; I, 818–820; Engels, *Socialism, Utopian and Scientific*, p. 57.

and the serf surrenders a definite amount in agricultural and handicraft products. When commerce develops to a larger extent, and money comes into greater use, he can pay his rent in the new medium.[27] In all these cases the peasant is not hindered from producing a surplus above his needs, from selling it in the market, and from accumulating wealth.

In the town, the artisan follows handicraft industry. He owns the raw material and other means of production as well as the completed product, and he is familiar with the market for which he produces. Here, too, the direct producer dominates his product. Engels paints idyllic pictures of guild production and muses over them with historical homesickness: the master with his small garden, with his cattle pasturing on the common, and the apprentice working more for education than for his pay in board and lodging, remind him of the charm of days that were but are no more.[28]

Now, as in antiquity, the sinister figure of the usurer is everywhere. Whenever personal accident or a bad season involves the small producer in difficulties, he turns to this person, who is in wait for him.[29] Another familiar figure is the merchant, who facilitates exchange between town and country. The merchant is at war with the usurer. Already in the twelfth and fourteenth centuries the merchants in Venice and Genoa form credit associations to finance their extensive land and maritime trade, and to free themselves from the clutches of the usurer.[30] The dominant forms of capital are the usurer's and the merchant's capital; it cannot turn into industrial capital because of the feudal restrictions in the country and the guild regulations in the town.[31] "While the country exploits the town politically in the Middle Ages, wherever feudalism has not been broken down by an exceptional development of the towns, the town, on the other hand, everywhere and without exception exploits the land economically by its

[27] Marx, *Capital*, III, 919, 923–925.
[28] Engels, *Socialism, Utopian and Scientific*, pp. 51–52.
[29] Marx, *Capital*, III, 699, 703.
[30] *Capital*, III, 706–707.
[31] *Capital*, I, 822–823.

monopoly prices, its system of taxation, its guild organizations, its direct mercantile fraud, and its usury." [32]

Slowly and persistently new elements develop within the bosom of this society. Serfdom is swept away in England in the fourteenth century. The semi-independent peasant pays his rent in kind, and later in money. He is no longer hampered by the restrictions attached to labor-rent; he can even buy himself free from the landlord for a lump sum of money. Many a guild-master or independent artisan begins to employ wage labor, and gradually becomes a small capitalist. The same is true, and to a higher degree, of the merchant, who takes to production by hiring and exploiting labor, and who develops new markets. But all this merely stands for faint beginnings of capitalism, sprouting out sporadically here and there in the fourteenth and fifteenth centuries. [33]

The new productive forces and the rising bourgeoisie are handicapped at each step by the old mode of production and social relations — by feudal restrictions, guild regulations, absence of freedom of contract, local legal provisions, diverse schemes of taxation, and the arrogant privileges of the hierarchical nobility. There is an insistent call for hired labor, but labor "free" for hire is tantalizingly scarce because of guild impediments and the independence of the peasant proprietor. Everywhere the worker possesses the means of production and works for himself. Likewise, "the money capital formed by means of usury and commerce was prevented from turning into industrial capital, in the country by the feudal constitution, in the town by the guild organization," complains Marx. At best, the bourgeois advances at "the snail's pace." The play of stronger forces is required to give a firm footing to the capitalistic system of production. [34]

## Capitalism

These forces do not fail to arrive. At the end of the fifteenth century great geographical discoveries startle the world. Over-

[32] *Capital*, III, 930.
[33] *Capital*, I, 787–788, 815, 822; III, 393, 395, 928.
[34] *Capital*, I, 786, 809–810, 822–823, 835; Engels, *Anti-Dühring*, pp. 116, 183.

sea trade is extended and faraway markets grow up. The demand for commodities rises progressively, and since the old form of production and the sluggishly developing new one are inadequate to meet the new requirements, fresh incentives and fresh energies receive a new impetus.

> The discovery of America, the rounding of the Cape, opened up fresh ground for the rising bourgeoisie. The East-Indian and Chinese markets, the colonization of America, trade with the colonies, the increase in the means of exchange and in commodities generally, gave to commerce, to navigation, to industry, an impulse never before known, and thereby, to the revolutionary element in the tottering feudal society, a rapid development —

chronicles the *Communist Manifesto* (page 13).[35]

However, while supplying perhaps the prime cause, the geographical discoveries do not represent the only element in this upheaval. Other factors as well figure in the far-reaching transformation. The process is, in brief, as follows.

Before capitalistic production can establish itself, certain conditions must be fulfilled. "In themselves, money, commodities are no more capital than are the means of production and of subsistence. They want transforming into capital. But this transformation can take place only under certain circumstances that center in this, namely, that two very different kinds of commodity possessors must come face to face and into contact." These two kinds are, on the one hand, the owners of money and means of production, eager to hire wage labor; and on the other hand, masses of workers, dispossessed, divorced from the means of production, owners of labor-power alone and eager to sell it for a wage. "With this polarization of the market for commodities, the fundamental conditions of capitalist production are given."[36] In other words, capitalism cannot arise without the antecedent expropriation of the many and the enrichment of the few.[37]

The realization of these two conditions is achieved by a process that Marx terms "original accumulation" (*ursprüng-*

[35] Marx, *Capital*, I, 469, 822; III, 391; Engels, *Anti-Dühring*, p. 115; Socialism, *Utopian and Scientific*, pp. 58–59.

[36] Marx, *Capital*, I, 785, 189.

[37] *Capital*, I, 624–625, 848, 684.

*liche Akkumulation*) — original, because it forms the "pre-historic stage," the basis and starting-point of capitalism.[38] Original accumulation begins in the last third of the fifteenth century. It is the expropriation of the independent farmer, an expropriation "written in the annals of mankind in letters of blood and fire." The drama is enacted in England, and there are various factors at work. The impoverished feudal nobility disband the numerous retainers who had thronged house and castle. At the same time, the enclosure movement is inaugurated by the lords who desire to turn arable land into sheep-walks; whole populations of independent peasants are uprooted from the soil and cast adrift in utter ruin. The Reformation imparts a "new and frightful impulse" to the process, through the suppression of monasteries and the dispersion of the serfs attached to them. The whole event is a succession of "the most shameless violation of the 'sacred rights of property' and the grossest acts of violence to persons"; "a whole series of thefts, outrages, and popular misery"; a display of "merciless vandalism . . . of passions the most infamous, the most sordid, the pettiest, the most meanly odious." [39]

Armies of homeless, enraged vagabonds are let loose, who, partly by need and partly by inclination, take to robbery and thieving. Thereupon comes the bloody legislation against them, inflicting severe punishment for idleness, and disciplining them to sell their labor at any price. "Thus were the agricultural people first forcibly expropriated from the soil, driven from their homes, turned into vagabonds, and then whipped, branded, tortured by laws grotesquely terrible, into the discipline necessary for the wage system." [40] A proletarian class is created, separated from the means of production, unfettered by feudal restrictions and guild regulations, and ready to be hired and exploited.[41]

---

[38] *Capital*, I, 784, 786. The English translation has "primitive accumulation." This is a misleading expression. "Original accumulation" is better. Marx himself employed this expression in an address delivered in English (see *Value, Price and Profit*, p. 74).

[39] *Capital*, I, 786–805, 835; *Poverty of Philosophy*, p. 149.

[40] *Capital*, I, 808–809.     [41] *Capital*, 817.

Simultaneously with these events there is at play another set of forces in this "original accumulation," meant to fulfill the other condition, namely, the formation of a bourgeoisie ready to exploit labor. Among these forces the geographical discoveries are once more of first significance. "One of the most indispensable conditions for the formation of the manufacturing industry was the accumulation of capital facilitated by the discovery of America and the introduction of its precious metals." America floods Europe with gold and silver; a tremendous rise in prices follows, with the ruination of the landlord and the laboring class, through the depreciation of rent and wages, and with the concurrent elevation of the bourgeoisie, through a rise in profits.[42] The "Christian colonial system" is marked by barbarities and revolting outrages, by the extirpation of the aborigines or their entombment in the mines. East India is conquered and looted, Africa is turned into "a warren for the commercial hunting of black skins," and "The treasures captured outside Europe by undisguised looting, enslavement, and murder, floated back to the mother country and were there turned into capital." [43]

The state takes an active part in these proceedings, and employs devious expedients to hasten the course of original accumulation in both of its phases. The state power is employed in pressing the newly formed proletariat into the workshop by Draconian laws against idleness, in forcing down his wage, in prolonging his workday, and in holding him in the proper degree of subjection.[44] The state launches elaborate schemes of national debts, or public credit, which, "as with the stroke of an enchanter's wand," endow "barren money with the power of breeding" and turning into capital. These public debts form a class of lazy annuitants; furnish improvised wealth to financiers and windfalls to tax farmers, merchants, and manufacturers; and foster joint-stock companies, stock exchange gambling, and the modern "bankocracy." Na-

---

[42] Marx, *Poverty of Philosophy*, p. 148; Engels, *Anti-Dühring*, p. 115.
[43] Marx, *Capital*, I, 823–826.
[44] *Capital*, I, 809.

tional loans have as their necessary complement the policy of increased taxation — a convenient mode of expropriating the masses. Then add the system of protection, which is an ideal "artificial means of manufacturing manufacturers, of expropriating independent laborers . . . of forcibly abbreviating the transition from the medieval to the modern mode of production." [45]

*Tantae molis erat* [summarizes Marx] to establish the "eternal laws of Nature" of the capitalist mode of production, to complete the process of separation between laborers and conditions of labor, to transform, at one pole, the social means of production and subsistence into capital, at the opposite pole, the mass of the population into wage laborers, into "free laboring poor," that artificial product of modern society. If money, according to Augier, "comes into the world with a congenital blood-stain on one cheek," capital comes dripping from head to foot, from every pore, with blood and dirt.[46]

The capitalist era is not introduced by technological inventions. There is merely a change in the grouping of laborers and in the ownership of the raw material and the other means of production. "The workshop of the medieval master handicraftsman is simply enlarged": the bourgeois employer gathers many laborers under his supervision, and makes them work for him. There is no deviation from the methods of production as pursued by the guilds, except in scale. This is, "both historically and logically, the starting-point of capitalist production." [47] By a "leap" quantity turns, dialectically, into quality.

Marx distinguishes two phases of productive organization in the capitalist era. There is a preliminary stage, which he terms coöperation, and defines as a gathering of numerous laborers working side by side on one and the same process or on different but connected processes, under the eye of the capitalist. Coöperation is a familiar phenomenon in the gens society, but there we see no capitalist; the workers own in common the means of production, and they produce directly for their own needs. There is also coöperation in the workshop of classical

[45] *Capital*, I, 826–830.
[46] *Capital*, I, 833–834.
[47] *Capital*, I, 353, 362, 367. Cf. Engels, *Socialism, Utopian and Scientific*, p. 83.

antiquity, but there the laborers are not "free," they are slaves. Likewise, we find coöperation in the house of the medieval guild-master, but it is on a smaller scale; moreover, the apprentice is not so much a provider of surplus-value to an exploiter as a pupil preparing himself to become master in due time.[48]

As an independent phase, however, coöperation does not prevail over a long period of time. The first genuine phase of capitalist production is the one that Marx names "manufacture" (hand-labor), and which lasts over two hundred years, from the middle of the sixteenth century to the last third of the eighteenth.[49] It begins as a twofold development. First, as in the case of simple coöperation, the employer assembles in the workshop a number of artificers, all of whom do the same work, and each one of whom goes through alone all the successive processes necessary for the completion of the product. Second, the capitalist employs simultaneously various craftsmen, who are engaged in the successive handicraft pursuits which contribute to a final product; thus he engages wheelwrights, harness-makers, blacksmiths, painters, and so forth, to coöperate in making carriages. In either case, sooner or later, an elaborate form of division of labor sets in, and what was previously performed by one handicraftsman is resolved into many elementary processes one or more of which claims the full attention of the worker. As time goes on, experience shows that the old tools are not well adapted to the minute tasks; they are therefore improved and turned into more specialized ones, to suit the detailed operations. In some cases the laborers are not assembled under one roof, but work independently in their homes. However, they are no more the free guildsmen of yesterday; they toil under the control, and at the beck, of the capitalist employer.[50]

Manufacture does not represent a radical departure from the medieval handicraft system. It depends, in the first place,

---

[48] *Capital*, I, 357, 361, 367.
[49] *Capital*, I, 368–369; Marx and Engels, *Selected Correspondence*, p. 142.
[50] Marx, *Capital*, I, 369–370, 374, 376–377.

on the rural community, for it does not make a complete separation between town and country. The raw material, like wool, flax, silk, used in production is prepared by a newly developing class of small villagers who follow agriculture as a mere accessory, and who devote themselves chiefly to domestic industry, selling their industrial product to the manufacturer, directly or through a merchant.[51] In the second place, even the detailed laborer is essentially the old craftsman. Each operation, whether complex or simple, is a handicraft operation depending on personal "strength, skill, quickness, and sureness," and on "muscular development, keenness of sight, cunning of hand," in manipulating the "dwarfish implements." Handicraft skill is the foundation of manufacture, and "the mechanism of manufacture as a whole possesses no framework, apart from the laborers themselves." Machinery plays an insignificant part and is used only sporadically. "The collective laborer, formed by the combination of a number of detail laborers, is the machinery specially characteristic of the manufacturing period." [52]

This whole mode of production "towered up as an economical work of art, on the broad foundation of the town handicrafts, and of the rural domestic industries." [53] It is incapable of satisfying the demands of an ever-expanding market. "When in England the market had become so fully developed that manual labor no longer sufficed to supply it, the need for machinery made itself felt. It was then that the application of mechanical science, which had been fully prepared during the eighteenth century, was thought of." [54]

The capitalist system of production existed for two hundred years without machinery or any other new technical development as its distinctive mark.[55] Technique does not intro-

[51] *Capital*, I, 818–820; *Poverty of Philosophy*, p. 152.

[52] Marx, *Capital*, I, 417–418, 371, 403, 383. "During the manufacturing period, handicraft labor, altered though it was by division of labor, was yet the basis" (*ibid.*, pp. 469, 372).

[53] *Capital*, I, 404.

[54] Marx, *Poverty of Philosophy*, p. 152.

[55] "That coöperation which is based on division of labor assumes its typical form in the manufacture, and is the prevalent characteristic form of the capi-

duce capitalism, nor does it characterize it during its first long phase of "manufacture." Only with the arrival of the second phase, at the end of the eighteenth century, machinery becomes the dominant characteristic. This phase Marx and Engels call "modern industry," and it is introduced by mechanical inventions.[56] The overmastering feature of modern industry is the factory.

The rest is familiar. It is the story of the flaming Marxian indictments against the present system with the enslavement of man to the machine, the remorseless grinding of surplus-value out of the exploited wage-slaves, the industrial reserve army, the increasing misery of the workers, and crises and panics. All this will receive attention in later chapters.

---

talist process of production throughout the manufacturing period properly so called. That period, roughly speaking, extends from the middle of the sixteenth to the last third of the eighteenth century" (Marx, *Capital*, I, 368–369).

[56] *Capital*, I, p. 430. "Machinery does away with coöperation based on handicrafts, and with manufacture based on the division of handicraft labor" (*ibid.*, p. 502). "Machinery properly so called dates from the end of the eighteenth century" (*Poverty of Philosophy*, p. 150). In *Anti-Dühring*, p. 182, Engels records that the weapon of the bourgeoisie in its struggle with the feudal nobility consisted in the economic power gained from "handicraft industry, at a later stage progressing to manufacturing [machine] industry."

# PART II
# THE HUMAN ELEMENT IN HISTORY

# CHAPTER IV

## MARX'S VIEW OF HUMAN NATURE

WHILE it is the predetermining causality of social phenomena, the mode of production obviously cannot by itself enact history. History is neither the automatic result of the productive system nor a mysterious entity, apart from man, using him as a tool to carry out its designs. History is the activity of man seeking to achieve his ends; but the ends are, in Marx's view, inspired and shaped by economic realities. Marx repudiates the construction which places man in "fantastic seclusion," in the rôle of a mere spectator of the historical drama.[1]

Man writes his history. But what is meant by man? Does Marx mean the multitude of wayfaring persons busy with their daily tasks? the many groups actuated by fluctuating motives? or the dominant classes moved by enduring and clashing interests? The answer is given by the declaration in the *Communist Manifesto:* "The history of all hitherto existing society is the history of class struggles." This answer is the explicit concomitant of his basic conceptions, and prominent among them is his conception of human nature.

### HEREDITY

In his and Engels' opinions of human nature one can discern some recognition of innate hereditary elements in man's constitution. They perceive that man has inborn abilities and inclinations. He possesses a "natural fertility of mind," which lies fallow, and is stunted or stimulated to growth, according as the environment is favorable or not. Marx indicates that social division of labor, as well as the minuter division in the manufacturing processes, is based on "their [the workers']

[1] E.g., Marx and Engels, *Aus dem literarischen Nachlass von K. Marx, F. Engels*, II, 179, 416; Marx, *Poverty of Philosophy*, p. 125; *The Eighteenth Brumaire of Louis Bonaparte*, p. 9.

natural and their acquired capabilities," on "natural endowments"; and it offers individuals the opportunity of finding employment suitable to their "various bents and talents." [2] At the same time, he and Engels complain that division of labor, by calling to constant exercise a single muscular or mental performance, slaughters "all other physical and mental faculties," and converts the laborer into a crippled monstrosity, because a "world of productive capabilities and instincts" are sacrificed to the acquisition of dexterity in a minute detail.[3]

They are also aware that abilities are not possessed by all individuals in uniform quantity and quality. Men are not born equal; they exhibit "differences of brains and intellectual capacities." [4] Two persons working side by side will spend different amounts of time on the production of a commodity, partly because of differences in "purely negative moral qualities, such as patience, impassibility, assiduity." [5] Division of labor rests on the inequalities among workers: one operation needs more strength, another more skill, another more attention; "and the same individual does not possess all these qualities in an equal degree." [6] Some persons lack the capacity for adaptation in a society based on division of labor, and they therefore remain idle and poor.[7] "A man without wealth, but with energy, solidity, ability, and business sense may become a capitalist . . . In a similar way . . . the Catholic Church in the Middle Ages formed its hierarchy out of the best brains of people without regard to estate, birth, or wealth." [8] Some men are born leaders, and Owen, a product of heredity and environment, is one of the few.[9] Aristotle is "a giant thinker," "the greatest thinker of antiquity." [10] Xenophon in his writ-

[2] *Capital*, I, 198, 383-384, 401, 436.
[3] Engels, *Anti-Dühring*, p. 318; Marx, *Capital*, I, 396.
[4] Marx, *Critique of the Gotha Programme*, p. 30; Marx and Engels, *Gesamtausgabe*, Part I, vol. 5, p. 526.
[5] Marx, *Poverty of Philosophy*, p. 58.
[6] Marx, *Capital*, I, 383.
[7] *Capital*, I, 706.
[8] *Capital*, III, 705-706.
[9] Engels, *Socialism, Utopian and Scientific*, p. 20.
[10] Marx, *Capital*, I, 94n., 445-446.

ings shows already a "characteristic bourgeois instinct."[11]
Watt was a genius.[12] John Bellers was "a very phenomenon
in the history of political economy."[13] Mandeville was "an
honest, clear-headed man."[14] The Venetian monk Ortes was
an "original and clever writer."[15] Engels assures us that he
himself was at best but talented, whereas Marx was a genius.[16]
Wilhelm Liebknecht tells us in his memoirs that Marx was a
believer in phrenology, and he would examine the heads of
his admirers before he would take them into his confidence.[17] This may point to a belief in inborn differences, for
Marx hardly expected that an acquired character would be
heralded by the arrival of a new bump. But we cannot be
certain.

Marx seems to believe in racial differences, and he is not
above racial prejudice. He talks of "race peculiarities" and
"inborn race characteristics."[18] In his essay on the *Jewish
Question* there are more than hints of prejudice.[19] In his first
thesis on Feuerbach he goes out of his way to use, irrelevantly,
the adjective "*schmutzig-jüdischen.*"[20] His letters to Engels,
and Engels' to Marx, when touching Ferdinand Lassalle, are
pockmarked with unsavory epithets.[21] He refers to the Mex-
icans as "*les derniers des hommes.*"[22] His references to the
small Balkan nationalities are equally shabby.[23]

Engels is worse than Marx. In his *Revolution and Counter-
Revolution* he disapproves of Bohemia's and Croatia's joining

[11] *Capital*, I, 402.
[12] *Capital*, I, 412.
[13] *Capital*, I, 535n.
[14] *Capital*, I, 674.
[15] *Capital*, I, 676n.
[16] *Feuerbach*, p. 93n. In a letter to J. P. Becker, Engels writes: "I have been doing all my life what I was fit to do, namely, to play second fiddle." Marx was first fiddle (*Der Kampf*, VI, 533).
[17] *Karl Marx, Biographical Memoirs*, p. 52.
[18] *Capital*, III, 919, 922; I, 562.
[19] Marx and Engels, *Gesamtausgabe*, Part I, vol. 1, e.g., pp. 601–606.
[20] *Gesamtausgabe*, Part I, vol. 5, p. 533.
[21] Marx and Engels, *Selected Correspondence*, pp. 120, 134, 146, 148, 151, 157, 158, 178, 338.
[22] Marx and Engels, *Gesamtausgabe*, Part III, vol. 3, p. 111.
[23] E.g., *New York Tribune*, April 7 and 21, 1853.

in a pan-Slavic movement for the emancipation from German domination. History, he says, necessitates the absorption of these feebler peoples by the "more energetic stock," the Germans, who have the "physical and intellectual power to subdue, absorb, and assimilate its ancient eastern neighbors," and to carry western civilization to Eastern Europe. Therefore, "the natural and inevitable fate of these dying nations" is to submit to absorption, instead of fighting the "historical tendency" and dreaming "that history would retrogress a thousand years to please a few phthisical bodies of men." [24] Engels speaks disparagingly of the Poles, and refers to Russian rule, "for all its Slavic dirt," as a civilizing influence in some of her territories.[25]

At variance with these pronouncements on individual differences are declarations by Marx and Engels which make one think twice before imputing to them the theory that heredity is the chief explanation. They consider division of labor a conspicuous cause of differences among men, and Marx quotes with approval from Adam Smith the famous passage which states that the difference in men's natural talents is much less than we think, adding the remark that "it is division of labor which has placed an abyss" between the porter and the philosopher.[26] In the *Deutsche Ideologie* they talk in the same vein about differences in artistic talents.[27] From the conflicting statements it may be reasonable to deduce that while heredity plays a part in the variations in individual capacities, division of labor is more generally the commanding cause. Similarly, racial and national differences are neither biological nor invariant. Discussing with Engels the theories of the French scientist, P. Trémaux, Marx expresses the belief that the geologic or geographic environment and resources provided a natural basis for differences of race or nationality.[28] In another place he re-

---

[24] Pages 91, 137–138. In another place he says: "Of course the Germans were a highly gifted Aryan branch" (*Origin of the Family*, p. 188).

[25] Marx and Engels, *Gesamtausgabe*, Part III, vol. 1, pp. 206–207.

[26] *Poverty of Philosophy*, p. 140.

[27] Pages 372–373.

[28] *Gesamtausgabe*, Part III, vol. 3, pp. 355–356, 361–363.

marks that even "natural" distinctions among men such as "racial differences . . . can and must be removed historically" [i.e., by human measures].[29]

One outstanding characteristic, of considerable weight in history, and apparently held by the two friends as inborn, is man's adherence to tradition. By and large, men are reluctant to make changes, except under pressure. What is, and especially what has existed for a long time, is endowed with a peculiar sanction and is not to be molested. Even when fighting for a change, people conjure up battle cries and mottoes of the past, and clothe present events and characters with the associations of old deeds in order to lend dignity and glory to the issue at hand. They try to derive vigor and ardor, not so much from the problems that led to the crisis, as from old names and watchwords and the spirits of by-gone days.[30] The old has a strong grip on people, and progress proceeds slowly. "Tradition is a great retarding force, is the *vis inertiae* of history." [31] "The tradition of all past generations weighs like an Alp upon the brain of the living." [32] Because of tradition and custom every new form of production retains for a long time vestiges of the old one. Elements of an antiquated system will cling to the framework of the new order until the latter is so fully developed that its vitality destroys the adhesive power of the old remnants. Similarly with a standard of living, with workers' wages, and with the determination of interest; custom and age hold the prerogative.[33]

A still more potent human trait is self-interest and its concomitants, greed and the thirst for power. Marx refers to it as "the most violent, mean, and malignant passions of the human breast, the Furies of private interest." [34] In its realization it displays man's most ignoble passions. To indicate the

---

[29] *Gesamtausgabe*, Part I, vol. 5, p. 403.

[30] Marx, *Eighteenth Brumaire*, pp. 9–10.

[31] Engels, *Socialism, Utopian and Scientific*, p. xxxvii.

[32] Marx, *Eighteenth Brumaire*, p. 9. *Alp* in German means also a nightmare.

[33] Marx, *Capital*, I, 190; III, 427.

[34] *Capital*, I, Introduction, p. 15.

lengths to which capital will go when it scents its profits, he quotes approvingly from P. J. Dunning:

> Capital eschews no profit, or very small profit, just as Nature was formerly said to abhor a vacuum. With adequate profit capital is very bold. A certain 10 per cent will ensure its employment anywhere; 20 per cent certain will produce eagerness; 50 per cent, positive audacity; 100 per cent will make it ready to trample on all human laws; 300 per cent, and there is not a crime at which it will scruple, nor a risk it will not run, even to the chance of its owner being hanged. If turbulence and strife will bring a profit, it will freely encourage both. Smuggling and the slave trade have amply proved all that is here stated.[35]

Self-interest is the cause of much suffering; but, as will be seen repeatedly in subsequent discussions, it is also a lever of social progress and change.

Only one period in the history of mankind was immune from the play of this monster. Self-interest did not visit primitive society to mar its idyllic happiness. But with the fall of this order the earth became the scene of turmoil. "Bare-faced covetousness was the moving spirit of civilization from its first dawn to the present day; wealth, and again wealth, and for the third time wealth; wealth, not of society, but of the puny individual, was its only and final aim." [36] When the curtain of history rises upon ancient Greece, we behold the mad rush for wealth; piracy on sea and plunder on land, the goal being "cattle, slaves, and treasure"; the farmer struggling in the clutches of the usurer; debtors and their children sold into servitude; the master and the slave.[37] The scene in Rome is not brighter. The blackmailing regents, the tax collectors, and the soldiers grinding the life out of the populace; the usurer-patricians living off the plebeians; the noble degrading the independent peasant into a serf in exchange for protection — these are some of the details.[38] In the Middle Ages the mien of the feudal lord mars the picture; usurer's and merchant's capital is the dominant form, and, with Marx, it always "stands

---

[35] *Capital*, I, 834n.
[36] Engels, *Origin of the Family*, p. 215.
[37] *Origin of the Family*, pp. 129, 134, 143.
[38] *Origin of the Family*, pp. 179, 182; Marx, *Capital*, III, 698, 703.

for a system of robbery, and its development . . . is always connected with plundering, piracy, snatching of slaves, conquest of colonies." [39]

The advent of capitalism intensifies the work of self-interest. Original accumulation, which, to recall, prepared the ground for the inauguration of this mode of production, is "written in letters of blood and fire," is marked by series of "thefts, outrages, popular misery," is an array of "murder, robbery and war." Born in the storm of blood and fire, the capitalist system, throughout its existence, remains true to its heritage. It imposes on the relations between man and man the "nexus" of self-interest, complains the *Communist Manifesto* (page 15). In the drive for wealth, all that is sacred is trampled upon, and nothing escapes violent hands. "Not even are the bones of saints, and still less are more delicate *res sacrosanctae extra commercium hominum* able to withstand this alchemy" of turning everything into gold.[40] The world becomes a market, with price as the universal language, and nationality is but the "guinea's stamp." [41] Only with the coming of socialism will the ravages of self-interest vanish. This order will furnish an environment devoid of stimuli that would call the black trait into exercise.

It is true that the two writers are aware that human beings also possess finer attributes. Engels mentions that "the mutual and reciprocal feelings of men for one another such as sexual love, friendship, compassion, self-sacrifice, etc.," are facts anyone can observe. He admits that at times men are impelled by "ideal motives, zeal for honor, enthusiasm for truth and justice, personal hate." [42] Yet these finer qualities are regarded as private, domestic virtues manifested in the humbler dealings of everyday life. They do not occupy a prominent position in social processes. There they are marginal, not focal. On the arena of history, the persistent human passion that plays a dominant part is self-interest.

---

[39] *Capital*, III, 389–390.                    [40] *Capital*, I, 148.
[41] Marx, *Critique of Political Economy*, pp. 207–208.
[42] *Feuerbach*, pp. 77–78, 105.

The play of self-interest is not confined to the economic sphere. As will be seen in later chapters, Marx and Engels put self-interest in a central place in nearly all other departments of civilization. Institutions are designed to serve the interests of the master class; ideas and ideals are charged with class interests. In both static and dynamic phases of social organization self-interest plays an outstanding part.

Viewed in such a comprehensive setting, self-interest in the Marxian corpus is a far cry from the "economic man" of the English classical school of economics. According to the exponents of this school, man is generally guided by self-interest only in one domain, economic dealings. They do not hold that people are largely actuated by such a motive in the many other spheres of life. Men like Adam Smith, Ricardo, and J. S. Mill hardly presume to maintain that in politics and law, ethics and religion, art and science self-interest is the keystone. In his *Theory of Moral Sentiments* Adam Smith subjects to severe criticism all the views which make self-interest the determining factor of social life and historical progress. He urges that the dominant force in society is, on the contrary, sympathy, or "fellow-feeling." [43] Similarly, J. S. Mill objects to the philosophers who maintain that "private, or worldly, interest" is the only ruling principle of government. He insists that no one single human trait can be made to explain social phenomena, but that "all the determining agencies" are to be studied carefully. "The phenomena of society do not depend, in essentials, on some one agency or law of human nature. . . The whole of the qualities of human nature influence those phenomena, and there is not one which influences them in a small degree." [44] Marx and Engels are remote from such views. If the older English economists assumed the economic man in pecuniary

---

[43] Adam Smith, *Theory of Moral Sentiments*, Part VII, sections ii, iii, and iv, pp. 542–611.

[44] J. S. Mill, *System of Logic*, II, 467, 469, 472; cf. p. 511. Cf. D. Ricardo, *Principles of Political Economy* (Everyman ed.), p. 83. See the suggestive article by Professor A. A. Young on "The Trend of Economics," in *Quarterly Journal of Economics*, XXXIX, especially pp. 175ff.

dealings, if Machiavelli constructed the "political man" in the domain of politics, Marx and his friend went further. With them, man is impelled by self-interest in nearly every phase of social life and culture. With them, man had been and still is, especially if he is not a proletarian, the apotheosis of self-interest.

It is not exactly clear whether self-interest is considered by Marx and Engels an inborn trait or a product of the environment. Such evidence as can be obtained on this question points, apparently, to their belief that it is innate. Engels praises the achievements of civilization, but he laments the fact that the *instinct* of self-interest was the moving force behind them: "But these exploits were accomplished," he complains, "by playing on the most sordid passions and instincts of man, and by developing them at the expense of all his other gifts." [45] In the primitive, communal gens war "reigned from tribe to tribe," and in time the cruelty of warfare was modified "simply by self-interest." [46] Already in this excellent society the leaders coveted the usurper's place, and the nobles sought wealth and power. In the dissolution of this order and in the introduction of classes self-interest played a commanding part. "The new system of classes is inaugurated by the meanest impulses: vulgar covetousness, brutal lust, sordid avarice, selfish robbery of commonwealth. The old gentile society without classes is undermined and brought to a fall by the most contemptible means: theft, violence, cunning, treason." [47] Introduce money into a communal society, and the social ties will break up, gradually introducing private production.[48] The question arises, How did such mean traits ever find their habitat in the human breast when the gens environment originally contained nothing that would produce them, since it was fit to raise only "splendid men and women"? It was a worthy society. "How wonderful," exclaims Engels, "this gentile constitution is in all its natural simplicity! No soldiers, gendarmes, and police-

[45] *Origin of the Family*, p. 215.
[46] *Origin of the Family*, pp. 118–119.
[47] *Origin of the Family*, p. 119.
[48] Engels, *Anti-Dühring*, p. 339.

men, no . . . prefects or judges, no prisons, no lawsuits, and still affairs run smoothly. . . There cannot be any poor and destitute. . . All are free and equal — the women included." [49]

It may therefore be taken, but we cannot be certain, that they regard self-interest as inborn. In primitive communism, up to its last days, environment gave this human trait no opportunity to emerge. But as exchange between neighboring tribes increased, and as opportunities presented themselves for the acquisition of wealth and prestige, it began to assert itself. Under socialism, presumably, the environment will once more provide no incentive for this instinct to come into action. It will slumber in the innermost recesses, cramped in by the nobler motives in full operation, and will languish for want of nourishment.

It is sad to reflect that so many thinkers since Plato and Aristotle have held generally pessimistic views of human nature. Of course, men like Godwin, Rousseau, and Condorcet are in the other camp. These optimists admit that human nature is unattractive as it displays itself in prevailing circumstances, but they are persuaded that it is capable of perfection in an improved environment. Marx and Engels range themselves among the optimists, perceiving a great future for the race under communism. But while many of the other optimists were convinced that human nature is inherently noble but is degraded by a shabby environment, it is probable that our two friends did not have an exalted opinion of human nature generically, but hoped for the superior setting of communism to elevate it to fine achievements. We find Engels quoting with approval: " 'One thinks he is saying something great,' Hegel remarks, 'if one says that mankind is by nature good; but it is forgotten that one says something far greater in the words: man is by nature evil.' " [50]

[49] *Origin of the Family*, p. 117.
[50] *Feuerbach*, p. 84.

## ENVIRONMENT

Such is human nature when viewed in the light of heredity. Men have capacities, individual differences, and certain persistent traits. However, according to Marx and his friend, human nature as it reveals itself in reality cannot be fully comprehended when a mere summation of such items is exhibited. Real human nature embodies the aggregate of concrete responses of definite people to a particular environment, as well as the mass of specific ideas, feelings, prejudices, experiences, and aims, nourished by a given age and place. Stripped of environmental data, human nature is a mere abstraction.[51] Human traits, moreover, do not constitute a fixed apparatus supplied at birth; on the contrary, they are constantly shaping themselves and are steadily undergoing modifications, under the impact of stimuli. Accordingly, human beings are not the same the world over and throughout history. "All history is nothing but a continual transformation of human nature,"[52] and anyone who would presume to criticize or evaluate human behavior ought to "deal with human nature in general, and then with human nature as modified in each historical epoch."[53]

One of the environmental agencies that mold human character relates to the geographical conditions. Marx and Engels, however, give this point insufficient attention. The indirect influence of the physical surroundings, through the effect on a mode of production, is readily acknowledged, but the direct influence receives little discussion. Engels remarks that the presence of domestic animals in certain regions of Asia had supplied, in the remote past, a milk and meat diet, and accounts for the superior development of the Aryans and the Semites; while the Indians of New Mexico had a small brain, because they were compelled to subsist on a vegetable diet. But he adds that he is not certain of the correctness of this view.[54] Marx indicates that where nature is luxuriant in her gifts, she

[51] Engels, *Feuerbach*, p. 83.
[52] Marx, *Poverty of Philosophy*, p. 160.
[53] *Capital*, I, 668n.
[54] *Origin of the Family*, p. 32 and n.

treats man like a child, and does not compel him to develop himself. But where she is parsimonious in the distribution of resources, she puts man on his guard, calls his abilities into constant exercise, and forces him to economize, to plan, and to enter upon all sorts of enterprizes.[55]

In the formation of man's character the foremost position is given, however, to a second factor, the power of work in general and occupation in particular. "By thus acting on the external world and changing it, he at the same time changes his own nature" and "develops his slumbering powers."[56] Work claims a big part of man's life and constitutes the major area of his experience. Accordingly, in proportion as his work is broad or narrow, stimulating or monotonous, it develops or stunts his abilities. We can differentiate, Marx and Engels assert, between man and animal by consciousness or whatever else we like, but man begins to differ from the animal only when he begins to produce his livelihood. What he is, they continue, depends on his production, on what and how he produces.[57] It is the division of labor in the factory which dwarfs the worker's capacities, and it is the dull work in the country that denies full development to the agricultural laborer.[58] The petty bourgeoisie in Germany is timid and vacillating. "The *mesquin* character of its commercial transactions and its credit operations are eminently apt to stamp its character with a want of energy and enterprise."[59] Only variety of work can develop the many sides of human ability and character, and this principle will guide the organization of labor in a communist society.[60]

The effectiveness of work looms so large in Engels' mind that he sees in it the principal factor in the evolution of the ape into the human being. This essay in anthropology is offered

[55] *Capital*, I, 563 and n., 564 and n. Cf. Marx and Engels, *Gesamtausgabe*, Part III, vol. 3, pp. 355–356, 361–363.
[56] Marx, *Capital*, I, 198. Cf. A. Marshall, *Principles of Economics*, pp. 1–2.
[57] *Deutsche Ideologie*, pp. 10–11.
[58] Engels, *Anti–Dühring*, p. 318. *Capital*, I, *passim*.
[59] Engels, *Revolution and Counter-Revolution*, p. 169.
[60] Engels, *Anti–Dühring*, p. 221.

in a notable article.[61] Ages ago a highly developed type of anthropoid apes, our ancestors, discarded the practice of moving on all fours and adopted the erect posture. "This was *the decisive step* in the transition from ape to man." [62] Already in climbing trees the hands performed somewhat different functions from those of the feet, and were also used to gather and hold food. But now the hands were freed for a gradually expanding scope of operations until the changed structure of the hands and their acquired dexterity, steadily inherited by the offspring, reached the perfection to conjure up Raphael's paintings, Thorwaldsen's statues, and Paganini's music.[63] With the change in the structure and functions of the hands a change took place in the structure of the whole organism, in compliance with the law of physiological correlation. Our simian forbears were always gregarious, but the rising mastery over nature attained by labor which their developing hands made possible reinforced the necessity of coöperation and alike created the need for communication. "The need led to the creation of its organ," and gradually the mouth organs developed, with the power of articulation.[64]

Under the constant stimulus of labor and speech, the brain began to expand until it reached the dimensions and quality characteristic of man. The growth of the brain was accompanied by the perfection of its instruments, the sense organs, like hearing, sight, smell, and so on. Parallel with this progress went the widening and deepening of the realm of consciousness, the power of abstraction and judgment, and the accumulation of knowledge. All these attainments in their turn gave stimulus to the further evolution of labor and speech. Thus the anthropoid ape evolved into man. With the transition to the estate of man, society becomes a powerful lever in the many-sided development of human nature. Engels sums up the difference between the band of tree-climbing monkeys and human society in

---

[61] "Der Anteil der Arbeit an der Menschwerdung der Affen," *Neue Zeit*, XIV, no. 2, pp. 545–554. Reprinted as chap. ix in *Dialectics of Nature*, pp. 279–296.

[62] *Dialectics of Nature*, p. 279. Engels' italics.

[63] *Dialectics of Nature*, p. 281.

[64] *Dialectics of Nature*, p. 283.

one italicized word, *Labor*.[65] "In a sense, we have to say that labor created man himself."[66] And he reproaches those thinkers who stress the mind as the central factor in the advance of human civilization.[67]

Immense influence in shaping man's nature is, thirdly, assigned to society and its institutions. Man breathes the atmosphere of his social environment, absorbs its traditions, assimilates its ways of looking at things, and forms his character in the process. Apart from society, man is a paradox. He must be within society before there can be reference to this nature. "Man is in the most literal sense of the word a *zoon politikon*, not only a social animal, but an animal which can develop into an individual only in society."[68] In each period human nature is a mirroring of the unique characteristics of the given social organization. Says Marx in his sixth note on Feuerbach: "But the essence of man is not an abstraction dwelling in each individual. In its reality it is the ensemble of the social conditions."[69]

Each society produces its own brand of human nature by casting man's potentialities into a definite configuration, and by implanting in him ideas and feelings peculiar to its own age. The primitive communal clan produces fearless, altruistic, liberty-loving individuals. The Germans, who triumph over decadent Rome, infuse better blood into decrepit Europe, and make history on its ruins, can achieve this, because they are a product of gens society, and not because of "an innate magic power of the German race," as the jingo historians would have it.[70] The eighteenth-century individual is a child of a society that saw the complete disappearance of feudalism, and was engaged in building the capitalistic order, which had been in formation since the sixteenth century.[71] The objection that socialism is impossible in practice would therefore be met by Marx and

---

[65] *Dialectics of Nature*, pp. 285, 18.     [66] *Dialectics of Nature*, p. 279.
[67] *Dialectics of Nature*, p. 289.
[68] Marx, *Critique of Political Economy*, p. 268.
[69] Marx and Engels, *Gesamtausgabe*, Part I, vol. 5, p. 534. Cf. *ibid*., pp. 27–28.     [70] Engels, *Origin of the Family*, pp. 188–189.
[71] Marx, *Critique of Political Economy*, p. 267; *Poverty of Philosophy*, p. 125.

Engels with the retort: You conjure up the ghost of the human nature that will have been sent to its grave by the tumbling ruins of the capitalist order; the human nature you have in mind is only the inevitable fruit of the present social organization; socialism will transform society, and human nature with it.[72]

Two modifications must be kept in mind at this juncture. To Marx, society is not an independent entity, but a resultant of the mode of production, which gives it a distinctive character. Therefore, when discussing Marx's view of the influence of society on man, one ought to remember that the system of production is subsumed as the basic force, and that it is the productive system which releases the elements characterizing society and building human nature. In the second place, with Marx and Engels society is too large and too general an entity to identify an individual by it. The direct, compelling influence on man's nature is exerted by the class to which he belongs. Society lays the broad foundations and imparts tonality to the general outlook and habits of man; but the specific traits are engraved by the class of which he is a member. In the strict sense, man is a product of his class. His ideas and interests, aims and attitudes, his modes of conduct, his whole psyche, are those of his class. In his preface to the first volume of *Capital* (page 15) Marx declares that it is not his intention to blame individuals when he depicts the capitalist and the landlord; they are merely the "personifications of economic categories, embodiments of particular class relations and class interests." The mode of production, the classes it engenders, the type of society it generates, and the social institutions it creates — these are implied when one talks of the action Marx and Engels ascribe to social environment on man's make-up.

### The Rôle of Individuals

The problem of the rôle of individuals in history would not down, and Marx and Engels, sometimes deliberately and some-

---

[72] A very able brief for the view that human nature is plastic will be found in Professor John Dewey's *Human Nature and Conduct.*

times unconsciously, refer to it. Their statements, however, do not reveal a consistent frame of reference; some pull one way, some the other way. Engels says that the "brilliant school of French materialists" made the eighteenth century, "in spite of all battles on land or sea won over Frenchmen by Germans and Englishmen, a preëminently French century, even before that crowning French Revolution." These thinkers are referred to as "great men" who prepared the minds of the French for the revolution.[73] Napoleon "brought about within France" the conditions necessary for a bourgeois society, and beyond the French frontier "he swept away" the feudal system.[74] Feuerbach's philosophy "made an epoch." [75] Hegel rendered "an epoch-making service" by presenting things as in a process of growth, and his system played "an incomparably greater rôle than any earlier system," although he was "somewhat of a philistine," and his cult of the Idea was not without "idealistic frippery" and "delirious phantasies." [76]

"Peter the Great overthrew Russian barbarism with barbarism." [77] Wyatt and Watt helped in introducing the Industrial Revolution.[78] Marx declares William Petty "the father of political economy," and Engels states that this science "arose in the minds of a few geniuses of the seventeenth century," but is essentially the product of the eighteenth because of the physiocrats and Adam Smith.[79] The discovery of the labor theory of value marks "an epoch in the history of the development of the human race": this doubtless alludes to British economists.[80] "Every real advance in England on behalf of the workers links itself to the name of Robert Owen. . . He introduced as transition measures to the *complete communistic organization* of

[73] *Socialism, Utopian and Scientific*, pp. xiii, 1–2.
[74] Marx, *Eighteenth Brumaire*, pp. 10, 148–150.
[75] Marx, *Poverty of Philosophy*, appendix, p. 194.
[76] Engels, *Anti-Dühring*, pp. 30, 49; *Feuerbach*, pp. 46, 96.
[77] Marx, *Poverty of Philosophy*, appendix, p. 201.
[78] Marx, *Capital*, I, 406, 412; Engels, *Socialism, Utopian and Scientific*, p. xxix.
[79] *Capital*, I, 299; *Anti-Dühring*, p. 182.
[80] *Capital*, I, 85.

society" coöperative societies and labor bazars.[81] Darwin's theory receives tribute for the advance it gave to science.[82]

On the other hand we find in our two writers an abundance of expressions which tend to belittle the achievements of individuals. An analysis of the inventions of the eighteenth century would demonstrate that they were due very little to the work of a single individual, says Marx.[83] "Man makes his own history, but he does not make it out of the whole cloth; he does not make it out of conditions chosen by himself, but out of such as he finds at hand." [84] Revolutions are not precipitated by the ill will of a few agitators, but by persistent social needs, the fulfillment of which is made impossible by outworn institutions; and the failure of an uprising is not to be ascribed to "the accidental efforts, talents, faults, errors, or treacheries of some of the leaders," but to the conditions of existence of the nations convulsed.[85] The dreams of the eighteenth-century French philosophers of justice, inalienable rights, and the rule of reason found their substance, after the Revolution, in the iniquities of the bourgeois order; for these philosophers "could, no more than their predecessors, go beyond the limits imposed upon them by their epoch." [86] Neither the statesman nor the thinker, neither the leader nor the revolutionary can make society raise itself by its bootstraps.

In general, Marx is critical in his estimates of important persons, and is inclined to minimize their significance. Where others would see cause for praise, he discerns weakness and faults, although often his criticism is well to the point — as far as it goes. Burke is "the celebrated sophist and sycophant," the "execrable political cant-monger." "This sycophant, who in the pay of the English oligarchy played the romantic *laudator temporis acti* against the French Revolution, just as, in the pay of the North American colonies . . . he had played the Liberal

---

[81] Engels, *Socialism, Utopian and Scientific*, pp. 25–26. My italics.

[82] *Feuerbach*, pp. 99, 101; *Anti-Dühring*, p. 83.

[83] *Capital*, I, 406n.

[84] Marx, *Eighteenth Brumaire*, p. 9.

[85] Engels, *Revolution and Counter-Revolution*, pp. 14–16.

[86] Engels, *Socialism, Utopian and Scientific*, pp. 3–4.

against the English oligarchy, was an out-and-out vulgar bourgeois." [87] Bentham is "the arch-philistine Jeremy Bentham, that insipid, pedantic, leather-tongued oracle of the ordinary bourgeois intelligence of the nineteenth century"; "a genius in the way of bourgeois stupidity." [88] Cobden and Bright are only "manufacturers"; just "Boring, Bright, and Company," in whom people have "their worst enemies and the most shameless hypocrites"; who are crusading for free trade only because it spells good profits.[89] Locke is "an advocate of the new bourgeoisie in all forms, the manufacturers against the working classes and paupers, the commercial class against the old-fashioned usurers, the financial aristocracy against the state debtors." [90] Malthus is "that master in plagiarism," the producer of a "pasquinade." [91] Macaulay is a "Scotch sycophant and fine talker," a "systematic falsifier of history." [92] McLeod, "who has taken upon himself to dress up the confused ideas of Lombard Street in the most learned finery, is a successful cross between the superstitious mercantilists and the enlightened Free Trade bagmen." [93] J. S. Mill is a vulgar economist on page 654, but is exonerated on page 669.[94] "He is as much at home in absurd contradictions as he feels at sea in the Hegelian contradiction, the source of all dialectic." [95] Ranke is the "little dwarf," "the bouncing little root-grubber"; his "spirit of history [is] facile anecdote-mongering and the attribution of all great events to petty and mean causes." [96] Count Rumford, the famous physicist, is "an American humbug, the baronized Yankee." [97] J. B. Say is the vulgarizer of Adam Smith; "the dull J. B. Say"; "this comical *'prince de la science,'* " whose

[87] *Capital*, I, 354, 833n.

[88] *Capital*, I, 668 and n.

[89] *Poverty of Philosophy*, appendix, p. 209; *Capital*, I, 19; *Klassenkämpfe in Frankreich*, p. 84.

[90] *Critique of Political Economy*, p. 93.

[91] *Capital*, I, 556n.; *Poverty of Philosophy*, p. 194.

[92] *Capital*, I, 300n., 788n.

[93] *Capital*, I, 70.

[94] *Capital*, I, 654n., 669n.

[95] *Capital*, I, 654n.

[96] Marx and Engels, *Selected Correspondence*, p. 159.

[97] *Capital*, I, 659.

"merits consisted rather of the impartiality with which he equally misunderstood his contemporaries, Malthus, Sismondi and Ricardo." [98] Senior is a vulgar economist who substituted "for an economic category a sycophantic phrase — *voilà tout*," of abstinence, and who presumes that "the world still jogs on solely through the self-chastisement of this modern penitent of Vishnu, the capitalist." [99] "Adam Smith applied the Scotch saying that 'mony mickles mak a muckle' even to his spiritual wealth, and therefore concealed with petty care the sources to which he owed the little out of which he tried to make so much. More than once he prefers to break off the point of the discussion, whenever he feels that an attempt on his part clearly to formulate the question would compel him to settle his accounts with his predecessors." [100] Thiers stands on a "mean, petty pedestal"; is an "historical shoeblack" of Napoleon I; is "a master in small state roguery, a virtuoso in perjury and treason, a craftsman in all the petty stratagems, cunning devices, and base perfidies of parliamentary party warfare; . . . with class prejudices standing him in the place of ideas, and vanity in the place of a heart; his private life as infamous as his public life is odious." [101] Arthur Young is "the unutterable statistical prattler"; his "reputation is in the inverse ratio of his merit." [102]

It is not easy to weave one's way among the different statements on personalities to a definite conclusion regarding their rôle. One point seems clear, however. No individual can resist the tide of conditions generated by the system of production, or turn historical currents away from their courses and direct

[98] *Critique of Political Economy*, p. 123.

[99] *Capital*, I, 654–655.

[100] *Critique of Political Economy*, p. 232. However, elsewhere he implies that Smith is an original thinker, and refers to his merits. See *Capital*, II, 451; III, 721, 891.

[101] *Poverty of Philosophy*, p. 200; *Civil War in France (Paris Commune)*, pp. 54–56. Thus to Thiers for having squelched the Paris Commune!

[102] *Capital*, I, 301n., 254n. See, however, Marx and Engels, *Selected Correspondence*, p. 57, for the reference to some of the economists on the above list as "the master-minds among the economists of Europe." Of Ricardo he speaks in high terms (same reference), but regards him as "the most stoical adversary of the proletariat."

them into new channels. Problems and solutions emerge only as conditions ripen them. "It is still true that man proposes and God (that is, the extraneous force of the capitalist mode of production) disposes." [103] If it is true, Engels writes, that a great man can lead to new deeds regardless of historical necessities, "he might just as well have been born five hundred years earlier, and would then have saved humanity five hundred years of error, strife, and suffering." [104]

On the question whether outstanding minds and characters can at least accelerate or retard the result, the answer seems conflicting. Marx writes to Kugelmann that accidents play a part in history, only they are compensated by the effects of other accidents, and that "acceleration and retardation are very much dependent on such accidents, and among these figures the accident of the character of the people who stand at the head of the movement." [105] In another letter to the same person he says that the material conditions in England are ripe for a social revolution, but the English lack revolutionary ardor; the leadership of the General Council of the First International would supply the deficiency "and thereby accelerate a truly revolutionary movement" in England, and consequently everywhere else. [106]

Then there are pronouncements of a different tenor. Acknowledging that each social epoch needs leaders, Marx agrees with Helvetius that if it does not find them it invents them. [107] In one of his last letters Engels is emphatic. That a great man appears at a given moment in a given country is pure accident, he states. Suppress him and a substitute will come. Napoleon was an accident, and in the absence of a Napoleon somebody else like him will appear. This is "proved," he continues, by the fact that each time the man was found when the need for him arose, e.g., Caesar, Augustus, Cromwell. Marx, he continues, discovered the materialistic conception of history, but Thierry, Mignet, Guizot, all the English historians prior to

[103] *Anti-Dühring*, p. 345.  [104] *Anti-Dühring*, p. 25.
[105] *Neue Zeit*, XX, no. 1, p. 710.  [106] *Ibid.*, XX, no. 2, p. 477.
[107] *Klassenkämpfe in Frankreich*, p. 70.

1850, and the American anthropologist, Lewis Morgan, demonstrated that the time was ripe for such a theory.[108]

In the same minimizing vein Engels treats the question of human will in history. Individual desires and plans, he says, far from flowing in one direction, cumulating into one movement and culminating in impressive events, run along numberless different paths, interfering with one another and modifying or canceling each other. In consequence, either "these ends are utterly incapable of realization"; or "the results of many individual wills produce effects for the most part quite other than what is wished — often, in fact, the very opposite"; or "the ends of the actions are intended, but the results which follow from the actions are not intended." The actual historical event, then, is not the product of human will. "That which is willed but rarely happens . . . the innumerable conflicts of individual wills and individual agents in the realm of history reach a conclusion which is on the whole analogous to that in the realm of nature — which is without definite purpose." [109]

This view is puzzling indeed. The individual wills either are or are not organically related to the economic situation. If they are, it is not clear why they should display enormous diversity or why, certainly, they should cancel out into nothing. If they are not, it is equally obscure why human wills should be at striking variance with surrounding realities. Assuredly, to Engels, man's strivings and plans are not born in a vacuum. Be it as it may as far as this statement by Engels is concerned, Marx incontestably holds that the historic action of human beings moves in integral connection with economic and social facts as the prime influence.

Thus in the conception of the two colleagues the individual is of negligible significance in shaping human destiny. The rôle of actors on the historic stage, the task of carrying out the dictates of the economic developments, are assigned to classes. Engels declares:

[108] Letter of January 25, 1894, in Marx and Engels, *Selected Correspondence*, p. 518.
[109] *Feuerbach*, pp. 104–106.

If, therefore, we set out to discover the impelling forces which . . . stand behind historical figures, and constitute the true final impulses of history, we cannot consider so much the motives of single individuals, however preëminent, as those which set in motion great masses, entire nations, and again, whole classes of people in each nation, and this, too, not in a momentarily flaring and quickly dying flame, but to enduring action culminating in a great historical change.[110]

## SUMMARIZING REMARKS

The conception of human nature is central to the thinking of a social scientist. In social phenomena, no matter what one's philosophy is about them, the individual is the unit of action, and what one thinks of the individual's make-up informs what one thinks of the drama of social events generally. Men make their history, says Marx. What is man that Marx is mindful of him? It is the purpose of this section to synthesize the components in Marx's theory of man's nature, with some attention to the distribution of emphasis. Some of the points briefly mentioned here anticipate what will be developed later.

It was suggested in the preceding paragraphs that Marx may regard as inherent to man certain mental capacities as well as self-interest and devotion to tradition. But one cannot be sure. When one reflects on the general picture given by the scattered elliptical statements on man's nature and when one is mindful of Marx's general attitude to such a question, one is brought to realize that to Marx man has no invariant substratum of attributes and no definite bundle of separate entities which could be classified as dispositions, abilities, emotions, and the like. What makes man is fluid and changing with the changing stream of events. Man is identified with his surroundings, the form of production, institutions, and ideas. Since these surroundings are man's work, man is what he does, thinks, and builds, in constant interaction with his natural and social environment. There is no such thing as human nature in itself. Man is a biological being that we can see and touch, but that is merely the animal part of him. The distinctly human aspect is not something residing in him, but what he expresses by action, thought, and attitude. What he is is a never-ceasing proc-

[110] *Feuerbach*, p. 108.

ess of development, and history is the spectacle of the continual transformation of human nature.

But if man is what man does, what is there in him that enables him to do it? To affirm that he is an empty vessel, but that somehow the complicated forms of production, institutions, ideas, artistic expression, and aspirations manage to spring forth and give us an index of his nature, does not seem to make sense. It is not necessary to insist on instincts or faculties, expressing themselves as constants and breaking through the environmental medium to invariable and predictable results. But there must be in his constitution such native potentialities as creativeness, criminality, ambition, inertia, and the complex of attributes that goes under the name of intelligence. Of course, the content of the expression of the potentialities varies. In Greece the thief steals tetradrachms, in the United States federal reserve notes. Sophocles writes of Oedipus and with a stylus on tablets, while Shakespeare deals with Hamlet, and uses quill and paper. Moreover, despite the shifting environment, there is a considerable aggregate of human traits that endure through time. There is no distinction, basically, between ancient drama, satire, philosophical speculation, and ours. In Herodotus, Thucydides, Gibbon, Macaulay, and Tolstoy's *War and Peace*, we see the same human beings, with the same capacities, emotions, temperaments, cunning, and wickedness.

Without an environment the potentialities are meaningless, but the environment without them is meaningless, too. There is an interaction between the two, and it is possible that in certain contexts the one or the other will have the upper hand. For instance, self-preservation is to many the supreme example of an inborn datum. Yet in certain circumstances it may yield to self-destruction, as in cases of heroism in saving a child or a friend, in the defense of a city under siege, or in going to the lions for one's faith. One may suggest that certain potentialities, as the power to think, to feel, to strive, to get "hunches" in scientific effort, may be largely or partly in the genes within the chromosomes, and are hereditary; while the direction which the potentialities take, their content, method, and means are largely environmental.

It is difficult to tell what Marx would say to this. He never probed into the problem. But should he allow that there are such potentialities, he would no doubt at once attach reservations. One, these powers, he would say, are in themselves amorphous, and only what they do in interaction with external data can tell us of their presence. Two, these capacities are not so many distinct entities, each going its own way, but constitute an integrated and mutually conditioning whole. Three, these potentialities are not initially wrought into the biology of our remote ancestors, but evolved by slow gradations through the ages past. Four, these capacities, even as they exist today, are, with the exception to be noted presently, no different qualitatively but only in degree from those in the higher animals.

There is apparently another gap in Marx's account of human nature, and it concerns the important fact of individual differences. Marx talks of some persons as having a superior brain, but his agreement with Adam Smith on the cause of the distance between the porter and the philosopher casts a shadow on the opinion that he believes in inherited differences. We do not learn from Marx what makes a Plato, Leonardo da Vinci, Shakespeare, or Newton, and people of lesser stature but yet of outstanding capabilities. Environment is important, but it may be doubted that it is enough always to account for differences in constructive imagination, ambition, or wickedness; yet such traits and differences play a part in propelling the small changes and little improvements in every walk of life, cumulating, in time, to dimensions which count in social evolution. There are numberless permutations and combinations of human traits in their interactions with the variegated aspects of the environment, so that no two persons are alike psychically just as no two persons are alike physically, and this fact deserves the attention of the investigator of social organization and social change.

Among the external data which shape man's nature, a preeminent place is given by Marx and Engels to labor. It is labor that starts the ape on the long and tortuous career of developing into a human being. Animals possess intelligence. They also work. They procure food, build homes, and engage in cooperative efforts. But because they have no hands, their work is condemned to a repetitive routine, and their nature stays unchanged for long periods. Labor is the cornerstone not only in anthropological origins but also in the unfolding destinies of mankind. It is ever present in shaping man's make-up, and it will doubtless continue in this function under communism. In labor man comes in contact with nature, with matter, and with stubborn facts. Labor baffles, fatigues, and challenges. It means tools, science, and human association. It is practice, and practice is to Marx, as we shall see, one of the sources of genuine knowledge. Of course, labor is not an abstraction but is cast into a definite mode of production, and it does not stand alone but implies correlative classes and appropriate institutions.

But human nature, like society, is too general a concept. To make it more or less specific, we have to project it, Marx would say, against the class background. Every form of production beyond the gens order and prior to communism splits society into classes. An individual is first of all a member of a given class. As such he takes his unique place in production, is associated with a particular group of people, and is motivated by a distinct set of interests. He is shaped by the class standard of living and by class experiences, emotions, outlooks, and strivings. His habitat is primarily the class world and only secondarily the social world generally. He sees things through class-glasses, darkly, except the modern proletariat who eventually acquires adequate understanding at least of some elements in the social scene. The individual is not conscious that his glasses are class-made, reflecting and refracting with a particular angle every experience. He regards his conduct, viewpoints, and feelings as normal and reasonable: the other people are prejudiced or ignorant. To step outside the class cocoon and to look at what is inside it objectively and critically is to practice the art of raising yourself by your bootstraps. He who can do this is a

scientist. Marx finds few scientists in the field of social phenomena.

It may contribute to the understanding of Marx's and Engels' conception of man if we inquire into the question whether
there is something in human nature that is not found in the
animal. As far as general intelligence is concerned, they see no
difference in kind but only in degree. Induction, deduction, abstraction, analysis, synthesis, and experiment "are absolutely
the same in men and the higher animals." But when it comes to
dialectical thinking, which explores "the nature of concepts,"
a sharp difference emerges. Self-examination, on the level of
procedures of thought, is the attribute of man alone.[111] Perhaps
this is what Engels has in mind when he says: "History is only
differentiated from natural history as the evolutionary process
of *self-conscious organisms*." [112] It may be observed that once
we grant as much intelligence to the animals as Engels does,
even this particular difference seems to savor more of a difference in degree than in kind.

Marx seemingly points to another difference. In his discussion of the labor process he indicates that with the animal labor
is instinctive, while man plans his activity, informs it with a
purpose and a will, and foresees the result in his imagination.[113]
But what Marx gives Engels takes away. Engels declares expressly that animals act in a "planned and premeditated fashion," and that "conscious, planned action" develops with the
nervous system of all animals.[114] We are told by the two
writers, in a very early work, that the distinction between man
and the animal begins as soon as man's labor graduates to the
level at which it can be called production;[115] but now we are
told that animals are also engaged in production, only without
a conscious design according to Marx, and with a conscious design according to Engels.

The difficulty may be resolved by the suggestion that Engels

[111] *Dialectics of Nature*, p. 203.
[112] *Dialectics of Nature*, p. 164. Engels' italics.
[113] *Capital*, I, 198.
[114] *Dialectics of Nature*, pp. 290–291.
[115] *Deutsche Ideologie*, p. 10.

means to attribute conscious and planned activity to the animal only with respect to the immediate elementary job and not with reference to remote consequences. Man foresees the result far ahead, e.g., the crops that will come from sowing and the advantage of keeping animals that will breed more animals, whereas the animal is concerned with the immediate purpose, as when the wolf devours the doe. Man's planning is not only conscious and intentional, but it ranges over a wider area and over a greater span of time. It is in this sense that Engels can declare that the ultimate distinction lies in the fact that the animal does not impress its will on nature, and uses nature without changing it, while man changes nature and makes it a servant to his ends.[116] The conditions of existence of the animal are given by nature, and the animal adapts itself to them. But the complex of conditions, natural and social, under which man lives are very largely man's own making. "Man is the sole animal capable of working his way out of the mere animal state — his normal state is one appropriate to his consciousness, *one to be created by himself.*" [117]

Since the mode of production is overwhelmingly responsible for human nature, and since our two writers favor only coöperative, socially planned production, one can surmise what their estimation of human nature as it actually exhibited itself in the successive productive orders is apt to be. They have admiration for the humans in the gens society, not without being mindful of their primitive ignorance. In classic slavery, they depict avarice, cruelty, oppression, graft, quarrels, and war. In the feudal centuries, they underscore the arrogance and callousness of the upper orders bent on keeping the masses in subjection, in brutalizing toil, and in abject ignorance. They indicate that the independent farmer or handicraftsman of the late Middle Ages exercised some initiative in his work, but they present him as petty, with a limited horizon, and of dwarfed intelligence. But their heartburning and eloquence are reserved for what capitalism does to human nature. The pages of the

---

[116] *Dialectics of Nature*, pp. 290–291, 285–286.
[117] *Dialectics of Nature*, p. 187. Engels' italics.

*Communist Manifesto, Capital, Class Struggles in France, Eighteenth Brumaire, Civil War in France,* and Engels' *Condition of the Working Class in England in 1844, The Housing Question,* and *Revolution and Counter-Revolution* are flaming with descriptions of and comments on the cunning, treachery, cruelty, and lasciviousness of the master classes, and of the pettiness, vacillation, shabbiness, hypocrisy, and chicken-heartedness of the middle classes. Especially are these pages groaning or thundering with pained outcries over the lot of the laboring poor, dehumanized, degraded, foul-mouthed, deprived of decent impulses, derelict, selling their wives and children into wage-slavery, reduced to automatons, to fractions of human beings, by the brutalizing toil amidst unwholesome and dangerous surroundings, by poverty, slums, saloons, brothels, and above all, by the fractionalized division of labor in the factory which makes of man not a producer but a flunkey to the machine.

Despite their striving for objectivity, they do not regard the human being with indifference, as the biologist regards the crayfish. They obviously feel for the underdog, they apologize for his shortcomings, and they are pleased over his successes. Back of their heads are normative conceptions of what ought to be the destiny of human beings, and they talk of "true," "genuine," "worthy" human nature. They imply an emphasis on dignity, freedom, decency, and reasonableness in human relations, and they disparage oppression and money-making alike as unworthy human goals. They expect of man what they do not expect of the animal, and they aim to exhort and to educate. This aim is the quintessence of their literary efforts. Education is, within limits, part of the environmental equation which determines human nature. In the third thesis on Feuerbach Marx states that while men are changed by circumstances, "circumstances are changed precisely by men, and the educator himself must be educated." [118] To evaluate Marx and Engels as no more than heartless firebrands is to misunderstand their lives and the aim of their labors.

[118] Marx and Engels, *Gesamtausgabe,* Part I, vol. 5, p. 534.

# CHAPTER V

## THE CLASS AND CLASS STRUGGLE

### NATURE OF A CLASS

WHAT is a class? What is the class struggle? What are the causes of such phenomena? Marx and Engels discuss these questions in many a connection, but leave much that is puzzling. Marx began an analysis of classes in notes which Engels put into the last chapter of the third volume of *Capital*, but the notes break off too soon.

Marx warns us in this chapter that the source of income does not distinguish classes. This criterion merely points to groupings which he calls "social division of labor," or division of labor by occupation. Physicians and lawyers are not distinct classes; nor are farm laborers and miners.[1] Republicans and democrats, conservatives and liberals, pacifists and militarists do not constitute classes. To Marx class and political party are not the same thing. A divergence of economic views would likewise fail to divide society into economic classes: free traders and protectionists, supporters of trade-unions and their opponents, those who favor monopoly and the exponents of competition, are not the classes he has in mind. Some define a Marxian class as a group of people who find themselves in the same economic condition. But this criterion is too general and vague. Organized labor with bargaining power is in a different economic condition from that occupied by the unorganized and the unskilled. The corporation lawyer with an extensive practice and the minister who depends for his living on the modest allowance of the parish are hardly in the same economic condition. Yet in neither case would Marx see two separate classes.

For the study of the nature of classes we must turn our attention to what Marx terms the economic or the social relations of production (*Produktionsverhältnisse*). He employs

[1] Marx, *Capital*, III, 1032.

this concept to designate two distinct facts. On the one hand, it comprises such general connections among the members of society or among the phenomena of a given era as are the peculiar resultants, and simultaneously the significant characteristics, of the prevailing system of production. For example, in present society division of labor, the workshop, money, capital, surplus-value are relations of production.[2]

However, this use of the term does not interest us here. It is the other fact to which this concept refers that is of special relevance: the fact of the personal relations among the producing agents. Under any mode of production the direct participators in the processes of making goods maintain various relations to one another, and on various terms.[3] In each productive enterprise and in the performance of their daily tasks not all men enjoy the same status. Not all perform the same functions and possess the same amount of freedom and authority. Some work, others supervise; some command, others obey; some own the property involved in the processes, others do not. The specific nature of these personal relations is vitally connected with the mode of production or with the productive forces. When these change, the relations will change. "Any change arising in the productive forces of men necessarily effects a change in their relations of production."[4] These relations define the character of the economic classes; and the considerations which give precision to these relations and serve as criteria of a class are two: property ownership and the degree of personal freedom attached to the dependent class.

[2] Marx, *Poverty of Philosophy*, pp. 87, 145; *Capital*, I, 839; III, 952.

[3] Marx, *Wage-Labor and Capital*, pp. 28ff.; *Capital*, III, 952.

[4] Marx, *Poverty of Philosophy*, p. 133. The English translation has "conditions of production," but the original, written by Marx in French, has *rapports de production*. See also *Capital*, I, 326; III, 919. The German word *Verhältnisse* may mean conditions as well as relations, and the expression *Produktionsverhältnisse* may designate conditions of production or relations of production. It is essential to distinguish which of these Marx had in mind, but there is no way of making the meaning certain. The context is not always a safe guide. The English translations are careless in some places, especially in *Poverty of Philosophy*, e.g., pp. 133, 175, and most likely, in the last pages of *Capital*, III, e.g., pp. 1022–1024, where "conditions of production" should, in some sentences, be replaced by "relations of production."

First, as to property. Property in general is not in question here. The humble wage earner may own a cottage, while the wealthy manufacturer may dwell in a rented mansion. The ownership of the means of production is meant, of buildings, raw materials, appliances, and machinery. This ownership gives the economic relations a definite stamp, and for this reason Marx employs the two (ownership and relations) interchangeably. "At a certain stage . . . the material forces of production in society come in conflict with the existing relations of production, or — what is but a legal expression for the same thing — with the property relations within which they had been at work before." [5] With him, "to define bourgeois property is nothing other than to explain all the social relations of bourgeois production." [6] To the question what were the relations of modern bourgeois property "one could only reply by a critical analysis of political economy, embracing the whole of the relations of property, not in their juridical expression as relations of will, but in their real form as relations of material production." [7]

The property relations enable one to identify the classes existing in the society of a given historical period. At a given time those who own the property needed in the processes of production constitute one class, and those who do not own it form another. The possession of the means of production places the owners in a position of power in relation to the nonowning workers. They dictate terms and exact a toll for the privilege of using their property. The result is that one class does not work, but obtains an income by filching part of the labor of the direct producers, while the other class does not receive the full product of its labor. Property is the right to appropriate other men's labor; it is an instrument of making the propertyless sweat for the owners. The peasant working on his own land receives a return which can be separated into wages, profit,

---

[5] *Critique of Political Economy*, p. 12.

[6] *Poverty of Philosophy*, p. 168.

[7] *Poverty of Philosophy*, appendix, p. 195. Cf. Marx and Engels, *Communist Manifesto*, p. 19, and *Capital*, I, 722.

and rent. The wages represent what he, as a hired laborer, could earn for his work. The other two portions represent surplus-labor which, if he were a hired laborer, he would have to relinquish to his employer. The reason he retains this surplus is not that he labors, but that he happens to be the owner of the land and the other property essential in the performance of his task.[8]

In the primitive gens all property was owned by the community, therefore there were no classes. Likewise, socialism will have no class stratification, and for the same reason. With the differences in property distribution, however, classes are introduced. Society becomes divided into upper and lower classes, into plunderers and plundered.[9] In capitalistic society, for example, some individuals own the means of production, while others do not. Hence two classes linked by a wage relationship; and, "So long as the relation of wage labor to capital is permitted to exist . . . there will always be a class which exploits and a class which is exploited."[10]

The relations, to repeat, based on private property enable us to discern the classes in a society under a given productive form. They do not aid us in distinguishing the classes as they existed in the various productive orders. Neither the slave in Greece, for instance, nor the modern proletariat owns the means of production. Yet they are not to be taken as members of one and the same class. When we talk of the slave and the proletariat, of the Greek master and the modern bourgeois, we are not dealing with two Marxian classes but with four. Why?

Here we come to the second element, closely allied with the first, which characterizes personal relations of production and gives a specific definition to classes; namely, the amount of freedom and authority enjoyed by the classes formed by the property relations. The ownership of the means of production not only bestows liberty on the owner, but also invests him with power over the freedom of the nonpossessors. The slave

---

[8] *Capital*, III, 1020–1021.
[9] Engels, *Anti-Dühring*, p. 165.
[10] Marx, *Poverty of Philosophy*, appendix, p. 224.

is not only a nonpossessor of the property needed in production, he is also deprived of the freedom to dispose of his person as he pleases. The master has complete control over him, and owns him like any other means of production. The slave is an object, a mere chattel. The modern laborer possesses no means of production, either, but he is a free agent. He has the liberty to conduct himself as he sees fit, and as a freeman he can enter into contractual relations with the capitalist.[11] Of course the capitalist can, by shutting the factory, withdraw the property indispensable in production, and deprive him of the means of gaining a livelihood. In other words, the employer has under his control the means of maintaining the worker's life. However, over his personal freedom he has no power; after work, the laborer can live as he pleases. The relations of production in the Middle Ages exemplify classes that occupy a middle position. The serf is not a slave, yet he is not as free as the modern proletarian; he is attached to the soil, and cannot leave his lord at will. The same holds, although in a different manner, of the journeyman. "Personal dependence here characterizes the social relations of production."[12] Likewise with respect to property. The serf possesses the land and the appliances he uses in his work, but he is not their absolute owner, for the lord has prerogatives in this matter.[13]

We arrive at this conclusion. A definite mode of production is correlated with particular individual relations among the participants in it. These relations are characterized primarily by the type of ownership of the property requisite in the processes of production, and by the degree of freedom exercised by the participating agents. These relations, and so characterized, furnish the key to the classes into which a given society is divided. One may define, then, a class as a group of people who, in a given society, with a given régime of production, are finding themselves in the same position with reference to two things: the ownership or nonownership of the property essen-

---

[11] *Capital*, I, 186–187.
[12] *Capital*, I, 89.
[13] *Capital*, III, 921.

tial in the labor-processes, and second, the personal freedom enjoyed or deprived of. Marx nowhere adequately explains this view, but that it is his view, scattered discussions make fairly certain. Each system of production implies a unique class structure. With a change in the mode of production, the relations of production change, and with them the type of classes.[14] Marx teaches that socialism will finally lead to "the abolition of class distinctions, the abolition of social relations of production on which they rest."[15]

It does not follow that a given society will necessarily have two classes only. In some historical periods the mode of production may not be homogeneous, but may fall into two distinct departments. In each department the relations of production may be different, and therefore in each one there is a set of two classes. In the Middle Ages agriculture and industry rested on foundations apart from one another. The country and the city were two provinces of production. Hence, two sets of classes, "lord and serf, guild-master and journeyman."[16]

It may seem that this theory of classes is faced with a difficulty. Marx talks of the struggle between the feudal nobility and the industrial bourgeoisie, and refers to them as two classes at war with each other. He also holds that the latter class was oppressed by the other, and therefore it sought emancipation. This case does not accord with the criteria of classes as advanced in the foregoing analysis. The bourgeoisie and the landed nobles were no participants in the same productive processes, and were not tied by relations of production. One class here did not have possession of the means of production that the other class needed in its work, nor did it exercise authority over the personal freedom of the members of the other class. The nobles and the bourgeoisie, in other words, were no allies in the productive tasks; the one class was in no position to exact any toll, like surplus-labor, for allowing the other the use of the means of production.

[14] Engels, *Socialism, Utopian and Scientific*, p. xix; *Anti–Dühring*, pp. 32, 174.                    [15] *Klassenkämpfe in Frankreich*, p. 94.
[16] Marx and Engels, *Communist Manifesto*, p. 12.

This is not a serious difficulty. Each society generates within itself the makings of its successor. When the old order begins to die out and the new one to gain in vigor, there is the inevitable struggle for supremacy between the upholders of the two orders. While the two systems overlap, the dominant classes of both systems find themselves side by side, the older class creating difficulties for the new class by frustrating its interests. At the end of the Middle Ages modern capitalism was born, and the bourgeois class appeared. The feudal lord, wielding his ancient, although waning, prerogative, sought to maintain the old system, whereas the bourgeois, hampered by the feudal institutions, sought to create conditions favorable to his prosperity. The two classes met at the juncture of the two régimes, and they clashed.

## THE EVOLUTION OF A CLASS

A class, in the Marxian sense, does not come into existence full-fledged. It has to go through a process of evolution. In a young, unsettled country classes cannot acquire a permanent character, because conditions are fluid. Spectacular opportunities are offered to energetic people, social groups continually change their nature, and individuals shift from one status to another.[17] But in a country more or less settled two stages are discerned in the development of a class. At first, the class is a class only because it is a group in contradistinction to another group which enjoys a different position in the relations of production. It is a class in so far as it finds itself facing another class. There is as yet no cohesion among the members composing it. There is no clear perception of the identity of their interests and no collective antagonism to the other class.

This stage prevails in the youthful period of an era of production, when the productive forces peculiar to it are not yet fully grown; when, consequently, the material conditions of existence do not define the nature of class exploitation and class interests, and do not point the way to class action. At such a stage Engels finds, for example, the German working class be-

---

[17] Marx, *Eighteenth Brumaire*, pp. 21–22.

fore the convulsions of 1848. It was, he says, as far behind the English and French workers in political and social development as the German bourgeoisie was behind its counterpart in the more advanced countries. In those days the capitalist mode of production had not progressed far enough in Germany to foster a strong proletarian class arrayed against a strong bourgeoisie. The two were classes merely because they found themselves as two distinct entities in the relations of production.[18]

Similarly, the agricultural groups everywhere are subject to conditions of work which tend to keep the producers at this unripe stage. Marx discusses the position of the French farming population before 1848. Although the interests of the farmers were identical, there was no recognition of this fact on their part, no organization, and no unity of conduct. Each farmer tilled his parcel of land, and was self-sufficient. He lived far from his neighbors, and had little social intercourse with his fellow beings. The family and the farm constituted a unit; a collection of these made a village; and a group of villages composed a department. The farmers as a whole represented a magnitude, "much as a bag with potatoes constitutes a potato-bag." They formed a class only in so far as they were facing another class in the population; but they were not a compact, self-conscious unit. Marx generalizes:

> In so far as millions of families live under economic conditions that separate their mode of life, their interests, and their culture from those of the other classes, and that place them in an attitude hostile toward the latter, they constitute a class; in so far as there exists only a local connection among these farmers, a connection which the individuality and exclusiveness of their interests prevent from generating among them any unity of interest, national connections, and political organization, they do not constitute a class.[19]

At this early stage the economic realities are inadequate to offer a class competent instruction regarding its immediate policies and legitimate historical mission. There are desultory collisions with the enemy class, haphazard schemes and half-hearted measures, but no consistent class strategy. The leaders

[18] *Revolution and Counter-Revolution*, pp. 22–25.
[19] *Eighteenth Brumaire*, pp. 144–145.

of the oppressed class improvise theories and weave utopias.[20] In the early days of capitalist England, Engels complains, the workers would turn a deaf ear to the cries of Saint-Simon, Fourier, and Owen that society was built on an unjust system of distribution. The material elements were too unripe to open their eyes to prevailing wrongs.[21] The contest is waged by individual members of the class or by small groups, against one or more members of the opposite class, but not against the whole exploiting class. Without a clear comprehension of their interests, the laboring population is divided and hesitant. "Thus this mass is already a class, as opposed to capital, but not yet for itself." [22]

The second stage emerges when the class becomes a class in itself. This occurs when "the mode of production . . . has already a good part of its declining phase behind it, when it has half outlived its day." [23] Then the productive forces begin to reveal the contradictions of the existing order, to furnish intimations of a better system, to prepare the materials that will go into the composition of the future society, and to suggest to the abused class the means of its emancipation. Mature economic conditions produce a mature proletarian class. Its members begin to think and to see their strength in terms of the class. But, Marx emphasizes, the proletarians will not become a class unless they are organized. "There is one element of success that the workers possess: its great numbers. But numbers will weigh in the balance only when united by organization and guided by knowledge." [24] The vehicles of organization are labor combinations and strikes. Well-developed means of communication, bringing workers together and acquainting them with their common interests, are of great service.[25]

Henceforth the course of action becomes clear. The progress-

[20] Marx and Engels, *Communist Manifesto*, pp. 54–55.
[21] Engels, *Anti-Dühring*, p. 166.
[22] Marx, *Poverty of Philosophy*, p. 189.
[23] Engels, *Anti-Dühring*, pp. 166.
[24] *Inauguraladresse der internationalen Arbeiter-Association*, p. 29
[25] Marx and Engels, *Communist Manifesto*, pp. 24–25; Marx, *Poverty of Philosophy*, p. 189; Engels, *Revolution and Counter-Revolution*, p. 20.

ively developing productive forces, destined to prepare the ground for a new society, are hampered in their growth by the old order. This antithesis teaches the class that the struggle for the abolition of the old system and for the establishment of a new one is the only means of its emancipation. Half measures and utopias composed by learned men are scorned from now on, and sporadic conflicts give way to purposeful struggles. A contest by a handful of members, in an isolated section of the country, is clothed with the dignity of a class war in behalf of class interests and as a step toward a new social order. Of course, these isolated collisions are intended to serve as training exercises for the final cataclysm. Strongly conscious of its interests, resolute in its struggle, ever pushing to its goal, unified, organized — this is a Marxian class.[26]

The impression prevails that Marx arbitrarily divides each society into two classes, but this is hardly a correct view. Where economic conditions have not assumed a definite pattern, society may consist of several classes. In 1848 Engels saw in Germany a variety of classes — the landed classes, like feudal lords, rich farmers, small freeholders, and feudal tenants; the industrial classes, like the bourgeoisie and petty traders; and the proletarians, including the agricultural laborers.[27] In Austria at the same period he found the serfs, the factory operatives, the journeymen, the merchants, the manufacturers, the intellectuals — and "not a single class satisfied." [28] In France, likewise, Marx discovered the financial aristocracy, the industrial bourgeoisie, the small traders, the parsons' class, the proletariat, the landlords, and the free farmers.[29]

However, this medley of classes does not endure in modern society. As capitalism advances, there is a convergence toward fewer classes, with some of the previous independent classes scaled down as mere subdivisions of the few outstanding cate-

---

[26] *Poverty of Philosophy*, pp. 136–137, 188–190; *Eighteenth Brumaire*, p. 145.

[27] *Revolution and Counter-Revolution*, pp. 17–25.

[28] *Revolution and Counter-Revolution*, pp. 60–61.

[29] *Eighteenth Brumaire*, p. 20 and *passim*.

gories. Marx is in the habit of stating that the "three great classes" of modern society are the landlords, the capitalists and the proletarians.[30] But he does not expect the landlords to endure as a separate category. With the progressive adoption of capitalistic methods in agriculture, the landlord turns capitalist. Already in 1852 Marx said: "Large landed property . . . has become completely bourgeois through the development of modern society." [31]

## THE MIDDLE CLASS

What of the celebrated middle class? There is such unanimity with respect of Marx's ideas on the subject that it is embarrassing to register a discordant note. It must be suggested, however, that his teachings on the subject are fragmentary and inconclusive. By the middle class he means all the groups occupying a position, as regards function and power, somewhere between the capitalists and the proletarians. Poised between the upper and lower layers of society, this class partakes of the nature of both and blunders along with confused interests. It looks up to the powerful bourgeoisie respectfully and jealously, but, squeezed by this upper tier, it is in fear of being reduced to the level of the proletariat. Uncertain of its ground, it gives its allegiance now to the capitalists and then to the laborers. It shrinks from direct responsibility when action is required and is satisfied with half measures. Marx and Engels waste no love on this class.[32]

Four categories of people may have title to membership in this class, in the Marxian scheme. One category comprises the small producers who work themselves and also employ some labor — the small manufacturer, the independent artisan, and the farmer. Next are those connected with what Marx terms

[30] *Capital*, III, 1031, 725; *Critique of Political Economy*, pp. 9, 305.

[31] *Eighteenth Brumaire*, p. 49.

[32] *Revolution and Counter-Revolution*, pp. 21, 154, 169; *Eighteenth Brumaire*, p. 57. "While the decline of former classes, such as knights, could furnish material for magnificent tragic works of art, the petty bourgeoisie, quite naturally, provides nothing more than feeble expressions of financial malice and collections of Sancho Panzian adages and maxims" (*Aus dem literarischen Nachlass von K. Marx, F. Engels*, III, 404).

the "circulation" of commodities (that is, marketing, buying, and selling), as middlemen, wholesalers, shopkeepers, speculators, and real estate dealers. A third group is composed of salaried persons working in factory and office, of those who "command in the name of capital" and their aids, like supervisors, managers and foremen, secretaries, bookkeepers, and clerks. Finally, comes the "ideological" category [33] of the professions, like doctors, lawyers, artists, newspapermen, and the clergy; and state servants, like officials, the military, and the police. With the exception of some in the first group and some in the third group, the members of the middle class are unproductive, in Marx's sense, inasmuch as they exist on the surplus-value yielded by the laborer in the factory and field and appropriated by the industrial capitalist and the landowner.[34]

One cannot be certain that Marx would insist on including all these elements in the middle class. There is no doubt about the first group, many in the third group, and most of the professions. But it is doubtful whether he would consider a millionaire lawyer, a wealthy physician catering to the rich, a large-scale wholesaler, a powerful politician, or even a high army officer as a member of the middle class, and not of the capitalist class; or whether he would group with this class, and not with the proletarians, the clerk, the letter-carrier, or the soldier drafted from the slums. When discussing the middle class, Marx generally refers to it as "petty bourgeoisie," "small capitalists," and "small proprietors."

There is equally no doubt about the fate of the first group, but what future Marx sees for the other groups is not altogether clear. With the unfolding of the productive forces the concentration of capital in individual firms proceeds at a swift pace, the methods of production become more complicated, and competition grows keener. The petty capitalist with his limited means and skill is unable to endure in the competitive struggle. He is pushed to the wall, and he sinks to the ranks

[33] *Capital*, I, 487.
[34] *Capital*, II, 142–144, 429, 531.

of the workers.[35] But the members of the other groups, far from dwindling, increase in numbers. With the rise of corporate organization, large-scale enterprise, and division of labor and specialization, the functions of the manager and supervisor, of the broker and the marketing agent, of the bookkeeper and the clerk become more widespread. The same holds of the "servants of the public," performing "social functions" pleasing to the bourgeoisie — the professions, the magistrates, and the entertainers.[36]

However, a rise in the membership of these groups does not guarantee the survival of the middle class, since the paramount question revolves around the status of these groups: do they stay on as members of the middle class, or does the evolution of capitalism doom them to a proletarian estate? On this question Marx says enough to raise doubts, but not enough to resolve them. He specifies that managers and "commercial laborers" (like clerks, salesmen, etc.) are mere wage workers whose remuneration is determined in the market, like any other wage; and he suggests that should the capital-labor nexus apply to the members of the professions, they too will become mere wage earners.[37] He mentions, further, that the wages of managers and commercial laborers suffer in a depression, and that, owing to the competition of numbers, their lot deteriorates. There is also a reference to the "poorly paid artists, musicians, lawyers, doctors, professors, teachers, inventors, etc." [38]

Such opinions encourage the deduction that the advance of capitalism is associated with the proletarianization of most members of the middle class. Corroboration of this deduction comes from explicit utterances in both early and later writings. The *Communist Manifesto* (page 16) recognizes that "the

[35] Marx and Engels, *Communist Manifesto*, pp. 23, 26, 45–46; Marx, *Wage-Labor and Capital*, p. 53; *Capital*, I, 687; III, 288.

[36] *Capital*, I, 364; II, chap. vi; III, 340ff., 352, 451, 454, 456; *Theorien über den Mehrwert*, I, 325.

[37] *Capital*, III, 454, 458, 344, 346; *Theorien über den Mehrwert*, I, 425–427, 259.

[38] *Capital*, II, 475, 531; III, 458, 354; *Theorien über den Mehrwert*, I, 325.

physician, the lawyer, the priest, the poet, the man of science" have been converted into "paid wage-laborers," and (page 46) that the petty bourgeoisie will in time be completely replaced by "managers, superintendents, and foremen." [39] It declares (page 13): "Society as a whole is more and more splitting up into two great hostile camps, into two great classes directly facing each other: bourgeoisie and proletariat." In the third volume of *Capital* (page 1031) he affirms that although even in England, the classical realm of capitalism, "middle and transition stages" blur class boundaries, modern society evolves "three great classes," the capitalists, the landlords, and the laborers. On the other hand, Marx seems to throw cold water on this inference by a declaration, made as late as the previous one in *Capital*, if not later, to the effect that "the constant multiplication of the middle classes which, situated between the workers on the one side and the capitalists and landlords on the other side, live mainly and directly on revenue and press like a heavy burden on the nether laboring class, enlarging the social security and power of the upper ten thousand." [40] We are thus left in the dark with respect to Marx's doctrine of the disappearance of the middle class.

One proposition stands out with sufficient clarity. The middle class, even if it thrives, has no place in Marx's theory as a factor in modern social evolution. This class is not integrated with the dialectic, and is of no particular importance in the final struggle for communism. The social synthesis of the future is achieved without reference to the middle class, which, in Marx's mind, has no political power, no coherent outlook, and no disposition to build a new order.

## The Rôle of Classes

The theory of class stratification is an indispensable component of Marx's interpretation of history. In the first place, classes throw light on the morphology of society. The aggre-

---

[39] For "managers, superintendents and foremen," the standard translation has "overlookers, bailiffs, and shopmen." The German is: *"durch Arbeitsaufseher und Domestiken übersetzt werden."*

[40] *Theorien über den Mehrwert*, II, No. 2, p. 368.

gate social relations of the producers and the resulting classes constitute the economic structure of a given society and stamp the community with a given character. Without an idea of classes society would present itself, from the Marxian viewpoint, as a conglomeration of people with diverse relations among themselves and toward nature, subjected to a complex of forces which their system of production originates. It would be difficult to orientate oneself in a given society and to discern the factors that govern its behavior and define the end towards which it is tending. Classes exhibit its internal organization and the underlying fundamentals. "Population," observes Marx, "is an abstraction if we leave out, for example, the classes of which it consists." [41] And, as he informs us, "It is always the direct relation of the owners of the conditions of production to the direct producers, which reveals the innermost secret, the hidden foundation of the entire social construction." [42]

The relations of production form accordingly the soil in which grow institutions and ideas. As will be shown later in some detail, classes and class interests explain why particular institutions exist and why certain ideas prevail in a society. In other words, they explain social life in its static aspects. For this reason Marx considers the mode of production and the class structure of equal effectiveness in generating the remaining institutional phases of an epoch; and in some formulations of his theory of history Marx and his friend mention either the mode of production as the commanding cause of the other historical phenomena,[43] or the relations of production.[44]

It is to be pointed out, however, that the more accurate view would be that they consider both as the foundation. The real basis upon which is erected the institutional superstructure consists of two tiers, the system of production and the economic

---

[41] *Critique of Political Economy*, appendix, p. 292.

[42] *Capital*, III, 919.

[43] Marx, *Critique of Political Economy*, p. 11; Engels, *Socialism, Utopian and Scientific*, p. 45; preface to *Origin of the Family*, pp. 9–10.

[44] Marx, *Critique of Political Economy*, p. 11; *Poverty of Philosophy*, p. 119; Engels, *Socialism, Utopian and Scientific*, p. xxxvii.

relations, or classes, which it calls into being. The former, or the lower tier, is the supporter and regulator of the upper tier; but the two together form the substructure. Therefore, in many of the more formal statements of their conception of history the two authors advance both the organization of production and the class relations as the composite mainspring of the other aspects of civilization.[45] They mean to emphasize that the mode of production, while supplying the motive power, cannot of itself produce historic events. Human agents are needed.

In the second place, classes are inseparably associated with the evolutionary processes of society. The march of civilization proceeds dialectically through the antithesis with which a given system of production is permeated and the eventual synthesis reflecting the union of the old thesis and the new opposing elements. But this march needs marchers: the work of the dialectic is the work of the opposing classes. "The history of all past society has consisted in the development of class antagonisms."[46] The class struggle is coördinated with the social dialectic.

The picture is as follows. The relations existing among the participants in production in a given era are to the advantage of the dominant class. This class is naturally interested in the preservation of the régime. But the exploited class is dissatisfied and is seeking the means of resolving its difficulties. Such is the case, for example, in the relations between the bourgeoisie and the proletariat, as Marx perceives them. The solution of the workers' problem cannot, however, be spun out of the mind or promoted by pious wishes. It can come to the awareness of the lower class and it can take shape only when the material conditions reach a stage of development at which they can point the way. This stage arrives when the growing productive forces can no longer thrive within the shell of cap-

---

[45] Marx, *Capital*, I, 94n.; Engels, *Anti-Dühring*, p. 32; *Socialism, Utopian and Scientific*, pp. xviii–xix, 41; preface to Marx and Engels, *Communist Manifesto*, pp. 7–8.

[46] *Communist Manifesto*, p. 40.

italism, and begin to give intimations of the possibilities of a
different social construction. Without knowledge of Hegel or
Marx, without doctrinal formulations, but by the light of economic realties, the proletariat wins its orientation. "The working class . . . has no fixed and ready-made utopias . . . It
has no ideals to realize; it has only to set free the elements of
the new society which have already developed in the womb of
the collapsing bourgeois society." [47] It begins to see that its
salvation awaits the dawn of a new order, and it girds its loins
for the fatal struggle.

Social dynamics and Marxian classes are thus interwoven,
and the pages of history are the pages of class struggles. A few
citations may emphasize this thought. "An oppressed class is
the vital condition of every society based upon the antagonism
of classes. The emancipation of the oppressed class, therefore,
necessarily implies the creation of a new society. In order for
the oppressed class to be emancipated it is necessary that the
productive powers already acquired and the existing social
relations should no longer be able to exist side by side." [48]
"From the very moment in which civilization begins, production begins to be based on the antagonism of orders, of states,
of classes, and finally on the antagonism between accumulated
labor [capital] and present labor. No antagonism, no progress.
That is the law which civilization has followed down to our
day." [49] "It is this rapid and passionate development of class
antagonism which, in old and complicated social organisms,
makes a revolution such a powerful agent of social and political progress." [50] "Revolutions are the locomotives of history." [51]

The doctrine of classes and class struggles is an integral
part of Marx's conception of history, and it cannot be severed
from the conception without seriously injuring it. The produc-

[47] Marx, *Civil War in France*, p. 80; Marx and Engels, *Deutsche Ideologie*,
pp. 205–206. See above, p. 39.
[48] *Poverty of Philosophy*, p. 189.
[49] *Poverty of Philosophy*, pp. 65–66.
[50] Engels, *Revolution and Counter-Revolution*, p. 64.
[51] Marx, *Klassenkämpfe in Frankreich*, p. 90.

tive forces and the mode of production embody the basic, but impersonal and objective, elements of history. The classes represent the living agents acting in obedience to the impulses propagated by these material realities. Classes provide the constituent elements of society; they form a component of the substructure on which institutions are based; and they are indispensable alike in the static and in the dynamic phases of history. It is amazing, therefore, that some writers on Marx's interpretation of history refer to Marx's idea of classes as a second theory of history, apart from the mode of production theory, or else omit the discussion of classes altogether. This is like *Hamlet* with Hamlet left out.

# PART III

# THE IDEOLOGICAL ELEMENT
# IN HISTORY

# CHAPTER VI

## THE DERIVATION OF IDEAS

THE substructure compounded of a given productive scheme and the correlative classes gives rise to a unique superstructure of institutions and ideas. The question emerges: By what mediating processes does the one lead to the other? As far as the mediating links with institutions are concerned, they will be considered in the following chapter. The present chapter will be concerned with the manner in which man builds his ideas; with the way, that is, in which existence leads to consciousness and being to thinking. This problem is a prominent part of Marx's philosophic thought, and only a student of materialism, of Hegel, and of the neo-Hegelians of Marx's day can feel sure of his ground. Much of what follows in this chapter is therefore not offered with the assurance that only such a specialist can possess.

### IMAGES

The first proposition emphasized by the two friends is that natural and especially social realities about us constitute the ultimate source of our ideas. Our mental world does not emerge by internal generation, but is derived from the outside material world, preëminently from the changing sensory phenomena engendered by the evolving system of production.[1] Indeed, so dependent are our ideas on the material conditions of existence that Marx denies them an independent history: shadows have no independent career.[2] As Marx proclaims in the introduction to his *Critique of Political Economy*, it is not our consciousness that determines our existence, it is our social existence that determines our consciousness, and mankind sets itself only such problems as it can solve, because the problem

---

[1] Marx and Engels, *Deutsche Ideologie*, p. 33.
[2] *Deutsche Ideologie*, pp. 16, 27.

itself is recognized only when the basis for its solution is emerging.[3]

In pure mathematics, Engels argues, it may appear that we are dealing with concepts independent of our experience, but such is not the case. Before such concepts evolved there were objects to measure, count, and compare, and there were shapes and surfaces, rectangles and cylinders to observe.[4] Equally, the defeat of mercantilism by the physiocrats and Adam Smith was not a victory of thought but a thought reflex of changed economic facts. Otherwise Richard Lionheart and Philip Augustus, instead of going on the crusades, might have introduced free trade and spared the world five hundred years of stupidity.[5]

How does reality become an idea in our minds? To begin with, by a process of photography. Reality mirrors itself in man's brain and emerges as an idea. Marx refers to Hegel's view of the real as the reflex of the Idea, and adds: "With me, on the contrary, the ideal is nothing but the material world transformed and translated in the human head (*das im Menschenkopf umgesetzte und übersetzte Materielle*)." [6] And Engels says: "We conceived of ideas . . . as pictures of real things." [7]

From the viewpoint of technical philosophy, it is not easy to discern precisely what part Marx allows the mind to play in the process of forming ideas. In 1845 he penned obscure notes on Feuerbach's philosophy, which deal largely with the theory of knowledge.[8] These notes, or "theses," seem to speak the language of the instrumentalist theory of knowledge held by

[3] Cf. Engels, *Anti-Dühring*, p. 32.

[4] *Anti-Dühring*, p. 45.

[5] Engels, letter of July 14, 1893, in Marx and Engels, *Selected Correspondence*, p. 512.

[6] *Capital*, I, p. 25.

[7] *Feuerbach*, p. 96. "The twofold social character of the labor of the individual appears to him, when reflected in his brain, only under those forms which are impressed upon that labor in everyday practice by the exchange of products" (Marx, *Capital*, I, 84–85). "The realities of the outer world . . . reflect themselves there as feelings, thoughts . . ." (Engels, *Feuerbach*, p. 73).

[8] These eleven brief "theses" are found in *Gesamtausgabe*, Part I, vol. 5, pp. 533–535.

modern pragmatists. But one is inclined to pause when one recalls that in 1845 Marx, in an early stage of transition from Hegel to new viewpoints as yet not fully crystallized, was still under the spell of his master. Perhaps these vague pronouncements point to a Hegelian frame of reference. The doctors disagree.[9]

The recurrent theme in these controversial theses is the proposition that reality or sense-perception is related to "activity, practice," is "practical activity," and that objective truth and its test are a matter of "practice." [10] Some see in these phrases the basic principles of pragmatism, while others see in them a variant of Hegelianism. One cannot be certain about the meaning of some of these "theses." For example, perhaps the least obscure, thesis XI, states: "Philosophers have interpreted the world in different ways; the point is to change it." Those who see pragmatism in Marx interpret this statement to mean that philosophy ought to function as an instrument of social change. But to others, Marx merely means to say: "Stop talking; do something."

### SCIENTIFIC KNOWLEDGE

In any event, it is necessary to stress that in opposition to the traditional materialism of his day, Marx does not treat the mind as a passive receptacle of sensory data. Only, with reference to the degree of mental activity involved in the formation of ideas, he makes a sharp distinction between the acquisition of knowledge by scientists and the superficial notions of the "ordinary mind," the majority of the people.[11]

Sense-perception and mental images are basic, but they are not enough. In fact, especially in the realm of social phenomena, they are inadequate even as far as they go. Appearances and ordinary common sense are deceptive. "Scientific truth is always paradox if judged by everyday experience,

[9] E.g., M. Eastman, *Marxism: Is it Science?*, appendix; S. Hook, *From Hegel to Marx*, chap. viii.
[10] Theses I, II, V, VIII, IX. Cf. Engels, *Dialectics of Nature*, p. 172.
[11] Cf. *Capital*, III, 1022–1023.

which catches only the delusive appearance of things." [12] Of "economic, political and other reflections" Engels writes that, as with the human eye, they pass through a convex lens and "therefore appear upside down, standing on their heads. Only the nervous system, which would put them on their feet again for representation, is lacking." [13] A commodity may seem easy to understand, but analysis reveals that it is charged with "metaphysical subtleties and theological niceties." [14] The same is true of other economic phenomena. "*Everything appears upside down in competition.* The existing conformation of economic conditions, as seen in reality on the surface of things . . . is not only different from the internal disguised essence of these conditions . . . but actually opposed to them, or their reverse." [15] "The thing which seems irrational to ordinary common sense is rational, and what seems rational to it is irrational." [16] There is a wide gulf between the "phenomenal form" of reality and the "hidden substratum" of its meaning. The task is to resolve the visible "external movement into the internal actual movement." This is the task of science.[17] In a letter to Engels Marx writes in 1867 that if the "*inner connection*" of phenomena were "reflected" in the brain as the "*apparent form*" is, "why would there be a need of *science* at all?" [18]

Accordingly in scientific procedure the energetic activity of the mind is required to penetrate through the appearance of phenomena to their essential core, to their interrelations, their variations, and their significance in the scheme of a larger totality. First of all, observation becomes an elaborate process

[12] Marx, *Value, Price and Profit*, p. 70; *Capital*, I, 591–592; III, 1010, 1016.
[13] Letter of October 27, 1890, in Marx and Engels, *Selected Correspondence*, p. 478.
[14] Marx, *Capital*, I, 81–82.
[15] *Capital*, III, 244, 263, 369, 807. Marx's italics.
[16] *Capital*, III, 905. "But sound common sense, respectable fellow . . . has most wonderful adventures as soon as he ventures out into the wide world of scientific research" (Engels, *Anti-Dühring*, p. 28).
[17] Marx, *Capital*, I, 594; III, 369.
[18] Marx and Engels, *Gesamtausgabe*, Part III, vol. 3, p. 404. Marx's italics. See also *Capital*, III, 951, and letter to Kugelmann in *Neue Zeit*, XX, no. 2, p. 222.

of assimilating sensory data, a process of experimentation and critical testing. Perhaps it is this that Marx has in mind when he states in his first note on Feuerbach: "The chief defect of all previous materialism . . . is that the subject (*Gegenstand*), reality, what is sensed, is conceived only under the form of the object (*Objekt*) . . .; but not as human sense-activity, practice, not subjectively." [19] The mind works by analysis and synthesis. As we examine a concrete economic phenomenon it presents itself to our senses as a general picture, as a complex resultant of processes; in other words, our senses confront ready-made objects.[20] But we cannot grasp the general picture unless we understand the elements composing it. The phenomenon is therefore broken up into its parts, and each part is studied in detail. We do not study the anatomy of the human body all at once, but move from part to part. In natural science minutiae are explored by experimentation, in social science by abstraction.[21] Finally we are ready for the synthesis or the interconnections of the constituent parts. It is by such mental activity that the aggregate grows in our apprehension and becomes a clear phenomenon. The senses and images give us awareness and raw material; thought penetrates to the meaning.[22]

Only in this sense, Marx teaches, is reality a product of thought. Reality is not, as with Hegel, merely the Idea transcribed in our minds. Reality is palpable, outside us; only it is comprehended and evaluated by thought. "The method of advancing from the abstract to the concrete is but a way of thinking by which the concrete is grasped and is reproduced in our mind as a concrete. It is by no means, however, the process which itself generates the concrete . . . The whole . . . is the product of a thinking mind which grasps the world in the only way open to it, a way which differs from the one employed by the artistic, religious, or practical mind." [23]

---

[19] Marx and Engels, *Gesamtausgabe*, Part I, vol. 5, p. 533.

[20] Marx, *Capital*, I, 87; *Critique of Political Economy*, appendix, p. 293; Engels, *Anti-Dühring*, p. 27.

[21] *Capital*, I, 12, 24–25.     [22] Engels, *Anti-Dühring*, p. 49.

[23] *Critique of Political Economy*, appendix, pp. 293–294.

Such is the scientific method, or dialectical materialism, as Marxians call it. "If we deduce world schematism not from our minds, but only *through* our minds from the real world, deducing the basic principles of being from what is," we need no philosophy; what we get is positive science.[24] The art of working with concepts is a difficult procedure, "is not inborn and also is not given with ordinary everyday consciousness." The true scientist is, above all, faithful to the dialectic method. He is mindful of the evolution and the interrelations of phenomena, and in exploring the social world he is alert for the conditions which generate the negation of what exists, paving the way for a new transformation.[25]

Since sense-experience is the mother of knowledge, the question arises as to what assurance we have that our senses are reliable conveyors of reality. May we not suspect that objects possess attributes inaccessible to our senses, so that the resulting ideas depart from truth? What of Kant's "thing-in-itself"? The proof of the pudding is in the eating, is Engels' view. We can turn the object to a use warranted by our idea of it, and if it yields the expected results our knowledge of it is valid. To use Engels' homely example, if our senses fool us into taking the shoebrush for a cow we discover our error when we repair to the object for milk. As long as science can reproduce objects out of their component elements and can discover distant stars and planets on the basis of calculations, we may be certain that our senses are reliable guides to reality and that the ideas induced by our perceptions are true. The "thing-in-itself" has no meaning, and its resurrection by the neo-Kantians is a step backward.[26]

---

[24] Engels, *Anti-Dühring*, p. 43. Italics not mine.
[25] *Anti-Dühring*, p. 19.
[26] Engels, *Socialism, Utopian and Scientific*, pp. xv–xviii; *Feuerbach*, pp. 60–62. Cf. Engels, *Dialectics of Nature*, pp. 159, 230. Perhaps the same idea is voiced in Marx's second note on Feuerbach: "The question whether human thinking can get at objective truth is not a question of theory but is a practical question. In practice man must prove the truth, that is, the reality and power, the 'this-sidedness' of his thinking. The dispute over the reality or nonreality of thought, apart from practice, is a purely scholastic question" (Marx and Engels, *Gesamtausgabe*, Part I, vol. 5, p. 534.)

### ILLUSIONISM

But very few are given to the quest for scientific truth. The generality of men are mentally sluggish. With the multitude, observation is a superficial performance, and appearances are allowed to pass undisturbed into an inactive mental medium. Personal whims and prejudices, and especially class interests, feelings, and habits of mind, persistently color observation and experience: this is the sorry counterpart of careful thinking in scientific effort. Much value is attached to haphazard observation of an instance or two, to common sense, to seeing is believing, to the personal, the tangible, the immediate, and the particular.

The result of the cult of appearances is that the ordinary person confuses cause and effect, and mistakes symptoms for causes; considers ideas as autonomous creatures and not as reflexes of reality; believes in eternal categories instead of seeing their fugitive nature; and fails to perceive that his beliefs are merely the product of class tradition and education, and that institutions are class tools for class purposes and not for man's glory or the general good. In brief, the "ordinary mind" exemplifies precisely what dialectical materialism repudiates. The "ordinary mind" lives in a world of illusionism.[27]

Who represents the "ordinary mind"? As far as the complexities of the economic world — the subject of investigation by professional economists — are concerned, the agents of production, the laborers, the capitalists, the merchants and bankers, are alike victims of illusionism. Prone to judge by surface phenomena and unaware of what does not meet the eye, they fail to understand the economic processes, which only scientific probing can achieve.[28]

As regards the attitudes to the general superstructure of institutions and ideas, we may distinguish between the ruling class and the proletariat. Institutions and ideas, the correlates of economic production, are fashioned by the upper class to serve its interests. But the upper class is unaware of the true

---

[27] See the succeeding reference.
[28] E.g., Marx, *Capital*, III, 369, 198, 199, 1016–1017; I, 591–592.

nature of the ideological superstructure, of its class character and its passing existence. It regards its "feelings, illusions, habits of thought, and conceptions of life" as independent eternal data and as the true premises of its conduct. Thus the Tories in England long imagined that they were enthusiastic about the monarchy, the English constitution, and the church, while they were really enthusiastic about ground rent.[29]

The case is less clear with the proletariat. There are conflicting statements. For instance, on page 27, the *Communist Manifesto* proclaims that the workers are sophisticated about law, morality, and religion, holding them as "so many bourgeois prejudices" in support of bourgeois interests. But, on page 39, it asserts, "The ruling ideas of each age have ever been the ideas of its ruling class"; and this proposition is voiced more than once. [30] In his essay on Hegel's philosophy of law, written in 1843, Marx put into circulation the well-known bromide: "Religion is the opium of the people." [31] But two or three years later he writes: "For the proletarians these theoretical notions do not exist . . . and if they ever had theoretical notions, e.g., religion, they have been long dissolved by circumstances." [32]

It is obvious that the proletariat must entertain some skepticism about prevailing institutions, if it is to fulfill the revolutionary part assigned to it by Marx. Perhaps it is reasonable to assume that, according to Marx, the proletariat dwells in a world of illusionism before new contradictory productive forces develop within the capitalist system, but with the emergence of these new realities, with the growth of the revolutionary movement, and with the tutelage of the sympathetic members of the intelligentsia,[33] there develops a critical and suspicious attitude towards institutions and the traditional articles of faith. "The existence of revolutionary ideas . . . always pre-

[29] Marx, *Eighteenth Brumaire*, pp. 48–49. Cf. Marx and Engels, *Deutsche Ideologie*, pp. 15–16.

[30] E.g., *Deutsche Ideologie*, pp. 35–36; letter to Kugelmann, *Neue Zeit*, XX, no. 2, p. 223.     [31] Marx and Engels, *Gesamtausgabe*, Part I, vol. 5, p. 607.     [32] Marx and Engels, *Deutsche Ideologie*, p. 30.     [33] Cf. Marx and Engels, *Communist Manifesto*, pp. 26, 30.

supposes the existence of a revolutionary class," assert the two writers.[34]

It follows as a matter of course that Marx and Engels have little regard for the opinions of the multitude. Marx advises the searcher for the causes of social transformation to pay no attention to the ideas and feelings of men, but to center his mind on the economic conditions of production, which can be determined with the precision of natural science. "Just as our opinion of an individual is not based on what he thinks of himself, so can we not judge of such a period of transformation by its own consciousness." [35] Marx concludes his first preface to *Capital* with the remark that scientific criticism he welcomes, but he cares little for the prejudices "of so-called public opinion," to which he never made any concessions; and he cites for his maxim Dante's *Segui il tuo corso, e lascia dir le genti.*[36]

## RELATIVITY

In obvious consequence of their basic conceptions, Marx and Engels are apostles of the relativity of ideas. The relativity of natural and social sciences will be specifically touched on in Chapter VIII, but here a few general remarks are pertinent. Ideas in the social realm are relative first of all to the modes of production, the landmarks of history. Since ideas are sublimates of social realities, and social realities are the fruit of economic production, ideas are subject to change with a change in the productive system. "Not criticism but revolution [in production] is the driving force" of ideas.[37] Within a given

[34] Marx and Engels, *Deutsche Ideologie*, p. 36. On the "vulgar economists" as weavers of illusions see Chapter VIII, below.

[35] Introduction to *Critique of Political Economy*, p. 12.

[36] *Capital*, I, 16; Engels, preface of 1892 to *The Condition of the Working Class in England in 1844*, p. xviii. Characteristic, perhaps, of Marx's attitude to the mentality of the average person is the following observation. Ask, Marx says, any well-meaning citizen what is the trouble with existing property relations, and "the worthy man will put his finger to his nose, draw two deep breaths of thought," and discourse significantly that it is a shame that many possess nothing at all while others roll in wealth, "not only to the detriment of the propertyless rabble but also to the hurt of respectable citizens." *Aus dem literarischen Nachlass von K. Marx, F. Engels*, II, 473.

[37] Marx and Engels, *Deutsche Ideologie*, p. 27. Marx, *Poverty of Philosophy*, p. 119.

order of production there is a determined chain of causality; but the pattern of the cause and effect series changes when a new type of economic activity sets in.[38] If certain forms of social consciousness have endured unchanged through the ages in face of changes in economic conditions, it is because certain elements of economic reality have persisted as a common denominator in the succession of productive systems; class exploitation, for example.[39]

Secondly, ideas are relative to the intellectual heritage of a given period. Our minds and efforts are limited, and it is not given to one generation to make all possible observations, experiments, and analyses; to formulate all hypotheses and construct all generalizations; to learn all about everything. We advance step by step, generation by generation. We continually gain new ideas, which destroy, delimit, or enlarge the ideas transmitted to us from the past. As our inherited stock of knowledge accumulates we acquire wider perspectives and deeper insights. Our present knowledge is not final. We should be distrustful of our present knowledge because the generations which will correct our ideas will be far more numerous than the generations whose ideas we are correcting.[40]

Thirdly, ideas are relative to each other. A conquest in one sphere of knowledge energizes other disciplines, and limited viewpoints in some branches restrict the approach in other branches. The materialistic philosophy of the eighteenth century was mechanistic because the natural sciences were then mechanistic; for the same reason this philosophy lacked the evolutionary outlook. When Darwin's theory of evolution appeared all the sciences became electrified with a fresh vitality.[41]

Two parenthetical observations may be given in closing. Marx does not seem to apply the concept of relativity to his

[38] Cf. *Capital*, I, 23–24.
[39] Marx and Engels, *Communist Manifesto*, p. 40.
[40] Engels, *Anti-Dühring*, p. 96; *Feuerbach*, p. 41.
[41] *Anti-Dühring*, pp. 27–31, 83; *Feuerbach*, p. 66; *Dialectics of Nature*, pp. 7, 13.

own doctrine of relativity. We do not find him speculating that the idea of relativity, itself presumably the product of certain economic conditions, may possibly give way to another theoretical overarching construction when the economic world will change. Too, Marx does not mean to confine scientific quality, or quality generally, only to those who happen to think as he does. A firm believer in his own conceptions, he respects the thinkers who profoundly and sincerely explore beneath the surface. He has a high regard for the Greek thinkers, for Petty, Quesnay, Ricardo, Hegel, Darwin, and many others, who did not walk in the way of Marx.

The representatives of the German historical school of economics also endorse the doctrine of relativity, but the relativity of Marx and Engels differs in some important respects. Our two authors hold that social life is subject to definite laws which reveal the operation of cause and effect in the sequence of events. For example, Marx's aim in his *Capital* is to disclose the "natural laws of capitalist production" and to "lay bare the economic law of motion of modern society." [42] The section in the third volume of *Capital* (pages 247ff.), where he discusses the tendency of profits to diminish, bears the title "The law of the falling tendency of the rate of profit"; likewise with the chapter on the "General law of capitalist accumulation." [43] But the historical school doubts whether social phenomena can be isolated out of their hopelessly tangled and chaotic milieu and made to display definite sequences where cause and effect can be traced. Even among those who would like to obtain laws from historical inductive studies, some despair of success.

Marx and Engels anchor the relativity of ideas, ultimately and primarily, to the narrow solid basis of material factors. Social ideas and institutions and all history move in accordance with economic reality. The historical school is not so clear here. It regards ideas in almost all spheres as interlaced among themselves and as determining each other. There is no single force which subordinates the rest. To understand one domain

[42] *Capital*, I, 13, 14.
[43] *Capital*, I, 671.

in science, it is essential to read the history and philosophy of everything else; to understand economics, one has to be omniscient. Then to the two friends the mainspring of the relativity of human thought is clear, and it follows logically from their general philosophy. Their philosophy of cognition yokes ideas to reality; and the causes of changes in reality will simultaneously present themselves as the causes of relativity. Such causes are the dialectic and class struggles. Their relativity is a concomitant of their theory of cognition and of their view of the dynamic forces in history. With the historical school the causes of relativity are not apparent.

Finally, with Marx and Engels the scope of relativity is defined. Each epoch has its mode of production, its classes, and class interests. Consequently, ideas and institutions vary with each epoch, but within a given epoch they maintain a more or less definite character. The social laws they speak of are the laws special to a certain economic era and to no other era. "Every historical period has laws of its own. . . . As soon as society has outlived a given period of development, and is passing over from one given stage to another, it begins to be subject also to other laws." Such is the summary by a Russian critic of Marx's views of laws, and Marx reproduces it with approval in his preface to the first volume of *Capital*.[44] Discussing the formation of a redundant population in modern society, Marx adds: "In fact, every special historic mode of production has its own special laws of population, historically valid within its own limits." [45] It follows that, viewed in the historical perspective, social thought and institutions are relative to the five economic epochs: primitive communism, ancient slavery, medieval feudalism, modern capitalism, and future socialism. The historical school indeed divides history into eras — Roscher, Hildebrand, Schmoller, Bücher, have their series of "stages" in history — but this school does not insist that thought and institutions are relative only with reference to these particular stages, and that they fall into sharply de-

44 *Capital*, I, 23–24.
45 *Capital*, I, 693.

fined categories parallel to these stages.[46] With the historical school relativity is, in the main, a constantly flowing stream, harnessed to no distinct epochs.

[46] Karl Knies, who was skeptical about economic "stages" and other historical "laws," holds, likewise, that thought and institutions are relative to time and place in general.

# CHAPTER VII

## THE NATURE OF INSTITUTIONS

THE preceding chapters examined the four pillars of Marx's theory of history — the mode of production, the principle of social dynamics (the dialectic), the class struggle, and the derivation of ideas. We are now ready to examine the applications of this theory as found in Marx and Engels. First, we shall take up their views of social institutions and human thought, namely, the state and law, morality and religion, science and philosophy. The first four of these subjects are the concern of the present chapter; the last two, of the next chapter.

### THE STATE

To the followers of the idealistic philosophy the state is the realization of the Idea, the manifestation of the Universal Reason. To others the state is a device of ensuring order and peace to the inhabitants of a given territory. To still others the state is preëminently the compromiser among the conflicting groups and interests which would otherwise tear society apart. To Aristotle the state is the highest good, to Hobbes it is the citadel of order and safety, to Hegel it is "the Divine Idea as it exists on earth."

The state is nothing of the kind, declare Marx and Engels. The state is rooted in economic soil and is presided over by economic forces. "I was led by my studies to the conclusion," says Marx, "that . . . the forms of the state could be neither understood by themselves, nor explained by the so-called general progress of the human mind, but that they are rooted in the material conditions of life." [1] The economic form in which unpaid labor is extracted from the direct producers "determines the relation of rulers and ruled"; this relation "determines its

[1] Introduction to *Critique of Political Economy*, p. 11; Marx and Engels, *Deutsche Ideologie*, pp. 22–23; Engels, *Feuerbach*, pp. 112–116.

[the community's] political shape," and also "reveals the innermost secret, the hidden foundation of the entire social construction and with it of the political form of the relations between sovereignty and dependence, in short, of the corresponding form of the state." Every form of production creates its own form of government.[2] In the general formulations of his conception of history, Marx places the state as the institution most sensitive to the mode of production and its unique classes.

By its nature the state is an apparatus of physical force and of oppression of one class by another.[3] The dominant class is the beneficiary of the prevailing mode of production and it needs an institution to guard its property interests. Not welfare of man but custody of wealth is the aim of the state. Throughout history (that is, class history) the population has been divided into groups on the basis of property, and each group has enjoyed political rights in proportion. "This is a direct confirmation of the fact that the state is organized for the protection of the possessing against the nonpossessing classes."[4] In each historical society the master class could proclaim: *l'État c'est moi.*

An outstanding characteristic of the state is found in the fact that its members are not bound by ties of kinship, as was true of primitive communities, but are grouped with reference to geographical sections. The constituent elements of the state are not the clan or the tribe but the province or the department.[5] Another "essential mark of the state consists in a public power of coercion divorced from the masses of the people."[6] Far from deriving its power from the people, the state super-

[2] *Capital*, III, 919; *Critique of Political Economy*, appendix, p. 273.

[3] Engels, preface to Marx's *Civil War in France*, pp. 19–20. The *Communist Manifesto* (p. 42) asserts that "Political power, properly so called, is merely the organized power of one class for oppressing another." "The aggregation of civilized society is the state, which throughout all typical periods is the state of the ruling class, and in all cases mainly a machine for controlling the oppressed and exploited class" (Engels, *Origin of the Family*, p. 214; cf. *ibid.*, p. 208, and *Socialism, Utopian and Scientific*, pp. 75–76).

[4] Engels, *Origin of the Family*, pp. 130, 209–210.

[5] *Origin of the Family*, p. 206.

[6] *Origin of the Family*, p. 142.

imposes itself as a power over the people. "The state presupposes a public power of coercion separated from the aggregate body of its members."[7] This force may be inconsiderable in communities where classes are undeveloped, or in isolated districts, as was once the case in the United States of America. But it is multiplied where, and in measure as, the class antagonism in sharpened. An independent authority, the state has at its disposal the army, the navy, and the police; the courts, the prisons, and the executioners. It maintains itself by taxation, protective tariffs, and national debts. Its executive mansions are swarming with courtiers, functionaries, and potentates; with taxing experts, tariff schemers, and bankers, who know how to keep the masses in subordination and how to drain the lifeblood of the poor.[8]

It may seem that all this does not apply to a democratic state, where officials are elected and held responsive to social interests. But such is not the case. In a democracy wealth is only officially not accepted as the test of political rights, but in fact it exercises enormous power. The rich corrupt officials with bribery and develop entangling connections with the government through banking operations, corporate control of transportation, the stock exchange, and public debt schemes.[9] Says Engels:

It is just in the United States that we can most clearly see the process through which the State acquires a position of independent power over against the society . . . There exists here no dynasty, no aristocracy . . . Nevertheless, we have here two great rings of political speculators that alternately take possession of the power of the State and exploit it with the most corrupt means and to the most corrupt purposes. And the nation is powerless against these men, who nominally are its servants, but in reality are its two overruling and plundering hordes of politicians.[10]

Marx, too, states explicitly that democracy, both ancient and modern, rests on the foundation of one sort of slavery or an-

[7] *Origin of the Family*, pp. 115–116.
[8] *Origin of the Family*, pp. 179, 182, 184, 208; Marx, *Capital*, I, 827, 829; *Klassenkämpfe in Frankreich*, p. 26.
[9] Engels, *Origin of the Family*, pp. 209–210.
[10] Preface to Marx's *Civil War in France*, p. 18.

other. To him "the existence of the state and the existence of slavery are inseparable." [11]

In the progress of time the repressive functions of the state are intensified, even if the state is democratic in form. As the growth of modern industry widens and deepens the antagonism between capital and labor, the despotism of the state over the working masses and its power as an engine of oppression rise in proportion.[12] The state continues as an apparatus of social enslavement even when it tends toward state capitalism through the assumption of ownership of certain industries: its employees remain proletarians, and its oppressive sway is merely extended in scope.[13]

While the resultant of economic situations, the state is not altogether a passive derivative. It can react on economic phenomena and exert some influence on them. State action may retard or accelerate the effect of economic forces, through a policy of protection or free trade, through good or bad financial measures, and through wars of aggression or internal strife. It cannot presume, however, to modify the irresistible economic currents or to turn them from their determined course. Nor are the motives and methods of the state inspired by any other than economic considerations. Whenever political power collided with the economic development of a country, "the contest has always ended with the downfall of the political power." [14]

Such is the theme. But scattered among the writings of Marx and Engels are statements which strike discordant notes. From categorical pronouncements that the state is the organized expression of class domination we come at times upon milder declarations. The state makes its appearance, says Engels, to prevent classes from exterminating each other and to preserve the class struggle within reasonable limits, although it is in no position to resolve the antagonisms provoked by economic in-

[11] Marx and Engels, *Gesamtausgabe*, Part I, vol. 3, pp. 15, 298.

[12] Marx, *Civil War in France*, section III, third paragraph.

[13] Engels, *Socialism, Utopian and Scientific* (New York, 1935), p. 67. Cf. Marx, *Capital*, III, 918–919.

[14] Marx, *Die Inauguraladresse der internationalen Arbeiter-Association*, p. 29. Engels, letters of October 27, 1890, and January 25, 1894, in Marx and Engels, *Selected Correspondence*, pp. 480–481, 517; Engels, *Anti-Dühring*, p. 202.

terests.[15] In exceptional cases, when the contending classes are even in power, the state holds the balance. Thus, Bonapartism of the first and second empires in France played off the proletarians against the bourgeoisie, and Bismarck played off the same classes, cheating both "for the benefit of the degenerate Prussian cabbage junkers."[16] Where the estates (*Stände*) are prominent but have not fully developed into classes, where, therefore, no part of the population has dominance over another part, the state is independent. Such is the case in Germany in the middle 1840's.[17]

At times our two friends talk of the state even in a classless society, embracing a view which they consistently disparage in others. In the polemic against Dühring the assertion is made that in primitive communal orders the "state power," in a rudimentary form, attended to social needs, and only with the appearance of classes did it become a class engine.[18] In his introduction to Marx's *Civil War in France*, Engels asserts that originally society created state organs for the provision of common interests, but in the course of time these organs "transformed themselves from the servants of society into its masters. . . . Against this transformation of the State and the State's organs from the servants of society into its rulers . . ."[19] In his discussion of the Gotha program Marx talks of the future classless commonwealth and asks: "What change will the form of the state undergo in communist society?"[20]

It is useless to attempt a reconciliation of such contradictory views. But, in the perspective of the basic conceptions of Marx and Engels and their many pronouncements on this subject, it is reasonable to conclude that they see the state only in class societies and treat it as a class tool, while in a classless society they envisage only an administrative apparatus attending to common needs. In this latter instance the prime question is

---

[15] Engels, *Origin of the Family*, p. 206.
[16] *Origin of the Family*, p. 209.
[17] Marx and Engels, *Deutsche Ideologie*, p. 52.
[18] Engels, *Anti-Dühring*, pp. 165, 198, 202.
[19] Pages 17–18. Cf. Engels, *Socialism, Utopian and Scientific*, p. 78.
[20] *The Critique of the Gotha Programme*, p. 44.

whether or not the administrative officials possess coercive power over the people. It is this question which distinguishes between the anarchist and the nonanarchist. But on this question we remain in the dark, so far as Marx is concerned.

## THE HISTORY OF THE STATE

To Engels' belief, history proves abundantly that the state is a summation of the desires of the class in control of production and is relative to economic eras.[21] The primitive clan was a homogeneous group with identical interests and without class distinctions. Every adult, male or female, had a voice in the election of officials, and the council at which adults met and voted was "the sovereign power in the gens." There was no force above and apart from the collective will of society, therefore no state. "No soldiers, gendarmes, and policemen, no nobility, kings, regents, prefects, or judges, no prisons, no lawsuits, and still affairs run smoothly." Such was the situation, for example, among the Iroquois Indians in North America.[22]

The same situation prevailed in the heroic epoch of ancient Greece. But eventually private property appeared, differences in wealth arose, the elected king began to covet the usurper's place, and the newly born aristocracy captured offices. Class distinctions unleashed turmoil and strife. Theseus arose to offer relief. He established at Athens a central administrative body, the general council; introduced a common law applying even to those outside the Athenian tribe, thus dissolving the ties of kinship; and divided the nation into classes of nobles, farmers, and tradesmen, giving the nobles the exclusive privilege of filling office. This was the first attempt to form a state in Athens.[23]

The new arrangement proved to be merely a tool in the hands of the nobility in their struggle with the debt-ridden farmer. Public offices multiplied, and soon the army and navy came into

---

[21] Engels, *Feuerbach*, pp. 113–114.

[22] *Origin of the Family*, pp. 107, 117 and chap. iii. Elsewhere Engels records that when the old communal system persisted, it built up "the most barbarous form of the state, oriental despotism, from India to Russia" (*Anti-Dühring*, p. 200).

[23] *Origin of the Family*, pp. 125, 129, 199–200, 132–133.

existence. Then came Solon, and the state developed further. He divided the population into four classes according to land property, with rights and duties graduated in proportion. The final blow was dealt by the constitution of Cleisthenes, 500 B.C. The population was no longer divided on the basis of kinship but into one hundred territorial districts, the prototypes of the American townships. Each ten of these districts formed a higher territorial unit which had to contribute to the national defense. Above all stood the Athenian council, elected by the citizens. The state was complete. It was a "democratic republic." From then on the state was used as a weapon by the masters against the slaves. How well it suited the social conditions was demonstrated by the ensuing prosperity of Greece.[24]

Rome went through a similar experience. It began its career with a gens organization. The king and the senate were elected from the patricians, and the laws were passed at public meetings. It was a military democracy, but not a state. Finally, the struggles between the patricians, who were gens members, and the plebeians, who were strangers, forced Servius Tullius to give a constitution, introducing democracy much after the Greek pattern. The power of the new state was used "against the slaves and the so-called proletarians." [25]

The German tribes who invaded Rome had begun, likewise, with the gens; but the vast territories wrested from the Romans could not be administered by this elementary organ. Accordingly the state arose. Only then, instead of the classical democracies, monarchies began to appear. The monarchs were the former military leaders who rallied about themselves booty-loving warriors and led them in private expeditions of warfare and plunder. Treating themselves as the owners of the conquered territories, the new rulers proceeded to distribute the public domain among their favorites, laying the basis of a new nobility. Too, the state became a lever of oppression of the poor farmer. By the ninth century, exhausted by exploitation and wars, the farmer had to seek the protection of the powerful

[24] *Origin of the Family*, pp. 139, 141–143.
[25] *Origin of the Family*, pp. 153–157.

nobles who in return assumed title to his property, compelling him to become a serf. "The new race, masters and servants" introduced medieval feudalism, with absolute monarchy "everywhere" the most fitting form of government.[26]

The feudal monarchy was the handmaid of the lord in suppressing the serf, of the guild-master in dictating to apprentice and journeyman, and of the country nobility in its contentions with the city guilds. Yet how well this state corresponded to the medieval system of production, how closely it was a "reflection" of economic reality, is not exactly clear with our two historians. We should expect absolute monarchy, the child of medieval production, to be incompatible with capitalism. But Marx and Engels go on making puzzling statements, sowing dragon's teeth. The *Communist Manifesto* (page 15) tells us that absolute monarchy was in continual strife with the barons for political supremacy, and, as soon as the bourgeoisie appeared on the scene, the state became eager to use the new class "as a counterpoise against the nobility." Engels teaches: ". . . and this always has been the fundamental principle of absolute monarchies, to rely for support upon two classes, the feudal landlords and the large stock-jobbing capitalists," and to employ either class to hold in check the other class.[27]

There is a Gordian knot here hard to cut. On the one hand we meet declarations that absolute monarchy and the bourgeoisie go hand in hand. During the period of manufacture, extending from the middle of the sixteenth to beyond the middle of the eighteenth century, the bourgeoisie is the "cornerstone of the great monarchies in general," states the *Communist Manifesto* (page 15). Appearing in the transition period between the death of the feudal orders (*Stände*) and the rise of the bourgeoisie, absolute monarchy took "a most active part in the destruction" of the former, favoring the new class.[28] On

[26] *Origin of the Family*, pp. 174–175, 184–188, 205; Marx and Engels, *Deutsche Ideologie*, p. 15.

[27] *Revolution and Counter-Revolution*, p. 52; *Origin of the Family*, p. 209; *Anti-Dühring*, p. 182.

[28] *Aus dem literarischen Nachlass von K. Marx, F. Engels*, II, 465, 463. "Royal power, itself a *product* of bourgeois development. . ." (*Capital*, I, 789).

the other hand, we are assured that the two are incongruous from the beginning: the bourgeoisie struggled with "the feudal lords and their protector, absolute monarchy"; the bourgeoisie "overthrew feudalism and monarchy in order to make of society a bourgeois society." [29]

In Marx's thought, if absolute monarchy is feudal, it ought to be antagonistic to capitalism and the bourgeoisie; if it is the expression of capitalism, we cannot expect it to be in full flower before capitalism, its progenitor, has become well established. In other words, while capitalism is struggling for a foothold, the capitalist state cannot already be in the saddle, and in a position to aid capitalism. It is strange therefore to come upon such assertions as the following. At the beginning of capitalism the demand of industrial undertakings for more capital than could be provided by a private concern "gives rise partly to state subsidies to private persons, as in France in the time of Colbert," and partly to state monopolies.[30] In seventeenth-century England the bourgeoisie employs "the power of the state . . . to hasten, hothouse fashion, the process of transformation of the feudal mode of production into the capitalist mode, and to shorten the transition." Capital in the embryo absorbs surplus-labor "not merely by the force of economic relations, but by the help of the state." [31]

Be it as it may, a century or two after the capitalist form of production arrives the new material conditions no longer find suitable expression in the monarchic state with its "medieval rubbish." The political state which is the "official expression of the old civil society" has to go. Hence, 1688 in England, 1789 in France, and similar upsets in other countries. The modern state is exemplified by democracies in one form or an-

---

"When in Western Europe the great monarchies developed *in consequence* of bourgeois civilization. . ." (Engels, "Der Anfang des Endes in Oesterreich," *Der Kampf*, VI, 394). "From the outset, therefore, firearms were the weapons of the towns, and of the *rising* monarchy drawing its support from the towns, against the feudal nobility" (Engels, *Anti-Dühring*, p. 185. Italics are mine).

[29] Engels, "Socialisme de juristes," in *Le mouvement socialiste*, XII, 99; Marx, *Poverty of Philosophy*, p. 189.

[30] Marx, *Capital*, I, 338; cf. *Civil War in France*, p. 70.

[31] *Capital*, I, 823–824, 297.

other.[32] Like its predecessors, it functions as the weapon of the ruling class against the proletarians. "The modern state, no matter what its form, is essentially a capitalist machine, the state of the capitalists, the ideal personification of the total national capital"; it is "the summarized, reflected form of the economic desires of the class which controls production." [33] Its executive "is but a committee for managing the common affairs of the whole bourgeoisie." [34] It is a symbol "of the national power of capital over labor, of a public force organized for social enslavement, of an engine of class despotism." [35]

It will go under. The modern state is the last in the historical series. Under socialism it is extinguished, because economic facts will no longer call for it. Till the present day, society could not well dispense with classes. Till the present day, the systems of production have not been adequately developed. The productive forces have been meager, and man has not learned to contend with nature so effectively as to gain from her the necessaries of life with the minimum of effort. He has therefore been compelled to expend so much of his time on the struggle for a living that he has had little leisure for the participation in functions of common interest. Accordingly, there was need for a division of labor in this particular, so that most of society followed their individual pursuits in quest of a livelihood, while a small number of people were left to look after general social affairs. This division of labor gave origin to classes, and created for the ruling class the opportunity to utilize its power for the exploitation of the masses. But at last the point of historical evolution has been reached when the productive forces have grown so abundant that each man has sufficient leisure for matters of common concern. The political domination of a particular class is no longer to be tolerated.[36]

[32] Marx, *Poverty of Philosophy*, pp. 132, 167; *Civil War in France*, p. 70; Engels, *Anti-Dühring*, p. 183; *Socialism, Utopian and Scientific*, p. xxii; *Feuerbach*, p. 123; *Revolution and Counter-Revolution*, p. 19.
[33] Engels, *Socialism, Utopian and Scientific*, pp. 71–72; *Feuerbach*, p. 114.
[34] Marx and Engels, *Communist Manifesto*, p. 15.
[35] Marx, *Civil War in France*, p. 71.
[36] Engels, *Socialism, Utopian and Scientific*, pp. 78–79; *Anti-Dühring*, p. 201.

In the socialist society there will be no classes, no oppression, and "As soon as there is no longer any social class to be held in subjection . . . nothing more remains to be repressed, and a special repressive force, a State, is no longer necessary." [37] "There will no longer be political power, properly speaking, since political power is simply the official form of the antagonisms in civil society." [38] Accordingly, "The society that is to reorganize production on the basis of free and equal association of the producers, will transfer the machinery of state where it will then belong: into the Museum of Antiquities by the side of the spinning wheel and the bronze axe." [39]

## LAW

Closely allied with the state is law. Legal enactments are the chief medium through which the state expresses its mastery and coercion over society. Like the state, law is not the product of ideas and reason, but is the shadow of economic conditions. "The jurist imagines he is operating with a priori principles, whereas they are really only economic reflexes," says Engels.[40] First appear economic facts, such as production and the corresponding economic relations; when they are solidified by experience and custom, law arrives to acknowledge and sanction the facts.[41] Law is nothing but a paraphrase of economic reality. "Truly it is necessary to be entirely innocent of all historical knowledge not to know that in all times sovereigns have had to submit to the economic conditions and have never made laws for them. Legislation, political as well as civil, could do no more than give expression to the will of the economic conditions." [42] For example, under the patriarchal, caste, feudal, and guild régimes there was division of labor according to

[37] Engels, *Socialism, Utopian and Scientific*, p. 76.

[38] Marx, *Poverty of Philosophy*, p. 190. Cf. Marx and Engels, *Communist Manifesto*, p. 42.

[39] Engels, *Origin of the Family*, p. 211. For further discussion of the state after the fall of capitalism see below, pp. 271–272, 275.

[40] Letter of October 27, 1890, Marx and Engels, *Selected Correspondence*, p. 482.

[41] Marx, *Capital*, III, 921.

[42] Marx, *Poverty of Philosophy*, p. 90.

appropriate regulations. But such regulations were not created by a legislator. "Originally born of the conditions of material production, it was not till much later that they [these forms of division of labor] were established as laws." [43] Similarly, as soon as labor combinations became a fact in England, the law of 1824 did not delay in pronouncing them legal, and the old restrictions against labor combinatons were relaxed.[44]

The content of law is the complex of economic facts bred by a given mode of production.[45] The spirit of law is protection of property. Each productive system supplies and governs the motives of the dominant classes. The masters have property to defend, enemies to subdue, interests to protect. They declare their desires to their servant, the state, and appropriate laws are enacted. "Your jurisprudence," cries the *Communist Manifesto* to the bourgeoisie, "is but the will of your class made into a law for all, a will whose essential character and direction are determined by the economic conditions of existence of your class." [46] This will is the will of property. "Does not the need for notaries presuppose a given civil right, which is only an expression of a certain development of property, that is to say, production?" queries Marx.[47] Montesquieu labored over the problem of the "spirit of laws." To Marx the problem is easy, and he could have spared him the trouble. Marx points out that "Linguet overthrew Montesquieu's illusory *Esprit des lois* with one word: '*L'Esprit des lois, c'est la propriété!*'" [48]

But it by no means follows that laws are considered by our two writers as inert shadows. Legal enactments react on the economic world.[49] Just as the state can produce an effect on economic conditions by hastening and nursing the process of transition and by consolidating the ground won, so can laws. The English Factory Acts are an example. The extension of

[43] *Poverty of Philosophy*, p. 147.
[44] *Poverty of Philosophy*, p. 186.
[45] Engels, *Feuerbach*, p. 117.
[46] Page 35. Cf. Engels, "Socialisme de juristes," in *Le mouvement socialiste*, XII, 119.
[47] *Poverty of Philosophy*, p. 45.
[48] *Capital*, I, 675n.
[49] Marx and Engels, *Selected Correspondence*, p. 482.

these laws crowds small enterprises out of existence and hastens their combination into large concerns; it destroys undertakings run by antiquated methods and brings them under the sway of capital. In this manner the law accelerates the concentration of capital and the predominance of the factory system, extends the opposition of the exploited classes to the power of capital, intensifies and spreads the anarchy and the diseases of capitalist production, and, by the destruction of the domestic industry, cuts off the last resort of the "redundant population." "By maturing the material conditions, and the combination on a social scale of the processes of production, it matures the contradictions and antagonisms of the capitalist form of production, and thereby provides, along with the elements for the formation of a new society, the forces for exploding the old one." [50]

Yet we must keep in mind that laws can possess such effectiveness only if they run with the economic current. These very English Factory Acts, Marx pronounces, are "just as much the necessary product of modern industry as cotton yarns, self-actors, and electric telegraph." [51] "They develop gradually out of the circumstances as natural laws of the modern mode of production." [52] Laws not based on economic conditions, or out of accord with them, are devoid of vitality. They vanish as the shadow vanishes when the substance is gone. French law attempts to perpetuate small-scale farming. But in vain, says Marx. "In spite of these laws land is concentrating again." The laws in England perpetuating large landed property are, however, of significance, because they are in agreement with the prevailing system of production.[53]

It follows that each new mode of production, carrying with it a realignment of property relations, changes the character of previously existing laws. " 'Positive' law may, and must, alter its decisions in proportion as the requirements of social, that is,

---

[50] Marx, *Capital*, I, 552. Cf. pp. 519–520, 522.
[51] *Capital*, I, 526.
[52] *Capital*, I, 310.
[53] *Critique of Political Economy*, appendix, p. 289.

economic development, change." [54] Each historical mode of production is bound up with its peculiar code of law. Laws are not eternal, they are relative.

The gens knows no law, in the strict sense. The primitive accepted ways of managing common affairs and of dealing with infractions are time-honored customs and traditions; they are not laws handed down by legislators and enforced by police and prison. With the dissolution of the gens, the "legal conception of free property in land arises," as well as laws of succession of property and paternal rights.[55] Already Theseus gave a "common Athenian law, standing above the legal traditions of the tribes and gentes." [56] Then came Solon and others. Greek law was the law of the creditor over the debtor, and of the master over the slave; the state permitted the class struggle "in a so-called 'legal' form." [57] Rome went much further in this direction and performed something of striking significance. With a system of commodity exchange less developed even than in Greece, it elaborated a body of law which is an "almost perfect expression of the juridical relations" corresponding to commodity production, and which could be easily adapted, some seventeen centuries later, to capitalist conditions. Roman law, says Engels, was founded and developed as the most perfect system of jurisprudence based on private property with which we are acquainted.[58]

In the Middle Ages law was an instrument favoring the feudal lords and the guilds. It was the dispenser of privileges for one class and of restrictions for the other. "Local privileges, differential duties, exceptional laws of all kinds," deluged society and impeded free movement. The right of the subject class to the pursuit of happiness was sacrificed to the interests of the dominant class, regardless and by means of law.[59]

As soon as capitalism established itself, it swept away the old

[54] Marx, *Capital*, III, 722n.
[55] *Capital*, III, 723; Engels, *Origin of the Family*, p. 146.
[56] *Origin of the Family*, p. 132.
[57] *Origin of the Family*, p. 205.
[58] Engels, *Socialism, Utopian and Scientific*, p. xxvii; *Feuerbach*, p. 115; *Anti-Dühring*, p. 114.  [59] *Anti-Dühring*, p. 116; *Feuerbach*, p. 87.

legal fetters on enterprise. The new class was stirred by new interests, and new interests gave birth to new laws.[60] Modern law appeared in varying forms in different countries. In Western Europe it was an adaptation of the old Roman law to the new conditions. The best example is France, where the Revolution made an entire break with feudalism and created the *Code Civil*, that "classical code for bourgeois society." Elsewhere, as in the case of the Prussian land law, "pseudo-enlightened and moralizing jurists" drew up a system of law to suit the particular conditions. Only in England, where the capitalists and the feudal nobility effected a compromise, there are considerable residues of the "barbarous language" of feudal common law, which corresponds to capitalism, "the thing expressed, just as English spelling corresponds to English pronunciation — *vous écrivez Londres et vous prononcez Constantinople*, said a Frenchman." Yet we must not forget, Engels admonishes us, that this old English law preserved through the ages the best part of the Germanic personal freedom and local self-government, and transmitted these safeguards to America and the colonies.[61] But no matter in what form modern law is found, it is the law of the stronger class. The bourgeoisie required noninterference in enterprise, unfettered competition and, as a corollary, equality of rights to freedom of contract. In essence, this equality of rights is nothing but the equal right of all the capitalists to exploit labor. Equality of rights means to the laborer the right to sell his labor for bare subsistence and to fare no better than the slave or the serf.[62]

What happens to law with the advent of socialism is not mentioned. But it may be reasonable to surmise that a society not cursed with class antagonisms, unencumbered with property entanglements, and informed with a spirit of coöperation, will hatch no litigations and will need no legislators and barristers' briefs.

[60] Marx, *Capital*, III, 723; Engels, "Socialisme de juristes," in *Le mouvement socialiste*, XII, 98, 102.
[61] Engels, *Feuerbach*, p. 115, *Socialism, Utopian and Scientific*, p. xxvii; Marx and Engels, *Deutsche Ideologie*, pp. 52–53.
[62] Engels, *Feuerbach*, pp. 87–88; *Le mouvement socialiste*, XII, 98.

## ETHICS

The domain of ethics, like that of politics and law, is found in close dependence on economic imperatives. Each mode of production, with its material conditions and class relations, creates a complex of facts which breed ideas and engender sentiments with respect to questions of right conduct. What is good and what is bad is not decided by criteria of eternal justice developed by some idle brain, but is judged in the light of this material reality into which man is born, and which is about him through life. The dominant class sets the standards, and that system of morality governs society which is in keeping with the rule of this class, and justifies and reinforces the interests of the exploiters. Morality is essentially class morality. "Men, consciously or unconsciously, derive their moral ideas in the last resort from the practical relations on which their class position is based — from the economic relations in which they carry on production and exchange." [63]

Economic actuality alone delimits our ideas of justice and imparts meaning to them. To talk of justice which has not been forged on the anvil of economic fact is to talk an incomprehensible language. To clamor for equitable compensation under the wage system "is the same as to clamor for freedom on the basis of the slavery system. What you think just or equitable is out of the question. The question is: What is necessary and unavoidable, with a given system of production?" [64] What harmonizes with economic conditions is moral; what does not is not. We express our indignation at slavery and are convinced that slavery is wrong. This attitude merely reflects the circumstance that our present economic system is incompatible with slavery. Had present conditions called for it, slavery would

---

[63] *Anti-Dühring*, p. 104. Up to the present time, Engels continues, all ethical theory has been in the last instance testimony to the existence of certain economic conditions in any community at a particular time. In proportion, he says, as society developed class antagonisms, morality became a class morality and either justified the interests and domination of the ruling class, or, as soon as a subject class became strong enough, justified revolt against the ruling class and sanctioned the interests of the subject class (*ibid.*, p. 105).

[64] Marx, *Value, Price and Profit*, p. 76.

not appear to us a scandalous institution. The Greeks did not think slavery wrong, nor did the southern cotton planters.[65] It all depends on the form of production. "The justice of the transactions between the agents of production rests on the fact that these transactions arise as natural consequences from the conditions of production. . . Slavery on the basis of capitalist production is unjust." [66]

The same basis underlies the charge of injustice leveled at existing institutions. While a given régime of production is in the flourishing stage of its development, everyone is content with it, even its victims. But as soon as it has traveled the larger part of its path, as soon as contradictions arrive, and signs of a new order disclose themselves, dissatisfactions emerge, the old institutions begin to appear unjust, and appeals are made to morality and justice. This change of mind, this appeal "is only proof that in the modes of production and exchange changes have silently taken place with which the social order, adapted to earlier economic conditions, is no longer in keeping." [67] It is an indication that the corrosive action of the antithesis has set in, and that the dawn of a new synthesis is not far off. It is a symptom; the task of science is not to join in the cry for justice, but to study the character of the wrongs, to point out that they are the manifestations of the inevitable dialectic, and to expound how, within the old society a new order is striking roots and is bringing a new promise. The feelings stirred up by poets are sounding brass and tinkling cymbal. Talk of justice is of no value. It guides to no comprehension of the disease, and it provides no cure.[68]

It follows that in matters of ethics the range of final truths is severely limited. There is no eternal moral law built on sovereign principles transcending time and place. Morality is rela-

---

[65] Engels, *Anti-Dühring*, p. 200. "If the moral sentiment of the mass regards an economic fact — as, formerly, slavery and serfdom — as unjust, that proves that this fact itself is a survival; that other economic facts are established, thanks to which the first has become insupportable, intolerable" (Engels, preface to Marx's *Poverty of Philosophy*, pp. 14-15).

[66] Marx, *Capital*, III, 399.

[67] Engels, *Socialism, Utopian and Scientific*, pp. 45-46.

[68] Engels, *Anti-Dühring*, p. 166.

THE NATURE OF INSTITUTIONS

tive to variations in material facts. As the mode of production changes, people apply a different set of standards, and render different judgments as to right and wrong conduct. New classes have new interests, and new interests require new sanctions, new ways of envisaging good and evil. When a subject class overpowers its rival, what was good before is good no longer, and what was regarded as wrong in the past may become right.[69] From people to people, from age to age, says Engels, there have been such changes in the ideas of good and evil that these concepts are contradictory in different periods and among different peoples.[70] Even within a given society and at a given time, every class, every profession, has its own code of morals determined by its own material conditions and interests.[71]

True, Engels observes, a "friend of humanity" may arise who claims to believe in finite principles of morality and justice. He explains that all former inventors of eternal truths have been fools and charlatans, and urges that he, "the newly arisen prophet," has at length evolved the only true system of morals valid for all ages and places. Yet, says Engels, his scheme is not what he claims for it. The best he can attempt to do is to construct his system out of material drawn, not from the external world, but from his consciousness. But what is the content of his consciousness? It is a store of moral ideals and philosophical concepts, not come out of the void, but derived from the social conditions of his environment or from learned treatises. Try as he may to divorce his system from a particular time and place, the historical reality around him, driven out through the door, comes in through the window. His system is merely the image of his age, invalid for any other time.[72]

However, despite the bold declarations, it is easy to discern that Engels' mind on this question is disturbed. He is aware that people will remark: "Good is still not evil and evil is not good; if good and evil are confused, all morality is abolished

[69] Engels, *Anti-Dühring*, p. 103.
[70] *Anti-Dühring*, p. 105.
[71] Engels, *Feuerbach*, p. 89.
[72] *Anti-Dühring*, pp. 99–100, 106–107.

and each may do what he will." Engels grapples with this objection. He argues that the problem of morality is not so easily settled as this remark implies, and that, in fact, we do not know what is evil and what is good. He points to the circumstance that in modern society there are three contemporaneous theories of ethics: the "Christian-feudal," a survival of the early days of faith, with its subdivision into Catholic and Protestant branches; the bourgeois; and the proletarian. (Thus the three classes of modern society have three distinctive systems of ethics!) This proves, he says, that it is not easy to find absolute truth regarding right and wrong. He admits that these systems have much in common. But this is only natural, since they all evolved through history and have a common historical foundation. "In similar or approximately similar stages of economic development moral theories must of necessity be more or less in agreement." For example, as soon as private property appears, the ethical precept "Thou shalt not steal" arrives. In a society in which the motive for theft does not exist only the weak-minded would steal, and the precept would be meaningless.[73] This explanation given, Engels seems to rest satisfied, and he leaves the question.

Foes of the state and religion, Marx and Engels are friends of morality. Their writings are charged with warm protests against exploitation, greed, and injustice; against the degradation of the laboring poor; against the heavy price falling on the masses for each step of progress; and against the distortion of values in a perverted civilization unworthy of man. But they are equally disdainful of the intoxication with brotherly sympathy, of universal forgiveness, and of the "old cant love one another, fall into each other's arms." Socialism will introduce a "really human morality which transcends class antagonisms." As compared with previous ethical systems, the socialist system will possess "the maximum of durable elements." Socialist ethics will rest on material conditions which will permit higher standards of human conduct.[74] In the meantime, rising

[73] *Anti-Dühring*, pp. 103–104.
[74] Engels, *Anti-Dühring*, pp. 103–105; *Feuerbach*, p. 89. Sometimes Marx

above the moralities of the capitalist community is the morality of the revolutionary effort for the better society of the future.

## RELIGION

On the surface religion appears as the fabrication of the mind which builds for itself "a realm in the clouds." It seems as though, in this sphere, man were "governed by the product of his own brain." But like any other ideology, religion cannot be abstracted from the "ensemble of the conditions of society" and from the course of history.[75] Religious conceptions are pictures and ideas which people formulate in response to their material environment. The prime mover of religion, as of any other conception, is not criticism but revolution. There is no such thing as the "religious spirit." Religion has no independent history, because it is the creature of productive forces; Christianity has no independent history, because all its forms are the product of empirical causes. Says Marx: "The religious world is but the reflex of the real world." [76]

In primitive days religion originates in the immaturity of the mode of gaining a livelihood. Man is in close contact with nature, and nature confronts him as an overpowering, mystifying presence. He worships what he does not understand. Thus religion is born, which is "nothing but the fantastic reflection in men's minds of those external forces which control their daily life. . . In the beginnings of history it was the forces of Nature which were at first so reflected." [77] Religion has "its

makes a direct appeal to justice. In his inaugural address to the First International he calls upon the workers to watch over the diplomatic activities of their countries, to prevent international crimes, and to "vindicate the laws of morality and justice which ought to regulate the relations among individuals as the supreme laws of intercourse among nations" (*Inauguraladresse der internationalen Arbeiter-Association*, pp. 29–30).

[75] Marx, Theses IV, VI, VII on Feuerbach, in Marx and Engels, *Gesamtausgabe*, Part I, vol. 5, pp. 533–535; *Capital*, I, 681.

[76] Marx and Engels, *Deutsche Ideologie*, pp. 15–16, 27, 134–135; Marx, *Capital*, I, 91; Engels, *Feuerbach*, pp. 119, 124–125. Religion is "the fantastic reflection of human things in the human mind" (*Dialectics of Nature*, p. 289).

[77] Engels, *Anti-Dühring*, p. 344; Marx, *Capital*, I, 91; Marx and Engels, *Deutsche Ideologie*, p. 20.

roots in the limited and ignorant ideas of savagery," "in certain erroneous and barbaric conceptions." [78] In the course of time other unaccountable forces make their appearance. Social in character, they assume importance in proportion as society adopts elaborate schemes of division of labor, roundabout processes of production, and the confusion of competition. The commodity begins to mystify and disturb man's consciousness. Man cannot grasp its nature, nor can he trace its course when it leaves his hands. Thrown into circulation and expressed in terms of money, the commodity functions as an impersonal entity, apart from the human labor that gave it birth, and cloaking the unique human relations involved in the processes of its production. This is the "fetishism" of commodities. Moreover, competition hides within its chaos "external coercive laws" of nature which exercise a dark power in industrial crises. The commodity dominates modern man as nature dominated primitive man. Man again reacts with the "misty creations of religion." [79]

Strong supporters of morality, they repudiate religion unequivocally, and seemingly for three reasons. First, religion is to them the antithesis of the rational. Religion is a collection of superstitions, a bundle of riddles. The word "religion" symbolizes to them delusion, worship of appearances, and unwillingness to understand. To place religion on a reasonable basis is like conceiving of modern chemistry as alchemy. It has become the fashion, Marx observes, to explain the progress of history by Providence. This "explains nothing. It is at most a declamatory form, one manner among others of paraphrasing the facts." It is "a complete negation of all reasoning." [80]

Second, religion deprives a person of his dignity and renders him servile and unfit for revolutionary activity. "How do you feel, gentle reader," ask Marx and Engels, "when you listen to

---

[78] Engels, *Feuerbach*, pp. 57, 118. In one of his last letters Engels is not so certain of himself and acknowledges only "a negative economic basis" for religion or philosophy (Marx and Engels, *Selected Correspondence*, p. 482).

[79] Marx, *Capital*, I, 81ff.; Engels, *Anti-Dühring*, pp. 344–345.

[80] Marx, *Capital*, III, 967; *Value, Price and Profit*, p. 13; *Poverty of Philosophy*, pp. 129–130; Engels, *Feuerbach*, pp. 79–80.

a priest," whose eloquence is restricted to setting his listeners' tearglands into action, and who "calculates on the *cowardice* of the congregation?" [81] Religion does provide solace to the lowly, but, says Marx, without removing the underlying causes of their distress. "It is the opium of the people. The abolition of religion as the illusory happiness of the people is the requirement of their real happiness." [82] "The social principles of Christianity preach cowardice, self-contempt, abasement, submission, humility, in brief, all the attributes of the canaille . . . but to the proletariat, its courage, its self-confidence, its pride, and its sense of independence are more essential than its daily bread." [83]

Third, they dislike religion for its hypocrisy. Professing lofty principles, it is always in alliance with the oppressor, and is always given to petty self-interest. They therefore refer to it with irony and cynicism. Marx is certain that "the English Established Church, for example, will more readily pardon an attack on 38 of its 39 articles than on 1/39 of its income." [84] The Greek poet hailed the water wheel as an invention that will lighten the drudgery of the slaves, and Marx exclaims: "Oh! those heathens! They understood . . . nothing of political economy and Christianity." They did not see, he continues, that machinery was the

surest means of lengthening the working day. They perhaps excused the slavery of one on the ground that it was a means to the full development of another. But to preach slavery of the masses, in order that a few crude and half-educated parvenus might become "eminent spinners," "extensive sausage makers," and "influential shoeblack dealers" — to do this, they lacked the bump of Christianity.[85]

[81] *Deutsche Ideologie*, p. 522. Italics in original.

[82] "Zur Kritik der Hegelscher Rechtsphilosophie," in Marx and Engels, *Gesamtausgabe*, Part I, vol. 5, p. 607.

[83] *Gesamtausgabe*, Part I, vol. 6, pp. 278, 18. The feeling of the dignity of human personality, says Marx, vanished with the dissolution of Greek civilization, and reappeared in the mists of heaven. "Only this feeling [of dignity] can transform a society into a community of free men" (*ibid.*, Part I, vol. 1, p. 561).

[84] *Capital*, I, 15.

[85] *Capital*, I, 446. "Tucker was a parson and a Tory, but, for the rest, an honorable man" (*ibid.*, p. 834n.). See *ibid.*, pp. 60, 115, 115n.

## HISTORY OF RELIGION

Religion flourished in gens society. Man was then in close contact with nature and he worshipped natural forces. Priests, rites, and sorcery were prominent elements in his world. Each tribe had its own gods and its own mythology. Gradually, by a "natural" process of abstraction the many gods of a tribe or a nation were consolidated into one god. Thus arose monotheism, the best example of which is "the exclusively national god of the Jews, Jehovah." [86] Little is said about religion in classical antiquity, save for some brief references to its eventual monotheism.[87]

When slavery gave place to the medieval type of production a new religion did not fail to come. But it was not a religion originated by the beneficiaries of the new productive system to serve their unique interests. Christianity was not the offspring of medieval production; it was born among the masses hurled together by Roman might, the indebted farmer, the lowly freeman, the slave, and the nationalities subjected by defeat. There was one thing in common to these peoples: misery and hopelessness. Glorifying life after death and promising, in the future world, retribution to the authors of iniquity and rewards for past sufferings, the new religion was an answer to their yearnings. Anton Menger, in his *Right to the Whole Produce of Labor*, asks why socialism failed to come upon the fall of Rome, inasmuch as it was marked by the same symptoms which in present capitalist society are taken as the heralds of socialism — like concentration of property and the increasing misery of the proletariat. Engels replies that Menger did not perceive that socialism did come indeed, only in the circumstances it could be the socialism of the future world, Christianity. A mass product and the child of conditions, the new religion, Engels continues, traces fortunes parallel to those of modern socialism: both make their start among the lowly, both struggle for a bet-

---

[86] Engels, *Origin of the Family*, pp. 106–112, 119–128, 146, 153, 172; *Feuerbach*, pp. 57, 119; *Anti-Dühring*, p. 345; Marx, *Capital*, I, 91.
[87] *Anti-Dühring*, p. 345; *Feuerbach*, pp. 119–120.

ter world, both are torn by sects, and both ultimately triumph.[88]

Here we come upon a singular development. This ideology, instead of being stamped out by the upper class, as any attempt of an exploited class to construct a system of its own is crushed by the ruling class, is ultimately adopted by the oppressors. In the reign of Constantine Christianity becomes the state religion of Rome. To Engels this merely proves that the new institution suited the times. "Enough," he exclaims, "the fact that after 250 years it was a state religion shows that it was a religion answering to the circumstances of the times." [89]

Christianity, when examined closely, is an earthly institution, and not the mother of elevated ethical ideals. It recognized but one equality, the equal taint of original sin. The fact that occasionally, in its early days, it endorsed common property and mutual aid was due more to the pressure of misery and persecution than to concepts of human equality.[90] As soon as it gained recognition by the state, the Church eagerly joined the ranks of those engrossed in sordid affairs, and enlisted itself as an agency of oppression. It took "part in the slavery of the Roman empire for centuries. It never prevented the slave trade of Christians later on, neither of the Germans in the North, nor of the Venetians on the Mediterranean, nor the negro traffic of later years." [91] In the ninth and tenth centuries it imitated the trickery of the nobles, requiring of the harassed small farmer who sought its protection to transfer to it the title to his land and to forfeit his independence. It thus helped in the process of reducing the free farmer to a serf, "for the greater glory of God." [92] The transmission of property by testament before death had been introduced early in Athens and Rome, but in Germany it was originated by the priests "in order that the honest German might bequeath his property to the church without any interference." [93] In the fourteenth and fifteenth centuries,

---

[88] Engels, "Zur Geschichte der Urchristentums," *Neue Zeit*, XIII, no. 1, pp. 4, 6–12, 36, 37, 40.

[89] *Feuerbach*, p. 120.  [90] Engels, *Anti-Dühring*, p. 114.

[91] Engels, *Origin of the Family*, p. 181.

[92] *Origin of the Family*, pp. 182, 186.

[93] *Origin of the Family*, p. 215.

when the German nobility oppressed the serfs with special vigor, "The spiritual lords helped themselves in a more simple manner. They forged documents by which the rights of the peasants were curtailed and their duties increased." [94] Throughout the Middle Ages the Church preached heaven, but strove to possess as much as possible of the earth.

The Church so well adapted itself to medieval economic conditions and pursued material interests with such zeal that it became the stronghold and the symbol of feudalism. It united feudal western Europe into one political system, bestowed on the feudal institutions the advantage of divine consecration, organized its own hierarchy after the feudal pattern, and owned one third of the soil inhabited by Catholics. In the realms of ideology its power was equally great. Everything bore a religious imprint. Philosophy, politics, and jurisprudence were saturated with theology and were subordinated to its authority. The voice of science was stilled, since it dared not overstep the boundaries set by faith.[95] The medieval mind was dominated by religion, and expressed itself only in terms of faith; and social movements, even social uprisings, wore a religious garb.[96] However, Marx reminds us that we are not witnessing here an independent ideological factor, Catholicism, exercising an influence over the lives of men. "The Middle Ages could not live on Catholicism, nor the ancient world on politics. On the contrary, it is the mode in which they gained a livelihood that explains why here politics, and there Catholicism, played the chief part." [97]

When the bourgeoisie came to power, it needed its own religion. The new religion appeared in the form of the protestant heresy, and first of all among the Albigenses in southern France in the period of the greatest growth of free cities.[98] The rising class, intent on demolishing the old order, had to direct its at-

[94] Engels, *Socialism, Utopian and Scientific*, appendix, p. 110.
[95] Engels, *Socialism, Utopian and Scientific*, p. xx; *Feuerbach*, p. 121; *Le mouvement socialiste*, XII, 97.
[96] Engels, *Feuerbach*, pp. 121, 80.
[97] *Capital*, I, 94n.
[98] Engels, *Le mouvement socialiste*, XII, 98; *Feuerbach*, p. 121.

tack on Catholicism, the citadel of medievalism. The first phase of the conflict came with the Lutheran Reformation in Germany. But the power of the bourgeoisie there was insufficient, and the revolt proved a miscarriage. "The Lutheran Reformation produced a new creed indeed, a religion adapted to absolute monarchy," but the victory was gathered by the landed gentry, instead of the bourgeoisie, and this circumstance removed Germany for nearly three centuries from the ranks of "independent, energetic, progressive countries." [99] Then came Calvin with his "natural French acuteness," and won the day.

Calvinism performed a great function during the second act of the bourgeois struggle, that is, during the Great Rebellion in England in the seventeenth century, and finally triumphed when it was incorporated, in large part, in the restored Established Church of England. True, in France it was subdued in 1685. "But what was the good?" Presently the freethinker, Pierre Bayle, became active; in 1695 Voltaire was born; before long the army of encyclopedists, equipped with the mordant materialism or with the deism imported from England and modified by Cartesianism, subjected all religion to the devastating fire of skeptical criticism and rationalism. The French bourgeois became atheistic. "Christianity entered upon the last lap of the race," and could no longer provide the religious clothing for revolutionary ardor.

The third act of the drama, the French Revolution, founded its appeal on political and juristic ideals, and scorned religion. Not Protestants, but freethinkers filled the National Assembly. No one saw the need of religion, and "everybody knows what a mess Robespierre made of the attempt" to introduce it.[100] How it came to pass that, despite this thoroughgoing atheism, capitalist France ultimately reverted to religion, and not to Protestantism even, but to feudal Catholicism, we fail to learn from Engels. He abruptly closes his history of religion, saying, "And that is enough on this part of the subject." [101]

---

[99] Engels, *Feuerbach*, p. 122; *Socialism, Utopian and Scientific*, pp. xix–xxi.
[100] *Feuerbach*, pp. 80, 123–124; *Socialism, Utopian and Scientific*, pp. xxii, xxvi.
[101] *Feuerbach*, p. 125.

Protestantism in its various forms is in spirit and application preëminently a religion of capitalism. In a society which produces commodities with their inherent fetishism, "Christianity with its *cultus* of abstract man, more especially in its bourgeois developments, Protestantism, Deism, etc., is the most fitting form of religion." [102] When the ancient world went under, the ancient religions were "overcome" by Christianity; when feudalism died, Christian sentiment "succumbed" to eighteenth-century rationalism, and the idea of "religious liberty and freedom of conscience merely gave expression to the sway of free competition within the domain of knowledge," even as free competition was reigning within the sphere of production.[103] Calvinism was the "natural religious garb" of the interests of the bourgeoisie. Its doctrine of predestination was no more than the reflection of the economic fact that in commercial competition success or failure did not depend on personal exertion and merit, but on "superior economic powers," incomprehensible and uncontrollable.[104]

Protestantism had a marked effect on the development of capitalism and in setting up states required by this new era of production. It aided England during the "bourgeois upheaval." "The process of forcible expropriation of the people received in the sixteenth century a new and frightful impulse from the Reformation." [105] By changing almost all the traditional holidays into workdays, it "plays an important part in the genesis of capital." [106] Calvinism freed Holland from German and Spanish rule. This creed was organized on democratic and republican principles, "and where the kingdom of God was republicanized, could the kingdoms of this world remain subject to monarchs, bishops, and lords?" Hence, the republics in Geneva and Holland and the active republican parties in England and Scotland — all founded by Calvinism.[107] But it must be em-

[102] Marx, *Capital*, I, 91.
[103] Marx and Engels, *Communist Manifesto*, p. 39.
[104] Engels, *Socialism, Utopian and Scientific*, p. xxii; *Feuerbach*, pp. 122–123.
[105] Marx, *Capital*, I, 792.
[106] *Capital*, I, 303n.
[107] Engels, *Socialism, Utopian and Scientific*, p. xxii; *Feuerbach*, p. 123.

phasized that Protestantism, like Catholicism, was not an agency creating institutions according to its own designs. It was the offspring of the bourgeois régime of production, and in all these performances it acted merely as the child doing the bidding of its progenitor.

As regards the attitude to class relations in society, Protestantism, like its predecessor, is found in the service of the oppressor. It does not uphold lofty principles fearlessly and steadfastly, but gives property priority over everything else, even religion. Atheism is *culpa levis* as compared with an attack on private property.[108] In England a worker would occasionally be imprisoned if he worked in his garden on a Sunday, but he is punished for breach of contract if he does not report to the factory on Sunday, "even if it be from a religious whim." Sabbath-breaking is a crime, but not "if it occurs in the process of expanding capital."[109] The Church winked at the unspeakable atrocities in the colonies, and tolerated Negro slavery.[110] The representatives and leaders of religion look down on the exploited masses, and join the ruling class and the state in maintaining the disinherited and the lowly in subjection. "The 'holy ones' . . . show their Christianity by the humility with which they bear the overwork, the privations, and the hunger of others."[111] Some of them supply the oppressors with a philosophy. Marx quotes Reverend J. Townsend, who wrote in 1786 that hunger is the best motive to industry; that it is a wise law of nature that the poor are improvident, since want forces them to do the servile and "ignoble" work of society, thereby relieving the "more delicate" from drudgery; and that the poor law tended to destroy the "harmony and beauty, the symmetry and order of that system which God and Nature have established in the world."[112]

In England the bourgeois spent in the nineteenth century great sums of money on "the evangelization of the lower or-

---

[108] Marx, *Capital*, I, 15.
[109] *Capital*, I, 291n.
[110] *Capital*, I, 824–825; Engels, *Origin of the Family*, p. 181.
[111] Marx, *Capital*, I, 291n.
[112] *Capital*, I, 710.

ders," and, not content with the "native religious machinery," he imported from abroad organizers "of religion as a trade." The bourgeois knew well that religion was effective in befuddling the workers and rendering them "submissive to the behests of the masters it had pleased God to place over them." Soon his counterpart on the Continent became also convinced "that religion must be kept alive for the people," and this explains why the French and German bourgeoisie silently dropped their freethought and became religious.[113] Religion represents the spiritual force of repression, just as the state represents the physical force.[114] It is the opiate that intoxicates the poor so as to make it easier to rob them. "The mortgage the peasant has on heavenly goods gives guaranty to the mortgage the bourgeois has on the peasant's earthly goods." The Church in France knew this well.[115]

But religion will not endure. The time will arrive when all phenomena under man's observation will become clear to his comprehension. Then the foundation of religion will be removed. Under capitalism the range of mystery is narrowed to a considerable extent; yet the basic facts that give rise to religious reactions still persist. Crises, poverty, and the fetishism of commodities still rage at large, and they cannot be controlled. Man proposes, but the "coercive force" of capitalistic production disposes. However, capitalism will fall, and man's subjection to the secret forces which cast a spell over his production processes will vanish. He will study carefully, plan systematically, and regulate wisely the productive forces. He will at last become master of the mechanism he sets up, and every social phenomenon will be transparent to him and no longer a tantalizing riddle. Under socialism the state disappears because of the obliteration of class distinctions, and religion is destroyed "for the simple reason that there will be nothing left to reflect . . . religion dies this natural death."[116]

[113] Engels, *Socialism, Utopian and Scientific*, pp. xxv, xxxi, xxxvi.
[114] Marx, *Civil War in France*, p. 74.
[115] Marx, *Klassenkämpfe in Frankreich*, p. 64.
[116] Engels, *Anti-Dühring*, pp. 345–346; Marx, *Capital*, I, 91–92.

# CHAPTER VIII

## SCIENCE AND PHILOSOPHY

THE state, law, morality, and religion are more in the nature of institutions than ideologies, although the latter designation is frequently applied to them by Marx and Engels. The ideologies proper are the reflections of these institutions and of the natural and social phenomena, formed in the brains of men. They are the ideas that people have of their environment, of the problems confronting them, and of the solutions to be adopted; they are theories and systems of thought formulated by the investigator; they are also the artistic reflections of reality. The ideologies proper may be taken as comprising natural and social science, philosophy, literature, and art.

### NATURAL SCIENCE

The main source of science, natural or social, and the impulse behind its development are to be sought in economics. The practical necessities and the daily problems in direct and close or indirect and remote connection with the productive processes stir men to scientific thought and investigation. There are natural forces to subdue, methods of production to perfect, wayward human skill to replace by obedient mechanical contrivances. There are problems of class relations and class domination to be resolved. The incentives that lead to study and search proceed primarily from self-interest. True, economists are concerned with rent as pure theory, and quite aside from the fact that, as spokesmen of the industrial capitalist, they are to wage battle against the landlord;[1] true, when humiliated by war, Germany devoted herself zealously and disinterestedly to the study of science and philosophy.[2] But to Marx and Engels these cases are far from typical. By and large, scientific study is promoted for practical needs and tangible results.

[1] Marx, *Capital*, III, 908.
[2] Engels, *Feuerbach*, pp. 126–127.

Marx and his friend do not believe, as Veblen does, that idle curiosity has been the driving motive of science.

The economic science that arose in the seventeenth century and received its positive formulation in the eighteenth, was the expression of the conditions and requirements of the time, says Engels.[3] "Like all other sciences, mathematics arose out of the *needs* of men; from the measurement of land and of the content of vessels; from the computation of time and mechanics."[4] The sporadic use of machinery in the seventeenth century supplied to great mathematicians a "practical basis and stimulant to the creation of the science of mechanics."[5] Material facts connected with the system of production create problems, pose questions, and encourage investigation. Egyptian astronomy owes its existence to "the necessity for predicting the rise and fall of the Nile," and explains as well the supremacy of priests as directors of agriculture.[6] After 1825 all the new mechanical inventions in England were induced by workers' strikes, for the capitalist was intent on breaking the power that individual skill conferred upon the worker, and the new machines were used as a weapon against labor that knew not to be meek.[7] If civilization witnessed progressive achievements of science and at times great productions in art, it was "due only to the fact that without them the highest emoluments of modern wealth would have been missing."[8]

A correspondent writes to Engels that technique depends on science. Engels replies that, if this is so, science depends still more on the state and the requirements of technique. A technical need, he says, will do more for the advancement of science than ten universities. All hydrostatics (Torricelli, etc.) had been born of the necessity to regulate the torrents in Italy in the sixteenth and seventeenth centuries. We know, he continues, anything rational about electricity only since the day

[3] *Anti-Dühring*, p. 168.
[4] *Anti-Dühring*, p. 46. Engels' italics.
[5] Marx, *Capital*, I, 383.
[6] *Capital*, I, 564n.
[7] Marx, *Poverty of Philosophy*, pp. 153, 183.
[8] Engels, *Origin of the Family*, pp. 215–216.

we discovered its technical use. Unfortunately, the German, he remarks, is in the habit of writing the history of the sciences as if they had fallen down from the sky.[9]

Human needs are the spur to scientific thought. That its content is rooted in material actuality, the philosophy of cognition and the dialectic, as was seen previously, emphatically testify. No ideas can be conceived in man's mind that have no basis in external materiality. The question is what general relation science, once sprung into life, has to this reality. Here Engels distinguishes three groups of sciences: natural sciences, like mathematics, physics, chemistry, astronomy, concerned with inanimate natural phenomena; organic sciences, like biology, interested in animate nature; and social, or "historical sciences," dealing with social conditions surrounding human life, and law, political thought, philosophy, religion. Economics is not mentioned specifically.[10]

The first two groups of sciences, the natural and organic, are engaged with phenomena that are not man-made and that do not alter their nature. In their occurrences and sequences such phenomena are always the same, and the laws governing them never change, despite the shifts in the modes of production in society. The blood circulation of an animal is not different under capitalism from what it was under ancient slavery. The behavior of acids and of parallel lines is the same in primitive communism and under feudalism. Atoms, heat, electricity, the movement of celestial bodies, obey constant laws that pay no homage to economic eras. These phenomena know no relativity. Nevertheless, these two groups of sciences yield but a small range of absolute truths. The reason is that, while the phenomena themselves are not relative, the knowledge of them as acquired by man is.

The fundamental cause of this relativity is found in the powerlessness of the human mind to penetrate the ultimate character of natural phenomena and of the laws controlling

---

[9] Letter of January 25, 1894, Marx and Engels, *Selected Correspondence*, p. 517.

[10] *Anti-Dühring*, pp. 97–99.

them. Science advances step by step, ideas are subject to constant revision, and conquests are made with great pain. Boyle discovered that at the same temperature the volume of a gas varies inversely with the pressure on it. Then Regnault found that this law is susceptible to significant limitations; further investigation may introduce further modifications. It took the long period from Galen to Malpighi to establish as simple a thing as the circulation of the blood of mammals. Even in mathematics new hypotheses and new ways of looking at things are crowding one upon another, and frequent controversies arise concerning matters that had been regarded as axiomatic; so that we are no longer certain of what exactly we are doing when we multiply and divide. Accordingly, the field of absolute certainty even in these two types of science is hardly extended far beyond such assertions as that two times two are four, birds have beaks, men must die. So speaks Engels, with Marx's approval.[11]

It may be claimed that these sciences are relative also to the modes of production. But relativity will have a special sense here. It will mean that one productive era may stimulate the advancement of science more than another. Greek art and science would have been impossible without slavery;[12] feudalism fettered independent thought; "the whole Renaissance from the middle of the fifteenth century was an actual product of the city, and therefore of bourgeois domination";[13] and socialism, we are assured, will offer the greatest opportunities for disinterested investigation in all fields of knowledge.

## Economics

Among the "historical" sciences Engels lists those concerned with "the conditions of human life," and with law, politics, philosophy, religion, art, etc.[14] The first obviously refers to such a field as economics. Marx declares that after 1830 economics as a science became impossible. In so far as it labors

[11] *Anti-Dühring*, pp. 97ff.
[12] *Anti-Dühring*, p. 200.
[13] Engels, *Feuerbach*, p. 118.
[14] *Anti-Dühring*, p. 99.

under the limitations of the bourgeois horizon, "political economy can remain a science only so long as the class struggle is
latent" or manifests itself sporadically. Such was the situation in England prior to 1830, when economics flourished and
Ricardo was its "last great representative." But the turning
point came in 1830, when in both England and France class
antagonisms assumed serious proportions. "It sounded the
knell of scientific bourgeois economy." Economists enlisted
from then on as the "hired prize fighters" and "the sophists
and sycophants" of the ruling class. The question was no longer
whether a proposition was true or false, but whether it was
"useful to capital or harmful, expedient or inexpedient, politically dangerous or not." After 1848 there also appeared among
them devotees of "shallow syncretism," reconcilers of the irreconcilable, of whom J. S. Mill was the "best representative."
Such is Marx's judgment in his preface to the second edition
of his *Capital*, volume I.[15]

The science, he complains elsewhere, became the playground
of "vulgar economy," which he defines as "nothing but a didac-
tic, more or less dogmatic, translation of the ordinary conceptions of the agents of production"; as a reflection in the brain
of only "the immediate *apparent form* of conditions . . . not
their *inner connection*." [16] Vulgar economists treat the capitalist system as natural, reasonable, and eternal, and they supply
the bourgeoisie with a "religion of everyday life." [17] In their
superficiality they do not see, for example, that the elements of
the "trinitarian formula" — capital, land, and labor — are as
unrelated as "lawyer's fees, carrots, and music," and that the
expression "price of labor" is as irrational as "a yellow loga-
rithm"; [18] they have "Mister Capital and Mistress Land carry
on their goblin tricks" in "an enchanted, perverted, topsy-

---

[15] Pages 17–20. On a later page he refers to economists as capital's Sancho
Panza (*ibid.*, p. 703).

[16] *Capital*, III, 967, 271; Marx, letter of June 27, 1867, in Marx and Engels,
*Gesamtausgabe*, Part III, vol. 3, p. 404. Marx's italics.

[17] *Capital*, I, 93n., 623, 703; III, 913, 915.

[18] Yet Marx himself uses this phrase. See, e.g., *Capital*, I, 611, 613, 615, 678,
697.

turvy world." [19] In a letter to Kugelmann Marx complains: "It shows what these priests of the bourgeoisie have come to, when workers and even manufacturers and merchants understand my book [*Capital*] . . . while these 'scribes' (!) complain that I make excessive demands on their understanding." [20] Among the vulgar economists he numbers McCulloch, Senior, and J. B. Say. [21]

The best spokesmen of classical economics move on a higher plane. Nevertheless, even they "remained more or less the prisoners of the world of illusion which they had dissolved critically. . . Consequently all of them fall more or less into inconsistencies, halfway statements, and unsolved contradictions." [22] Adam Smith and Ricardo failed to see the many sides of exchange-value. Simple as the law of the falling rate of profit is, all economists, beginning with Adam Smith, "cudgeled their brains in tortuous attempts" to fathom its mystery; but in vain. No wonder, however, that they failed to solve the "riddle" when we consider that political economy "up to the present" had been merely "tinkering" with the distinction between constant and variable capital, that it never perceived the true nature of profit and surplus-value, and that it never thoroughly analyzed the organic composition of capital. [23] At times "Classical political economy nearly touches the true relation of things, without, however, consciously formulating it. This it cannot [do] so long as it sticks in its bourgeois skin." [24]

Economics and other social sciences are relative in the same sense as natural sciences are, but unlike the latter, they are also relative to the mode of production. Natural phenomena are invariant, but social phenomena, man-made, exhibit sequences varying with each productive order. Rent does not arise before capitalism, and Ricardo errs when he associates rent with landed property: rent comes from society, not from

[19] *Capital*, III, 947, 967, 952, 966.
[20] *Letters to Dr. Kugelmann*, p. 75.
[21] *Capital*, I, 572n., 654–655.
[22] *Capital*, III, 967.
[23] *Capital*, I, 92–93n.; III, 249–250.
[24] *Capital*, I, 594.

land.[25] Each form of production creates a new social world, with new types of division of labor and with property defined by new social relations. "Political economy, therefore, cannot be the same for all countries and for all historical epochs." [26]

But within each era of production there are definite economic laws, which Marx defines as tendencies.[27] "Every historical period has laws of its own. . . As soon as society has outlived a given period of development, and is passing over from one given stage to another, it begins to be subject also to other laws." As was mentioned earlier, in his preface to *Capital*, volume I (pages 23–24), Marx cites approvingly this summary by a Russian critic of his, Marx's, position. Marx's aim in *Capital* is to disclose "the natural laws of capitalist production" and to "lay bare the economic law of motion of modern society." [28] Each "mode of production has its own law of population." [29] He frequently talks of the law of value, the law of increased productivity, and other economic laws.[30]

## PHILOSOPHY

Philosophy is classed as an "historical," social science.[31] Like law, politics, and religion, it is a form in which the social consciousness expresses itself.[32] Respecting its genesis and connection with the economic world, it occupies the same position as religion. It is furthest removed from the economic basis because of the many intervening links, and it did not originate in response to economic needs, as the other sciences did. It arose in prehistoric times, and it had an absurd content, because, with the economic development at a rudimentary stage, men could not help generating extravagant ideas of man and nature. The history of natural science is the history of the gradual destruc-

[25] Marx, *Poverty of Philosophy*, pp. 119, 139, 168, 174; *Capital*, I, 95. And yet Marx recognizes the existence of rent in feudal society. See *Capital*, III, 917ff.
[26] Engels, *Anti-Dühring*, p. 163.
[27] *Capital*, III, 206.
[28] *Capital*, I, 13, 14
[29] *Capital*, I, 693.
[30] E.g., *Capital*, I, 612; III, 212, 308.
[31] Engels, *Anti-Dühring*, p. 99.
[32] Marx, *Critique of Political Economy*, p. 12.

tion of these prehistoric absurdities, and their systematic replacement by lesser absurdities. Each newly born economic epoch finds a heritage of philosophical ideas, and employs them as a starting point. This circumstance explains why countries economically backward may be advanced in philosophical speculation.[33]

But even in philosophy the potency of economic forces is manifest. Only their influence is frequently indirect, and for the following reason. The raw material that gives rise to philosophical reflection is frequently not economic reality immediately, but the ideologies that had issued from this reality, especially politics, law, morality. The economic elements do not affect directly anything in philosophy; they act first on these ideologies, and through them determine the foundations of and the variations in the philosophical heritage bequeathed to a given era.[34]

It follows that philosophical speculation is not only relative in the same sense in which all social sciences are, but is also contingent upon the stage of progress of these social sciences. Further, philosophy is dependent a good deal on natural science, providing an example of how all sciences are intertwined. The Greek philosophy of the world was naïve; it was the "primitive natural materialism." But it could not be otherwise, since all branches of science were in their infancy. Exact observation of nature began in the Alexandrian period, and experienced further development at the hands of the Arabs in the Middle Ages. However, true natural science began to flourish in the middle of the fifteenth century, and the new points of view were carried by Bacon and Locke into philosophy. Eighteenth-century materialism and metaphysics were mechanical and static in their fundamental postulates, because natural science had the mechanical and nonevolutionary orientation. Since then the philosophy of materialism underwent significant changes collateral "with each epoch-making discovery in the

[33] Engels, *Feuerbach*, p. 117.
[34] Engels, letter of October 27, 1890, Marx and Engels, *Selected Correspondence*, pp. 483–484.

department of natural science." Hegel had ideas of change and progress; yet, although "with Saint-Simon, . . . the most encyclopedic mind of his age," he could not come upon the laws of the development-process because, among other things, of the limitations of contemporary knowledge. In the nineteenth century science devoted much attention to the processes and principles of change. Physiology, embryology, and geology are examples. Then came the three great discoveries: the cell as the unit of plant and animal life, the transformation of energy, and Darwin's theory of evolution. Consequently, philosophy accepted soon a broader materialism, which embraced these "more recent advances of natural science." The proof of the materialistic dialectic was found in nature, and science deserves much credit for having accumulated the data for the argument.[35]

Like institutions, science and philosophy have repercussions on the economic world. In this respect, a distinction is to be made, however, between natural and social sciences. Natural science, as was seen earlier, is prominent as a constituent of the mode of production, and is identified with the productive forces. Accordingly it serves, although indirectly and through the system of production, as a regulator of human history. It also plays its part in liberating man from the blind domination of nature, and in elevating him from the domain of necessity to the realm of freedom, by strengthening him with the knowledge of the laws governing his natural environment.[36] In its future progress science will dissolve many a mystery and will at last dispel all "antagonism between spirit and matter, man and nature, soul and body." [37]

On the other hand, philosophy, and even social sciences, generally does not seem to be classed as an active factor in history. But neither is it entirely a passive element. It sheds a glamor over men's achievements, lends color to historical periods, marks turning points in human events, and helps in breaking

[35] Engels, *Anti–Dühring*, pp. 26–31, 152, 17; *Feuerbach*, pp. 65, 67, 98–101.
[36] Engels, *Anti–Dühring*, p. 125.
[37] *Neue Zeit*, XIV, no. 2 (1895–1896), pp. 552–553.

the ground for great movements. The brilliant school of French materialists "made the eighteenth century, in spite of all battles on land and sea won over Frenchmen by Germans and Englishmen, a preëminently French century, even before that crowning French Revolution." [38] The scientific discovery that products, as values, are the expression of human labor embodied in them marks "an epoch in the history of the development of the human race." [39] The French philosophy supplied the principles and battle cries, the "theoretical flag," of the French Revolution, and prepared men's minds for it.[40] "Just as in France in the eighteenth, so in Germany in the nineteenth century, revolutionary philosophic conceptions introduced a breaking-up of existing political conditions." [41] "The German working-class movement is the heir of the German classical philosophy," and modern socialism, in its theoretical aspects, has its roots in the teachings of the French philosophers of the eighteenth century.[42]

But once more, it should not be forgotten that whatever influence ideology exerts on human history, it remains the product of economic forces. In the last instance, the economic forces assert their supremacy, and drag in their train all other phases of social life, notwithstanding retardations and slight modifications imposed by institutions and systems of thought. Whatever concessions are made at times, this is the position from which neither Marx nor Engels ever departs. The economic reality is primary and decisive.[43] The more, Engels teaches, a

[38] *Socialism, Utopian and Scientific*, p. xiii.

[39] Marx, *Capital*, I, 85.

[40] Engels, *Socialism, Utopian and Scientific*, pp. xxvi, 1–2.

[41] Engels, *Feuerbach*, p. 37.

[42] *Feuerbach*, p. 128; *Socialism, Utopian and Scientific*, p. 1.

[43] Concerning the whole range of social sciences the *Communist Manifesto* (p. 39) expresses itself as follows:

"Does it require deep intuition to comprehend that man's ideas, views, and conceptions, in one word, man's consciousness, changes with every change in the conditions of his material existence, in his social relations, and in his social life?

"What else does the history of ideas prove than that intellectual production changes in character in proportion as material production is changed? The ruling ideas of each age have ever been the ideas of its ruling class.

"When people speak of ideas that revolutionize society, they do but express

given sphere is removed from the economic province, and the more it approaches abstract ideology, the more zigzags its curve of development will display. But the longer the period under observation and the larger the domain under study, the more will the curve tend to be parallel to the curve of economic development.[44]

Philosophy, the ideology remotest from the economic basis, is no exception. "But all the same," Engels contends, "they [the philosophers] themselves remain under the dominating influence of economic development." Hobbes, the first modern materialist, was a partisan of absolutism; Locke was in religion and politics the son of the compromise of 1688. The English deists and their successors, the French materialists, were the philosophers of the bourgeoisie; and the materialism of these French philosophers "was nothing more than the idealized kingdom of the bourgeoisie." No more than their predecessors could they go beyond the limits imposed upon them by their epoch.[45] The post-Renaissance philosophy, the English and French philosophy of the eighteenth century, and the Hegelian school were alike "only the philosophical expression of the thoughts corresponding with the development of the small and middle bourgeois into the great bourgeois." "The German petty bourgeois runs through German philosophy from Kant to Hegel, sometime positively and sometime negatively." The philosophers from Descartes to Hegel, and from Hobbes to Feuerbach, were by no means guided by pure reason. What really impelled them was the steady march of natural science and industry.[46]

What destinies Marx and Engels would prescribe for the various sciences when socialism comes is, one may believe, not difficult to surmise. Natural science will flourish, unobstructed by the interests of the bourgeoisie. Men of science,

---

the fact that within the old society the elements of a new one have been created, and that the dissolution of the old ideas keeps even pace with the dissolution of the old conditions of existence."

[44] Marx and Engels, *Selected Correspondence*, p. 518.

[45] *Selected Correspondence*, p. 483; Engels, *Socialism, Utopian and Scientific*, pp. 2–4; *Anti-Dühring*, pp. 23–24.

[46] Engels, *Feuerbach*, pp. 118, 62; Marx and Engels, *Selected Correspondence*, p. 483.

no longer the "paid wage laborers" doing the bidding of the capitalists, will dedicate themselves to the study of the ways of nature in order to hasten man's ascent to freedom. The fate of the social sciences will not be so cheerful. Some of them will receive their death warrant. All theorizing concerning the state will most probably vanish, for socialism will know no state or property. The study of religion will be abandoned, as there will remain no mysteries to trouble the human mind. The socialist world will be devoid of such phenomena, and the corresponding sciences will have nothing to observe and to "reflect." Such sciences as economics, psychology, and ethics will undoubtedly prosper, since economic activities will expand in scope, human beings will find fullest self-expression, and morality will move on a superior plane.

Philosophy, however, is doomed to a bitter end. Its task has been heretofore to "devise" interrelations among the phenomena of nature or society, and to indicate how facts fit into the great totality of things. But with the advance of future science, these interconnections will be sought rather in the phenomena themselves, and not in the "empty imaginings" of the philosopher's mind. Each science will examine the interdependence of the particular phenomena within its own confines, and also their association with the phenomena under scrutiny in all the other sciences. The emphasis will fall on external facts and not on speculation. Positive science will reign everywhere. Philosophy had rendered great service in its day, but it is no longer needed. In its stead the laws of thought will come to power, logic and especially dialectics.[47]

## ART

The subject of art receives brief attention in an obscure corner.[48] It appears to many, Marx says, that periods of the highest development of art stand in no direct association with the general development of the community or with its material basis. Examples are ordinarily drawn in support of this view

[47] Engels, Feuerbach, pp. 101, 125; Anti-Dühring, p. 43; Socialism, Utopian and Scientific, p. 39.

[48] Marx, Critique of Political Economy, appendix, pp. 309–312.

from the Greeks or the Elizabethans, comparing their attainments with those of modern days, when the economic development reached a higher scale. But appearances deceive, suggests Marx, and the connection is there nevertheless. Greek art sprang from the soil of its mythology, and it would have been impossible without a mythology. Now mythology thrives when the forces of nature are an enigma to man. He then contrives to master them in and through his imagination. Nature, and even forms of society, are then molded "in popular fancy in an unconsciously artistic fashion." Greek art employed Greek mythology as its material, and such art could not originate in a society which excludes mythological conceptions of nature. It could appear only under "unripe social conditions."

As soon as man gains mastery over his natural environment, mythology disappears, and art like that of the Greeks can no longer prevail. In an age of automatic machinery, railways, locomotives, and the electric telegraph such views of nature and social relations as had been formed by Greek imagination and Greek art are inconceivable.

Where does Vulcan come in as against Roberts and Company; Jupiter, as against the lightning rod; and Hermes as against the Credit Mobilier? . . . What becomes of the Goddess of Fame side by side with Printing House Square? . . . Is Achilles possible side by side with powder and lead? Or is the *Iliad* at all compatible with the printing press and the steam press? Do not singing and reciting and the muses necessarily go out of existence with the appearance of the printer's bar, and do not, therefore, disappear the prerequisites of epic poetry?

"But," continues Marx, "the difficulty is not in grasping the idea that Greek art and epos are bound up with certain forms of social development." It consists rather in the question why they still furnish us esthetic enjoyment and even serve as standards "beyond attainment." Marx offers an explanation. A man cannot become a child, yet he enjoys the artless ways of the child, and strives to reproduce its truth "on a higher plane." Similarly, the social childhood of mankind holds forth the charm of an age that will never return. The Greeks were normal children, and they exhibited "the most beautiful development" of the social childhood. Therefore their art has an irresistible charm for us. At this point the manuscript ends.

In the *Deutsche Ideologie* [49] we find the following views. Leonardo da Vinci was conditioned by the social environment of Florence. Not everybody can be a Raphael, but he "who has a Raphael in him" should be given the opportunity to develop freely. Like every other artist, Raphael was conditioned by the technical advances in art before him and by the organization of society and the division of labor in his day. Whether an individual like Raphael can develop depends on demand, and demand depends on division of labor and the educational conditions. "The exclusive concentration of artistic talent in a few individuals and its correlative suppression in the masses are an effect of division of labor." Under communism the artist is not confined to local or national limitations, nor is the individual artist either a painter or a sculptor. "In a communist society there are no painters but first of all men who, among other things, paint."

In various connections, the accent is put on the idea that capitalism degrades art and is ill calculated to permit its genuine development. The indictment of the *Communist Manifesto* [50] is unsparing. Equally harsh is Marx's pronouncement in *Zur Judenfrage* [51]: "What lies hidden and abstract in the Jewish religion, namely, the disdain for theory, for art, for history, for man as an end in himself, becomes the *real, conscious* standpoint and virtue of the moneyed man," the capitalist.

[49] Pages 372–373.
[50] Pages 15–16. Cf. Marx, *Theorien über den Mehrwert*, I, 382.
[51] Marx and Engels, *Gesamtausgabe*, Part I, vol. I, pp. 603–604. Marx's italics.

# PART IV

# THE TREND OF HISTORY

# CHAPTER IX

## MARX'S CONCEPT OF CAPITALISM

### UTOPIAN AND SCIENTIFIC SOCIALISM

As the founder of scientific socialism, Marx is convinced that socialism is not the product of benevolent efforts of well-disposed people, but that the evolution of society moves towards socialism, inexorably and independently of dreamers. He and his friend scorn as utopian the theories sponsored by their predecessors for the regeneration of society. Ever since the appearance of capitalism and its evils, there had been, they say, no want of well-meaning persons who sought to build a better world. In the sixteenth and seventeenth centuries writers painted beautiful pictures in utopian climes. In the eighteenth century Morelly and Mably bred schemes for the obliteration of class distinctions and for political and social equality; and they proposed a Spartan communism as a substitute for capitalism. Then came Sismondi with his cry "back to medievalism"; then "the three great utopians," Saint-Simon, Fourier, and Owen.[1]

The theories of these reformers Marx and Engels stamp as the fantastic visions of utopian socialists who lived during the youth of capitalism, when the proletariat was barely emerging as a class, and when material conditions were too immature to reveal the causes of existing evils and to suggest lasting solutions. Accordingly the reformers sought refuge in their minds, improvising far-fetched schemes. They proceeded from the assumption, Marx and Engels continue, that the sense of justice was so firm in the human character that an appeal to it would bring miracles. Instead of laboring as the defenders of the oppressed class, they posed indiscriminately as the emancipators of all mankind. They meant to harmonize the

[1] Engels, *Socialism, Utopian and Scientific*, pp. 5–6; Marx and Engels, *Communist Manifesto*, p. 46.

interests of the divergent classes and to reconcile the irreconcilable contradictions of society. Their remodeling schemes
did not call for the eradication of the conditions which fostered the evils. They planned to graft upon the material
foundations of the existing order the alien measures of their
dreams.[2]

To these constructions Marx called a halt. His theory of
social development emphasized that history was the history
of class struggles, and that classes were the product of the
modes of production. "From that time forward," says Engels,
"socialism was no longer an accidental discovery of this or
that ingenious brain, but the necessary outcome of the struggle" between the proletariat and the bourgeoisie. The task,
Engels continues, was no longer to invent a perfect system,
but to examine the "historico-economic succession of events"
that produce the class struggle and bring it to a happy end.
It became essential, first, to indicate that capitalism, while
historically unavoidable, has a transient career, like any other
system; and, second, to reveal how the workings of the present order specifically condemn it to dissolution. The materialistic conception of social life accomplished the one task, and
the "discovery" of surplus-value performed the other task.
"These two great discoveries," Engels teaches, ". . . we owe
to Marx. With these discoveries socialism became a science."[3]

These two discoveries are not isolated achievements, but
are closely connected with each other. The materialistic conception of history expounds that no economic order is eternal,
that capitalism is no exception, and that socialism will triumph
on its ruins. It appeared to Marx essential to demonstrate
that such is the inexorable course of modern history. It was
important to him to indicate the contradictions of capitalism
and the germs of the future socialist order already to be discerned; to explain, that is, the antitheses embedded in our
society and the future synthesis that is bound to arise. This

[2] Marx, *Poverty of Philosophy*, pp. 136–137, 197; Marx and Engels, *Communist Manifesto*, pp. 53–54; Engels, *Socialism, Utopian and Scientific*, pp. 6,
11–27.

[3] *Socialism, Utopian and Scientific*, pp. 42, 44.

he did in his monumental work, the three volumes of *Capital*. In a larger sense, therefore, we may regard *Capital*, and his other economic writings, as a part of his interpretation of history, as an intensive elaboration of one of its momentous claims.

Such a view comes reluctantly to the reader's mind. *Capital* is a comprehensive work, and we are accustomed to regard it as an independent body of thought, privileged, like the tub, to stand on its own bottom. Yet, the more one reflects upon Marx's works and ideas the more one wonders whether they do not constitute one system with the materialistic theory of history as its core. In the preface to the *Critique of Political Economy*, a work published in 1859, Marx explains that philosophical questions involved in the policies of the French socialists had led him to a critical revision of Hegel's *Philosophy of Law*, and that these studies had brought him to the conviction embodied in the materialistic view of historical processes. After these studies he turned to economics, and he confesses that this conception of history "continued to serve as the leading thread" in this new pursuit.[4] Why should an author of a book on economics preface it with his philosophico-evolutionary credo respecting world history, and why should his theory of history function as a guiding principle in his economic studies?

In the preface to *Capital* he declares that his ultimate aim is "to lay bare the economic law of motion of modern society" and to study its "natural laws," or the "tendencies working with iron necessity towards inevitable results."[5] The movement of capitalism toward a particular goal seems uppermost in his mind. In the first paragraph of the text of the same work he announces: "Our investigation must therefore begin with the analysis of a commodity," the unit of wealth in capitalist society. To what purpose he begins this analysis is revealed on the last page of the penultimate chapter,[6] where we read:

[4] Pages 10–11.

[5] *Capital*, I, 13, 14.

[6] *Capital*, I, 837. It is really the last page of the *last* chapter, since the following chapter on "The Modern Theory of Colonization" may be regarded as an appendix, or as a return to a thesis maintained in an earlier chapter.

"The knell of capitalist private property sounds. The expropriators are expropriated . . . But capitalist production begets, with the inexorability of a law of nature, its own negation," and the outcome is "coöperation and the possession in common of the land and of the means of production . . . . What the bourgeoisie therefore produces, above all, are its own gravediggers." He begins with the analysis of the commodity; explores the fundamentals of capitalism; outlines its origin; shows how the dialectic labors for its extinction; and lastly reads its death warrant. His theory of history seems to preside over the pages of *Capital.*

We shall accordingly find it profitable to examine Marx's views on the nature and fate of capitalist society as presented in his economic writings. The findings will throw light on his interpretation of history. The characteristics of a mode of production, the contradictions undermining it, the nature of the warring classes, the transition to a new order, all these elements take on concrete and dramatic form in his diagnosis of capitalism.

### THE MEANING OF CAPITALISM

First of all, what is capitalism? Marx never gave a thoroughgoing discussion of the distinctive earmarks of the object of his lifelong attention, and it is not easy to break a path to a definitive conclusion through the tangle of statements bearing on the question. But an attempt can be made to formulate what he very likely had in mind. The upholders of the technological interpretation of Marx's conception of the mode of production may answer that with him capitalism is distinguished by the pervasive use of machinery in production. But we recall that, according to him, capitalism rose in the sixteenth century while machinery came into use at the end of the eighteenth century. As was indicated in Chapter III, above, capitalism, in Marx's view, went through the stages of coöperation and "manufacture," lasting for over two centuries, before the advent of "modern industry" with its machine technique.

On the basis of the varied pronouncements by Marx, it seems reasonable to conclude that the main features of capitalism are three: commodity production, surplus-value, and "free" labor. The first two, as will be seen presently, are not unique to capitalism and only became more prevalent and more typical under capitalism, while the third is peculiar to capitalism and may be taken as its distinguishing mark. This point deserves a little more attention.

First, as to commodity production. Marx distinguishes between a product, or an article made for use by the producer, and a commodity, or an article produced as merchandise, for sale.[7] Commodity production had been known before capitalism. There was exchange of goods on the boundaries of neighboring tribes even in the days of archaic communism.[8] Marx and Engels relate that commerce had flourished, money had circulated, and usurers had plied their trade, long before Christ, in Phoenicia, in Carthage, and in Greece and Rome. Bankers were known in the Middle Ages. All these agencies suggest the exchange of goods: "Merchant's capital is older than the capitalist mode of production . . . and its function consists exclusively in promoting the exchange of commodities."[9] Under capitalism, however, commodity production becomes more typical by far. "The mode of production in which the product takes the form of a commodity . . . is the most general and the most embryonic form of bourgeois production . . ."[10]

Similarly with the second attribute of capitalism, surplus-value. Surplus-value does not make its maiden appearance under capitalism. According to Marx, commerce had been known since antiquity. Commerce implies, generally, a surplus product, a product over and above the consumption of

---

[7] See, e.g., *Capital*, I, 48, 188; II, 159.

[8] *Capital*, I, 100; III, 209, 374.

[9] *Capital*, III, 382, 383, 385, 391; II, 125–126; Engels, *Origin of the Family*, pp. 131, 135, 200, 214; *Anti-Dühring*, pp. 179–180.

[10] Marx, *Capital*, I, 94. "The monetary system correctly proclaims production for the world market and the transformation of the product into commodities . . . as the prerequisite and condition of capitalist production" (*ibid.*, III, 911. See also *ibid.*, I, 639n.; II, 125–126, 163).

the direct producer; it obviously implies, too, the exchange of the surplus product, or its transformation into a commodity. Such surplus commodities represent surplus-value, since, typically, commerce involves the exchange of products filched by the master from the slave and by the lord from the serf, or of products obtained in a hard bargain by the medieval merchant from the independent artisan.[11]

But commerce is not the only index of surplus-value in precapitalist days. When discussing exploitation by the usurer, Marx observes that in the past usury commonly devoured the whole of the surplus labor of the victim, and "hence it is very absurd to compare the level of this interest, which assimilates all surplus-value," with the modern rate of interest, which represents only part of surplus-value.[12] Similarly with ground rent. With reference to the serf, who works a number of days each week on the lord's estate, Marx observes that here "rent and surplus-value are identical," that here "surplus-value obviously has the form of surplus-labor . . . it still exists in its visible, palpable form"; while under capitalism it is concealed.[13] It goes without saying that in capitalist society surplus-value is a more widely prevalent phenomenon than in any previous era.

In a different category is the third attribute of capitalism, "free" labor. Here seems to lie the unique trait of capitalism. In modern society the laborer is free, and in two senses. First, unlike the slave or serf, he is personally independent; he is at liberty to dispose of himself and his labor as he sees fit and to contract with anybody he chooses: a Marxian version of the change from status to contract. Marx talks of coöperation and comments that while it is common to all modes of production, it is distinguished under capitalism by free labor: "The capitalistic form, on the contrary, presupposes from first to last the free wage laborer, who sells his labor-power to capital."[14]

---

[11] *Capital*, I, 559; II, 44; III, 366, 383–384, 389–391, 394, 395. "Every process of commodity production at the same time becomes a process of exploiting labor-power" (*ibid.*, II, 44–45).

[12] *Capital*, III, 699.

[13] *Capital*, III, 917, 919–920.                    [14] *Capital*, I, 367, 186.

Second, unlike the independent peasant or artisan, the average laborer is "free" from the possession of the property indispensable to production, except his labor-power. To live, he must offer his labor-power for hire to those who own the means of production. Under the previous forms of production only products might be commodities, or merchandise. Under capitalism, a new kind of commodity makes its appearance, labor-power. Two commodity owners confront each other on the market: "on the one side, the possessor of the means of production and subsistence; on the other, the possessor of nothing but labor-power." The "polarization of the market" with these two commodities constitutes the essence of capitalism.[15] Free wage labor is the "basis," the "starting point," the "fundamental constitution," the "specific character," of the capitalist mode of production.[16]

The expropriation of the peasant and independent artisan from their means of production was achieved by developments treated by Marx as "original accumulation" (Chapter III, above). Once achieved, this "freedom" of the worker from the ownership of productive property is made thorough and lasting by the exacting requirements of capitalist production. The general use of enormous masses of capital, the elaborate division of labor, and the progressive employment of science doom the laborer with unequivocal dependence on the capitalist for employment. Under slavery and serfdom the property requirements for independent production were minor, and a freed slave or serf could hope to become an independent peasant or artisan. But capital towers over the laborer as an overwhelming, hostile power, perpetuating his status of dependence on the capitalist for a livelihood.[17]

Even when considering the other two features of capitalism Marx has in mind free labor as their foundation. On the last pages (1025–1028) of the third volume of *Capital* he names commodities and surplus-value as the "two peculiar traits" of

[15] *Capital*, I, 624, 785.
[16] *Capital*, I, 189, 470; II, 44, 444.
[17] *Capital*, I, 396–397, 786, 835, 840, 843; III, 699.

capitalism. Regarding commodities he adds, rather abstrusely, that in themselves they do not distinguish capitalism from other orders, that the unique mark of capitalism rests rather on a double fact here. First, the article produced is a commodity, but the striking fact to note is that the laborer himself becomes a seller of his labor-power as a commodity, "so that wage labor is the typical character of labor . . . the relation between wage labor and capital determines the entire character of the mode of production." The second fact is that the commodity is the product of capital; and here it is sufficient to recall that, in Marx's thought, means of production are not capital when used by the independent craftsman; they become capital only when used to pump surplus-value out of free wage labor.[18] Thus free labor is central. In other connections, too, Marx specifies that the precondition of the production of commodities as the universal practice centers in "free" labor.[19]

A similar note is struck in his observations on surplus-value as "the other specific mark" of capitalism. He indicates that surplus-value stands as a component of value only because of the twin fact that labor is in the character of wage labor, and the means of production are in the character of capital (and, once more capital is such only when it exploits labor "free" from the possession of capital); and he adds that ". . . the form of labor, as wage labor, determines the shape of the entire process and the specific mode of production itself . . ."[20] "Free" labor is central again.

Labor, free legally but implicitly subordinated to the owner of the accumulated equipment involved in production, seems to be the specifically distinguishing hallmark of capitalism. But as a concept or as an economic system, capitalism symbolizes, of course, something vastly more comprehensive. It stands for an enormous structure of many integrated parts: private property; freedom and obligation of contract; produc-

[18] *Capital*, I, 785; III, 207.
[19] *Capital*, I, 643, 189n.; II, 43.
[20] *Capital*, III, 1027–1028; II, 444–445.

tion primarily for exchange and not for use; the capitalist owner of the means of production; the "free" wage laborer; the relations of the capitalist and proletarian classes; the undisputed prominence of industrial over mercantile and usurer's capital; the annexation of surplus-value, and the re-creation and accumulation of capital from it; the workshop in the early phase of capitalism, and the factory and the machine in the later phase; the prevalence of an elaborate system of division of labor; marketing and financing operations on an elaborate scale; large-scale production; the amassing of immense fortunes; monopoly; and so on.

# CHAPTER X

## THE BASIC PRINCIPLES OF CAPITALISM

### VALUE

FOR a proper understanding of capitalist society and its tendencies we have to turn first of all to Marx's analysis of value. Capitalist production results in commodities that are exchanged in the market. There must be a law regulating the exchange. Thus we can assert that one quarter of corn equals *x* hundredweight of iron, to use Marx's example. Why? He decides that there must be a third entity dwelling in equivalent amounts, in weight, in these units of corn and iron to govern the equation. The quest of this third entity becomes the opening problem of *Capital*. He reasons by the process of elimination. It cannot be, he says, "either a geometrical, a chemical, or any other natural property of commodities"; nor is it their use-value. Therefore, "the only one common property left" is the fact that commodities are the product of labor. The amount of labor, in units of time, spent on the production of articles controls their exchange.[1]

By labor he means "social labor," that is, the labor in the long chain of making the tools, machinery, raw materials, as well as the labor of shaping the finished product. He means, further, not any amount of inefficient labor that happens to be spent on a commodity, but "socially necessary labor," labor of normal efficiency, applied under normal conditions, by the bulk of substantial firms, in accordance with the prevailing industrial arts. The concept points to the representative firm; there is no reference to marginal costs.[2] Finally, he means abstract, homogeneous, unskilled labor; skilled labor is resolved into multiplied simple labor, the exact reduction having been established by a "social process" and fixed by

[1] *Capital*, I, 44–45.
[2] *Capital*, I, 46, 612; *Value, Price and Profit*, p. 62.

custom.[3] Such is his theory of "natural" or long-run value; of course, there are temporary deviations, in response to fluctuations of supply and demand.[4] This theory of value is to Marx "the basis of political economy." [5]

At times this labor theory of value is applied ingeniously. Suppose the supply of linen is so large that it cannot be sold at the normal price expressive of the labor-time put into its production. This means, says Marx, that an excessive amount of labor had been apportioned by the community to weaving. "The effect is the same as if each individual weaver had expended more labor-time upon his particular product than is socially necessary." [6] Likewise, if the price of cotton rises, the value of the previously produced cotton held in stock rises also. "This last-named cotton then represents by indirection more labor-time than was incorporated in it." [7] Marx apparently does not perceive that he is in a circle in both cases. If the price of linen is determined, like the price of any other commodity, by the labor-time expended on it, he cannot infer the labor-time to be properly expended on it from the lower price. In the second instance, he does not stop to inquire why the price of cotton rose. It evidently rose because of an increased demand. Then the amount of labor spent on the cotton held in stock is irrelevant; and, again, as the cause of price, the amount of labor cannot be determined from the supposed effect, the increased price. If, possibly, the rise in the price of cotton is occasioned by an advance in the costs of the marginal farms, then we deal with such rudimentary aspects of the marginal analysis as are found already in Ricardo, and Marx's explanation that the price of cotton held in stock rises because there is, "by indirection," more labor-time in it, is inadequate and circular.

Aside from exchange value, Marx puts special emphasis on what may be termed intrinsic or absolute value. A com-

[3] *Capital*, I, 52.
[4] *Capital*, II, 156, 160, 164, 168, 170, 172.
[5] *Capital*, II, 384, 429, 531.
[6] *Capital*, I, 120.
[7] *Capital*, II, 133.

modity has value, is a value, by virtue of the fact that it embodies a given quantum of labor-time. "As values, all commodities are only definite masses of labor-time." [8] Exchange value is the "form of value," while value itself, or the "volume of value," is the labor-time dwelling in the article; or is the article itself as the symbol, the bearer, of the labor-time in it.[9] The quest for the common substance governing the exchange value of corn and iron leads to "the value that lies behind it." [10] What is said in these paragraphs of labor ("socially necessary labor," "social labor") and of value (exchange value, intrinsic value) applies to surplus-labor and surplus-value, concepts which will be touched on presently.[11]

Not all labor creates value. Marx draws a distinction between production and circulation, or mere buying and selling, the mere conversion of commodities into money or money into commodities. Circulation is necessary but unproductive, and this applies to the labor of merchants, bookkeepers, bankers, salesmen, and their hired help; to storage and to the production of gold and silver as money. The agents engaged in circulation obtain their compensation out of the surplus-value provided by the laborers making the commodities.[12] The manufacturer sells to the wholesaler, the latter to the retailer, and he to the consumer, each at a profit, which is part of this surplus-value; these profits, put together, are equal to the whole surplus-value embodied in the price paid by the final consumer. However, Marx allows an exception of one type of circulation: he considers productive the labor needed to form a steady flow of the supplies of already produced raw materials, capital goods, and consumer goods, to insure orderly and uninterrupted production. For such purposes, storage and transportation add to the value of the product.[13] It may

[8] *Capital*, I, 46, 106, 108.

[9] *Capital*, II, 121.

[10] *Capital*, I, 55. "The common substance that manifests itself in the exchange value of commodities, whenever they are exchanged, is their value" (*ibid.*, I. 45, 59; III, 194, 206).

[11] E.g., *Capital*, I, 241.

[12] *Capital*, II, chap. vi, also pp. 142, 144, 232; III, 340–354.

[13] *Capital*, II, 156, 160, 164, 168, 170, 172.

be noticed, parenthetically, that unproductive too are the members of the "third class," kings, state officials, soldiers, priests, members of the professions, and prostitutes. They live on the surplus-value turned over to them in the form of taxes or fees.[14] Where the worker obtains the surplus-value to pay his doctor or lawyer, or to send his daughter to a private business school, we do not learn.

This theory of value is commonly regarded as the legacy of the classical school of economics, notably Ricardo. But this is not quite Ricardo's theory of value. Ricardo has constantly in mind exchange value, relative value, while Marx emphasizes, besides, intrinsic value, value as the quantum of congealed labor in the commodity. This idea of value as labor filling the interatomic spaces of a product Ricardo once or twice seems to hint at, but he never puts the focus on it. Veblen suggests that with Hegel spirit is the ultimate reality, while with Marx material labor energy imparts meaning and value.[15] It is for this reason, perhaps, that Marx denies value to a commodity not produced by labor. Land, animals, virgin forests have a price, he says, but no value. There is no jellified labor in them.[16]

It may be pertinent to remark here that some Marxians see striking significance in intrinsic value as the expression of the social relations among the producers in a given, historically conditioned society. The value lodged in the commodity by virtue of the labor-time in it defines, they claim, a society with private property and division of labor, which latter implies, of course, coöperation of labor or that people work for one another. This view, even if it may have Marx's sanction, is not convincing. Since time out of mind goods have been the product of labor, and they promise to continue to be the product of labor, while social relations have been changing and will continue to change. The fact, then, that goods embody labor is a constant, like use-value; and, like use-value, it

[14] *Capital*, II, 384, 429, 531.
[15] T. Veblen, *Place of Science in Modern Civilization*, p. 420.
[16] *Capital*, I, 47, 114–115, 227.

cannot portray the particular social relations of producers in a specific historical context. Indeed, the fact that the labor-time dwelling within goods assumes significance is only a reflex of the fact that there are such problems as exchange, valuation, and the allocation of resources. Such problems are not special to capitalism: in varying degrees, they apply to Robinson Crusoe and all social organizations, including communism.

Again, it must be emphasized that Ricardo recognizes the time element, or the rôle of capital, in the determination of the exchange value of a product: of two commodities in which the same amount of labor is contained, the one which was produced with more durable capital, or with more fixed capital relative to circulating capital, or the one that had to be stored away for some time to mature and improve its qualities before it was fit for sale — possesses more relative value.[17] In a letter to McCulloch he says: "I sometimes think that, if I were to write the chapter on value again which is in my book, I should acknowledge that the relative value of commodities was regulated by two causes instead of by one, namely, by the relative quantity of labor necessary to produce the commodities in question, and by the rate of profit for the time that the capital remained dormant, and until the commodities were brought to the market."[18] But Marx recognizes no element besides labor. Even in the third volume of *Capital*, where he modifies his theory, he maintains that fundamentally labor, and nothing else, is the basis of value.

### SURPLUS–VALUE

In intimate association with value and of indispensable importance in Marx's system is the celebrated concept of surplus-value. The capitalist spends money on the production of a given article, and then he sells it. This activity is represented by the formula $M - C - M^1$. With money ($M$), he buys the

[17] Ricardo, *Principles of Political Economy*, chap. i, sections 4 and 5.
[18] *Letters of David Ricardo to J. R. McCulloch*, ed. by J. H. Hollander, p. 71.

commodities $(C)$ needed for production, and then sells the finished product for money $(M^1)$. Money, it may be noted, is merely a universal equivalent, a way of measuring value, and when we say that a thing costs two dollars, we mean, says Marx, that as much labor was spent on making this thing as is spent ordinarily on mining two dollars' worth of gold. It is evident that $M^1$ is larger than $M$, else the whole process would involve no more than gratuitous trouble to the capitalist. $M^1 = M + \Delta M$. The capitalist realizes more money than he had laid out; he gains $\Delta M$. This is surplus-value. Our "friend Moneybags" buys the elements essential for production at their value and sells the finished article at its value, that is, on the basis of the amount of socially necessary labor-time lodged in it. Yet in the end he procures more value than he had put in.[19] How did $M$ expand into $M^1$, and where did this surplus-value originate?

Marx again reasons by the process of elimination. The increment of value does not proceed from the money $(M)$ itself, for "as hard cash, it is value petrified, never varying"; "just as little" can it originate in $C - M^1$, that is, in the sale of the produced commodity, since the sale is merely a transformation of the article into its money form. "The change must, therefore, take place" in the first act, $M - C$, when the requisite commodity is purchased. In this particular transaction the increase cannot originate in the value of this requisite commodity, because equivalents are exchanged here. "We are, therefore, forced to the conclusion" that the change comes about in the *use-value* of the requisite commodity bought. Surplus-value originates in the use of a commodity which, bought at its value, has the property of yielding for the purchaser more value while it is being consumed. There is involved here, in other words, a commodity with a use-value exceeding its exchange-value.

Such a commodity is labor, or labor-power.[20] The capitalist employer buys labor-power at its value, which is, in common with all commodities, the amount of labor spent on the produc-

---

[19] *Capital*, I, 184–185.
[20] *Capital*, I, 185–186.

tion of this labor-power — customary subsistence of the laborer, his education, and the expense of rearing his children. We see here Marx's theory of wages.[21] It may take the laborer six hours of work daily to produce the equivalent of this value of labor-power. But the employer uses him twelve hours a day. The first six hours are "necessary labor-time," the additional six hours are surplus labor-time, and the commodities produced in this extra period are surplus product and their value, represented by these extra six hours, is surplus-value. The consumption of labor-power is at once production of commodities and of surplus-value. Commodities are thus bought and sold in the whole series at their value, but the worker is forced to yield more labor than is needed to produce his wage. The value that labor creates for the employer exceeds the value that it obtains from him in payment.[22]

Surplus-value is the evidence and measure of the exploitation of the laborer by his employer. However, Marx is anxious to indicate that he is not dealing with a question of justice or ethics. He does not intend to postulate that the worker is entitled to the full product of his labor, nor is it his purpose to underscore the iniquities in the distribution of wealth in a capitalist society. He has in mind to depict how the mode of production stands for class relations based on exploitation, and to present facts that will disclose the mainspring of the alignment of class interests. The employer is not a robber, and the laborer is not robbed. Both are the agents and victims of the system. This is the only "just distribution" possible under capitalism.[23] Marx does not claim for the laborer the right to

[21] Capital, I, 189–191, 612. "The value of labor is in every country determined by a *traditional standard of life*," established by social conditions. Over short periods there may be deviations, governed by fluctuations of supply and demand for labor. (*Value, Price and Profit*, pp. 117, 44–45. Marx's italics.) For the cyclical and secular aspects of wages, see below, Chapter XI, section on Increasing Misery.

[22] Capital, I, 232. It is interesting to recall Adam Smith: "The value which the workmen add to the materials, therefore, resolves itself in this case into two parts, of which one pays their wages, the other the profits of their employer, upon the whole stock of materials and wages which he advanced" (*Wealth of Nations*, Book I, p. 42).

[23] Critique of the Gotha Programme, p. 26. Cf. Capital, I, 216, 641.

the whole product of labor, argues Engels against Menger. Marx never posits a right of any kind, his friend insists. Marx recognizes the "historical legitimacy," within certain epochs, of certain modes of appropriation and of certain social classes; only he claims that capitalist exploitation no longer functions as a lever of social evolution but rather as an impediment to progress.[24] It is true, nevertheless, that while ostensibly no appeal is made to feelings of fairness and justice, many of Marx's expressions are charged with moral indignation and arouse emotion. Marx does not always convey the impression of a dispassionate chronicler of facts; and it may be suggested that it is not always easy to stay objective when recording and commenting on the facts which Marx reveals touching on man's inhumanity to man.

Labor is the source of surplus-value. To bring this conception into prominence as well as to progress with his analysis of capitalism, Marx divides the capital advanced for purposes of production into two parts. In one part he puts the fixed and circulating capital, which either is used up gradually through wear and tear, like machinery, or is consumed directly as it is used in production, like coal. This part he calls constant capital ($c$). In the other part he puts the wage-bill, the capital advanced to labor as wages, and he calls it variable capital ($v$).[25] The proportional composition of the values, in labor-time, of the constant and variable constituents of a given capital he names the organic composition of capital. The organic composition is high when the ratio, in value, of the constant capital to the variable capital is high, and conversely. As far as the value of a particular commodity is concerned, it is important to distinguish between $c$, the total constant capital invested in the business, and $c_1$, that part which is consumed in the production of the given commodity. The outlay for a particular commodity is, then, $c_1 + v$; but from the sale of this commodity the capitalist realizes surplus-value ($s$) in addition to the outlay. In other words, he sells the commodity for $c_1 + v + s$. The

[24] Engels, "Socialisme de juristes," *Le mouvement socialiste*, XII, 109–110.
[25] Marx, *Capital*, I, 232–233.

rate of profit, however, is calculated on the full investment $c + v$, as will be indicated presently.

The source, the creator of surplus-value is not the constant but the variable part of the expense; not the means of production, but labor. The reason is as follows. For the constant capital the employer pays the full value; therefore, there is no possibility of an augmentation of value here. It is the seller of constant capital (machinery, raw materials, and so forth) who gains surplus-value on it, not the purchaser. But it is different with variable capital. The employer buys labor at one value, but he extracts from the laborer more than he pays for.

The rate of surplus-value is its proportion to the variable capital, or $\frac{s}{v}$, or $\frac{\text{surplus labor}}{\text{necessary labor}}$. The rate of surplus-value is an exact formulation of the degree of exploitation of the laborer by the capitalist. The higher the exploitation, the greater the rate.[26] The total mass of surplus-value derived in a given factory is equal to the amount of surplus-value obtained from one laborer multiplied by the number of laborers. However, the employer is not thinking in terms of the rate of surplus-value when he makes his calculations. It serves him no purpose to divide his outlays into constant and variable parts. Both parts are an expense to him, and on both he expects a profit. The rate of *profit*, therefore, is the proportion of surplus-value to the *total* capital invested, $\frac{s}{c + v}$.[27]

Marx deduces three laws here. First, the mass of surplus-value $(S)$ equals the total variable capital $(V)$ advanced, multiplied by the rate of surplus-value, or $S = V \times \frac{s}{v}$.[28] This implies the second law, namely, that the number of laborers may decrease, or, which is the same thing, the total variable capital may diminish, and yet the total mass of surplus-value may not decrease, provided there is a rise in the rate of ex-

[26] *Capital*, I, 239, 241, 332.
[27] *Capital*, III, 55.
[28] *Capital*, I, 332.

ploitation of labor, that is, in the rate of surplus-value.[29] The third law is an obvious consequence: the greater the variable capital, or the number of laborers, or the wage-bill, the greater will be the mass of surplus-value, provided the rate of exploitation stays the same. In other words, the masses of surplus-value yielded by two equal capitals but of different organic compositions will vary directly with their variable constituents.[30] The larger the wage-bill in a factory, the larger its profits; the larger the proportion of the variable to the constant part of capital, the larger the rate of profit — other things remaining equal. It means, then, that it is to the best interest of the capitalist to keep as large a number of workers as possible and as small an outlay on fixed and circulating capital as possible.[31]

This obviously contradicts experience. Capitalists do not prefer a business where the chief outlay is on wages to one where it is on means of production. The rates of profit of capitalists producing various commodities do not vary with the proportion wages bear to the total outlay. Under competition, the rates of profit are rather more or less uniform, or are distributed around a "central tendency," for plants in a given industry and even for different industries. The establishment that employs much labor and less constant capital, or much $v$ and less $c$, will not have a larger mass of profit than an establishment using the same amount of capital but apportioning it between

[29] *Capital*, I, 332–334.
[30] *Capital*, I, 334.

[31] Examples. Given a rate of surplus-value $\frac{s}{v} = 50\% = \frac{1}{2}$:

If capital $= 100 = c\ 80 + v\ 20$, then surplus-value $= v \times \frac{s}{v} = 20 \times \frac{1}{2} = 10$,

and rate of profit $= \frac{s}{c+v} = \frac{10}{100} = 10\%$.

If capital $= 100 = c\ 70 + v\ 30$, then surplus-value $= v \times \frac{s}{v} = 30 \times \frac{1}{2} = 15$,

and rate of profit $= \frac{s}{c+v} = \frac{15}{100} = 15\%$.

Here the variable part is smaller in the first case than in the second; therefore both surplus-value and the rate of profit are proportionately smaller.

more constant capital and a smaller wage bill. The organic composition of capital is no guide to the rate of profit prevailing in economic life.

This discrepancy between his theory and realities did not escape Marx's eye, and after expounding the above third law he delcares: "This law clearly contradicts all experience based on appearance." [32] He does not, however, proceed to resolve the contradiction. He merely observes that for the removal of "this apparent contradiction many intermediate terms are wanted," just as in algebra intermediate terms are called for "to understand that $\frac{0}{0}$ may represent an actual magnitude." In the next paragraph he adds, irrelevantly to the issue at hand, that for society as a whole, given the rate of exploitation, the total mass of surplus-value does vary directly with the total variable capital, or the laboring population in employment. The source of the "contradiction" lies, of course, in the precarious analysis of exchange value, of wages, and of surplus-value. In actual life commodities do not exchange according to the labor-time contained in them, wages are not confined to subsistence, and profit, interest, and rent cannot be dismissed as unpaid labor. "Intermediate terms" will be of little avail as an oxygen tank for an analysis out of touch with life.

Of the same cast is another difficulty. It is of the essence of a competitive equilibrium that the rate of profit on the invested capital is the same, by and large, for all the producers, and an analysis which comes to the result that different rates of profit prevail in the different spheres of industry has something wrong with it. The labor theory of value yields precisely this awkward result. This point needs explanation.

The labor theory of value is compatible with the same rate of profit throughout the economy only on one assumption: namely, that the organic composition of capital is identical in all branches of production. This proposition is grounded in the mathematics of the situation: the rate of profit $\frac{s}{c+v}$ can

[32] *Capital*, I, 335.

be the same in all lines of industry only if $c:v$ (the organic composition) is the same in all of them. For example, let the investment in the production of one commodity be $c+v$, and the investment in the production of another commodity $mc + mv$. The organic composition is identical in both. If the rate of surplus-value, which under competition is the same throughout industry, is, say, 100%, the surplus-value realized on the first commodity is $s = v$, and on the second commodity $ms = mv$. We assume, for simplicity, that in both cases the investment $c$ and $mc$ is fully consumed in the production of these commodities; and the same assumption is made in the example in the next paragraph. The two commodities will exchange, then, in the ratio $(mc + mv + ms):(c + v + s) = m:1$; and the rate of profit is the same in both enterprises,

$$\frac{s}{c + v} = \frac{ms}{mc + mv}.$$

That the labor theory of value is incompatible with the same rate of profit when the organic composition differs can be shown by a numerical example. Consider two commodities embodying the same expenditure of labor and capital, and with the same rate of surplus-value, again 100%, but with a different composition of capital. Let one commodity represent $60c + 20v + 20s = 100$, and the other $20c + 40v + 40s = 100$. According to Marx these commodities are even in exchange for one another, each embodying 100 units of labor. But the producer of the first commodity makes $\frac{20}{60 + 20} = 25\%$ profit,

while the producer of the second makes $\frac{40}{20 + 40} = 66\frac{2}{3}\%$.

Obviously this is far from the state of affairs in a competitive equilibrium.

In the world of actuality the organic composition of capital is not uniform. The many types of industry employ different combinations of labor and capital; even different firms in the same industry do so. The proportion of labor to capital is governed by such factors as the size of the market, division of labor, the state of the arts in a given industry, mass production or the emphasis on handicraft skill, and the type of management. If we apply Marx's labor theory of value to an economy with different compositions of capital in the many lines of production, we get a variety of rates of profit instead of the uniform rate characteristic of a competitive equilibrium.

Marx recognizes this difficulty. At the end of the chapter in which he discusses different compositions of capital and the rates of profit in different branches of industry, in the perspective of the labor theory, he summarizes the difficulty as follows:

We have demonstrated that different lines of industry may have different rates of profit, corresponding to differences in the organic composition of capitals . . .; the law (as a general tendency) that profits are proportioned as the magnitudes of the capitals, or that capitals of equal magnitude yield equal profits in equal times, applies only to capitals of the same organic composition, with the same rate of surplus-value, and the same time of turnover. And these statements hold good on the assumption, which has been the basis of all our analyses so far, namely, that commodities are sold at their values. On the other hand there is no doubt that . . . a difference in the average rate of profit of the various lines of industry does not exist in reality, and could not exist without abolishing the entire system of capitalist production. It would seem, then, as if the theory of value were irreconcilable at this point with the actual process, irreconcilable with the real phenomena of production.[33]

### PRICE OF PRODUCTION

To the resolution of these contradictions he addresses himself in the ninth chapter of the last volume of *Capital*; and he presents a different theory of value. This change of front led to an outburst of controversy as to the contradiction between the third and the first volume of this work, some maintaining that there is no contradiction, and others, notably Böhm-Bawerk, claiming that the third volume is an unequivocal abandonment of the theory of value as presented in the first.[34]

[33] *Capital*, III, 181.

[34] Böhm-Bawerk, *Karl Marx and the Close of His System*. To cite only two recent writers, G. F. Shove, in "Mrs. Robinson on Marxian Economics," *Economic Journal*, LIV (April, 1944), 48, regards the difference between the two theories as a "flat contradiction," while Dr. P. M. Sweezy, in *The Theory of Capitalist Development*, chap. vii, considers them as organically related. Contradictory or not, and related or not, these are two different theories of value.

Marx's new position on value may be best explained by means of the following table, which is a condensation of the tables presented by him on pages 183–186:

| I | II | III | IV | V | VI | VII | VIII |
|---|---|---|---|---|---|---|---|
| Capitals<br><br>$C$  $V$ | Rate of Surplus Value | Surplus Value $S$ Also Rate of Profit | Used Up Constant Capital $C_1$ | Cost Price<br><br>$C_1+V$ | Value of Commodities<br><br>$C_1+V+S$ | Price of Commodities or "Price of Production" (*Produktionspreis*) | Deviations of Price from Value |
| 80+ 20 | 100% | 20 | 50 | 70 = 50+20 | 90 = 70+20 | 92 = 70+22 | + 2 = 92 − 90 |
| 70+ 30 | " | 30 | 51 | 81 = 51+30 | 111 = 81+30 | 103 = 81+22 | − 8 = 103−111 |
| 60+ 40 | " | 40 | 51 | 91 | 131 | 113 = 91+22 | −18 = 113−131 |
| 85+ 15 | " | 15 | 40 | 55 | 70 | 77 = 55+22 | + 7 = 77− 70 |
| 95+ 5 | " | 5 | 10 | 15 | 20 | 37 = 15+22 | +17 = 37− 20 |
| Total 390+110 | | 110 | | | | | +26= 26= 0 |
| Average 78+ 22 | | | | | | | |

We assume here five different branches of production, each employing the same amount of capital but of different organic compositions, as in column I. The rate of surplus value is assumed to be the same in each, 100 per cent. In each branch the amount of surplus-value depends entirely on the amount of the variable constituent, and is equal to 100 per cent of this variable portion; while the rate of profit is obtained by dividing the surplus-value gained in each case by the capital invested, or 100. The rate of profit will therefore differ in each case (column III). We shall assume that in each branch only parts, and different parts, of the constant capital are worn out in a given period of time, say one year (column IV). The "cost price," or the sum of the costs actually incurred in production, equals the amount of constant capital actually used up added to the variable capital, $C_1 + V$ (column V). The value of the commodities produced annually in each branch of production equals the amount of constant capital used up plus the variable part laid out in wages plus the surplus-value which represents time spent by the laborer for which he is not paid, or $C_1 + V + S$, as in column VI. Thus far the labor theory of value has been followed.

But such values will not prevail in actual economic experience. In reality, to the cost price is added, not the particular surplus-value realized in the given branch of production (column III), but a fixed average rate of profit applied to all branches and obtained by averaging up all their respective profits. The five capitals, in other words, are regarded as constituents of one large capital of 500, with an organic composition of $390 c + 110 v$, and with a total surplus-value of 110. The average organic composition of each capital will be one-fifth, or $\frac{390 c}{5} + \frac{110 v}{5} = 78 c + 22 v$, and the average rate of profit will be $\frac{110}{500} = 22\%$. In each branch of production the price of the commodities will be equal to the "cost price" plus this fixed average rate of profit on the total capital invested in the business, and not merely on the portion actually consumed. This Marx calls *price of production* (*Produktionspreis*) (column VII).[35] Thus commodities do not sell at their value. Those with a higher composition than the average (that is, where the proportion of $c$ to $v$ is higher than $78 c : 22 v$) sell above the value, and those with a lower sell below, as is seen in column VII. All commodities sell, not according to the labor lodged in them, but at their "price of production," which is Adam Smith's "natural price" and Ricardo's "cost of production."[36] But all deviations of the "prices of production" from the values are mutually canceled, as is seen in column VIII.

The example of these five employments of capital epitomizes the situation prevailing in industry as a whole. All the amounts of surplus-value realized in separate industries are fused into a total mass, and its ratio to the total social capital advanced in all the industries determines the average rate of profit. Each capitalist produces in his factory a given amount of surplus-value and profit, but he pockets neither this surplus-value nor this profit. What he receives is a profit resulting from applying this average social rate of profit to his total capital outlay.

[35] *Capital*, III, 185–186.
[36] *Capital*, III, 233.

Each capitalist is like a shareholder in the total social capital, and his profit bears the same proportion to the total mass of social surplus-value that his capital bears to this total social capital.[37] "Capitals of the same magnitude must yield the same profits in the same time," whatever their organic composition.[38] The costs are individual, but the rate of profit is this average social rate. Only if the composition of a given capital happens to be identical with the average composition of the total social capital, will the "price of production" equal the value of the commodity and the profits coincide with the surplus-value produced by this particular capital. Such a case would be a miniature, a "sample," of the total social situation.[39]

The amount, then, of surplus-value appropriated will be dependent on the variable capital only if we calculate for the *total* volume of capital in society; and only the total volume of commodities produced in all industries can be said to sell according to the mass of socially necessary labor incorporated in it. In individual cases, commodities in one branch of production will sell at less, and in another at more, than the value according to the labor theory. But these deviations compensate each other, as we should expect, since the deviations of the items from their arithmetic average will always cancel out, algebraically, as in column VIII.[40]

The forces in economic life which bring about the sale of commodities at their price of production instead of their value, and which agglomerate the individual surplus-values and profits into one uniform average rate of profit cause Marx a good deal of concern. He devotes to them long pages where the ideas are as abstruse as they are ingenious, and where appeals to arith-

---

[37] *Capital*, III, 186–187.

[38] *Capital*, III, 245.

[39] *Capital*, III, 186–187, 203–204.

[40] It follows that all the concepts elaborated in the first volume, as, e.g., necessary and surplus labor-time, the value of the constant and variable parts of a given capital, suffer distortions on account of the deviations of the "price of production," or the selling price, from the value. Thus the variable capital is no longer estimated by the amount of necessary labor-time spent on the maintenance or wages of the laborers, because this maintenance sells not at its value, but at the "price of production" (*Capital*, III, 190).

metic, especially averages, and not to facts, are quite in evidence.[41] Out of the welter a few claims can be discerned clearly. Commodities sold at their values, and the average rate of profits was unknown, only in the days before capitalism.[42] But under capitalism the situation is twisted by the operation of competition. If one sphere of production, selling its commodities at their values, realizes much surplus-value and a high rate of profit according to the organic composition of its capital, another sphere employing a capital of a different composition and reaping a smaller rate of profit will immigrate into the first branch.

> By means of this incessant emigration and immigration, in one word, by its [capital's] distribution among the various spheres in accord with a rise of the rate of profits here, and its fall there, it [capital] brings about such a proportion of supply to demand that the average profit in the various spheres of production becomes the same, so that the values are converted into prices of production.

In an advanced capitalist society, with mobility of labor and capital, this equilibration is accomplished in a more or less perfect degree.[43]

Yet, even under capitalism, Marx emphasizes, the first theory of value is the foundation of the second theory, and to assert categorically that commodities exchange according to their prices of production is to see the surface of things and to disregard their "internal and disguised essence"; it is to behave like the blinded capitalist himself, or like his Pindar, the vulgar economist. "Everything appears upside down in competition"; phenomena point to the second theory, but in substance they obey the first.[44] In the first place, the average rate of profit is merely a resultant of compounding the masses of surplus-value, and the higher the volume of surplus-value in individual branches of production, the higher this average rate of profit, and conversely.[45] In the second place, the "price of production" is only a derivative, although a complicated, imperfect, and remote one, of their values. A change in the labor-

[41] *Capital*, III, 203–234.
[42] *Capital*, III, 207–209.
[43] *Capital*, III, 230.
[44] *Capital*, III, 244–245, 369.
[45] *Capital*, III, 232–233.

time spent on the production of commodities will ultimately register a change in the "price of production." [46] In the third place, in so far as the migration of capital does not penetrate all the nooks and crannies of industry, and in so far as an average rate of profit or a change in its magnitude fails to establish itself promptly and smoothly, the price of commodities here and there, now and then, is for short periods dominated by the labor-time concealed within them.[47]

Marx summarizes his contention in statements like the following. "In short, under capitalist production, the general law of value enforces itself merely as the prevailing tendency, in a very complicated and approximate manner, as a never ascertainable average of ceaseless fluctuations." [48] "Values . . . stand behind the prices of production and determine them in the last instance." [49] He does not claim that the two theories are identical, but he urges that the first is still the heart and soul of the second, and that therefore the labor theory enunciated in the first volume is not abandoned in the third.[50]

### ACCUMULATION

Surplus-value represents what belongs to the laborer but what he does not get. Any income but the laborer's, any expenditure not made by labor comes out of surplus-value. Interest, rent, and profit; the receipts of the merchant and banker and all the labor hired by them; the income of the doctor, professor, or actor, of the judge, policeman, or soldier; and the expenditures on schools, parks, and battleships, all come from surplus-value. It is evident that in so far as the laborers obtain free an education, medical care, old-age pensions, and the

[46] *Capital*, III, 211.
[47] *Capital*, III, 196.
[48] *Capital*, III, 190.
[49] *Capital*, III, 244, 221, 1002. Cf. I, 86.
[50] The idea that Marx discovered the failings of his labor theory of value after the publication of the first volume of *Capital*, and tried to straighten himself out in the third volume, is without foundation. Already in 1862, five years before the appearance of the first volume, Marx outlines the price of production theory as it is presented in the third volume. See the letter to Engels, August 2, 1862, in Marx and Engels, *Selected Correspondence*, pp. 129–132. Cf. *ibid.*, pp. 240–245.

services of libraries, roads, and playgrounds, they have part
of the surplus-value refunded to them; thus, not all surplus-
value is robbery. Marx does not touch on this idea. He teaches
that under communism deductions are made from the product
of labor for the following purposes: the maintenance of capital, capital for the expansion of production, insurance reserves
against mishaps, "general costs of administration," the common needs, such as schools and health, and the relief of those
unable to work.[51] Of course Marx would say that all these deductions are, in a communist society, for the benefit of the
laboring masses exclusively; but, condemning all surplus-
value as proletarian tribute for the use of the means of production, he ignores, if he does not deny, that under capitalism
at least part of the surplus-value returns to benefit the laborer.

Surplus-value is the matrix of the key phenomenon, capital
accumulation. Marx draws a distinction between simple reproduction, or reproduction on the same scale, on the one hand,
and, on the other hand, expanded reproduction, reproduction
on an enlarged scale, or accumulation.[52] Simple reproduction
means that no investment is made beyond mere replacement
of worn-out capital. There is no extension of capital or production; in more recent terms, there is neither a deepening
nor a widening of the capital structure. Is the replacement
derived from surplus-value, or does surplus-value emerge
*after* replacement is taken care of? The answer depends on
the page you read. In some places Marx states that a bourgeois may accumulate capital by his own labor, but in time
the capital is used up and is replaced by funds from surplus-
value. This makes all capital a derivative of surplus-value, a
principle which Marx expresses more than once.[53] But more
frequently, and correctly, he indicates, by numerical examples
or general statement, that surplus-value appears only after
the deduction for replacement.[54] This latter view squares with

[51] *The Critique of the Gotha Programme*, pp. 27–28.
[52] *Capital*, I, 619, 634; II, 580, 592.
[53] E.g., *Capital*, I, 623–624; II, 367–368.
[54] *Capital*, I, 217, 237, 635, 637; II, 592.

the value formula given before: value $= c_1 + v + s$, where $c_1$ stands for replacement.

More common than simple reproduction is accumulation. Part of the surplus-value is consumed by the capitalist and part is accumulated, spent on additional capital, that is, on additional variable capital and additional constant capital. The expenditure on constant capital is investment proper. Thus, the progressive building up of instruments for the exploitation of labor rests on unpaid labor as the foundation; the laborer forges his own chains. Marx is aware of the theory of abstinence in saving, but he dismisses with scorn this "unparalleled sample . . . of the discoveries of vulgar economy." [55]

Accumulation presents two phases. A "special phase" stands for the amassing of capital of the same quality, requiring a proportionately larger number of workers to set it in motion as it grows in quantity. Investments in constant and variable capital move together, and the organic composition remains unchanged.[56]

But capitalism is dynamic, and this stationary phase is scarcely exemplified in reality. Division of labor grows more complex, more skilled and profitable use of the forces of nature is discovered, and better machinery and superior processes are adopted. Labor becomes more productive, and the same number of laborers will transform more materials and machinery into commodities than before. The organic composition of capital in a typical plant rises; that is, $c:v$ is greater. This is Marx's "law of the progressive increase of constant capital in proportion to the variable." [57] Of course, while the variable constituent falls relatively to the constant part, it rises absolutely. To use Marx's example, a capital of £6,000 may have a composition of 50:50. When it grows to £18,000 the composition may change to 80:20, or £14,400:£3,600. The variable capital has fallen relatively but has grown absolutely from £3,000 to £3,600.[58] What these phases of accumulation

[55] *Capital*, I, 654–656; III, 420.
[56] *Capital*, I, 672, 681.
[57] *Capital*, I, 663, 682; III, 248, 882; *Wage-Labor and Capital*, pp. 44–45
[58] *Capital*, I, 683.

mean to the fortunes of labor and to the curve of the rate of profit will be discussed in the next chapter.

Marx gives two reasons for accumulation. He talks, in the first place, of the "love of power," the "desire to get rich," "sordid avarice," and the "passion for accumulation." [59] "Accumulate, accumulate! That is Moses and the prophets." [60] To ask the capitalist to consume more is to misunderstand alike the capitalist and capitalism.[61] "Capitalism is destroyed in its very foundation" if we assume that enjoyment, and not accumulation, is its motive.[62] This does not permit the inference that the capitalist is uniquely abstemious. Luxury and prodigality grow unrestrained with mounting surplus-value, but ever-increasing amounts are left for accumulation.[63]

Second, the compelling immediate reason for accumulation lies in competition. In the struggle for sales and profits the best weapon is to lower the cost of commodities, and this implies greater productivity of labor, or a higher proportion of constant to variable capital. There is accordingly unceasing pressure for a widening scale of plant in the search for what now would be called internal economies, and for the introduction of improvements. The innovator can sell below the prevailing price, or "social value," and yet above his own diminished costs, at once taking away trade from his rivals and reaping larger profits. This advantage he can enjoy only temporarily, because in time his rivals are forced to adopt the new methods if they are to survive. Then the selling price declines for all producers in the market, forming a new starting-point for further rivalry and improvements. "This is the law which continually drives bourgeois production out of its old track, and compels capital to intensify the productive powers of labor." [64] Whether he is to initiate an improvement or to follow

[59] *Capital*, I, 649 and n., 650–653.
[60] *Capital*, I, 652.
[61] *Capital*, II, 588; III, 302.
[62] *Capital*, II, 136.
[63] *Capital*, I, 650–651, 667; II, 475.
[64] Marx, *Wage-Labor and Capital*, p. 46.

suit, the capitalist realizes that a fund of accumulated money-capital is an indispensable necessity.[65]

It is obvious that this second reason is basically a mere implementation of the first reason. The capitalist recognizes the need of accumulation if he is to stay in business in a competitive field; and he is eager to stay in business to earn profits in order to accumulate for the purpose of satisfying his greed and maintaining his position of wealth and power. What of the profit motive in this picture? The profit motive does not serve as a third reason for accumulation, but is rather intimately identified with these two reasons, or, to put it differently, is their graphic and symbolic expression. Besides, profit is the exclusive source of accumulation.[66]

## CONCENTRATION AND CENTRALIZATION

In close association with accumulation is the double phenomenon of concentration and centralization. Concentration is Marx's term for large-scale production, for the large business firm. Large-scale production goes together with greater productivity of labor, greater surplus-value per laborer, a greater mass of surplus-value, and greater accumulation. Accumulation and concentration of capital are mutually interacting and accelerating elements. There is no mention that economies of size are realized only up to a certain point, beyond which the diseconomies cancel the economies, with rising unit costs as the sequel. To Marx, evidently, the cost curve for the firm is a descending curve as output increases, and not the much-discussed U-shaped curve. However, to Marx, concentration does not march with undisputed sway over the economy. Small new capitals are born here and there, and large single capitals are split, within families and in other ways, into smaller capitals. Along with concentration there is the fractionalizing of capital units, especially in spheres not fully invaded by Modern Industry.[67] But the trend, Marx predicts, is unmistakably toward steady concentration.

---

[65] Marx, *Capital*, I, 348–351; III, 287, 310–311; *Wage-Labor and Capital*, pp. 44–47.

[66] Cf. *Capital*, III, 283, 304.      [67] *Capital*, I, 685–686; III, 257.

Hand in hand with concentration goes centralization, or the fusion of several independent capitals or firms into one management or firm. We are dealing here with the celebrated prediction by Marx that the evolution of capitalism fosters a progressive decline of competition and a steady rise of monopoly. In the competitive struggle the large business unit has an inevitable advantage over the small unit. Harassed by the continual cheapening of commodities initiated by the big concern, the small firm is eventually forced to the wall, and the large rival takes over its property and market. Centralization means the expropriation of the small capitalist by the large capitalist. One capitalist "decapitalizes" another, "one capitalist kills many." [68] By this process, in each industry capital becomes centralized into gigantic aggregations, under a few heads, ripe for easy expropriation by the nascent socialist state. Here, too, Marx sees no limit to the advantages of amalgamation, and without reservation he asserts that centralization may progress until each industry, and even the whole economy, finds itself under the domination of "one single capitalist" or "one single corporation." [69] Centralization, unlike concentration, entails a redistribution of the existing capital into fewer hands, and not necessarily new accumulations of capital. However, it accelerates and intensifies the effects of accumulation (to be discussed in the following chapter) by raising the organic composition on its own account; for centralization implies not only the unification of individual capitals but also their reorganization into a coherent, more scientifically managed unit with a higher proportion of the constant to the variable capital.[70]

The corporation, as can be readily seen, plays an outstanding part in accumulation, concentration, and centralization,

---

[68] At times Marx makes centralization mean, not expropriation of capitalist by capitalist, but a voluntary massing of many small capitals into huge aggregates of capital for great enterprises like railway building. By centralization he therefore has in mind sometimes simply the large corporation. See *Capital*, I, 688–689.

[69] *Capital*, I, 688.

[70] *Capital*, I, 686–689, 836; III, 288–289.

and Marx pays his respects to it in terms strikingly prophetic of recent criticisms of this institution. He was obviously familiar alike with Adam Smith's onslaughts on the joint-stock companies [71] and with corporate malpractices generally. He talks of the control by the few insiders over the enormous capital compounded of the small savings of the many; of the separation between management and ownership, for most stockholders; of the board of directors' using their position only as "a pretext for plundering the stockholders"; of the corporation's breeding parasites and an aristocracy in the persons of promoters, directors, and bankers; of stock speculation and swindling; of recklessness with other people's money; of the illusory character and imaginary wealth of securities; of the artificial inflation of dividends by accounting devices; and of the connections between the national debt and adventures in stock dealings.[72]

[71] *Wealth of Nations*, pp. 127ff., 136–137, 219–241.
[72] *Capital*, III, 456, 458, 516–522, 560–561; II, 203, 205, 362; I, 827.

# CHAPTER XI

## THE WEAKNESSES OF CAPITALISM

### THE CONTRADICTIONS OF CAPITALISM

VALUE, surplus-value, and the accumulation of capital with the attending changes in its composition are essential in explaining the mechanism of capitalism. These principles also aid in disclosing the nature of the disintegrating forces functioning within the system, and of the consuming maladies which doom it to certain extinction. The conception that capitalism itself generates the enormities which bring about its dissolution is the distinctive mark of scientific socialism. Not free will and aspirations will make the transition to a new order, but the inexorable natural laws of the modern system. Not teleology, but mechanistic cause and effect condemn capitalism to death and proclaim the birth of socialism.

The capitalistic régime rests on a foundation of three fatal contradictions which ultimately release the dialectic forces that disrupt it. First, the aim of society is gain and accumulation. The compelling motives are not production for use and the development of human beings, but production for profit and self-seeking. Profits to the individual rather than social needs and benefits are the criteria of capitalist successes. "Modern society, which, soon after its birth, pulled Plutus by the hair of his head from the bowels of the earth, greets gold as its Holy Grail, as the glittering incarnation of the very principle of its own life." [1] With such an ideal the expansive development of the productive forces is incompatible. Hence, disastrous collisions.[2]

Second, while the present system depends increasingly on socialized production, private control of the productive processes and private appropriation of their fruits remain the

[1] Marx, *Capital*, I, 149.
[2] *Capital*, III, 293, 303.

ruling canons. Division and coöperation of labor implemented by science and inventions render the part which the laborers play in the productive process a social enterprise. The individual handicraftsman, the independent producer of an article, has vanished, and the laborer has become a link in a long, complicated chain. Likewise with capital. In joint-stock companies it is gathered from the many small owners associated in the enterprise, and the continual concentration and centralization of capital represent immense aggregates of social resources. In general, capital is a product of social labor, "a collective product," a "social power."[3] Yet, whereas production is social, the control of industry is in the hands of private capitalists, who supervise the processes, decide upon policies, and, on considerations of personal interests, determine the channels into which the social productive energy will flow. Moreover, the products resulting from the collective productive forces are not appropriated socially, but become the property of the capitalist who disposes of them as he pleases. Production is social in character, but the appropriation of the wealth created is private.[4]

A third contradiction consists in the fact that two diametrically opposite principles operate within the factory and outside, in society. Inside the factory there is order, coöperation, coördination of processes, and careful planning. But outside, in society at large, the production of the means of satisfying the wants of the community is not pursued on the basis of sensitive responsiveness to the genuine social needs. There is no carefully studied apportioning of the social resources, and no planned, orderly direction of them into appropriate avenues. Among individual plants and enterprises complete anarchy reigns. Each capitalist first produces whatever his fancy chooses, and as much as he pleases; then he begins to search for markets. One capitalist competes with another for the opportunity to dispose of the commodities. There is order

[3] Marx and Engels, *Communist Manifesto*, p. 32.
[4] Marx, *Capital*, III, 310, 312, 516; Engels, *Socialism, Utopian and Scientific*, p. 55.

within the factory, but among the industrial enterprises there is *bellum omnium contra omnes.*[5]

These contradictions embody the principles and the spirit of capitalism. Production for gain and not for use, social production but private appropriation, and complete anarchy in enterprise; greed, grab, and competitive combat; exchange, private gain, and the chaos of atomism: these are its articles of faith.

Yet Marx realizes that this creed accomplished a good deal, especially during the early days of capitalism, and he joins his friend in paying tribute to its achievements. Capitalism is an enormous advance over the preceding eras, and the above principles supplied it with a powerful urge for noteworthy attainments. The *Communist Manifesto* acknowledges that "The bourgeoisie, during its rule of scarce one hundred years, has created more massive and more colossal productive forces than have all preceding generations together," and, after enumerating some of them, questions: "What earlier century had even a presentiment that such productive forces slumbered in the lap of social labor?" "It [the bourgeoisie] has been the first to show what man's activity can bring about. It has accomplished wonders far surpassing Egyptian pyramids, Roman aqueducts, and Gothic cathedrals." [6] But all this is true only up to a certain point, and while the contradictions are latent. Soon the stage is reached when they begin to assert themselves as an insurmountable obstacle to the further development of the productive forces.

The contradictions generate consequences which afflict the capitalist organism with three fatal diseases that finally seal its doom: the misery of the laborers; the tendency of profits to fall, undermining the very ground on which the capitalist thrives; and the crises which throw the whole system into periodic convulsions.

---

[5] *Capital*, I, 391; *Socialism, Utopian and Scientific*, p. 59.

[6] Marx and Engels, *Communist Manifesto*, pp. 18, 16. "The bourgeois society is the most highly developed and most highly differentiated historical organization of production," says Marx (*Critique of Political Economy*, appendix, p. 300).

## The Machine Versus the Worker

First, as to the fate of the workers. The present régime is antagonistic to, and incompatible with, the welfare of the masses, the proletarians; the further the system progresses, the more miserable becomes their lot. Surplus-value is the source of gain for the capitalist, and his single life purpose is to absorb the maximum of surplus labor, "to extract the greatest possible amount of surplus-value, and consequently to exploit labor-power to the greatest possible extent." [7] This explains the long working day and the "civilized horrors of overwork." It explains why the establishment of the normal working day by law is the result of centuries of struggle, and why the history of the struggle is filled with the most astute devices for evasions and the most stubborn attempts to frustrate the legal efforts to lighten the burden of the proletariat.

This history Marx chronicles in detail and with appropriate remarks.[8] He prefaces it with the following indictment:

Time for education, for intellectual development, for the fulfilling of social functions and for social intercourse, for the free play of his bodily and mental activity, even the rest time of Sunday . . . — moonshine! But in its blind unrestrainable passion, its werewolf hunger for surplus labor, capital oversteps not only the moral, but even the merely physical maximum bounds of the working day. It usurps the time for growth, development, and healthy maintenance of the body. It steals the time required for the consumption of fresh air and sunlight. It higgles over a meal-time. . . It reduces the sound sleep needed for the restoration, reparation, refreshment of the bodily powers to just so many hours of torpor as the revival of an organism, absolutely exhausted, renders essential [9] . . . To the outcry as to the physical and mental degradation, the premature death, the torture of overwork, it answers: Ought these to trouble us since they increase our profits? [10]

In the machine the capitalist finds a powerful ally in the art of exploiting labor, and added opportunities for pumping out surplus-value.[11] Not demanding great muscular strength, the

[7] *Capital*, I, 257, 363.
[8] *Capital*, I, 297–330.
[9] *Capital*, I, 291.
[10] *Capital*, I, 296–297.
[11] *Capital*, I, 430ff.

machine permits the employment of women and children.
While before, the head of the family worked and supported it,
now the whole family slaves. The laborer sells his wife and
child to the capitalist. "He has become a slave dealer." [12] This
"coining of children's blood into capital" [13] exacts a fearful
toll of the tiny victims. It brings on physical deterioration, it
multiplies infant mortality, it robs the "immature human being" of the opportunity to develop its faculties, and it induces
intellectual desolation by turning the child into a machine for
the fabrication of surplus-value. [14]

A special product of the machine is the prolongation of the
working day "beyond all bounds set by human nature." [15]
For this there are a number of reasons. The capitalist is interested in using the machine as much as possible, for a machine during idle hours undergoes depreciation, but fetches
no profits. [16] Then, an old machine is subject to a potential
"moral depreciation," because it is rendered worthless as soon
as a better one is invented. The capitalist is therefore anxious
to reproduce its value in the quickest possible time. Exploitation of a doubled number of workers would require twice the
amount of machinery, but the exploitation of the same number of workers for longer hours does not involve a proportionate increase of machinery and other types of constant
capital; so that more surplus-value is obtained with almost
the same overhead expense. [17] Further, the sporadic use of a
new machine by an astute capitalist before it is employed by
his competitors nets him an excess of surplus-value, because
his "individual value" is lower than the normal "social value"
prevailing in the market. He is therefore in haste to exploit
"his first love," before the universal adoption of the new invention wipes out his advantage. [18]

In general, idle capital is a loss to the owner. When the
laborer rests, the capitalist loses. Capital stands in perpetual

[12] *Capital*, I, 431, 432; *Poverty of Philosophy*, p. 153.
[13] *Capital*, I, 298.
[14] *Capital*, I, 434, 436.
[15] *Capital*, I, 440.
[16] *Capital*, I, 441.
[17] *Capital*, I, 442–443.
[18] *Capital*, I, 444.

need of labor to exploit. "Capital is dead labor that, vampire-like, lives only by sucking living labor, and lives the more, the more labor it sucks." [19] Accordingly, "the excessive prolongation of the working day turned out to be the peculiar product of Modern Industry." [20] This robs the laborer of leisure. "Time is the room of human development. A man has no free time to dispose of, whose whole lifetime . . . is absorbed by his labor for the capitalist, is less than a beast of burden. He is a mere machine . . . broken in body and brutalized in mind." [21] The machine also offers facilities for the intensification of the toil. The machine can be speeded up, or more machines can be placed under the care of a laborer.[22]

The machine is also an implacable enemy of the worker in his struggle against oppression, and a ruthless competitor for employment. The machine is the favorite means of suppressing strikes and curbing the power of insubordinate labor. "It would be possible to write quite a history of the inventions, made since 1830, for the sole purpose of supplying capital with weapons against the revolt of the working class." [23] If wages rise, the way to lower them is the introduction of more machinery.[24] The appearance of a new machine in an industry renders superfluous the workers previously engaged, and deprives them of their livelihood. Marx strongly believes that machinery and inventions displace labor and cause unemployment, and on this question he argues strenuously against the classical economists. He will hear none of the talk that the introduction of machinery may prove but a "temporary inconvenience," except in the sense that it turns the laborers out of this "temporal" world.[25]

In general, the machine, the factory, "exhausts the nervous system to the uttermost"; "confiscates every atom of freedom,

---

[19] *Capital*, I, 257.

[20] *Capital*, I, 560.

[21] Marx, *Value, Price and Profit*, p. 109.

[22] Marx, *Capital*, I, 450.

[23] *Capital*, I, 476; *Poverty of Philosophy*, pp. 153, 183.

[24] Marx, *Value, Price and Profit*, p. 122.

[25] *Capital*, I, 471, 478ff.

both in bodily and intellectual activity"; "deprives the work of all interest"; creates a "barrack discipline" with a "factory code in which capital formulates, like a private legislator . . . his autocracy over the workpeople," with "fines and deductions," with injury to "every organ of sense" caused by the raised temperature, dust-laden atmosphere, and deafening noise, and with "danger to life and limb among the thickly crowded machinery which, with the regularity of the seasons, issues its list of the killed and wounded in the industrial battle." [26] The laborer has no choice but submission, because his special skill "vanishes as an infinitesimal quantity before the science, the gigantic physical forces, and the mass of labor that are embodied in the factory mechanism." [27] Intent on savings which would lower his "price of production," the capitalist is economical about his machinery but allows "the most outrageous squandering of labor power" and "prodigality in the use of the life and health of the laborer," scorning all provisions that would "render the process of production human, agreeable, or even bearable." [28] "As a producer of the activity of others, as a pumper out of surplus labor and exploiter of labor-power, it [capital] surpasses in energy, disregard of bounds, recklessness, and efficiency, all earlier systems of production based on directly compulsory labor." [29]

Marx does not blame the machine or the factory, but the spirit of capitalism. He realizes that the machine represents the triumph of man over natural forces, and that it affords the opportunity of shortening the labor-time, of lightening human toil, and of increasing the wealth of the masses. But in the hands of the capitalist, it stands for the direct opposite: long hours, great drudgery, poverty, the "martyrdom of the producer," and the means of crushing his "individual vitality, freedom, and independence." [30] Marx also acknowledges that legislation curbs more and more the avarice of the capitalist and tends to diminish the laborer's sufferings. But he wishes

---

[26] *Capital*, I, 462–466.
[27] *Capital*, I, 462.
[28] *Capital*, I, 581; III, 103–104.
[29] *Capital*, I, 338–339.
[30] *Capital*, I, 482, 555.

to emphasize that capitalism per se, with profits and not service as its inspiring aim, promotes all these evils and displays them in lurid light whenever the arm of the law is absent or fails to reach.

## INCREASING MISERY

Such would be the plight of the worker if conditions under capitalism were to remain static. But they do not remain static. Society is dynamic, and capital runs the spiral of accumulation, concentration, and centralization. Therefore he encounters more harassing conditions still, and his life is beset with new troubles. With the progress of capitalism the laborer becomes the victim of "increasing misery."

The theory of increasing misery has caused considerable uneasiness to socialist interpreters of Marx, because facts seem to contradict the prediction of their master. With the advance of the present order, the misery of the proletariat is not increasing. On the contrary, a good case can be made out that his lot is improving. But to some socialists Marx cannot be wrong, and they strain their faculties in the effort to attach peculiar meanings to this theory. Kautsky, for example, urges that it means *relative* misery, and that Marx claims only that, while the condition of the worker does improve, it does not improve as rapidly as wealth accumulates. The laborer is better off, but when he is compared with the upper classes, the difference in fortunes is steadily rising.[31]

But Kautsky is in error. The distinction between the two phases of accumulation must be kept in mind. During the "special phase," when the organic composition of capital stays unaltered, an increase in capital implies a proportionate increment in its variable constituent, which, to recall, is the wages of labor. Therefore, the demand for labor increases, and sooner or later a point is reached when "the demand for laborers may exceed the supply," and a rise in wages follows. Such was the case during the fifteenth and the first half of

---

[31] Kautsky, in *Neue Zeit*, XXVI, no. 2, pp. 542–543.

the eighteenth century.[32] Under such conditions the dependence of the worker on capital is more endurable.

Marx assures us, however, that this circumstance in no way
changes the fundamental character of wage-slavery, and by
no means offers any hope of emancipation. The system is not
threatened. It only means that the chain tying the laborer to
capital "allows of a relaxation of the tension of it." There is
no cause for exultation. Suppose the rise in wages encroaches
on surplus-value to such an extent as to slacken accumulation
of capital. Then the check comes automatically; the demand
for labor slows down, and wages fall back to their previous
level. Exploitation of labor is not imperiled, and the foundations of capitalism remain intact.[33]

Marx emphasizes these ideas in his *Wage-Labor and Capital*, and from a different viewpoint. He tries there to demonstrate that the interests of capital and labor are always in
sharp opposition. He is discussing first the "special phase" of
accumulation, saying: "And, to assume even the most favorable case, with the increase of productive capital there is an
increase in the demand for labor. And thus wages, the price
of labor, will rise." But this rise, he continues, does not free
the laborer from relative misery. As capitalism progresses,
the worker's house may "shoot up"; but if the neighboring
palace "shoots up" in the same or in greater proportion, the
occupant of the smaller dwelling "will always find himself
more uncomfortable, more discontented." Similarly, an increase of capital results in an advance in wages; but it also
calls forth a rapid rise "in wealth, luxury, social wants, and
social comforts." Although the comforts of the laborer have
increased, the satisfaction he derives is diminished, because
he witnesses the far greater comforts enjoyed by the rich.
"The material position of the laborer has improved, but it is

---

[32] Marx, *Capital*, I, 672; *Value, Price and Profit*, pp. 120–121. This may be
regarded as a supplement to his subsistence theory of wages (see above, p. 188).
In the long run there is a tendency of wages to conform to subsistence; but
over short periods there may be deviations, according to conditions of the supply
of labor and the demand for it.

[33] *Capital*, I, 672, 677–680.

at the expense of his social position. The social gulf which separates him from the capitalist has widened." [34] It is on these statements that Kautsky bases his interpretation of "increasing misery" as meaning relative misery.

But we must remember that this psychological misery applies only to "the most favorable case," the special phase of accumulation. Kautsky seems to neglect this. He refers to page 35, but he does not take into account what Marx says on page 42, when he leaves the special phase and turns to the typical situation. "We can hardly believe," Marx says, "that the fatter capital becomes the more will its slave be pampered. . . We must therefore inquire more closely into the effect which the increase of productive capital has upon wages." [35] This closer inquiry appears in greater detail in *Capital*, volume I, than in *Wage-Labor and Capital*, and the conclusions are the same.

The general condition of labor under capitalism is basically associated with Marx's doctrine of overpopulation and the industrial reserve army. Accumulation, centralization, inventions, and improvements, by diminishing the variable capital in relation to the constant capital, reduce "the relative demand for labor." New capital attracts fewer laborers "in proportion to its magnitude," and old capital, when replaced, repels more and more of the laborers previously connected with it.[36] The variable capital rises absolutely, yet the demand for labor "falls progressively with the increase of the total capital, instead of, *as previously assumed*, in proportion to it." [37] The demand for labor is on the increase, but it fails to keep pace with the ratio of the growth of capital.[38] It is not that the laboring population is rising, as Malthus would have it; it is rather capitalist accumulation that produces "a relatively redundant population of laborers, i.e., a population of greater extent than suffices for the average needs of the self-expan-

[34] Marx, *Wage-Labor and Capital*, pp. 35, 42.
[35] *Wage-Labor and Capital*, p. 43.
[36] *Capital*, I, 689.
[37] *Capital*, I, 690. My italics.
[38] *Value, Price and Profit*, p. 124.

sion of capital, and therefore a surplus population." [39]   The displacement of man by the machine is an integral part of the phenomenon. "Machinery always produces a relative over-population, a reserve army of laborers, and this increases the power of capital." [40]

The relative surplus population, employed and discharged at will, is alike an effect and a necessary condition of the accumulation of capital. With the expansion of industry, credit, and markets, with the inflow of capital into fresh spheres or old branches of industry, and with the upward swing of the cycle, part of this reserve army is recruited into employment. When the outbursts of activity subside, part of this army is discharged. Without a reserve of laborers to draw upon, these adventures of capital would be unthinkable. "This is the law of population peculiar to the capitalist mode of production." [41] Malthus was wrong.

It is difficult to see how this theory accounts for a surplus population as a rising trend. Laborers live on wages and not on ratios, and, since the total social wage bill rises absolutely, as Marx repeatedly asserts,[42] the population can rise with it, ignoring the falling ratio of the variable to the constant capital. In other words, labor displaced by the machine or otherwise is promptly reabsorbed. We may have cyclical unemployment, but no steadily rising curve of the unemployed. In this connection two remarks made by Marx are of significance. He indicates that as the wage bill rises, more labor is needed, but not more laborers, in view of the mounting exploitation of the laborer and the substitution of women and children for regular workers. The overwork of the employed swells the reserve army, and the competition of the reserve army makes the overwork more acute. Let England, says Marx, treat labor reasonably in respect of hours of work, age, and sex, and the working population will immediately become insufficient for

[39] *Capital*, I, 691–692; III, 260.
[40] *Theorien über den Mehrwert*, II, no. 2, 343, 351; *Capital*, I, 702, 705. Cf. Ricardo, *Principles of Political Economy*, p. 266.
[41] Marx, *Capital*, I, 692–694.
[42] E.g., *Capital*, I, 683, 690; III, 253, 261.

the existing volume of production.[43] This remark, however, does not dispose of the problem. With the progress of capitalism not merely the amount of labor but the number of employed wage workers has been steadily rising, and Marx is aware of this fact.[44]

A second remark is more enlightening, but is damaging to his analytical position. He states that high wages will raise the laboring population by encouraging marriages and lowering infant mortality, and that low wages are equally a hothouse for multiplication, "since . . . poverty propagates its kind." [45] Centering the locus of infection on the biological behavior of the laboring masses and not on the effects of accumulation, Marx is here dangerously close to Malthus.

To continue with the argument, this intermittent attraction and repulsion of laborers is the tragedy of the proletariat. The movement of wages is governed by the magnitude of the "relative surplus population," the ratio of the reserve to the active army, the expansion or contraction of the reserve army through the phases of the business cycle. The forces of supply and demand operate; but the area on which they play is the "relative surplus population." [46] Eager for employment, the idle are in competition with those in the active army; and the larger the reserve, the greater the competition. Consequently, those employed are compelled to overwork and to submit to any terms dictated by the capitalist. The overwork deprives others of employment, and swells the ranks of the reserve. In Marx's thought, the bargaining power of labor has much to do with wages, but the reserve army has much to do with breaking this power. Still other circumstances conspire to enlarge the reserve: the all-pervasive machine displaces more and more workers; with the progress of capitalism division of labor becomes so elaborate and the processes so simple that one man can accomplish the tasks which five men

[43] *Capital*, I, 696–698; *Wage-Labor and Capital*, pp. 49–50.

[44] *Capital*, III, 309, 255, 257.

[45] *Capital*, III, 256, 299; I, 706 and n.

[46] *Capital*, I, 699, 701–702; *Value, Price and Profit*, p. 120. This is the cyclical aspect of his theory of wages. For the main theory see above, pp. 188, 213–214.

performed before; and the centralization of capital crowds out the petty employer and casts him into the ranks of the proletariat. All this renders the struggle for employment exceedingly severe.[47] "The industrial reserve army, during the periods of stagnation and average prosperity, weighs down the active labor army; during the periods of overproduction and paroxysm, it holds its pretentions in check."[48] This play of competition and of supply and demand completes the despotism of capital and works havoc with wages.

Marx's conclusions on this question, both in *Wage-Labor and Capital* and in *Capital*, are unambiguous. In the first work we read: "To sum up: *the faster productive capital increases the more do the division of labor and the employment of machinery extend . . . so much the more does competition increase among the laborers, and so much the more do their average wages dwindle.*"[49] In the second work he talks of the "ruinous effects" of capitalistic accumulation on the working class,[50] and concludes:

Pauperism is the hospital of the active labor-army and the dead weight of the industrial reserve army . . . along with the surplus population, pauperism forms a condition of capitalist production and of the capitalist development of wealth. . . The relative mass of the industrial reserve army increases therefore with the potential energy of wealth. . . The more extensive, finally, the lazurus-layers of the working class, and the industrial reserve army, the greater its official pauperism. *This is the absolute general law of capitalist accumulation.* Like all other laws, it is modified in its working by many circumstances.[51]

He then cites from economists who saw the disastrous effect that capitalist accumulation has on the workers. The citations refer to "absolute privation of the first necessaries of life," to "hunger," and to "degradation of the masses."[52] He

---

[47] *Capital*, I, 698, 701–702; *Wage-Labor and Capital*, pp. 48–53.

[48] *Capital*, I, 701.

[49] *Wage-Labor and Capital*, p. 52. Marx's italics. On the same pages he says: "*Exactly as the labor becomes more unsatisfactory and unpleasant, in that very proportion competition increases and wages decline*" (p. 49. Marx's italics). "And thus the forest of arms outstretched by those who are entreating for work becomes ever denser and the arms themselves grow ever leaner" (p. 53).

[50] *Capital*, I, 702–703.

[51] *Capital*, I, 707. Marx's italics.          [52] *Capital*, I, 709–711.

then offers numerous illustrations of this law, all dealing with abject poverty, low wages, fearful living conditions, and deterioration.[53]

It is reasonably clear that by increasing misery Marx means precisely what he says, physical impoverishment, and not psychological dissatisfaction, as Kautsky would have it. Statements made in other connections bring additional evidence. The Gotha program asserts that, as wealth accumulates, "poverty and neglect develop among the workers" in proportion. Marx comments on this: "This has been the law in all history up to the present." [54] In his speech on Free Trade he avers that "the minimum of wages is constantly sinking." [55] The *Communist Manifesto* proclaims (page 29): "The modern laborer, on the contrary, instead of rising with the progress of industry, sinks deeper and deeper below the conditions of existence of his own class. He becomes a pauper, and pauperism develops more rapidly than population and wealth." In *Value, Price and Profit*, devoted largely to a discussion of wages, the final conclusion is: "The general tendency of capitalist production is not to raise but to sink the average standard of wages" (page 127). Engels, too, talks of "the underconsumption of the masses," of their "sinking to the level of the Chinese coolie," of the "retrogression in the condition of the oppressed class." [56] Perhaps it is necessary to add that Marx understands, of course, that a rise in the productivity of labor makes it arithmetically "possible" for both wages and profits constantly to rise. But increasing misery is to him a matter of stark realities and not of arithmetical possibilities. He also allows that here and there, owing to particular circumstances, and especially during the cyclical periods of prosperity, wages do rise. This is, in fact, an integral part of his theory of wages.

But here, too, Marx does not fail to produce declarations that run with the hares and hunt with the hounds. One can

[53] *Capital*, I, 711–783.

[54] *Critique of the Gotha Programme*, p. 23.

[55] Reprinted in *Poverty of Philosophy*, appendix, pp. 223–224. See also his *Inauguraladresse der internationalen Arbeiter-Association*, pp. 18–25.

[56] *Anti-Dühring*, pp. 312, 174; *Origin of the Family*, p. 216.

find in Marx two statements suggesting *relative* misery. In 1864 he says: "Everywhere the great mass of the working class sinks more deeply into poverty, at least in relation to the rise of the upper classes in the social scale." [57] The other statement is in comment on Gladstone's assertion, for the period 1842–1861, that "While the rich have been growing richer the poor have been growing less poor." Marx retorts: "If the working class has remained 'poor,' only 'less poor' in proportion as it produces for the wealthy class 'an intoxicating augmentation of wealth and power,' then it has remained relatively just as poor. If the extremes of poverty have not lessened, they have increased, because the extremes of wealth have." [58] Whatever weight one may be inclined to give these pronouncements, the balance of evidence rests, I believe, with the interpretation of increasing physical misery. Marx seems to be convinced of a trend of physical impoverishment, but when in a given period of time the lot of the laborer fails to deteriorate, he remains unimpressed, pointing to the relative impoverishment, in face of the enormous advances of the rich.

No better summary can be given, in conclusion, of Marx's view concerning the promise of capitalism to the laborer than his own:

Within the capitalist system all methods for raising the social productiveness of labor are brought about at the cost of the individual laborer; all means for the development of production transform themselves into means of domination over, and exploitation of, the producers; they mutilate the laborer into a fragment of a man, degrade him to the level of an appendage of a machine, destroy every remnant of charm in his work and turn it into a hated toil; they estrange from him the intellectual potentialities of the labor-process in the same proportion in which science is incorporated in it as an independent power; they distort the conditions under which he works, subject him during the labor-process to a despotism the more hateful for its meanness; they transform his life-time into workingtime, and drag his wife and child beneath the wheels of the Juggernaut of capital. . . . It follows, therefore, that in proportion as capital accumulates, the lot of the laborer, be his payment high or low, must grow worse. The law, finally, that always equilibrates the relative surplus population, or industrial reserve army, to the extent and energy of accumula-

[57] *Inauguraladresse der internationalen Arbeiter-Association*, pp. 24–25.
[58] *Capital*, I, 715–716.

tion, this law rivets the laborer to capital more firmly than the wedges of Vulcan did Prometheus to the rock. It establishes an accumulation of misery, corresponding with accumulation of capital. Accumulation of wealth at one pole is, therefore, at the same time accumulation of misery, agony of toil, slavery, ignorance, brutality, mental degradation, at the opposite pole, that is, on the side of the class that produces its own product in the form of capital.[59]

## THE FALLING RATE OF PROFIT

Another organic malady, a menace to the whole system, is the tendency of the rate of profit to fall: profit here embraces all categories of surplus-value, that is, interest, rent, and profit proper. As was seen above, in the course of accumulation there is a reorganization of capital, so that the constant capital (in value terms) grows in relation to the variable capital. In approaching this problem Marx assumes a constant rate of exploitation, that is, a constant $\frac{s}{v}$, or a constant ratio of profit to wages. When, for the economy as a whole, $\frac{c}{v}$ is rising, while $\frac{s}{v}$ stays fixed, $\frac{s}{c+v}$ must fall. To put it differently, with the growth of capital, $\frac{v}{c}$ drops, and so does $\frac{v}{c+v}$, and since the total mass of surplus-value or profit $(s)$ is a fixed ratio of $v$, $\frac{s}{c+v}$ must decline. This principle Marx calls "the law of the falling tendency of the rate of profit." There is no implication of a fall in the absolute volume of surplus-value or profit; on the contrary, Marx teaches that a rise in the mass of surplus-value is inherent in the workings of capitalism.[60]

In this development the passion for gain and competition play their part. A capitalist would not introduce a new method of production and thereby a capital of a higher composition when common experience teaches that such a move ends in lowering the rate of profit. But he is lured by the extra profits which he expects to harvest while his price of production is

[59] *Capital*, I, 708–709.
[60] *Capital*, III, chap. xiii, and pp. 311–312.

below the market price still based on the old methods; that is, in the interval before the improvement gains general adoption, precipitating a drop in the rate of profit.[61] Too, the powerful capitalists are eager to expropriate the small ones in order to compensate for the declining rate of profit by an increment in the mass of profit obtained from the larger centralized capitals after the expulsion of rivals who were unable to endure the race. Thus accumulation and centralization accelerate the fall of the rate of profit, and the fall of the rate of profit hastens accumulation and centralization.[62] Centralization, we recall, means oligopoly or monopoly. We are told, then, by Marx that monopoly, far from checking the fall of the rate of profit, tends to accelerate it.

One may wonder, says Marx, why in face of the enormous accumulation of capital the fall of the rate of profit has not been more rapid. The reason lies in six countervailing factors "which thwart and annul the effects of this general law." This explains why he calls the phenomenon a "tendency, that is, a law whose absolute enforcement is checked, retarded, weakened by counteracting influences." [63] Three of these influences are connected with the exploitation of labor and increasing misery. First, the intensification of the toil caused by the speed-up of the machinery and particularly by the prolongation of the working day, raising the rate of surplus-value, without raising proportionately, if at all, the organic composition, tends to boost the rate of profit. Second, the "depression of wages below their value" is specified as "one of the most important causes checking the tendency of the rate of profit to fall," primarily by advancing the rate of surplus-value. Third, the idle reserve army permits both old and new lines of production to persist in backward methods which rely more on labor and less on capital equipment. In such lines "the variable capital constitutes a considerable proportion of the total capital and wages are below the average, so that the rate

[61] *Capital*, III, 310.
[62] *Capital*, III, 283.
[63] *Capital*, III, 272, 275, 280.

and mass of surplus-value are exceptionally high." The high rate of profit in these backward spheres pushes up the average rate for industry as a whole.[64]

Of the other three counterbalancing causes, one refers to the reduction in the value of the constant capital induced by the greater productivity of labor associated with the greater use of machinery, so that as the organic composition rises with accumulation the rise in terms of value is less than the rise in terms of physical capital. Another counteracting factor relates to foreign trade, which by cheapening alike the constant and variable capitals acts both to raise the rate of surplus-value and to lower the organic composition of capital. (For more detail on this point, see below, p. 227.) The sixth and remaining element is of no particular significance.

The dark offspring of the same forces which are responsible for the increasing misery of the proletariat, the falling rate of profit, blunts the incentive of the capitalist and is therefore fatal to the career of capitalism. The vitality of the economy depends on accumulation and investment, and these depend on profits. The specter of a diminishing scale of returns menaces the numerous small capitals "seeking an independent location," and if the formation of capital becomes the function of large capitalists, who alone can find compensation in the mass of profit for the low rate of profit, "the vital fire of production would be extinguished. It would fall into a dormant state." The English economists, he states, were understandingly concerned over the prospect. That it should worry Ricardo "shows his profound understanding of the conditions of capitalist production." The falling rate of profit demonstrates that capitalism creates its own limits, and that by the laws of its own processes it is doomed to dissolution.[65]

As Marx is aware, in exploring this problem he walks in the tradition of the orthodox economics of his day. Since Adam Smith economists speculated about declining profits and the stationary state. With Adam Smith the fall of profit is induced

[64] *Capital*, III, chap. xiii, sections i, ii, iv.
[65] *Capital*, III, 304, 283.

by the accumulation of stock and competition among trades-men, that is, by the conditions of supply and demand of loan-able funds. To Ricardo profits are in inverse relation to wages, and when a rising population brings about diminishing returns on land and rising prices of food, wages rise and prof-its shrink. In accounting for his stationary state, J. S. Mill is, characteristically, eclectic. Marx addresses himself to the problem from the angle of a rising composition of capital. Marx has a high opinion of his analysis. He observes that economists since Adam Smith vainly "cudgeled their brains" over this question, but in view of the faulty approach of politi-cal economy, "up to the present," to surplus-value and the organic composition of capital, "we no longer wonder at its failure to solve the riddle." [66] In a letter to Engels in 1868 he refers to his theory — already developed in notes which Engels later put into *Capital*, volume III — as "one of the greatest triumphs over the *pons asini* of all economics up to the pres-ent." [67]

Little does he suspect that his analysis of the problem rests on a precarious foundation. His twin assumptions of a rising organic composition and of a constant rate of surplus-value carry implications which are incompatible with some of his key theorems. The first assumption means that the laborer, handling more machinery and raw materials per unit of time, is more productive, and the national income rises. The second assumption implies that the proletarian, receiving a constant proportion (and this is what a constant rate of surplus-value means) of this rising national income, shares with the capitalist the fruits of progress in a capitalist society, so that while the rate of profit declines the real wage steadily climbs. This will be readily perceived as a striking contradiction by those who find in Marx the doctrine of increasing physical misery, al-though it will not be recognized as such by those who inter-pret increasing misery in relative terms, and therefore com-patible with a mounting scale of real wages.

[66] *Capital*, III, 250.
[67] Marx and Engels, *Gesamtausgabe*, Part III, vol. 4, p. 48.

However, these two assumptions create a difficulty which must be credited even by those inclined to the latter position with regard to Marx's idea of the steady impoverishment of the proletariat. A *constant* rate of surplus-value coupled with a rising composition of capital and consequently with a rising productivity of labor is incompatible with another basic teaching of Marx. In his thought, the development of the productive forces and the accumulation of capital are associated with a *rising* and not with a constant rate of surplus-value. As the productivity of the laborer increases, the number of hours needed to produce his wage ("necessary" labor-time) diminishes, so that, without a lengthened working day, the unpaid or "surplus" labor-time rises. The rate of surplus-value rises even if real wages are pushed up, inasmuch as they are not pushed up in proportion to the advance in productivity.[68]

From these difficulties Marx cannot be extricated by changing his assumption from a constant rate of surplus-value to a rising rate. On this new assumption, the mathematics of his formula for the rate of profit $\frac{s}{c+v}$ suggests that a falling rate of profit can result only if the rise in the organic composition of capital ($c:v$) is greater than the rise in the rate of surplus value ($s:v$); otherwise $\frac{s}{c+v}$ will not be a declining magnitude. But the organic composition (in value terms) may or may not rise faster than the rate of surplus-value. There is no logical necessity involved here. It is a matter of empirical situations, and Marx's law gives indeterminate results. Marx is in a dilemma. If he is to demonstrate a falling rate of profit, he must make assumptions incompatible with basic premises of his system. If he makes assumptions in harmony with his teachings, he cannot establish the necessity of a falling rate of profit. As Mrs. Joan Robinson states at the conclusion of her chapter on this problem: "His explanation of the falling tendency of profits explains nothing at all." [69]

[68] *Capital*, I, chap. xii, and pp. 405, 662.
[69] *Essay on Marxian Economics*, chap. v. See also P. M. Sweezy, *Theory of Capitalist Development*, pp. 100ff.

## Imperialism

The celebrated socialist doctrine of imperialism, multiplying the strains and stresses of capitalism, extending oppression and international rivalries, and precipitating large-scale wars with their enormous and penetrating dislocations, was elaborated in many variants by his followers, but received little direct treatment from Marx. Of course, he laid the foundations for his disciples by his theories of accumulation, the rising tide of monopoly, increasing misery, the falling rate of profit, underconsumption, and crises; which all suggest that, with large profits as the prime objective, the domestic market is insufficient alike for the disposal of the enormous volumes of commodities which modern industry is capable of producing, and for the investment of the huge accumulations made possible by the massive exploitation of labor. But, specifically, neither colonization nor foreign trade and investment receives extended exploration by Marx. The same is true of Engels: he does not address himself explicitly to the question of imperialism, but he makes statements suggestive to future camp followers.[70]

We know that in Marx's presentation colonies play a commanding part in the establishment of capitalism. As was seen in Chapter III above, colonies provided, during the sixteenth and seventeenth centuries, by slave trade, by precious metals, and by the exploitation of the aborigines, the "original" accumulation of capital essential to the exploitation of wage-labor, thereby providing the basic precondition of the present order. Too, as the *Communist Manifesto* and other writings tell us, the destruction of feudalism and the formative impulse to capitalism came from the expansion of markets induced by colonies which created a demand for goods that could not be met by the medieval mode of production.[71]

But we scarcely find in Marx an emphasis on the necessity of colonial empires after the infancy of capitalism. He has something to say on foreign trade in general. Viewed from

[70] E.g., his footnote in Marx, *Capital*, III, 574.    [71] Cf. *Capital*, III, 391.

one angle, foreign trade is very important; viewed from another angle, it has only temporary effects. Capitalism, for instance, is essentially a system given to the conversion of goods into commodities, and foreign trade and a world market facilitate the conversion. A world market, says Marx, is the "basis and vital element of capitalist production."[72] Foreign trade also gives fuller dimensions to the play of capitalist forces and greater possibilities for the mature development of the system. Commerce dissolves, under suitable conditions, the elementary orders of backward countries, supplanting them by more advanced organizations.[73] It converts, in due course, the whole world into one capitalist stage on which the drama of "contradictions" is enacted with greater sweep and intensity, to the predetermined fatal end. Marx is in favor of free trade because of its revolutionary effects. "It breaks up old nationalities and carries the antagonism between proletariat and bourgeoisie to the uttermost point. In a word, the system of commercial freedom hastens the social revolution."[74]

The implications of its effect suggest, however, that from the viewpoint of long-range analysis, foreign trade is hardly of major significance. It extends and intensifies the enormities and maladies of capitalism — it "only transfers the contradictions to a wider sphere," says Marx — but it introduces no new principles into the equations. Accordingly at some stages of his analysis he sees no advantage in introducing the problem of foreign trade, considering the introduction a "disturbing subsidiary circumstance" and preferring to treat "the whole world as one nation."[75]

However, its rôle as a temporary factor is not to be minimized. Foreign trade is a considerable influence in counteracting the tendency of the rate of profit to fall, and in several ways. First, an industrial country obtains its raw materials at lower prices for the double reason that, one, agricultural countries

[72] *Capital*, III, 131, 280; *Theorien über den Mehrwert*, II, no. 1, pp. 147–148.
[73] *Capital*, III, 389–391.
[74] *Free Trade*, reprinted in *Poverty of Philosophy*, p. 227.
[75] *Capital*, II, 546; I, 636n.

produce them more cheaply, and, two, agricultural peoples are generally "forced to sell their product below its value." This tends to reduce $c$ in $\dfrac{s}{c+v}$. Second, because of the cheapness of the imported food products, the paid part of labor-power shrinks in relation to the unpaid part, given the length of the working day, and relative surplus-value rises. The purpose of the free trade movement in England before the repeal of the Corn Laws in 1846 was, says Marx, to reduce the price of bread "in order to reduce wages and . . . the profits of capital would rise."[76] Third, foreign investments are prominent in this picture. The rate of profit is higher in backward countries, owing to the low standard of living of the laboring population; to the greater submissiveness of labor to exploitation, as through a long working day; to the higher ratio $v:c$, characteristic of undeveloped regions; and to the fact that the commodities produced by the invested capital can sell above their value and yet undersell the exploited country's own products on account of its inferior facilities of production.[77] Moreover, investments abroad diminish the pressure of the overproduction of capital at home, with the effect of tending to maintain there a greater scale of returns. The combined influence of all these circumstances is to produce a higher average rate of profit on the total investments at home and abroad.[78]

Some socialist writers, notably Rosa Luxemburg, attempt to build a theory of imperialism with Marx's doctrine of underconsumption as the keystone. The encouragement which Marx can give such theorists is of precarious value. There is no want of statements in Marx to the effect that capitalism demands ever-expanding markets. Because of a surplus of commodities at home, he says, a demand must be sought for it abroad. The overaccumulation of capital and the overproduction of goods stimulate alike the search for new outlets. In

[76] *Free Trade*, reprinted in *Poverty of Philosophy*, p. 215.
[77] Cf. *Capital*, I, 613–614.
[78] *Capital*, III, 127, 278–279, 300; *Theorien über den Mehrwert*, II, no. 2, pp. 240–241, 252, 305–306.

fact, overproduction is often brought into focus in relation to the dimensions of the market. The mere admission, Marx teaches, that markets must be expanded testifies to the possibility of overproduction.[79]

But such declarations are inadequate to sustain the weight of the theory which Rosa Luxemburg intends to build on them. It is necessary to resolve the elementary question of how foreign trade can function as a corrective of overproduction in face of the truth that, in the main, exports are paid for by imports. The overproduction of commodities is not neutralized, then; for domestic goods seeking a buyer are substituted the imported goods. The importation of raw materials in exchange for *finished* goods does not alter the argument. This problem Marx does not undertake for analysis, but a suggestion or two may, perhaps, be discerned in his discussions of other or allied problems. In his treatment of accumulation in the last chapter of *Capital*, volume II, he decides that the surplus of consumption goods can be disposed of by exporting them against gold.[80] This, however, is not an enduring solution because of a variety of repercussions of gold imports. For instance, if the price level of the gold importing country rises, its exports will decline and its surplus goods will glut the market. Too, as far as the issue at hand is concerned, this suggestion cancels the incentives to imperialism in general by converging the incentives to the limited interest in gold-producing regions. There is also a hint, and perhaps more than a hint, that foreign investments mitigate the overproduction of consumption goods by diminishing the volume of capital utilized at home, thereby establishing a more balanced proportion there between investment and consumption.[81] However, it is necessary to pursue this point further and demonstrate, among other things, how the investing country obtains interest without a resurgence of overproduction, perhaps in an aggravated form. This Marx does not touch on.

---

[79] E.g., *Capital*, III, 301–302, 287; *Theorien über den Mehrwert*, II, no. 2, p. 305.                                        [80] *Capital*, II, 593, 610.

[81] Marx, *Theorien über den Mehrwert*, II, no. 2, pp. 304–305.

To summarize, Marx gives prominence to colonial empires in the genesis of capitalism, but he does not elaborate on imperialism as a permanent adjunct of capitalism, nor as a satellite of mature capitalism. Foreign trade is always of importance, but Marx does not seem to equate it to imperialism, although he mentions that trade with backward regions is not on the basis of equality but is charged with privileges to the advanced country which manages to reap excessive profits. Foreign trade ultimately brings up the less developed regions to the level of those with superior economic organizations. Then its function as a corrective of some of the capitalist maladies evaporates, and its function as an agency contributing to the disintegration of capitalism becomes immanent and evident.

With such ideas as a frame of reference, the followers of Marx (and non-Marxians as well!) have built up a literature on the socialist doctrine of imperialism in many ramifications: the struggle for colonies and markets, monopolistic exploitation of backward peoples, corporate and banking finance on an international scale, tariff policies, militarism, war, penetration, spheres of influence, power politics, mandates, and the like. There are polemics on whether imperialism is a special phase of capitalism or a perennial attribute; whether the impulse behind it is the struggle with underconsumption or the quest of "super-profits" on investments; whether the capital is industrial or "finance capital." The reader is usually assumed to take it for granted that imperialism was unknown until capitalism came, that capitalism was predominantly competitive until well towards the end of the nineteenth century, that monopoly began to characterize capitalism a couple of decades before the present century, that *laissez faire* was an impressive reality over the larger part of the career of capitalism, that fascism is an unavoidable phase of decadent late capitalism, and that modern wars, where Russia is not involved, are imperialistic wars.[82] All, or nearly all, these writings seem to agree that imperialism will in time cease to be the solvent of

[82] Cf. J. A. Schumpeter, *Capitalism, Socialism, and Democracy*, pp. 49ff.

some of the difficulties of capitalism, and that capitalism will then hasten to its dark end. Some of the prominent names in this literature are R. Hilferding, J. A. Hobson, V. I. Lenin, Rosa Luxemburg, F. Sternberg, and lately P. M. Sweezy.

# CHAPTER XII

## MARX'S THEORIES OF CRISES

To Marx crises are not minor incidents extrinsic and collateral to capitalism, as the economists of his day (and of a later vintage, too) were in the habit of thinking, but major catastrophic events organic in the functioning of the present system. Crises temporarily purge capitalism of accumulated disorder, expose the pathological contradictions festering within it, and reinforce the agencies tending to undermine it. It is during a crisis that the final revolution and the death of capitalism are expected to come. Prominent as the subject was in his mind, he never gave it systematic treatment. Scattered through his writings are numerous observations, and only in two places is the discussion given some length, in Chapter XV of the third volume of *Capital*, and in a long chapter in an inaccessible work edited by Kautsky.[1]

His discussions center on a number of conceptions, and accordingly the following theories, hardly any one adequately presented, may be imputed to him: the underconsumption theory, the falling rate of profit theory, and the disproportionality theory.

### J. B. Say's Law

If judged by the amount of space it receives, and especially by the persistently repeated references to it early and late in his and Engels' writings, the underconsumption theory seems to dominate over the other theories. The outlines of this theory are sketched in Marx's reactions to J. B. Say's law of markets and in other pronouncements, indicated shortly. First about J. B. Say's law and Marx's comments on it.

Say's law (summarized by Ricardo in his *Principles*, chapter XXI) affirms that there is a necessary equivalence between

[1] *Theorien über den Mehrwert*, II, no. 2, pp. 262–318.

total demand and total supply, that supply creates demand and demand creates supply. Basically, it claims, commodities and services exchange for commodities and services. The production of goods creates the wherewithal of paying for them; production constitutes an effective demand for production. As Ricardo has it, if you desire to purchase a commodity, produce something that people want, and you will have created a supply with which to satisfy, to match, your demand. The goods produced by a person constitute his income, and he may spend part of it and save part. The first part he exchanges for consumption goods, the second part for capital goods. A theory developed later may be taken as an addition to, not as a modification of, Say's law. It is the theory that the rate of interest equilibrates the demand for capital (or the marginal productivity of capital) and the supply of capital (or the marginal time preference of savers), bringing savings and investments into equality.

The use of money does not change the situation to the followers of this law. The cost of producing a commodity is resolved into income to the factors of production, and directly or indirectly these costs or incomes are used to buy all the commodities produced; no matter how much is produced, it can be disposed of at a profit. To the modern economist the crucial implications of this law are that income spent and saved is translated respectively into consumption and investment, that savings and investments are equal, that costs of production are recouped by sales proceeds, that the only source of saving and investment lies in lessened consumption, that purchasing power is indestructible, being fully spent on consumption goods and capital goods, and that the phenomenon of unemployment does not threaten the economy except as a temporary possibility.

A corollary of this law is the proposition that while partial overproduction is possible general overproduction has no meaning. In a given branch of industry miscalculation may beget overproduction with the concomitant unfavorable exchange for other goods and with inevitable loss or decline of profits. But general overproduction can only mean that everybody has more goods to exchange for more goods. Everybody is better off. "Could we suddenly double the productive powers of the country," says J. S. Mill, "we should double the supply of commodities in every market. . . Everybody would bring a double demand as well as supply: everybody would be able to buy twice as much, because everyone would have twice as much to offer in exchange." [2]

Such views are not the exclusive property of J. B. Say, nor was he their originator. They are integral to the economics of Ricardo, the two Mills and their followers, and indeed to academic economics, by and large, up to the great challenge of J. M. Keynes. The first challenges to this law came from Chalmers, Lauderdale, Malthus, and Sismondi, who refused to acknowledge the impossibility of a general glut. The controversy between the two camps is an interesting chapter in economics. Marx joined the rebels, although intellectually he was cool if not hostile to them, especially Malthus, but with the notable exception of Sismondi, from whom (as well as from Malthus), it may be added, Marx evidently borrowed much on the underconsumption theory of crises. In his argumentation against this law, Marx turns principally to Ricardo's defense of it.

This law, he declares, is the child of premises which remove all difficulties by emasculating capitalism of some of its indigenous earmarks. To Ricardo, in Marx's interpretation of him, capitalism is the simple economy of small-scale production wherein the individual business proprietor produces for a well-ascertained limited market with an assured demand. Ricardo assumed further that although money is in use the exchange of goods is only formally different from barter, and money introduces no complications of its own; that the limit of demand is production, and the limit of production is the volume of available capital.[3]

[2] *Principles of Political Economy*, p. 558.
[3] *Theorien über den Mehrwert*, II, no. 2, pp. 267, 309, 296, 275–278, 292, 311, 299.

But, Marx insists, the picture of capitalism is considerably more complicated. The overshadowing aim of capitalism is exploitation of labor, exchange of commodities, and accumulation of capital. The congruity which Ricardo postulates between producers and consumers does not exist. The laboring masses produce vastly more than they consume, and conversely, the landlords and all owners of capital consume but do not produce. There is no validity, Marx asserts, to the possible retort that employers merely represent the workers when obtaining capital; that, in other words, in a society without employers the laborers themselves would have to procure capital, even as the capitalists do now. There is a fundamental difference, he insists. The laborers, in the society referred to, would be interested in recovering only wages, materials, and fixed capital, whereas the capitalists, under the driving objective of surplus-value, will seek much more; there the trouble lies.[4]

Equally fallacious, in Marx's view, are the reduction of capitalist exchange to barter, the equation between purchase and sale, and the identification of supply and demand. Money is not a neutral medium, but an instrument which splits exchange into two acts independent of one another spatially and temporally. Such a split is impossible only under barter, where producing is selling, and selling is buying. Under capitalism there is the far-reaching separation between producing and selling, on the one hand, and the reconversion of the money receipts into new materials of production, on the other hand. If, because of inadequate profits, the capitalist holds on to his money instead of spending it on labor and materials, the circulation process $M–C–M^1$ is disrupted, production is curtailed, and a crisis may set in. In his neglect to consider this possible separation, Ricardo abstracts outright, Marx urges, the essentials of crises. Furthermore, the circulation of capital, $M–C–M^1$, is a process stretching over a long period of time, during which disintegrating changes may occur in the market, in the productivity of labor, and in the value of goods. We deal,

[4] *Theorien über den Mehrwert*, II, no. 2, pp. 263–264, 296–299.

Marx says, with equating the value of goods in one period with their value in a later period, and before the circulation of capital is completed disturbances can accumulate. The essentials of a crisis can be hatched in the circulation process, in the attempt to realize value or surplus-value.[5]

### THE UNDERCONSUMPTION THEORY

To Marx, overproduction has no relation to the notion of the satiation of wants. He quotes Ricardo's argument that general overproduction is impossible since human wants are unlimited, and comments: "Can there be more childish reasoning?" Should overproduction emerge only after all wants have been gratified there would never be partial or general overproduction, for even during a glut there is not enough "to satisfy the wants of the great mass decently and humanely."[6] Nor is it adequate for Ricardo to advise that all that a person in need of goods has to do is to produce something and thereby supply the means of procuring, by exchange, the articles needed. The very commodities which are overproduced, Marx replies, had been produced by the laboring masses, and are needed by them; and yet they have not the means of paying for what they need.[7]

Overproduction, to Marx, is related to remunerative prices. There is no reason, he says, why all commodities, except money, cannot be overproduced and depressed in price below the "price of production." The need of conversion into money may confront all commodities, and there may be obstacles in the way of achieving this conversion without losses. Back of Ricardo's reasoning is the identity of supply and demand. But in a given situation, says Marx, the supply may exceed the demand in the sense that the demand for the universal commodity, money, may be more intense than the demand for goods, and the urgency to transform commodities into money

[5] *Theorien über den Mehrwert*, II, no. 2, pp. 274–286, 264–267, 316. See the important statement embodying these ideas in *Capital*, I, 127–128.
[6] *Capital*, III, 302.
[7] *Theorien über den Mehrwert*, II, no. 2, pp. 293–295.

may be acute.[8] At low prices, during a slump, the market could indeed absorb all the commodities available for sale, but the prices would be "ruining prices," short of the "price of production" which prevailed at the peak of prosperity when the goods were produced. At such low prices there is a destruction of the value of capital, business men cannot meet obligations, surplus-value lies idle as money in the bank, and accumulation, and even replacement, of capital may contract.[9]

Marx points to the narrowness of the consumption market as the fundamental cause of overproduction. In *Theorien über den Mehrwert* he specifically raises the question of what starts overproduction in the first place, and proceeds to the answer in a section with the suggestive title, "The expansion of production and the expansion of the market." [10] The argument runs as follows. Production is constantly mounting in volume as the productive forces grow and as the accumulations of surplus-value provide new capital. The widened stream of goods needs a widened market, "but the market grows slowly." In the cycle which the reproduction of capital runs ("spiral" is a better term, Marx observes) a moment arrives when the market becomes too narrow for production. Admit, says Marx, that the domestic and foreign market is limited, and you admit overproduction — the market is overtaken by production.

Ricardo, Marx continues, denies the necessity of expanding the market to meet the rising tide of capital and production, holding that all capital, no matter what its size, can be profitably employed at home (provided wages do not rise); and he, Ricardo, argues against Adam Smith who maintains that

[8] A general fall in prices, precipitated by a universal rise in the production of commodities while the volume of money is held constant, was immaterial to classical economists. They were interested in relative values, and the exchange of commodities for one another would not be deranged, they thought, when all prices decline proportionately. It is interesting, however, to note J. S. Mill's statement: "Besides, money is a commodity; and if all commodities are supposed to be doubled in quantity, we must suppose money to be doubled too, and then prices would no more fall than values would" (*Principles of Political Economy*, p. 558).

[9] Marx, *Theorien über den Mehrwert*, II, no. 2, pp. 292–293, 266, 268, 288. Cf. *Capital*, II, 87.

[10] Vol. II, no. 2, pp. 304ff.

foreign trade is an indication that the country is overstocked with capital. For once it is evident that Marx favors Smith against Ricardo.

Then we come upon the following interesting pronouncement.[11] In ancient slavery the mass of producers were limited to subsistence, and yet overproduction was unknown on account of the double fact that the productive forces did not develop considerably, and the surplus product was not transformed into capital clamoring for profits, but was used up in public consumption in the form of art and buildings. There was no overproduction because there was public "overconsumption." One recalls J. M. Keynes's reference to the Egyptian pyramids.[12] In modern times, however, steadily rising production is compelled to yield profits on the enormous accumulations of capital, in face of a distribution of wealth which confines the masses to sheer necessities. Overproduction is the inevitable result.

In the same work he opens the discussion of crises with the section titled *Krisenursachen*, and forthwith announces that the whole process of accumulation is resolved in overproduction, preparing an immanent basis of crises, and that the measure of this overproduction is capital and the capitalist's drive for wealth (an obvious overstatement even within Marx's framework). He closes his lengthy exposition of crises on a similar note, and with evident emphasis on limited markets and limited consumption.[13] The narrowness of the consumption market is also stressed in the other place in which Marx

---

[11] *Theorien über den Mehrwert*, II, no. 2, p. 310.

[12] *General Theory of Employment, Interest, and Money*, pp. 131, 220.

[13] *Theorien über den Mehrwert*, II, no. 2, p. 263. On p. 318, *ibid.*, the conclusion reads as follows: "Overproduction has specifically for its condition the general law of the production of capital — to produce according to the mass of productive forces, that is, *according to the possibility to exploit with a given mass of capital the greatest possible mass of labor, without considering the existing limits of the market*, of needs paid for; all this proceeds by continual extension of reproduction and accumulation, by the constant retransformation of revenue into capital, while on the other side the mass of producers remains restricted — and on the basis of the capitalist system of production must remain restricted — to an average quantum of wants." Italics not in the original.

See two other important statements in the same work, I, 377–379, and III, 55.

discusses crises at some length, in Chapter XV, *Capital*, volume III; although, as we shall see, other views are voiced there as well. Early in this chapter (pages 286–287), we find the following declaration:

As soon as the available quantity of surplus-value has been materialized in commodities, surplus-value has been produced. But this production of surplus-value is but the first act of the capitalist process of production. . . Now comes the second act of the process. The entire mass of commodities, the total product . . . must be sold. *The conditions of direct exploitation and those of the realization of surplus-value are not identical. They are separated logically as well as by time and space. The first are only limited by the productive power of society, the last by the proportional relations of the various lines of production and by the consuming power of society.* This last-named power is not determined either *by the absolute productive power* nor by the absolute consuming power, but by the consuming power based on antagonistic conditions of distribution, which reduce the consumption of the great mass of the population to a variable minimum within more or less narrow limits. The consuming power is furthermore restricted by the tendency to accumulate, the greed for an expansion of capital and a production of surplus-value on an enlarged scale. . . The market must, therefore, be continually extended. . . *But to the extent that the productive power develops, it finds itself at variance with the narrow basis on which the conditions of consumption rest.* (Italics mine.)

Marx ends this chapter with a summary of three important earmarks of latter-day capitalism. Commenting on the "creation of the world market" as one of them, he declares: "the stupendous productive power . . . and the increase . . . of capital values . . . contradict the basis, which, compared to the expanding wealth, is ever narrowing. . . This is the cause of crises." The "basis" is the consumption market.[14]

This defiance of the principle of traditional economics concerning the equivalence of production and consumption (plus investment), and the emphasis on limited consumption facing larger production as a fatal malady of capitalism, Marx repeats in all its variations. Consumption lags behind production; production is not commensurate with the limited consumption, but keeps pace with the expansion of capital; production does

[14] It is significant to add that in *Capital*, II, 363n., Engels cites some notes jotted down by Marx for further elaboration, which, clearly, deal with underconsumption as a disruptive "contradiction" of capitalism.

not heed the limits of the market; capitalism requires an ever-widening market; there is a contradiction between mounting production and restricted consumption; the realization of surplus-value is frustrated by inadequate consumption and requires extended markets; the expansion of capital meets a barrier in limited consumption and narrow markets.[15]

As one would expect, Engels has similar ideas, and one reference will suffice. In his preface of 1886 to the first volume of *Capital* he predicts (page 31) that the "decennial cycle" will finally give place, in England, to a chronic depression and a period of disintegration. The industrial system of England, he continues, impossible without a constant "extension of production and therefore of markets," is suffering everywhere severe checks because of foreign competition. "While the productive power increases in a geometric ratio, the extension of markets proceeds at best in an arithmetic ratio," rendering the final crisis (that is, the breakdown of capitalism) inevitable.

It is not difficult to see the picture which Marx seems to have in mind. The masses live on a customary subsistence level which rises somewhat only in prosperity.[16] If, on account of improvements, the goods meant for consumption by the proletariat decline in price, the money wage is generally lowered.[17] Real wages vary cyclically within narrow limits, and trace in their variations a declining trend. Further, the standard of consumption of the capitalists, although rising with their wealth, is not high enough to absorb a considerable part of their income; the apotheosis of their ambition is accumulation.[18] As additional capital is accumulated out of surplus-value, throwing on the market larger and larger volumes of consumption goods, the problem accordingly arises: to whom to sell

[15] E.g., Marx and Engels, *Communist Manifesto*; Marx, *Capital*, II, 363n.; III, 278, 286, 293, 301, 568; *Theorien über den Mehrwert*, II, no. 2, pp. 301, 304–305.

[16] ". . . the majority of the people, the laboring population, can extend their consumption only within very narrow limits" (*Theorien über den Mehrwert*, II, no. 2, p. 263).

[17] *Capital*, III, 999.

[18] The "phrase that there is too much capital means nothing but that too little is consumed as revenue" by the capitalists bent on accumulation (*Theorien über den Mehrwert*, II, no. 2, p. 318).

these goods, and at a profit? Surplus-value, the symbol of the basic maldistribution of income in our society, is the villain of the piece. It epitomizes alike the restricted real wages of the masses and the swollen incomes of the few, used mainly for investment; it stands guard over the key contradiction between the great capacity to produce and the small capacity to consume. In order to be consumers, Marx teaches, the laborers must function as overproducers: to produce their livelihood, they are forced to produce surplus-value, out of which issues the glut-producing capital.[19] To put it differently, the restricted consumption of society entails a limited demand for capital goods to produce consumption goods; the large output of capital goods, made potential by the rising volumes of surplus-value, far outruns the demand for constant capital arising from the limited output of consumption goods industries.

The picture is scarcely different to those who refuse to see in Marx the idea of increasing *physical* misery. They perceive that, to Marx, surplus-value rises at a faster rate than wages. They present then the theorem that, parallel to surplus-value, the investment and capital equipment and therefore the output of consumption goods rise at a faster rate than the rate of growth of the demand for consumption goods.[20] There is thus inadequate purchasing power available to buy the rising volumes of consumer goods at profitable prices. In either interpretation of increasing misery, a glut develops, investment becomes unprofitable, and a crisis arrives.

Defined and analyzed in a certain way, an underconsumption theory may have validity, and the blanket dismissal of all underconsumption theory is hardly justified. The problem of underconsumption is very intricate, and it refuses to be liquidated by the simple propositions of J. B. Say's law. Marx's underconsumption theory, however, is too elementary and incomplete. First, it ignores the rôle of interest in this problem, and it does not succeed in adequately establishing the interconnections among such important elements as income, con-

[19] *Theorien über den Mehrwert*, II, no. 2, p. 299.
[20] P. M. Sweezy, *Theory of Capitalist Development*, pp. 182, 187.

sumption, saving, investment, the rate of interest, and profit. Nowhere, for instance, can one discern in Marx the recognition of the significance of the relationship and discrepancies between saving and investment. Second, Marx does not clarify how and why purchasing power is hoarded, or shrinks, or fails to be paid out to the factors of production. Objecting to J. B. Say's law, he merely states that sales proceeds may be kept idle instead of being used immediately for purchases. In volume II of *Capital*, as we shall see, he talks of an accumulation of money, temporarily held idle before an amount is gathered sufficient·for replacement of or for additions to capital goods; and there he points to disproportionality as the cause of crises, and not to production outrunning total (effective) demand. Third, by positing limited consumption of laborers and capitalists alike, of the former because of subsistence wages and of the latter because of the greed for wealth and the imperative of competition to accumulate and invest, he reduces a problem of complex functions to one in arithmetic, simple and unrealistic.[21] And there are other inadequacies.[22] It is to be remembered, of course, that the second and third volumes of *Capital* do not represent the finished elaborations of Marx's ideas, but the incomplete and unorganized posthumous notes edited by Engels.

The underconsumption theory, to repeat, seems to occupy a prominent place in Marx's treatment of crises, although not to the exclusion of other theories. But aid and comfort are not withheld from those inclined to tone down such a theory in him. We find Marx giving as strong an endorsement of this theory as the following: "The last cause of all real crises always remains the poverty and restricted consumption of the masses as compared to the tendency of capitalist production to develop the productive forces in such a way that only the absolute power of consumption of the entire society would be

[21] For profounder issues involved, see the masterful article by O. R. Lange, "The Rate of Interest and the Optimum Propensity to Consume," in G. Haberler, ed., *Readings in Business Cycle Theory*.

[22] See, for example, Mrs. Joan Robinson, *Essay on Marxian Economics*, pp. 59–60, 113–114.

their limit." [23] But he also makes this impressive pronouncement:

It is pure tautology to say that crises are caused by the scarcity of solvent consumers. . . But if one were to attempt to clothe this tautology with a semblance of a profounder justification by saying that the working class receive too small a portion of their own product, and the evil would be remedied by giving them a larger share of it, or raising their wages, we should reply that crises are precisely always preceded by a period in which wages rise generally and the working class actually get a larger share of the annual product intended for consumption.

And he (or is it Engels?) adds in the footnote: "Advocates of the theory of crises of Rodbertus are requested to make a note of this." [24] One may suggest that Marx does not mean to repudiate here the underconsumption theory as he conceives it. Even if wages rise in prosperity, underconsumption is, in his opinion, certain to emerge as long as there is surplus-value beyond replacement of capital and the consumption of the capitalists and their "hangers-on." But we cannot be sure.

Engels does not lag behind Marx in contradictions on this question. He argues against Dühring's underconsumption theory of crises, urging that overproduction, the variable (because it is only a modern phenomenon), is the cause, and not underconsumption, known through the ages and therefore a constant. "The underconsumption of the masses is therefore also a necessary condition of crises, and plays in them a rôle which has long been recognized; but it tells us just as little why crises exist today as why they did not exist at earlier periods." [25] Yet in the same work he states that "large-scale industry, which hunts all over the world for new consumers, restricts the consumption of the masses at home to a starvation minimum and thereby undermines its own internal market." [26] This statement is similar to the wording of the underconsumption theory used at times by Marx; it is also close to Sismondi's phrasing of it in a quotation from him given by Engels.[27] Of

[23] *Capital*, III, 568. Cf. p. 303.
[24] *Capital*, II, 475–476.
[25] *Anti-Dühring*, p. 312.
[26] *Anti-Dühring*, p. 300.
[27] See Marx, *Capital*, II, 26n.

the same cast is a pronouncement made by Engels years later: "This overproduction [meaning underconsumption] engendering either periodical gluts and revulsions, accompanied by panic, or else a chronic stagnation of trade. . ." [28]

## BUSINESS REVIVAL

The underconsumption theory, or either of the two other theories, attempts to explain why a depression occurs. But there is also in Marx a brief account of the circumstances which induce a revival. There are three factors which tend to nurse a depression into a gradual upturn of activity. First, there is the depreciation of capital. During the slump, on account of the low yields, a large capital earns as little as a small capital normally does, and to all intents and purposes a large equipment is equivalent to a small one. The capitalized value of fixed capital and of the corresponding securities alike is lowered and the denominator in $\frac{s}{c+v}$ with it. We recognize here one of the influences which Marx enumerates, in another connection, as counteracting the tendency of the rate of profit to fall.

Second, labor becomes submissive to drastic wage cuts, and for two reasons. One, labor is suffering from unemployment. Two, during prosperity marriages among laborers multiply and infant mortality is lessened; and while the working force is not increased thereby, the effect, says Marx, is the same as if "the numbers of the actually working laborers has increased." The result is lower wages ($v$) and higher surplus-value ($s$). Third, the low level of prices and the intensified competition provoked by dull trade compel the capitalists to introduce improvements in the attempt to depress costs below the "social value" of the goods in the market. Under these three stimuli profitable business is gradually restored, and production livens up with rising momentum, ready for another sequence of "average activity,

[28] Introduction to Marx's *Free Trade*, reprinted as an appendix to *Poverty of Philosophy*, p. 192.

production at high pressure, crisis and stagnation," to use Marx's own phases of the business cycle (see *Capital*, I, 694).[29] "The industrial cycle," says Marx, "is of such a character that the same cycle must periodically reproduce itself once that the first impulse has been given." [30]

## THE FALLING RATE OF PROFIT THEORY

A second theory of crises, urged by some as the only one that Marx intends to offer, is centered on the "law of the falling tendency of the rate of profit," discussed in the foregoing chapter. The gist is, we recall, that, coördinated with the poverty of the masses, is the excessive flow of surplus-value, which fosters the overaccumulation of capital; that concurrently and interacting with accumulation go improvements, concentration, and centralization; that these latter aspects of the dynamics of capitalism find their common focus in the increased productivity of labor, in the steady rise of constant over variable capital, and in a relative overpopulation; and that despite counteracting influences, all this adds up to a tendency for the rate of profit to decline.

Surplus-value is the villain here too. Overproduction of commodities and overproduction of capital are the two sides of the same coin: less consumption, more accumulation. Overproduction of capital does not mean an excess of means of production beyond the requirements of full employment. As usual, it is a matter of profits. There is overproduction of capital when profit falls below "a certain rate," when the mass of profit is insufficient to permit the growth of capital.[31] The decline in the rate of profit "promotes overproduction, speculation, crises"; "calls forth disturbances and stagnations in the process of capitalist production, crises." [32]

But a slow trend of a declining scale of profit can hardly be expected to induce *cyclical* disturbances. Marx associates falling profit rates and crises, but he does not seem to indicate

---

[29] *Capital*, III, 296–299.
[30] *Capital*, III, 574.
[31] *Capital*, III, 302–303, 299–300.
[32] *Capital*, III, 283, 300.

how the trend and the cyclical fluctuation are causally connected. What seems to be in his mind is the idea that this drop in the scale of profit is charged with stresses and contradictions which, in their turn, precipitate *periodical* slumps. Each slump then runs its course, breeding the elements of a revival and a new upsurge of accumulation, with a repetition of the stresses and the resurgence of the crisis. It is in such a context that Marx declares: "Periodically the conflict of antagonistic agencies seeks vent in crises. The crises are always but momentary and forcible solutions of the existing contradictions, violent eruptions which restore the disturbed equilibrium for a while." [33]

What the contradictions specifically relevant to this question are is not clear. Obviously, if he lets the falling rate of profit symbolize, or be intimately connected with, the *general* "contradictions" characteristic of capitalism, the law of the falling profit scale cannot be regarded as a theory of crises, inasmuch as it does not reveal a specific cause of crises. What we seek is a set of contradictions organically and uniquely related to this law of falling profits and producing cyclical fluctuations. Perhaps Marx means to suggest them on pages 290–293 in the troublesome Chapter XV of *Capital*, volume III. Perhaps he has them in mind on page 303, the same chapter, where he says that the "barrier" of capitalist production rests on the fact that "the development of the productive power of labor creates in the falling rate of profit a law which turns into an antagonism of this mode of production at a certain point and requires for its defeat periodical crises." It is to be observed, however, that in this Chapter XV underconsumption, too, is represented as underlying the contradictions repeatedly referred to in it.[34] We are in the dark. Chapter XV is a potpourri of obscure and incomplete although suggestive notes which Engels, the editor, put together into a chapter.

In view of modern developments of cycle theory, one is

---

[33] *Capital*, III, 292.

[34] Underconsumption theory appears often in this chapter; see pp. 286–287, 293, 301, 302, 303, 312–313.

tempted to unite Marx's underconsumption theory and his law of the falling rate of profit into a modern pattern. The synthesis may run as follows. The limited consumption of the population and, therefore, the consumption goods industries, do not make an adequate contribution to employment. If there is to be full employment, investment, or the capital goods industries, must compensate for the inadequacy of the consumption goods industries. But the capital goods industries are equally inadequate because the declining marginal efficiency of capital (which may be urged merely as a modern version of Marx's declining profit rate), in face of the current interest rate, is insufficient to give a desired return on marginal investments. Such investments are therefore not made. The result is a deficiency in effective demand, and unemployment. The result is that, roughly, Marx had Keynes's doctrine before Keynes was born.

There is no evidence that Marx attempted a synthesis of this sort and little evidence that he prepared the ingredients for it. First, as was seen in the preceding chapter, the law of the falling rate of profit is analytically defective, and if there is such a phenomenon as a declining trend in the rate of profit, Marx fails to account for it. Second, even if we ignore this objection, the question comes up why the falling rate of profit is a barrier to investment. Marx talks about a "certain rate" as the minimum, but does not tell us what the minimum must be and why. In the Keynesian scheme, the interest rate is determined by specific factors, and investment will not proceed in spheres where the marginal efficiency of capital does not exceed the prevailing rate of interest. But Marx does not touch on determinants of the rate of interest; he regards it as an accidental and wayward category inconceivable under communism (see below, Chapter XIV). Nor does he oppose interest and profit; that is, he does not regard interest, in connection with his law of the falling profit rate, as eating into profits. On the contrary, in this law profit stands collectively for all the shares of distribution aside from wages: it includes interest. Marx, moreover, specifically indicates that a consideration of the constituents of profit in relation to the law is of no consequence.[35] This is not to deny affinity between Marx and Keynes. Those familiar with the work of both will notice that in several important respects their thoughts run in parallel lines, although the analytical distance between the parallel lines is great. A further discussion of the two men appears below in Chapter XIX, section on Marx and Keynes.

Recently two economists drew attention to a variant of the falling profits theory of crises, found specifically in Chapter XXV of the first volume of *Capital* and on certain pages of Chapter XV of the third volume.[36] The theory is brief and simple. In prosperity the demand for labor rises, the reserve army is gradually depleted, and wages mount to such a degree that profits sink and the incentive to production is smothered. A crisis results; in the ensuing depression the reserve army accumulates once more, and the consequent low wages, together with other favorable factors already mentioned in the section of business revival,[37] restore profits and prosperity. It is essentially a changes-in-cost theory.

The imputation of such a theory of crises to Marx rests on uncertain ground. In Chapter XXV of the first volume of *Capital* he takes up the rise in wages occasioned by accumulation, but he says that the rise may not interfere with the progress of accumulation. If it does interfere, accumulation "slackens" because of the fall in gains; the very slackening of accumulation lowers, as a matter of course, the demand for labor, and wages fall, uneventfully redressing the balance. "The mechanism of the process of capitalist production removes the very obstacle that it temporarily creates." There is no mention of crises; Marx's language is in the vein of the usual up-and-down temporary adjustments. "The very nature of

---

[35] *Capital*, III, 284–285. To Marx, in Mrs. Joan Robinson's words, "the rate of interest plays no part either in governing the capital structure or in influencing the inducement to invest" ("Marx on Unemployment," *Economic Journal*, LI, June–September, 1941, 237).

[36] Robinson, "Marx on Unemployment," *Economic Journal*, LI (June–September, 1941), p. 238. Sweezy, *Theory of Capitalist Development*, pp. 149ff.

[37] See above, p. 244.

accumulation," he repeats, "excludes . . . every rise in the price of labor which could seriously imperil" progressive accumulation.[38] Later in the same chapter, when discussing the idle reserve army, the synonym, to be emphasized, of chronic unemployment, he stresses that in prosperity the frantic ventures of the freshly accumulated capitals need idle labor to draw upon without impinging on the labor already in exploitation. He comments that the "decennial cycle," characteristic of modern industry, "depends on the constant formation, the greater or less absorption, and the reformation of the industrial reserve army" (page 694). Finally, when touching on the cyclical aspects of wages, he mentions that their movement is regulated by the expansion and contraction of the reserve army, "and these again correspond to the periodic changes of the industrial cycle" (page 699). There is no declaration on these pages that in prosperity rising wages devour profits and precipitate a crisis.

An advance in wages may come at the height of the cycle because capitalists are bidding for labor, and/or because labor, through trade-unions or in other ways, contend for higher pay. As to the first possibility, the presence of the industrial reserve army prevents wages from rising to a considerable height. Marx talks of the "greater or less absorption" of the idle reserve during prosperity (page 694): the industrial reserve army is not completely absorbed, it stands for a chronic trend of unemployment and not for idleness only in depressions. As to the second possibility, Marx indicates that in a boom the industrial reserve army "holds its [employed labor's] pretensions in check" (page 701), and that in "conflicts as to the rate of wages. . . Adam Smith has already shown that . . . taken on the whole, the master is always master" (page 678). Throughout the cycle, Marx tells us, the reserve army of the idle confines the operation of the law of supply and demand for labor "within limits absolutely convenient to exploitation and domination by capital," and "completes the despotism of capital"

[38] *Capital*, I, 678–680.

(pages 701, 702). It is hard to see such a theory of crises in Chapter XXV.

As far as Chapter XV of the third volume of *Capital* is concerned, only page 295 seems to be of specific relevance. The succeeding few pages, 296–299, to which Mrs. Joan Robinson and Dr. Sweezy refer, describe the course of the depression and the circumstances occasioning a revival. There is no reason to assume that this description of depression and revival applies only to one particular theory as to what causes the antecedent crisis, and not to his other theories as well. On page 295 Marx does talk of wages eating drastically into profits, but he avowedly does not talk of realities. He states that in order to clarify the concept of overproduction of capital, he assumes "absolute" overproduction (page 294), and he refers to this assumption as one "under the extreme conditions" (page 299). It is not his typical case of overproduction of capital. The typical case involves an increase in the productivity of capital, and he returns to it on page 300. By this unusual "absolute" overproduction of capital, he means that in prosperity climbing wages depress profits to such a low level that in every industry the total capital, enlarged by accumulation, earns no greater volume of profits than did the smaller capital previously at the higher rate of profit (page 295). In modern phraseology, the marginal revenue is zero.[39]

It is, of course, not intended here to deny that rising wages during an upswing sooner or later contribute to falling profits. The issue is whether Marx offers a theory that rising wages cause a crisis. Such a theory, it may be added, does not square with Marx's emphasis, repeated times without number, on the weakness of labor when facing the power of capital, and with his teaching that labor legislation or the success of trade-union strategy is fundamentally the measure of concession and tolerance which the capitalists think they can afford. Indeed, to

[39] Marx does not realize that this may or may not be so. It depends on the elasticity of the curve representing amounts of capital ($x$) and corresponding rates of profit ($y$). Only if the elasticity is consistently either unity or less than unity will the total profit on a large capital not exceed the total profit on a small capital.

assume that labor has the power to force wages which would
threaten profits, or that the demand for labor, in a context of
more or less chronic unemployment, can achieve the same end,
is to assume that periodically there is a sort of exploitation in
reverse, of capital by labor. Dr. Sweezy wonders why writers
on Marxian economics have neglected this theory.[40] It seems
that there is legitimate doubt that such a theory of crises appears in Marx.

Perhaps it is worth noting that this theory of crises has little
to sustain it, as Mrs. Joan Robinson indicates.[41] To put it
simply, when profits fall because wages rise, there is merely
a transfer of purchasing power from the capitalists, who would
invest it, to the laboring masses, who would spend it on consumer goods. The rise of activity in the consumer goods industries and the capital goods industries back of them will compensate for the lower *rate* of profit and for the diminished
activity in investment. There is no "destruction" of purchasing
power and no drop in the effective demand. There is no reason
for a slump in total employment. It is of more than passing
interest to note that Marx is quite familiar with this elementary
kind of analysis, and this he amply demonstrates in connection
with another problem.[42] However, his familiarity with the
analysis which can invalidate such a theory of crises is not to be
urged as conclusive evidence that he could not possibly have
sponsored it. Marx is not distinguished for his consistency,
and often he knew better than he builded.

### THE DISPROPORTIONALITY THEORY

This theory is concerned with the maladjustments and disproportionalities traced to the anarchy of competition; to the
blundering, incoördinated moves of multitudes of individual
capitalists; to the complexities of the many elements which
must fit into each other in an enormously complex world, and
which will do so by sheer accident if not by planned design;

[40] *Theory of Capitalist Development*, p. 149.
[41] "Marx on Unemployment," *Economic Journal*, LI (June–September, 1941),
238.
[42] See *Capital*, II, 391.

and to the vagaries of wind and weather. To what extent Marx means to stress this theory it is hard to tell, for as often as not he weaves it into the pattern of his other two theories of crises. The evidence is as follows.

Marx refers to the familiar contention that general overproduction has no validity on the ground that it merely signifies a growth of prosperity, with all fields of production maintaining the proper relation to each other. To him this is sophistry. The insistence that there is no overproduction when there is concerted expansion in all industries predicates, he argues, that all industries experience simultaneously and to the right degree the growth of division of labor, of machinery, of markets, and of mass production; and that all countries dealing with each other continue properly to complement each other. But, he insists, there is overproduction precisely because all these pious wishes are not realities. The assumption of coördination comes from the false identification of capitalism with the planned production of socialism. "This fiction stems chiefly from the inability to see the specific form of bourgeois production." Under capitalism, coördination of production is not brought about by the smooth effect of conscious social effort, but is periodically enforced by the "blind laws" which burst into the violent expression of a crisis.[43]

This argument against the assumption of proportionality Marx does not need to sustain his theory of underconsumption, grounded as it is on the nature of capitalist distribution of income and restricted consumption. His introduction, in this connection, of the idea of disproportion suggests that it is of some importance in his mind. At times he gives it greater prominence, as when he stresses the effects of weather and variability of crops. An overproduction of cotton and the consequent slump in the cotton industry will set in motion a complex of disturbances. It will injure the cotton planters, the spinning and weaving concerns, the manufacturers of spindles, the coal and iron industries, and many other enterprises. The revenue in these fields will diminish, their demand for goods will de-

[43] *Theorien über den Mehrwert*, II, no. 2, pp. 312, 315, 311; *Capital*, III, 301.

cline, and in many a sphere prices will drop. Overproduction in a leading industry thus proliferates into general overproduction, with crises as the sequel.[44]

Equally disturbing is a crop shortage. The consequent rise in the prices of raw materials necessitates larger expenditures on constant capital, leaving less for variable capital, or wages. Too, when there is less material to be worked up, fixed capital and labor alike will in part be forced into idleness. The rate of profit will tend to fall: in general the rate of profit, $\dfrac{s}{c+v}$, varies, according to Marx, inversely with the fluctuation in the prices of raw materials, since the constant capital ($c$) is directly affected by this fluctuation. Finally, the reproduction of capital is disturbed in this case by the effect on consumer goods. High prices of raw materials cause the prices of consumer goods to advance. If these goods are commonly used by labor alone, there is a distortion in the apportionment of variable capital; if they are destined for general consumption, sales will decline because of the high prices, and eventually prices will be forced down. "Violent fluctuations of price therefore cause interruptions, great collisions, or even catastrophes in the process of reproduction. It is especially the products of agriculture, raw materials . . . which are subject to such fluctuations of value in consequence of changing yields." [45] "As Tooke remarked, weather plays an important part in modern industry." [46]

Disproportionality is of significance in intensifying the malady of the overaccumulation of capital. With the growing formation of capital the demand for the constituent materials rises, and their prices and the price of capital goods are alike advanced. The overproduction of machinery emphasizes in this manner a relative underproduction of raw materials, and the rise in prices contributes to the disruption of the price

[44] *Theorien über den Mehrwert*, II, no. 2, pp. 284, 302–303.

[45] *Capital*, III, 140.

[46] *Theorien über den Mehrwert*, II, no. 2, pp. 290–291, 316; *Capital*, III, 125–127, 305.

structure and of the reproduction of capital, aggravating the reactions and convulsions. Furthermore, the higher price of capital reflects, Marx indicates, a lower rate of interest, and a lower rate of interest encourages daring and speculative undertakings.[47]

There is, finally, some emphasis on maladjustment in the notable last two chapters, perhaps the most original in Marx's economics, of the second volume of *Capital*, where he elaborates on the law of the reproduction of capital, and where there is frequent occurrence of the suggestive phrases "equality," "balance," "proportionality," and "dovetailing." [48] It is to be kept in mind, however, that the involved argument in these chapters does not stress proportionality as the sole factor, but combines it with hoarding, overproduction, and other phenomena into a complex whole.

The theme is intricate, and only a few ideas will be traced here. Marx assumes first simple reproduction (where all surplus-value is consumed as income, and net investment is zero), and divides production into departments I and II, producing production goods and consumption goods respectively. The value (in labor-time) of the goods produced in each department is as usual, $c + v + s$, where $c$ stands for depreciation and used-up materials.[49] The output of department I is used only for replacement of capital; the output of department II represents the consumption of the whole society.

If the exchange of goods between these two departments is to be in equilibrium, certain conditions must be fulfilled. Thus $Ic$ (the constant capital of department I) is needed to replace itself as worn-out capital, by exchange with producers in this department; and only production goods equivalent to $I(v + s)$ are available for exchange with II. In II, $v + s$ is consumed, and only the consumption goods represented by $IIc$ are available for exchange with I. It follows that, in equilibrium, $IIc = I(v + s)$. This is the first condition of equilibrium.

[47] *Theorien über den Mehrwert*, II, no. 2, p. 266; *Capital*, III, 141.
[48] E.g., pp. 529, 432, 546, 577, 578, 579.
[49] *Capital*, II, 459–460.

If $IIc < I(v + s)$, there is overproduction of capital goods, and the "surplus would remain unused." If $IIc > I(v + s)$, there is overproduction of consumption goods, and "it would be impossible for II to reproduce its entire constant capital." In either case there is the possibility of crises.[50]

Equilibrium is not assured, however, even if $IIc = I(v + s)$. Part of $IIc$ represents fixed capital which wears out gradually over a period longer than one year. Accordingly part of the money received from the sale of goods reflected in $IIc$ is kept as a hoard and spent eventually in a lump sum in the purchase of new capital from I. While this money is hoarded as a depreciation reserve it fails to sustain the demand for $I(v + s)$. Hence another condition of equilibrium: the money value of the new fixed capital purchased with the accumulated hoards, or section 1 of $IIc$, is to coincide annually with the money hoards set aside against the depreciation of the old fixed capital, or section 2 of $IIc$. Marx is more than skeptical that these two conditions of equilibrium can be fulfilled, demanding as they do, among other things, the preservation of subtle proportionalities in a system of haphazard production. He observes that ". . . disproportion can and must arise even on the assumption of an ideal and normal production on the basis of a simple reproduction of the already existing capital of society."[51] If section 1 of $IIc$ is greater than section 2 of $IIc$, there is a surplus of money which is not converted into commodities; if smaller, there is a deficit of money and a surplus of goods. Imports of foreign goods will be necessary in the first case, and exports will be necessary in the second case. But, Marx observes, foreign trade does not remove the "contradictions" and only transfers them "to a wider sphere." Either case would present no difficulty in a socialist society, but under capitalism the imbalance aggravates the "anarchy," and causes crises.[52]

The possibilities of crises are multiplied when the assump-

---

[50] *Capital*, II, 465, 472, 578, 587, 608; III, 975.
[51] *Capital*, II, 546–547.
[52] *Capital*, II, 524, 528, 534, 541, 542–547.

tion of simple reproduction is dropped and the actual condition of capitalism, accumulation (signifying that part of the surplus-value turned into additional capital), is taken into consideration. Now part of I$s$ and II$s$ is saved, and I($v + s$) exceeds II$c$ by an amount equivalent to that part of II$s$ which is invested. Now more hoarding is involved, since the saved part of surplus-value is kept idle before the accumulation is adequate for the expansion of operations; now there are more one-sided transactions — sales without compensating purchases and purchases with hoarded money; and there is more opportunity for overproduction. If these one-sided purchases and sales would balance in value, no trouble needs to arise; but "balance is an accident." The reader of these pages is impressed with the variety and complexity of factors which must fit into each other if economic activity is to proceed smoothly. Marx sees many possibilities of overproduction, hampered reproduction, "abnormal movements," "abnormal deviations," a "break in the reproduction," a "great crash." [53]

In these two final chapters of *Capital*, volume II, and elsewhere, Mrs. Joan Robinson sees an explicit anticipation of the modern idea of effective demand.[54] That Marx is somewhere at the edges of this idea and that sometimes he hints directly at some of its important elements admit of little doubt. But one must read into some of his statements more than they carry, and one must put together statements scattered here and there into a pattern of propinquity and emphasis hardly intended by Marx, before the claim can be urged that he definitely foreshadowed this modern doctrine in its salient aspects. One is inclined to share the skepticism of G. F. Shove on this point, for the reasons which he offers and for other reasons.[55]

## CREDIT AND CRISES

What of the rôle of credit? Only brief, stray remarks are available, and it is hardly possible to distill from them a reliable

---

[53] *Capital*, II, 578–579, 587–589, 605.

[54] *Essay on Marxian Economics*, chap. vi.

[55] G. F. Shove, "Mrs. Robinson on Marxian Economics," *Economic Journal*, LIV (April, 1944), 47–48.

formula. Credit plays a part in the trade cycle, but it does not rank among the causal factors. Credit is a powerful lever in the centralization of capital; it promotes new enterprises, encourages speculation and reckless ventures, strains production to the utmost, accelerates overproduction, intensifies the crises, and, presumably, aids in recovery. Credit is "one of the most potent instruments of crises and swindle." Credit gives impetus to enormous undertakings like railway building which may promote booms and crises. It is to be noted parenthetically that in these references he generally uses credit in the sense of corporate securities, and only at times in the sense of commercial bank credit; more than once it is hard to tell which type of credit he has in mind.[56] In any event, he does not regard credit as a determinant of crises. "The superficiality of Political Economy," Marx teaches, "shows itself in the fact that it looks upon the expansion and contraction of credit, which is a mere symptom of the periodic changes of the industrial cycle, as their cause." [57] A crisis on the money market, he says, merely masks "abnormal conditions in the process of production and reproduction." [58]

[56] *Capital*, I, 687, 693; II, 361–363; III, 298, 359, 497, 522, 652, 713; *Theorien über den Mehrwert*, II, no. 2, p. 289.

[57] *Capital*, I, 695; III, 575–576.

[58] *Capital*, II, 365.

# CHAPTER XIII

## THE TRANSITION TO COMMUNISM

### THE DECLINE OF CAPITALISM

LIKE every other social order, capitalism experiences two phases, the expanding phase and the declining phase. During the expanding stage the productive forces flourish, progress is rapid, and the maladies, like poverty, underconsumption, the falling rate of profit, and crises, do not assume threatening proportions and do not engrave themselves in the minds of the working people, who are as yet not thoroughly class conscious. During this stage the thesis is being consolidated, and the contradictions, breeding and growing, are not yet in full vigor. But the scene changes when capitalism has reached the stage of maturity and decline, the stage which Marx and Engels see in full force already in 1848, as the *Communist Manifesto* well testifies.[1] Then the contradictions begin to play with disruptive power. Then the mode of production, solidified together with its supporting institutions and inflexible in its support of vested interests, becomes incompatible with the growing dimensions of production. At odds with the productive forces, the stuff of which it is made, the mode of production is in conflict with itself. In Marx's language, "From forms of development of the productive forces these relations [of production] turn into their fetters."[2] The barrier to capitalism is capitalism.

In parallel with such realities, the capitalist class, personifying these relations, begins to appear as the pretentious symbol of a failing system. This class benefits enormously, but offers little in return. The trustee of social wealth,[3] it controls the whole economy, the lifeblood of the community. It is allowed to amass fortunes in capital, which is labor filched from the

[1] E.g., pp. 19–20, 29.
[2] Introduction to *Critique of Political Economy*. See above, Chapter II, section on Economic Dynamics.
[3] Marx, *Capital*, II, 312.

oppressed; it is allowed to own the natural resources, which, as a gift of Nature, are the common possession of men; and it is allowed to appropriate the priceless acquisitions of science, which represent a field of social and "universal" labor.[4] It enjoys the protection of institutions and the praise and approval of respectable people. But it shows a cynical disregard of the obligations which such extravagant privileges impose. It pockets the gains of its enterprises, ravishes the natural resources, cheats on the goods it produces,[5] laughs at the laws, and deludes the people through its mouthpieces, the educators, the clergy, and the journalists.

Daily the capitalist class demonstrates its incapacity to perform the functions it assumed. "It is unfit to rule," cries the *Communist Manifesto*, "because it is incompetent to assure an existence to its slave within his slavery" (page 29). It cannot maintain an uninterrupted increase of capital and a steady development of the productive forces, and periodically it rocks the economy with convulsions and breakdowns. The "historical task and privilege" of the capitalist class is to foster the productive forces to a state in which they can serve as the elements of a higher order. Such a task it has already achieved, and it is incapable of making further use of them.[6] It is now "a class under whose leadership society is racing to ruin like a locomotive whose jammed safety-valve the driver is too weak to open." It is increasingly becoming not only a superfluity but a social impediment, and "like the nobility in the past," it is assuming

---

[4] "Once discovered, the law of the deviation of the magnetic needle in the field of an electric current, or the law of magnetization of iron, around which an electric current circulates, costs never a penny" (*Capital*, I, 422). "Such a development of the productive power is traceable in the last instance to the social nature of the labor engaged in production; to the division of labor in society; to the development of intellectual labor, especially of the natural sciences. The capitalist thus appropriates the advantages of the entire system of the division of social labor" (*ibid.*, III, 98). See also *ibid.*, III, 753–754.

[5] *Capital*, I, 556; III, 100.

[6] *Capital*, III, 304, 522. "It is one of the civilizing sides of capitalism that it enforces this surplus labor in a manner and under conditions which promote the development of productive forces, of social conditions, and the creation of elements for a new and higher formation better than did the preceding forms of slavery, serfdom, etc." (*ibid.*, 953). Cf. I, 649.

the position of a mere revenue-consuming class.[7]  A radical change must come.

It will come. But skillfully planned utopias will not bring it about. The change to a new order is an historical resultant of our present order, a cause-and-effect process like the processes of nature. Modern society moves within the vicious circle of its own contradictions; "this circle is gradually narrowing . . . the movement becomes more and more a spiral, and must come to an end, like the movement of the planets, by collision with the center."[8]  As the capitalist system contains the seeds of its own destruction, so it harbors ingredients which will go into the composition of the new system. This refers not only to the productive forces which the future society will take over but to intimations within the capitalist organization of the context into which the productive forces will be placed under socialism.

These intimations find their expression in the joint-stock company with its "social capital," social because it is supplied by multitudes of investors and because it represents a "social enterprise," and in the coöperative establishments, where "associated laborers" plan their work without benefit of the obsolescent capitalist.[9]  The coöperative movement is a good omen in the eyes of Marx. In his inaugural address to the First International in 1864, he hails this movement as a "triumph of the political economy of labor over the political economy of capital." The value, he continues, of these "great social experiments" cannot be overestimated. They demonstrate that production can proceed on a large scale and in keeping with modern science without a master class; that to produce goods, the means of production need not be monopolized as means of exploitation; and that, like slave-labor and serf-labor, wage-labor is only a temporary form "destined to disappear before associated labor, which brings to its task a willing hand, a vigorous spirit and a joyful heart."[10]

---

[7] Engels, *Anti-Dühring*, pp. 174, 183, 201.
[8] Engels, *Socialism, Utopian and Scientific*, p. 60.
[9] Marx, *Capital*, III, 516–517, 521, 712–713.
[10] *Die Inauguraladresse der internationalen Arbeiter-Association*, pp. 27–28.

The fact, however, that socialism does not come upon us like a meteor, from outside, but is generated by our own history does not imply that the event comes off by itself. There must be human agencies to take charge of its arrival, or to hasten it, in accordance with conditions. Here is where the proletarian class becomes significant. The turn has come for the capitalists to relinquish their place to the workers as the star performers in history. The worst sufferers from the present system, the proletarians become growingly convinced that capitalism has nothing to offer them and stands in the way of furthering their interests. Apparently they are not victims of "illusionism," and are not perverted by "vulgar" economics. Apparently the silent forces that create disorder in modern society and the contradictions and maladies that consume it are clear to their view. Humiliated, starved, exasperated, they acquire the conception that history entrusts them with the high mission of building the new social synthesis. They discipline and prepare themselves for the task of fulfilling the mandate of the dialectic. The means they will employ are the standard historical means, the class struggle.[11]

### The "Breakdown" of Capitalism

Ever since Engels' death incessant controversies have been waged among Marxians over the breakdown (*Zusammenbruch*) of capitalism. Issues have been raised whether the end of our order comes by revolution or reform, as a result of a severe crisis or as the end of a protracted stagnation, with underconsumption, the falling rate of profit, an imperialist war, or something else as the stimulating cause. In the main, the controversies generated more heat than light. In any event, our concern is not with Marxists but with Marx and his alter ego, Engels. On these questions the two writers do not develop an explicit and coördinated attitude, but the general position seems to be that capitalism meets its doom in a class struggle during a crisis or a prolonged depression. The two parts of this for-

[11] Marx, *Capital*, I, 836–837 and n.; *Civil War in France*, p. 80; Engels, *Anti-Dühring*, pp. 174–175.

mula, the struggle and the timing of it, will be briefly taken up in turn.

First, as to the class struggle. The question that interests the socialist and nonsocialist alike is whether by the final contest Marx means a sensational bloody battle or the dramatic climax of a course of peaceful reform compelled by the pressure of mass suffrage. The answer cannot be suggested a priori by a guiding principle. True, in Marx's thought, the dialectic process is at once the principle of social evolution and the power behind the class struggle. But the dialectic cannot inform us whether the future social synthesis will be achieved by a revolutionary cataclysm or by a peaceful transition. The dialectic permits either method. It may be presumed that the capitalist thesis is too narrow to withstand the force of the antagonistic elements pressing on it, and it bursts, suddenly and violently. Or, it may be conceived that the dialectic may not operate in a bloodthirsty manner, and that a new synthesis is wrought by the gradual amalgamation of aspects of the old thesis with aspects of the evolving antithesis.

We must turn, then, to direct evidence in Marx's utterances. We find conflicting statements with ample accommodations for each side. However, a bird's-eye view of the statements reveals a trend line with fluctuations about it. As regards the fluctuations, up to the early 1850's it seems that Marx and Engels put great stress on violence, almost giving the impression of relishing it; while from the 1860's on they begin to allow that at least in certain countries a peaceful method, the ballot, may be both available and preferable. The trend line is unmistakable: the two writers recognize revolution as an essential historical instrument, and while the prospect of bloodshed is distasteful to them, they accept it as inevitable and necessary. For this basic attitude three reasons stand out. First, they are convinced that the ruling class will not relinquish its power without a desperate struggle. Second, the building of communism demands a change of heart on a mass scale, and only in the shock of revolution can this change be wrought; only the baptismal fire of conflict can cleanse even the radical class of "all the old rubbish," and fit it "to found a new society." Third, revolution shortens the pains of transition. When the disorders of 1848 were over, Marx writes that the "fruitless butcheries" and the "sacrificial debauch" during the turmoil, and the "cannibalism" of the counterrevolution will convince people that there is only one way to shorten "the death agony of the old society and the birth pains of the new society — revolutionary terrorism."[12]

It is not necessary to catalogue all the pronouncements they make on both sides of the question, but some references in support of the conclusion of the foregoing paragraph are pertinent. In 1847 Marx concludes his *Poverty of Philosophy* as follows:

Would it, moreover, be a matter for astonishment if a society based upon the *antagonism* of classes should lead ultimately to a brutal *conflict*, to a hand-to-hand struggle as its final *dénouement?* . . . It is only in an order of things in which there will be no longer classes or class antagonism that *social evolutions* will cease to be *political revolutions*. Until then, on the eve of each general reconstruction of society, the last word of social science will ever be: "Combat or death; bloody struggle or extinction. It is thus that the question is irresistibly put." [13]

The *Communist Manifesto*, written in the first month of 1848, is full of revolutionary threats, and among its last sentences we read: the communists "openly declare that their ends can be attained only by the forcible overthrow of all existing social conditions. Let the ruling class tremble at a communistic revolution." [14] Marx talks in the same vein in his historical sketches written in 1850 and 1851.[15]

But even at this period, when bloody revolution appeared as the only expedient, they did not gloat over violence, but

[12] Marx and Engels, *Deutsche Ideologie*, p. 60; "Der Fall Wiens," in *Aus dem literarischen Nachlass von K. Marx, F. Engels*, III, 199.

[13] *Poverty of Philosophy*, pp. 190–191. Marx's italics.

[14] Marx and Engels, *Communist Manifesto*, p. 58. The *Manifesto* states that in the early phases of the development of the proletarian class the struggle is but "veiled civil war"; but ultimately the stage will be reached "where that war breaks out into open revolution, and where the violent overthrow of the bourgeoisie lays the foundation for the sway of the proletariat" (p. 28). See also p. 52.

[15] See *Klassenkämpfe in Frankreich*, p. 85, for example, and *Eighteenth Brumaire*, p. 141.

regarded it as a distasteful although unavoidable instrument. In 1847 Engels prepared a catechism of socialism. Question 16 asks whether the abolition of private property in a peaceful way is possible. The answer states: it is much desired that this were possible, and the communists would be the last ones to stand against it; they know that revolutions are not made purposely and willfully, but are the necessary consequences of circumstances independent of the will of parties and classes; they see that the development of the proletariat is violently suppressed in almost all civilized countries, and that thereby the opponents of the communists pave the way to a cataclysm; if the oppressed proletarian is finally driven to revolution, the communists will stand by him.[16]

In the later years, along with declarations favoring revolution, we begin to come upon such reservations as that there is no one prescribed instrument of effecting social change; that the means vary with the country, circumstances, and institutions; that peaceful parliamentary measures are quite possible and are indeed preferable in lands where democratic institutions prevail. In 1864 Marx praises the beneficent effects of protective labor legislation. He assures the workers that coöperative production, extended to a national scale, will finally liberate them; and in order that they may propagate the coöperative movement by "national means," and counteract the many impediments which the bourgeoisie will seek to place before them at each step, he exhorts them to conquer political power through the political organization of workers' parties.[17] In 1867 he writes that on the Continent the conflict can be brutal or humane, depending on the development of the proletariat, and that society can shorten and lessen the birth pangs.[18] At a meeting of the Congress of the International at the Hague in 1872 he says:

We know that the institutions, the manners and the customs of the various countries must be considered, and we do not deny that there are coun-

[16] *Grundsätze des Kommunismus*, p. 23.
[17] *Inauguraladresse der internationalen Arbeiter-Association*, pp. 26, 28–29.
[18] *Capital*, I, 14. In 1871 he writes to Kugelmann that on the Continent the

tries like England and America, and, if I understood your arrangements better, I might even add Holland, where the worker may attain his object [that is, "capture political power"] by peaceful means. But not in all countries is this the case.[19]

In 1891 Engels declares that in countries like the United States, France, and England, where the majority rules, and where the power is vested with the representatives chosen by the people, the old society can grow into the new in a peaceful manner.[20] In 1894 he writes as follows: as soon as the socialists come into possession of political power, they will expropriate both the industrial manufacturers and the landowners; whether the expropriation will proceed with or without compensation will depend, not on the socialists, but on circumstances; "under no conditions do we regard indemnity as inadmissible; very frequently Marx expressed to me the opinion that the cheapest way would be to buy off the whole gang."[21]

In 1895, a few months before his death, he summarizes in his introduction to Marx's *Class Struggles in France* the lessons that could be drawn from the socialist movement since 1848. He admits that Marx's and his ideas around 1848–1850 pertaining to the proletarian conflict were based largely on the examples of the French revolutions of 1789 and 1830, but that history has exposed their views as "an illusion . . . it has also completely transformed the conditions under which the proletariat has to fight."[22] First of all, it is clear, he says, that the old style of rebellion, the sudden enthusiastic onslaught on the military forces, has become obsolete; insurgents behind barricades are merely so much fodder for the cannons handled by trained soldiers.[23] There is a new method

military bureaucratic machinery cannot be taken over, but must be broken — on the Continent, but not elsewhere, in England or America, for instance. Marx and Engels, *Selected Correspondence*, p. 309.

[19] Quoted by Kautsky in his *Dictatorship of the Proletariat*, p. 10; also by G. M. Stekloff, *History of the First International*, p. 240. Cf. Marx, *Capital*, I, 32.

[20] *Neue Zeit*, XX, no. 1, p. 10.

[21] *Neue Zeit*, XIII, no. 1, p. 305.

[22] Introduction to *Class Struggles in France*, p. 13.

[23] Introduction to *Class Struggles in France*, pp. 21, 25.

of proletarian warfare to be followed and it is a better weapon: the ballot. This the German socialist party had demonstrated. "They supplied their comrades of all countries a new weapon, and one of the sharpest, when they showed them how to use universal suffrage." [24] Propaganda, organization, votes for laws favorable to the worker, the election of government officials out of his own midst, and the gradual acquisition of political power are the tactics to be pursued. Then it will be only a matter of time before the organized proletariat will become "the decisive power in the land before which all other powers will have to bow . . . The irony of world history turns everything upside down. We the 'revolutionaries,' the 'rebels' — we are thriving far better on legal methods than on illegal methods and revolt . . . we, under this legality, get firm muscles and rosy cheeks and look like eternal life." [25]

But it must be stressed that even during this later period violence as an expedient is not abandoned. In 1867 Marx says in *Capital*: "Force is the midwife of every old society pregnant with a new one." [26] In the speech at the Hague Congress of the International (1872), referred to already, he says that in most Continental countries "It is to force that in due time the workers will have to appeal if the dominion of labor is at long last to be established." [27] In 1878, with a nod from Marx, Engels contends against Dühring that force is the instrument by which "social development forces its way through and shatters the dead, fossilized political forms." [28] In 1884 Engels argues strenuously against the renunciation of recourse to the right of resistance, arms in hand.[29] In his introduction to Marx's *Class Struggles in France* the accent is clearly on peaceful tactics, but violence is by no means excluded. In view of new military developments, he says, street fighting must be

[24] Introduction to *Class Struggles in France*, p. 20.
[25] Introduction to *Class Struggles in France*, pp. 27–28.
[26] *Capital*, I, 824.
[27] Quoted by G. M. Stekloff, *History of the First International*, p. 241.
[28] *Anti-Dühring*, p. 203.
[29] Letter to A. Bebel, November 18, 1884, in Marx and Engels, *Selected Correspondence*, p. 429.

modified; but he does not suggest its abandonment. He relates that "the German example of utilizing the suffrage" has been imitated by several countries in Europe, without, however, surrendering the right to revolution. "The right to revolution is, after all, the only real, 'historical right.' " [30]

We can now turn to the second part of the formula, the timing of the revolution. It seems that they expect the final cataclysm during a crisis or a war, or during a chronic stagnation of the economy. The immediate reason for the upheaval of 1848 Marx perceives mainly in the crisis of 1847, and he is of the opinion that the revival of industry after 1848 accounts for the political reaction that swept the Continent. A genuine revolution, he adds, can come only during a crisis, and the one is as certain to come as the other; this in 1850.[31] In 1854 he predicts a revolution, for which the signal will be given by "the impending European war." [32] In September, 1856, with signs of an approaching crisis, Marx writes to Engels that he expects a European revolution on an unprecedented scale, and that he and Engels would have to play an active part in it. "Even the fact that I have at last got to the point of furnishing a house again and sending for my books proves to me [!] that the 'mobilization' of our persons is at hand." A year later, during the depression of 1857, Engels writes to Marx, expressing the hope for a prolonged crisis, so that the proletariat would be hammered into greater unity and greater determination for the decisive struggle. He feels happy over the crisis. "The crisis will do me as much good physically as a sea-bathe; I can see that already." He is certain that the final revolution is near, and "This makes my military studies more practical at once." [33] In January, 1873, Marx sees the approaching crisis, and he is confident that "by the universality of its theater

---

[30] Pages 23–26. The publications of this introduction known to me at the time of the preparation of the first edition of this book inexcusably omitted all of Engels' reservations regarding the use of force, making of Engels a convert to peaceful methods. I was therefore misled in my interpretation of Marx's and Engels' attitude to violence in their later years.

[31] *Klassenkämpfe in Frankreich*, pp. 9, 101–102.

[32] *The Eastern Question*, p. 220.

[33] Marx and Engels, *Selected Correspondence* (New York, 1935), pp. 85–86.

and the intensity of its action it will drum dialectics even into the heads of the mushroom-upstarts of the new, holy Prusso-German empire." [34]

There are also declarations that crises will grow in severity, finally graduating into a chronic stagnation which will sooner or later touch off the decisive revolution. The *Communist Manifesto* (pages 20–21) warns that crises are placing capitalist society on trial, "each time more threateningly," and that the corrective measures which may be applied will merely pave "the way for more extensive and more destructive crises," and will reduce "the means whereby crises are prevented." In 1886 Engels states that the "decennial cycle" recurrent between 1825 and 1867 has culminated in England in a "permanent and chronic depression." He predicts that the "sighed-for period of prosperity will not come," and he warns that "we can almost calculate the moment when the unemployed, losing patience, will take their own fate into their own hands." [35]

## The Dictatorship of the Proletariat

When political power has been won by the proletariat, his "historical mission" is by no means ended. A given society cannot be turned into a radically different one at a single stroke. Once in power, the worker has before him the laborious task of gradually dissolving the capitalistic strongholds, institutions, and mechanisms, and of supplanting them with organs of the new order. It requires a long period for the old to die out and for the new to accumulate vitality for a vigorous, independent existence. Therefore, between the ascent of the workers to the political helm and the complete establishment of the communist régime there intervenes a period of social transformations.[36]

This is the period of the dictatorship of the proletariat. The experiences of '48 and of the Paris Commune convinced Marx and Engels that the victorious workers cannot take over the

---

[34] *Capital*, I, 26.

[35] Engels, Preface to *Capital*, I, 31; Engels' note, *Capital*, III, 574. Cf. *Capital*, I, 26.

[36] Engels, *Grundsätze des Kommunismus*, questions 17 and 18.

capitalist state machinery and employ it as an instrument of building a communist system. The old state must go, and, for the transition period, a new political form must be instituted, the dictatorship of the proletariat.[37] This expression was probably first employed by Marx in 1850 in *Klassenkämpfe in Frankreich*. On page 94 we read: "This socialism [that is, "revolutionary socialism"] . . . is the class dictatorship of the proletariat as a necessary transition to the abolition of class differences." In a letter to Weydemeyer in 1852 he writes that "the class struggle necessarily leads to the *dictatorship of the proletariat*," which is the transition to the classless society.[38]

The expression "dictatorship of the proletariat" suggests a despotic government headed by ruthless persons who rob the people of all choice save submission to decrees from above. But this Marx and Engels never had in mind. By such a form of government they mean no less than a democratic republic. This is clear in all their utterances. The *Communist Manifesto* teaches: "the first step in the revolution by the working class is to raise the proletariat to the position of the ruling class; to win the battle of democracy."[39] In his criticism of the Ehrfurt program Engels says explicitly: "If anything is well established, it is this: our party and the working class can come to mastery only under the form of a democratic republic. This is the specific form of the dictatorship of the proletariat, as the great French Revolution had already shown."[40] Marx describes the Paris Commune as a truly democratic experiment and as a steppingstone to socialism.[41] And in the

[37] Introduction to *Communist Manifesto*, p. 9; Marx, *Civil War in France*, p. 80, Engels' introduction, p. 17. "Between capitalist and communist society lies a period of revolutionary transformation from one to the other. There corresponds also to this a political transition period during which the state can be nothing else than the *revolutionary dictatorship of the proletariat*" (Marx, *Critique of the Gotha Programme*, p. 44. Marx's italics).

[38] Marx and Engels, *Selected Correspondence*, p. 57. Marx's italics.

[39] *Communist Manifesto*, p. 40. Likewise, in Engels' *Grundsätze des Kommunismus* the answer to question 18, concerning the phases of the revolution, states: "It will first of all set up a democratic political constitution."

[40] *Neue Zeit*, XX, no. 1, p. 11.

[41] Marx, *Civil War in France*, pp. 78, 84, 85, 80.

introduction to this work Engels exclaims: "Well, gentle sirs, would you like to know how this dictatorship looks? Then look at the Paris Commune. That was the dictatorship of the proletariat." [42]

The first steps that will be taken by the victorious dictatorship in order to prepare the ground for the socialist régime are outlined in the *Communist Manifesto*. This document advocates successive "despotic inroads on the rights of property." It recognizes that the measures will vary in different countries, but "in the most advanced countries" the following are recommended: abolition of land property and of inheritance; a heavy progressive income tax; state control of banking, credit, transportation, and other means of communication; equal liability of all to labor; and so forth. These measures, it adds, will "necessitate further inroads upon the old social order," until the new system is completely established. [43]

However, these measures are declared later to be antiquated, and referring to them in their joint preface of 1872, Marx and Engels confess that "That passage would, in many respects, be very differently worded today." [44] Instead, the activities of the Paris Commune are urged as the example to follow. The organization and undertakings of the Commune are outlined by Marx. It was composed of municipal councilors elected in the various wards and revocable at will, and it functioned simultaneously as a legislative and executive body. It instituted universal suffrage, suppressed the standing army, and substituted the "armed people"; the judges, police, and officials in all government departments were elected by the masses, and served as the responsible agents of the Commune, subject to recall at any time; they were all made public servants and at workers' wages; the educational institutions were opened free to everybody; it abolished night work for the bakers; prohibited employers from reducing wages; and the workshops and factories closed by the capitalists were, "under

[42] *Civil War in France*, p. 20.
[43] Marx and Engels, *Communist Manifesto*, pp. 41-42.
[44] *Communist Manifesto*, preface of 1872, p. 9.

reserve of compensation," taken away and turned over to "associations of workmen." [45] It was "the political form at last discovered under which to work out the economic emancipation of labor," once its political emancipation had been achieved. Marx assures us that the workers of the Commune had no ready-made utopias to further, and they understood that the higher society would come only after a "series of historic processes, transforming circumstances and men." [46] Toward the end of his life he acknowledges in a letter that the Commune, representing the uprising of a single town, under exceptional conditions, and with most insurgents as nonsocialists, could not accomplish a good deal. Evidently, in retrospect, the Commune fails to impress Marx as a model to follow, and we are left without a blueprint from his pen for the steps in the introduction of socialism, the preliminary phase of communism. [47]

This dictatorship of the proletariat is still a political state, in the view of our two writers. Marx expressly declares that the transition period between capitalism and communism is the dictatorship of the proletariat, and that it is a state. [48] Engels, likewise, says that the Commune merely eliminated the bad features of the state, but that the state can be completely abolished only in the future when a new race of men is born. [49] This is quite in harmony with their political theory. The dictatorship still coincides with the existence of classes, the dying bourgeoisie and the triumphant proletariat. Some kind of organized force is still needed to subdue a possible revolt of the class that is being expropriated. [50] Herein lies one of the chief differences between our two revolutionaries and the anarchist. The latter desires the abolition of the state immediately after

[45] Marx, *Civil War in France*, pp. 9–10, 74–75, 85.

[46] *Civil War in France*, pp. 78–80.

[47] Marx and Engels, *Selected Correspondence*, p. 387.

[48] *Critique of the Gotha Programme*, pp. 44–45.

[49] Engels, Preface to *Civil War in France*, p. 20. The *Communist Manifesto* says (p. 41) that the instruments of production will be centralized "in the hands of the State, i.e., of the proletariat organized as the ruling class."

[50] Marx, *Neue Zeit*, XXXII, no. 1, p. 40; Engels, letter to A. Bebel, reprinted in the latter's *Aus Meinem Leben*, II, 322.

the proletariat has won supremacy. But Marx and Engels maintain that political authority is indispensable during the period in which society is being transformed into a socialist commonwealth. Engels asserts that, if the Commune had not armed itself, it would not have lasted a day.[51]

It is apparent, however, that this proletarian state is not as rigorous as its predecessor, the capitalistic state. Engels says about the Commune that it was not a state "in the proper sense." [52] The dictatorship represents the proletarian class, the bulk of society. Therefore, to this extent at least, such a government is congruous with society and is not a force superimposed over it, while under capitalism the state is the machine of the minority against the majority. Again, this proletarian state is transitory, and it is fully aware of this fact. It does not strive for self-perpetuation, but, on the contrary, directs all its activities toward the building of a society wherein it will become entirely superfluous. Finally, the ruling class in possession of the state power in this case is not based on economic strength. It does not draw its energy and prestige from a superior position in class relations between participators in production; in other words, the proletariat is not economically the dominant agent, and the bourgeois is not the subordinate agent, in the processes of commodity manufacture. The state here is therefore not rooted in the mode of production; it is merely a temporary political expedient essential in the labors of establishing a new system.[53]

## SOCIALISM

When the dictatorship of the proletariat has accomplished its work of transformation, the era of communism dawns on this world. But as yet it is not genuine communism — for that a new race of men completely ignorant of the fleshpots of capitalism is required. "The present generation is like the Jews whom Moses led across the desert. It has not only a

[51] *Neue Zeit*, XXXII, no. 1, p. 39.
[52] In the above-mentioned letter to Bebel, p. 322.
[53] Cf. Lenin, *Staat und Revolution*, pp. 60, 84; Mautner, *Bolschewismus*, p. 153.

new world to conquer — it must perish in order to make room for men who will have been reared into a new world." [54] This new society has just issued from the lap of capitalism. It still harks back in some respects to the old order, and "economically, morally, and intellectually" it bears some of its features. This society Marx terms the first phase of communism, a phase that is generally called socialism. It knows no private property, little of classes, and no exploitation; everybody is obliged to work, and production is carried on by "associated" laborers. But distribution still bears the stamp of the capitalistic conception of equality of rights. From the aggregate of commodities that society produces two funds are, first of all, subtracted: one for productive purposes, as replacement of capital and a reserve against accidents, and another for the cost of administration (which Marx promises will decline as society advances), and for schools, sanitation, and invalids. Of the remainder each laborer obtains a share in proportion to the amount of work he has rendered.

On the surface, this is in accordance with equality of rights, since labor is measured for all by the same standard of duration and intensity. But under this dispensation, Marx urges, some may receive more than they need, while those with large families may need more than they receive. This principle of distribution is premised on inequality of enjoyments. It cannot be different, however, Marx observes, while the new society is still tainted with capitalist imperfections. [55]

Because Marx did not say much on the question, the presentation of the steps in the transition from capitalism to communism skates on thin ice. The position taken on these pages is that the transition breaks into three stages. To sum up, first comes the period of radical transformations. Capitalist strongholds and outposts are razed, and new institutions are introduced. The multitude of complicated capitalistic mechanisms and processes in production, finance, and exchange are partly replaced by new devices and partly simplified or abol-

---

[54] Marx, *Klassenkämpfe in Frankreich*, p. 85.
[55] *Critique of the Gotha Programme*, pp. 29–30.

ished. The dictatorship of the proletariat, which, to repeat, is a democracy to the proletarians but a dictatorship in relation to the bourgeoisie, is established. Next comes socialism or the first phase of communism. The new institutions are consolidated, and new outlooks and scales of value are slowly working on human minds. But there are still landmarks of capitalism, especially in the inequalities of wages; there are still lingering remnants of the bourgeoisie and of bourgeois viewpoints; and there is still the suspicion of the possibility of sabotage or even a revolt. The dictatorship of the proletariat continues. Third, the second phase of communism, or genuine communism, arrives, with a new race of men and new conceptions, as will be indicated in the next section.

But one cannot be sure about these stages. It is not certain, for example, whether the dictatorship of the proletariat is confined only to the first stage or extends through the second stage, socialism; whether, that is, those of bourgeois persuasion completely disappear, and, therefore, the state is extinguished already in the second stage, or only in the third stage, complete communism. Nor can we be certain that the transition falls in three stages and not into two stages. Marx's thought may be that upon the proletarian victory over the capitalist class comes at once socialism, or the first phase of communism, with the dictatorship of the proletariat, the gradual dissolution of capitalism, and the building of a new society; and that next comes thoroughgoing communism with new concepts of justice in the distribution of wage-income and a new ethical and intellectual orientation. Not least in contributing to the uncertainty is the fact that Marx and Engels use the term socialism to designate communism, and in their pronouncements on the future society it is not easy to distinguish when they refer by socialism to the first phase of communism and when to the second and final phase. Likewise in their use of the term communism they never indicate which of these two phases they have in mind.

## COMMUNISM

In the progress of time the higher phase of communism appears. No traces of capitalism, the bourgeoisie, and the bourgeois frame of mind are left. The state, the symbol of class society, vanishes. "The government of persons," Engels teaches, "is replaced by the administration of things, and by conduct of the processes of production. The state is not 'abolished.' *It dies out.*"[56] Only a few administrative functions remain, to guard the public interest.[57] On the ashes of the old state rises a commonwealth, devoted to the tasks of production and other social concerns, and united by the conviction that the way to deal with nature and to develop human beings in all directions is not through competitive atomism but through coöperative effort. This is the *societas perfecta* that Marx is dreaming of, the masterpiece which history seeks to achieve.

It is a society worthy of human nature. The contradictions of the old order are gone. Gone at last is the mastery of man over man. Society pools its assets in labor, natural wealth, capital, and science; calculates the diverse needs of its members; and apportions the resources among the multiple industrial channels, to insure an uninterrupted and rich flow of products for every want. Coördinate with social production is social enjoyment of the income. After the necessary deductions for public purposes, the social storehouse is shared by all, not according to their contribution, but in the light of a principle transcending the capitalist idea of equitable distribution. Emblazoned on the flag of communism is the motto: "From each according to his capacity, to each according to his need."[58]

The master principle of capitalism is the accumulation of wealth. Men are secondary; they are means, not ends. But in this "new and better society" the towering ideal is the free development of the individual, the expansion of his intellectual

[56] Engels, *Socialism, Utopian and Scientific*, pp. 76–77. Engels' italics.
[57] Engels, *Neue Zeit*, XXXII, no. 1, p. 39.
[58] Marx, *Critique of the Gotha Programme*, p. 31.

and social capabilities, and the enrichment of his personality.[59] "In bourgeois society, living labor is but a means to increase accumulated labor [capital]. In communist society, accumulated labor is but a means to widen, to enrich, to promote the existence of the laborer." Society becomes "an association in which the free development of each is the condition for the free development of all." [60]

But man does not gain a new dignity and a new freedom only because of the development of his capacities. He is also free in a more profound sense. For the first time in history he becomes master of his environment. In capitalist society, with competition and exchange the ruling principles, man is under the sway of his product. "Blind, coercive laws" impress their will on his enterprise, and conjure up unpleasant results which he has not anticipated. Capitalism is the reign of the "fetishism of commodities." It is different in the new society. Thanks to the social planning of the productive processes, to the richer knowledge of the social and natural environment made possible alike by the greater leisure after a shorter working day and by the unhindered growth of science, men no longer live in the dark but act in full consciousness of the causal connections governing each step they take.

This is the essence of freedom. Freedom is not independence of law, nor is it unaccountable conduct. Freedom means the comprehension of the principles involved, the intelligent application of them to desired ends, and the foreknowledge of the results to come. Marx opens the first volume of *Capital* with a consideration of the commodity, which dominates man under capitalism. On one of the last pages of the last volume of the trilogy he prophesies: "The associated producers regulate their interchange with nature rationally, bring it under their common control, instead of being ruled by it as by some blind power; . . . they accomplish their task . . . under conditions most adequate to their human nature and most

[59] Marx, *Capital*, I, 581, 649, 652; Engels, *Anti-Dühring*, p. 320.
[60] Marx and Engels, *Communist Manifesto*, pp. 33, 42.

worthy of it." [61] To Hegel history is a progressive march toward freedom. So it is with Marx. To Hegel it is the march of the Absolute Idea. To Marx history is the progressive development of production, the means, that is, of achieving this freedom for human beings, in their daily lives. The ultimate means finds its expression in the socialization of production. This final mode of production proclaims "the ascent of man from the kingdom of necessity to the kingdom of freedom." [62]

[61] *Capital*, III, 954.
[62] Engels, *Anti-Dühring*, pp. 125, 310; *Socialism, Utopian and Scientific*, pp. 56, 72, 80–82.

# CHAPTER XIV

## MARX AND ECONOMIC CALCULATION [1]

### THE ROLE OF PRICE

THE integrating principle of economics lies in maximizing satisfactions by the use of available scarce resources, in man-hours and the bounties of nature, as well as in savings resulting in capital. The allocation of these resources among the various spheres of enterprise, the combination of varieties of one resource with varieties of another resource, the substitution of one resource for another, and the division of income between consumption and saving, are central in achieving maximum satisfaction with the resources at hand.

Under capitalism the guide to the distribution of resources among the channels of economic activity is price, the price of consumer goods and the price of the resources, labor, land, and capital, in a setting of free enterprise and competition. We balance utilities against costs. To use a few simple examples, in competitive equilibrium the fact that price equals minimum average cost implies that the least expenditure of resources is incurred to obtain a utility; the assertion that the inefficient producer drops out of competition means that the producer who uses up more resources than other producers in order to get the same result is eliminated; and when a high cost and high price are associated with small purchases of a given commodity the idea is that because a given utility necessitates a large use of resources it is enjoyed sparingly.

It is doubtful whether Adam Smith, Ricardo, and their early followers, from whom Marx learned much of his economics, put this principle at the heart of economic analysis. To Smith the central problem of political economy was efficient production, to Ricardo the exploration of the principles of the distribution of income. The place of utility was not prominent

[1] Reprinted, with permission, from the *American Economic Review*, XXXVI, no. 3 (June, 1946), 344–357.

in their minds. Smith goes no farther than to mention that all production is evidently for purposes of consumption;[2] Ricardo goes no farther than to state that if goods are to be produced at all they must be useful. To Marx economics is preëminently a study of class exploitation in a given society in its evolution to the next, higher, social order, and the object of the economics of capitalism specifically is the investigation of the principles governing the exploitation of the proletariat, the fatal maladies of the system, and its dialectic disintegration into socialism and communism. However, more than any of his predecessors and even contemporaries, he was conscious of the problem, in any type of economy, of the distribution of labor and means of production among the various departments of enterprise to satisfy the wants of the community.

Marx teaches that for Robinson Crusoe and in a capitalist economy alike the controlling principle in the allocation of resources rests on labor-value; and that under capitalism the instrumentality which gives effect to this principle is competition. "Chance and caprice," he says, "have full play in distributing the producers and their means of production among the various branches of industry. The different spheres of production, it is true, constantly tend to equilibrium: for, on the one hand, while each producer of a commodity is bound to produce a use-value, to satisfy a particular social want, and while the extent of these wants differs quantitatively, still there exists an inner relation which settles their proportions into a regular system; . . . and, on the other hand, the law of the value of commodities ultimately determines how much of its disposable working-time society can expend on each particular class of commodities." This equilibrium, he continues, is constantly upset, but there is "an a posteriori, nature-imposed necessity controlling the lawless caprice of the producers" by the enduring work of value and competition.[3]

However, the law of labor-value presiding over the pages of *Capital*, volume I, asserts itself merely as a norm. In the de-

[2] *Wealth of Nations*, II, 155.
[3] Marx, *Capital*, I, 390–391, 88; III, 213, 226–227, 1026.

veloped stage of capitalism the "price of production" of volume III dominates the market. The business man seeks a profit on his investment, and capitals of equal magnitudes, whatever their organic composition (i.e., the ratio of capital to wages, in terms of labor-time) will have to bring equal profits. Otherwise the capital that yields a smaller rate of profit, because the labor employed, the source of surplus-value, bears a smaller ratio to the capital invested than is the case in another branch of industry, will migrate to this other branch, until the rate of profit is equalized in all productive spheres. The migration of capital from sphere to sphere transforms value into price of production.[4] Accordingly we find Marx alluding at times to prices of production as controlling the apportioning of resources, although he hastens to add that labor-value is the matrix of prices.[5] To him, "The exchange, or sale, of commodities at their value is the rational way, the natural law of their equilibrium."[6]

It is worth emphasizing that he had a poor opinion of the way in which price and competition operate in a capitalist society. Although performing, after a fashion, a coördinating function, price and competition are synonymous with anarchy and planlessness, underscoring the antithesis between the order inside the plant and the chaos outside, in the market at large. The quest for profits is to him antagonistic to production for the "satisfaction of social needs." The desire for gain is a perverting influence, and there is "no necessary but only an accidental connection between the volume of society's demand for a certain article and the volume represented by the production of this article."[7] A scheme of production based on the personal calculations and independent decisions of self-seeking individuals for unascertained markets not only breeds maladjustments but has to rely on "blind laws" to impress some order upon "the lawless caprice of the producer," generally through the pressure of competitive self-interest and periodically through crises. Competition stands for anarchy; it is

[4] *Capital*, III, 186, 206, 212, 230.
[6] *Capital*, III, 221.
[5] *Capital*, III, 745.
[7] *Capital*, III, 220, 303, 724n.

*bellum omnium contra omnes.*[8] Genuine organization in production postulates deliberate collective planning. "The point of bourgeois society," writes Marx, "consists precisely in this, that a priori there is no conscious social regulation of production."[9]

In view of his low esteem of calculation under capitalism, his unconcern over monopoly and protection as injurious departures from the optimum distribution of resources is not to be wondered at. To him monopoly profit is merely a redistribution of the loot, surplus-value; what one monopolist seizes another exploiter of labor fails to pocket. Inasmuch as wages are determined by the irreducible customary standard of living of the working population — and this is essentially Smith's, Ricardo's and Mill's theory — if laborers have to purchase monopolized articles their money wages are correspondingly advanced. Only if the wage is above the customary minimum will it fail to rise and the laborers will be hurt by monopoly.[10] In Marx's writings there is no counterpart of Smith's attacks on monopoly. Similarly with free trade. It is desired by manufacturers for the reason that imports cheapen food, so that wages can be lowered and profits raised. Marx favors free trade only because it spreads capitalism abroad, intensifies it at home, and, deepening its antagonisms, hastens the revolution.[11]

### The Entrepreneur

His reluctance to see in the work of entrepreneurs an organizing aspect of production is emphasized by his treatment of profits. To his mind, profits in the strict sense, that is, the share left after the deduction of interest and rent from surplus-value, stands for robbery, like the rest of surplus-value There is no specific function in a capitalist economy for which profits can be claimed as a reward.

[8] *Capital*, III, 301, 1026; II, 196; I, 391. That he is familiar with the functioning of price, supply and demand, and competition is clear to anyone who reads him. See, e.g., *Capital*, III, chaps. ix, x, xli, and II, 392–393.

[9] *Letters to Dr. Kugelmann*, p. 74. Cf. Engels, *Dialectics of Nature*, p. 19.

[10] *Capital*, III, 1003.

[11] Speech on *Free Trade*, reprinted as an appendix to *Poverty of Philosophy*.

He is familiar with the function of management inside the factory. The labor process demands the use of hands and head. The two were applied by the same person in the days of the independent craftsman; but capitalist production makes a separation. The workers are treated as automatons, while "the knowledge, the judgment, the will" are concentrated in the capitalist. Whenever production is "social" in character, entailing the coöperation of many workers, a "directing authority," a "commanding will" is needed to articulate the multitude of tasks in a comprehensive scheme of division of labor. Marx likens this function to that of the general of the army or the leader of an orchestra.[12] Too, the employer attends to the purchase of the proper quantity and quality of materials and labor; he takes care that the work is performed efficiently.[13]

But, Marx contends, these functions can be delegated to a hired manager for modest "wages of superintendence," as is the practice in workers' coöperatives and joint-stock companies. If the capitalist claims the role as the guiding genius of production he is doing so because he is the owner of capital and, moreover, under false pretenses, inasmuch as the tasks which he affects to perform are discharged by his managers. "It is not because he is a leader of industry that a man is a capitalist; on the contrary, he is a leader of industry because he is a capitalist. The leadership of industry is an attribute of capital, just as in feudal times the functions of general and judge were attributes of landed property." Wages of superintendence and profits proper are distinct categories. The former go to the hired managers, the latter to the idle capitalist.[14]

Aside from the ordinary work of factory management he sees no place for the entrepreneur. He mentions that the costs of running a concern based on a new invention are high and that "the first leaders in a new enterprise are generally bank-

[12] *Capital,* I, 557, 396–397, 363; III, 451.
[13] *Capital,* I, 205, 219.
[14] *Capital,* I, 213–215, 364–365; III, 449–458.

rupt," and only those who buy them out at bargain prices reap profits. "It is, therefore, generally the most worthless and miserable sort of money-capitalists who draw the greatest benefits out of the universal [i.e., scientific] labor of the human mind." [15] But we do not find him voicing the idea that judgment and risk are involved in the introduction of innovations, and that inventions, though they may represent interesting scientific achievements, may not be economical in view of market situations. On the contrary, inventions are, in his view, merely the gratuitous fruit of "social labor." Discussing the general improvements which reduce the cost of the constant capital of a given employer, he observes: "Such a development of the productive power is traceable in the last instance to the social nature of the labor engaged in production; . . . to the development of intellectual labor, especially of the natural sciences. The capitalist thus appropriates the advantages of the entire system of the division of social labor." [16]

There is likewise no discussion of the business man's uninsurable risks in introducing new commodities, in formulating long-range plans for his place in industry, in contending with shifts in demand and costs, and in facing other varieties of uncertainty in a dynamic world, while his commitments to the hired, borrowed, and leased resources are fixed beforehand. The *Communist Manifesto* pays tribute to the enormous achievements of capitalism prior to its maturity, but there is no intimation in his writings that the entrepreneur as such deserves credit for these achievements, and that risk-taking is a coördinating and dynamic function.

## CALCULATION UNDER COMMUNISM

Of a superior character is, to Marx's mind, economic calculation in a communist society. Under capitalism, he teaches, the commodity and production dominate society; under communism production is brought under "common control as a law understood by the social mind," and "socialized man, the

---

[15] *Capital*, III, 124.
[16] *Capital*, III, 98, 753-754; I, 422.

associated producers, regulate their interchange with nature rationally, bring it under their common control, instead of being ruled by it as by some blind power." [17]

The objectives which the "social mind" will aim to achieve are two: one, the allocation of labor-time to various industries in accordance with social demand; and, two, the distribution of the total income among the producers in accordance with the labor-time expended by them. In both cases value serves as the underlying principle. Says Marx: "Only when production will be under the conscious and prearranged control of society, will society establish a direct relation between the quantity of social labor-time employed in the production of definite articles and the quantity of the demand of society for them." [18] "In the case of socialized production" producers receive paper-checks entitling them to "a share corresponding to their labor-time." [19]

The independent handicraftsman or peasant, Marx observes, needs no bookkeeping in the management of his affairs, but it is essential in capitalist production "for the control and ideal survey (*Zusammenfassung*) of the process"; bookkeeping is "still more necessary in coöperative (*gemeinschaftlicher*) than in capitalist production." [20] The bookkeeping, he indicates, will run in terms of labor-time, and value, in labor-time, will endure as the governing principle in the allocation of labor among the various employments. [21]

In the absence of the capitalist and his claim to a return on the investment, value as a guide to the allocation of resources does not suffer in a communist society what Marx would call a distortion into "price of production." It is to be noted, however, that in this regard value is even less satisfactory than Marx's "price of production." Among its inadequacies note may be taken of the following. Two articles may embody equal amounts of labor, but one of them may have required the use of more natural resources, which although not the

[17] *Capital*, III, 301, 307, 954.

[18] *Capital*, III, 221; *Theorien über den Mehrwert*, II, no. 2, p. 311.

[19] *Capital*, II, 412. Cf. I, 90.

[20] *Capital*, II, 153.                    [21] *Capital*, III, 992.

product of labor, are not free goods and must be economized. While of equal value in terms of labor costs these two commodities must be priced differently to prevent the waste of natural resources. Equally, while capital accumulation is going on, i.e., before saving and investment become undesirable in a society, and while inventions take place, the marginal productivity of capital is greater than the marginal productivity of labor. Accordingly, commodities with equal costs in labor-time may yet differ in the amounts of instruments used in their production, and must be valued differently.[22]

Marx is not familiar with the marginal analysis, although the works of Jevons, Walras, and Menger appeared ten years before his death; and without marginal analysis a theory of calculation necessarily suffers unless criteria unknown to traditional economics are contemplated for the new society. He is even unmindful of the intensive cultivation of better than marginal land. In a communist society, he states, instead of allowing the value of wheat to equal the labor cost on the poorest land under cultivation, the value will be the average labor cost of the wheat, per quarter, raised on the land of all the different grades.[23] He does not perceive that it would be more economical to use the better grades of land intensively until the marginal product is the same on all grades. In Marx's solution, a dollar's worth of labor applied to land of lower than average quality will produce less than a dollar's worth of wheat; and labor will be partly wasted in farming while it could be used where it will yield a dollar's worth of product.

Some writers are in the habit of citing passages from Marx in which he designates value as the criterion of calculation in the future society and of concluding that this is his definitive position. But we cannot be sure. Doubt is imported from at least two sources: first, passages that either repudiate this proposition or throw cold water on it; and, second, certain general considerations.

First, as to passages. In *Die Deutsche Ideologie* Marx and

[22] O. R. Lange, "Marxian Economics in the Soviet Union," *American Economic Review*, XXXV, no. 1 (March, 1945), 132. [23] *Capital*, III, 773.

Engels write in 1845 that supply and demand exert a dominant influence under capitalism, but under communism "the power of supply and demand dissolves into nothing."[24] In *Anti-Dühring*, embodying mainly Marx's ideas, and the manuscript of which was read to Marx before publication,[25] Engels specifies that in a communist order "society will also not assign values to products."[26] Then comes the curious statement: "The useful effects (*Nutzeffekte*) of the various articles of consumption, compared with each other and with the quantity of labor required for their production, will in the last analysis determine the plan. People will be able to manage everything very simply, without the intervention of the famous 'value.'"[27]

It is likely that, engaged as he is on these pages in hair-splitting differentiations between labor-time embodied in goods, on the one hand, and value as a concept infected with price and exchange connotations, on the other hand, he uses, in the above citation, value in this latter sense, denying the existence of the evil connotations under communism. However, the paragraph following this citation is far from giving aid and comfort to this suggestion. There Engels reverts to value as labor-time, charges that this concept stands for all the ugly aspects of capitalism, and at the end of the paragraph pronounces that it would be absurd "to set up a society in which at last the producers control their products by the logical application of an economic category [value] which is the most comprehensive expression of the subjection of the producers by their own product." In a letter to Kugelmann, Marx writes that the allocation of labor in definite proportions "corresponding to the different needs" is a necessity in any system of production, only it changes its form with each particular system; and that under capitalism the form in which the distribution of labor operates is the exchange value of goods. The implication is clear that in the future society the principle of the allocation of labor will assume a different form from exchange value.[28] Finally,

---

[24] Marx and Engels, *Gesamtausgabe*, Part I, vol. 5, p. 25.

[25] See Engels' statement in *Anti-Dühring*, preface, p. 13.

[26] *Anti-Dühring*, p. 337.                    [27] *Anti-Dühring*, p. 338.

[28] *Letters to Dr. Kugelmann*, letter of July 11, 1868, pp. 73–74.

we cannot ignore Marx's disapproval, in his appraisal of A. Wagner's *Allgemeine oder theoretische Volkswirtschaftslehre*, of "the presupposition that the theory of value, developed for the explanation of bourgeois society, has validity for the 'socialist state of Marx.' " [29]

Second, there are general considerations casting doubt on Marx's adherence to labor-value as the principle of calculation in a communist society, and outstanding among them are his views on division of labor, and the distribution of income in a communist society. We are familiar with his attacks on division of labor under capitalism as stultifying human capacities and degrading human dignity.[30] There will be none of it in the new order. In their early days Marx and Engels write that in a communist system the individual will hunt in the morning, fish in the afternoon, rear cattle in the evening, and criticize after dinner, without specializing in any one of these occupations.[31] Toward the end of his years Marx allows Engels, in *Anti-Dühring*, to insist on the same idea. "The old form of division of labor," says Engels, "must be done away with, above all." During the working hours each person will be given the opportunity to develop his physical and mental faculties in all directions. A race of men will be raised who will receive comprehensive training in the scientific basis of production and will be given practical experience in many branches of production from the first step to the last. To institute division of labor in accordance with the natural aptitudes of the worker, and to have "porters" and "architects," is to perpetuate the capitalistic crippling of humanity. After half an hour of architecture the architect will devote his talents to barrow-pushing. "It is a fine sort of socialism which perpetuates the professional porter!" [32] Marx talks in the same vein on "variation of work," but in measured language.[33]

---

[29] Quoted by Raya Dunayevskaya, "A New Revision of Marxian Economics," *American Economic Review*, XXXIV, no. 3 (September, 1944), 535.

[30] See, e.g., *Capital*, I, 396, 461. Cf. Adam Smith, *Wealth of Nations*, II, 264.

[31] Marx and Engels, *Deutsche Ideologie*, p. 22.

[32] *Anti-Dühring*, pp. 320–324, 221–222.

[33] *Capital*, I, 533–534.

The implications of this antagonism to division of labor for the conception of the optimum employment of resources need no elaboration. The loss of the advantages of division of labor; the expenditure of resources to train each individual in several trades; the huge amount of bookkeeping required for the functioning of such a scheme; and the incompatibility of the one criterion, production and utility, with the other criterion, the development of the physical and intellectual capacities of the worker — these are some of the considerations that come to mind. The fact that Marx is unimpressed by such considerations argues that labor-value is not what he has in mind as the guide to the productive organization under communism.

Of the same order is his principle of the distribution of income. In his critique of the Gotha program he makes a distinction between two stages of communism. In the early stage, commonly designated as socialism and still marked by the imperfections of capitalism, a worker is rewarded in proportion to his contribution. He receives a voucher to draw on the social storehouse a quantum commensurate, in terms of hours, with the labor he has rendered. But this conception of right does not appeal to Marx. It is indeed superior to the bourgeois idea of right inasmuch as it excludes surplus-value and exploitation; but it is still burdened with capitalistic postulates. People are unequal physically and mentally. Some can work longer and more intensively, and receive greater remuneration although their wants may be smaller; while others, married or with larger families, have needs exceeding the compensation which they draw for their work. This standard of "equal rights" becomes a standard of "unequal rights for unequal work," Marx declares.[34]

Accordingly, "In a higher phase of communist society, after the tyrannical subordination of individuals in the division of labor and thereby also the distinction between manual and

[34] *Critique of the Gotha Programme*, pp. 29–30. Already in the *Deutsche Ideologie* Marx and Engels declare that it is one of the principles of communism to insist that differences in brains do not constitute differences of stomach and physical needs, and that a difference in occupation "gives no basis for inequality, for *privilege* in possession and enjoyment" (p. 526. Italics not mine).

intellectual work, have disappeared, . . . after the productive
forces have also increased and all the springs of social wealth
are flowing more freely, along with the all-round development
of the individual, then and then only can the narrow bourgeois
horizon of rights be left far behind and society will inscribe on
its banner: 'From each according to his capacity, to each according to his need.' " [35] This principle of distribution would
present no difficulties only if all conceivable goods were produced in such abundance as to stand ready to satisfy every
"need" fancied by anyone; or if needs refer to a minimum of
basic requirements supplied in enormous volume. Marx's allu-
sion to "increased" productive forces and wealth flowing "more
freely" hardly suggests such a profusion of goods.

That he is apt to associate needs for individual development
with production short of superabundant is seen in a paragraph
in *Capital*, volume III. He assumes a communal society barely
emerging from capitalism, in which wages come out of the producer's product and consumption is freed from capitalist "limitations" in that it is "extended" to the volume "permitted, on
the one hand, by existing productivity of society . . . and, on
the other hand, required by the full development of his individuality." [36] The "full development" of the individual is a big
order: it postulates production of munificent dimensions, and
yet the context suggests no such happy state.

In general, such a theory of wages or distribution, so long
as goods are not free, takes us far away from the idea of coördinating economic activity as commonly discussed in economics.
If wages are not brought in accord (in the Marxian scheme)
with value, and are allowed to fluctuate for a given worker with
marriage and divorce, with births and deaths in his family, and
with the imponderable needs of his personal development, the
manager of a communist plant — when he is not fishing or
criticizing — is hardly left with a meaningful guide for the
substitution of one factor for another in seeking the best com-

[35] Marx, *Critique of the Gotha Programme*, p. 31. The translation has been
slightly revised: see the translation in the appendix of the same work, p. 109.
[36] *Capital*, III, 1021.

bination of resources, or for the optimum scale of production. Cost of production, as a measure of disutility or as a determinant of price, loses meaning; so does the equilibrium of supply and demand.

Where are we? If Marx had indicated in all the passages dealing with the allocation of resources which stage of the future society he had in mind, the socialist or the communist stage, the path to a conclusion would be easier. Instead, with the lone exception of his observations on the Gotha program, he refers in such passages to a communal society generally, without specifying the stage of its development; and we confront a maze of contradictory pronouncements.

We must rely, therefore, on general considerations to guide us. We know that he harbors an acute dislike of vestiges of capitalism in the new order, especially where principles of human relations are concerned; that despite his competent knowledge of the equilibrating effects of price he is not well disposed to the functioning of supply and demand and the decisions of the market, stressing instead the superiority of social planning; that he is a firm advocate of the relativity of distribution, and what we should call justice, to the prevailing base of productive organization. On this basis one may venture the following interpretation of Marx's position. For a period of time after the fall of capitalism value will endure as a criterion of the distribution of resources, but as soon as possible, even before the arrival of the higher stage of communism, other criteria, not defined by him, should be elaborated. As for present Soviet Russia, it may be remarked parenthetically that, in view of the fact that her revolution came long before capitalism and its productive forces ran their full course, Marx would probably hold that the reign of value and correlative principles may prevail longer than in a society which abandoned capitalism after its maturest development.

## INTEREST

Integral to the problem of the ideal allocation of resources is the question of interest. Nowhere in Marx's writings is there mention that interest can be a guide in the use of resources for making consumption goods or capital goods, or in balancing present and future enjoyments. With reference to timber growing in a communist society, he says that the question is "simply how much land the community can spare . . . for forestry." [37] Under capitalism, he observes, the upsurge of economic activity associated with railway building may be accompanied by a crash when activity subsides with the completion of the project. This disturbance cannot occur in a communistic régime, where it is "simply" a matter of calculating how much labor, means of production, and subsistence society "can utilize without injury" for undertakings demanding a long period of construction. [38] In a communist economy annual deductions will be made from the total product for the expansion of industry, but the guide to the magnitudes of resources assigned for this additional capital is vaguely referred to as "social need." In one place he mentions that the deduction for this purpose as well as for replacement and insurance against natural mishaps "can be determined by existing means and forces, and partly through the calculation of probabilities." [39] What he means by "existing means and forces" is obscure. That he does not imply interest is evident from the fact that he denies its very existence in a communist economy.

Marx sees no valid reason for interest as a category in distribution under capitalism or communism. Senior is ridiculed for perceiving abstinence in capital; Adam Müller is dismissed sarcastically for suggesting that interest is payment for time. [40] To term interest the price of capital is to use "an irrational expression," because capital, even in the form of goods, represents a "sum of values" measured by price; and the phrase "price of capital" accordingly refers to price apart from the price embodied in the capital — "an absurd contradiction." [41] Far

[37] *Capital*, II, 278.    [38] *Capital*, II, 361.

[39] *Critique of the Gotha Programme*, p. 27.

[40] *Capital*, I, 654; III, 420.

[41] *Capital*, III, 417. However, he himself uses the expression: see *ibid.*, pp. 430–431, 433.

from functioning as a unique factor of production, as in ortho-dox economics, capital is to Marx the broad symbol of a com-prehensive social phenomenon in a definite historical period. It symbolizes "command over the labor of others"; it is a certi-ficate sanctioning the levy of tribute. Capital does not repre-sent savings, it stands for robbery. If the workers were in possession of all the means of production, the concept of capital would disappear together with the phenomenon of interest, profit, and rent.[42]

Interest owes its existence to the fact that there are bor-rowers and lenders of funds; that is, under capitalism, the in-dustrial capitalists and the money capitalists are not the same individuals. The use of money helps to generalize the rate of interest; but even in the absence of money interest would endure. Only, "If there were no money at all, there would certainly be no general rate of interest." [43] He emphasizes, too, that "if all capital were in the hands of the individual capi-talists, there would be no interest and no rate of interest," inasmuch as borrowing would cease.[44] Surplus-value arises

[42] *Capital*, III, 418–419, 207, 597. It is easy to get the impression that Marx is dealing only with the money-rate, in the short-term money market. However, while in certain chapters Marx deals exclusively with this rate of interest, he also has in mind the long-run rate in his discussion as a whole. In fact, his treatment embraces all kinds of borrowing and lending. In chapter xxi he de-velops the essentials of his theory of interest, and in chapter xxiv he gives emphasis to the idea of money-lending as cloaking the underlying aggregate of capital goods which epitomizes the social relations of exploitation, providing the surplus-value out of which interest is paid. In chapter xxiii he stresses the dis-tinction between capital goods as functioning and exploiting in the reproduction process and the loanable money as mere ownership. Too, there are corroborating brief statements throughout the discussion. For instance, his reference to the retired wealthy people living on interest and commanding part of the supply of loanable money obviously refers to long-term lending (pp. 425, 599). To calcu-late the average rate of interest, it is necessary to compound the rate which fluctuates through the business cycle and "the rate of interest in such investments as require loans of capital for a long time" (p. 426). The supply of loan-capital would be identical, he says, with the supply of the "elements of production for the industrial capitalist" if, instead of possessing money, "the lending capitalists were in possesison of machinery, raw materials, etc." which they would lend to the industrial capitalists (pp. 609–610). For his ideas on interest before capital-ism, see chapter xxxvi. All the references in this note are to the third volume of *Capital*.

[43] *Capital*, III, 495, 605.

[44] *Capital*, III, 443, 445, 435.

from the private ownership of the means of production, interest from the ownership of loanable funds. The employer exacts a tribute for the use of the former, the money lender for the use of the latter. In both instances the claim is based on ownership, but Marx sees a difference in the implications.[45] Were interest to vanish, surplus-value would not diminish and profits (in the strict sense) would rise correspondingly. Preëminently a property attribute, interest will be extinct under communism alike as an entity and as a habit of thought.

It is not surprising, therefore, to learn that in Marx's organon there is no determinant of the rate of interest and no "natural" rate of interest. Interest occupies a position at variance with that of price, wages, profits, or rent. These latter are governed by laws which set long-run limits to their magnitudes. The fluctuations of the supply of and the demand for commodities regulate the deviations of their price from the norm. When supply and demand are in equilibrium, "they cease to explain anything," Marx asserts, and it is then that the underlying determinant of value comes to expression — the immanent criterion of socially necessary labor or "the price of production" of the revised version. The same with wages. The oscillations of the market price of labor-power play around the gravitational focus, the value of labor-power as embodied in the goods constituting the customary standard of living. Further, in the apportionment of wages and profits (in the full sense of surplus-value) there is the inherent principle, according to Marx, of arriving at unpaid labor by deducting from the value of, say, the day's product the value of labor-power for the day. Similarly the dimensions of rent are validated by distinctive considerations governing its nature.[46]

Not so with interest. When the supply of loanable money,[47] offered by banks, temporarily unemployed funds of business men, or private savings, is in balance with the demand for short-term means of payment or purchase,[48] or for long-run

[45] *Capital*, III, 437–448.
[46] *Capital*, III, 223, 419, 428, 431, 439, 741.
[47] *Capital*, III, 589, 594–596.
[48] *Capital*, III, 601–605.

investments, there is no determinant of the rate of interest innate in the necessities of the process of production. At times it may be high enough to absorb all profit, and it may fall "to any depth." It "becomes a matter of arbitrary and lawless estimation"; "its determination is a matter of accident, purely empirical." In what proportions the lending and investing capitalists divide the surplus-value (aside from rent) is governed by the arbitrary opinion of borrower and lender, but principally "directly and indirectly . . . by the proportion between supply and demand," with the sanction of "custom and legal tradition" as a self-asserting background, and with the average rate of pure profit as a prominent influence.[49]

[49] *Capital*, III, 419–423, 426–432, 601.

# PART V

## CRITICAL OBSERVATIONS ON MARX'S THEORY

# CHAPTER XV

### A SUMMARY OF THE CRUCIAL CLAIMS OF THE THEORY

THE critic of Marx is assured beforehand of a host of opponents. The socialists and communists resent attempts to lay violent hands on the dicta of their leader. Marx is *their* man, and the materialistic view of history is an important article of their faith. They are hostile to the intruder upon the hallowed grounds.[1] They forget that this theory of history is of importance to the nonsocialist student of economics, history, politics, anthropology, sociology, and philosophy, and that, as a contribution to social science, it is subject to examination by those interested in these fields of knowledge. A physicist may be a socialist, but that should not deter nonsocialist physicists from analyzing his studies in physics and from pointing out weaknesses. By their intolerance to outsiders socialists underscore the religious character of their beliefs.

The socialists insist that outsiders consistently misinterpret and misrepresent Marx. Whatever the critic holds to be Marx's view, the socialists strive to prove the contrary, if it suits their purpose, by citing a passage from Marx which gives, or seems to give, a different view. But are the critics to blame? Marx took insufficient pains to make himself understood. Lenin and Kautsky were lifelong students of Marx, yet they disagreed radically with respect to his views on the state, the class struggle, imperialism, and other questions. The socialist journals are full of controversy over the meaning of concepts and laws enunciated by Marx. When an author is obscure, careless in expression, and contradictory, he will be interpreted in different ways. Pareto is right when he likens Marx's statements to bats: you can see in them something that looks like a mouse and something that appears like a bird.[2]

---

[1] This statement, made in the first edition, was borne out by the abusive letters which came to me from some who read the book.

[2] *Systèmes socialistes*, II, 332.

The confirmed Marxian exhibits the behavior of a mind possessed by emotional conviction. If an idea of Marx's is criticized, he asks for the reference. When the reference is produced, he replies that one statement is insufficint evidence. When more statements are indicated, the retort is made that Marx is not proved or disproved on the quantitative basis. What you need, he will instruct you, is an intellectual regeneration, such as J. M. Keynes, "who was coming around," was beginning to experience. A person laboring with the bourgeois habit of mind, he will tell you, speaks a different language and has a different mode of thinking from Marx's. It is necessary, he will continue, to penetrate to Marx's cast of thought and look at him without traditional prejudices and, above all, as a whole. What you need is the dialectic. Without the baptismal bath of the dialectic, you are opaque to Marx's ideas and attitudes. With the aid of the dialectic, however, all becomes clear and acceptable in its brilliant richness.

Without a doubt the socialist is sincere in this attitude. Emotion, and the unconscious and subconscious impact of a warm desire to agree, are solvents of doubts and of the cool-headed critical attitude. Too, there is a personal equation in the academic student of Marx. The student moving in conservative circles, trained in a conservative atmosphere, pessimistic about the noble potentialities of human beings, and inclined to look with a quizzical eye at proposals of radical departures in social construction, is apt to approach Marx in a demanding and fault-finding frame of mind. Many a classic would lose some of its luster and many a good treatise would be scaled down if it were approached with the same calculated, critical disposition and the same hardheadedness with which the conservative student scans the utterances of Marx.

To undertake a comprehensive criticism of Marx's theory of history would call for omniscience, since it touches on every phase of human knowledge. The critic would have to be familiar with the genesis and nature of such institutions as the state, law, family, religion, morality; he would have to feel at home in anthropology, biology, economics, history, sociology, psychology, philosophy, literature, and art; and he would have to be clear alike about the nature of the forces that determine the progress of civilization and the ends toward which human destinies are moving. The criticism which follows is planned on a modest scale, and will deal only with a few phases of Marx's conceptions. After an introductory summary of his crucial contentions, observations will be made on some of the weaknesses of the most important components of the theory — the mode of production, classes, the state, law, religion, science, and philosophy. Then a few words will be said about the general significance of Marx's construction.

### The Connection Between the Substructure and Superstructure

As a preliminary to an attempt at criticism it is necessary to bring into focus the relation to each other of the major components of Marx's theory of history, and to indicate the scope of its application. One of the questions that need to be examined is the exact connection which he and Engels see between the mode of production and the other social phenomena. In what relationship do the institutional and ideological elements stand with respect to this economic factor?

In the direct formulations of their philosophy this connection is designated in a number of ways. At times they assert that the régime of production and the correlative class relations constitute the foundation (*Grundlage*) upon which all institutions are erected, and from which all ideas irradiate.[3] If by foundation they imply only a habitat or container, such declarations would carry little meaning. A habitat does not account for the phenomena taking place in it. A glass containing a liquid or a powder has little to do with the nature of these substances, their chemical composition, or their behavior under various conditions. It is clear, however, that by foundation they do not mean a passive habitat, but something causally associated with the superstructure. After mentioning produc-

---

[3] *Communist Manifesto*, Engels' preface of 1883, reprinted in Sombart's *Grundlagen und Kritik des Sozialismus*, I, 128; Marx, *Critique of Political Economy*, p. 11; *Capital*, I, 94n., 200 (n. 2).

tion as the basis of the other phases of civilization, they generally add that with a change in the foundation a corresponding change will occur in the whole superstructure; [4] that this foundation alone "explains" all the institutions and ideas of a given epoch; [5] that definite (*bestimmte*) social forms of consciousness correspond to (*entsprechen*) the economic basis; [6] and that economic conditions are the determining (*bestimmende*) basis of the history of society.[7]

We also meet pronouncements to the effect that "in the last instance" and "ultimately" economic production is the controlling factor in history. Such expressions can only mean that when we probe below the surface and make a thorough effort to disentangle the elements at work in history, we discover that, after all, production is the paramount agency, and that all the phases of civilization can be traced to the mode of production as the primary fact which gave them initial impulse. It is clear that these expressions are charged with causal connotations.

Lastly, in nearly all the other direct general announcements of their conception there is either a clear implication or a definite statement of a causal connection. Marx states that principles, ideas, and categories are "conformable" with the social relations fostered by production; [8] that the mode of production conditions (*bedingt*) the social, political, and spiritual life process in general (*überhaupt*); that social existence determines (*bestimmt*) the consciousness of men; [9] and that the state and the ideological conceptions are determined (*bestimmt*) by material production.[10] Engels declares that all "historical transactions are very easily explained" with a sufficient knowledge

[4] Marx, *Critique of Political Economy*, p. 12; "Marx to P. V. Anenkov," reprinted as appendix to *Poverty of Philosophy* (New York: International Publishers, no date), pp. 152–154.

[5] Engels, *Communist Manifesto*, preface of 1888, p. 7; *Anti-Dühring*, p. 32; *Socialism, Utopian and Scientific*, p. 41.

[6] Marx, *Critique of Political Economy*, p. 11; *Capital*, I, 94n.; III, 919; *Eighteenth Brumaire*, pp. 48–49; Marx and Engels, *Deutsche Ideologie*, pp. 15–16, 27.

[7] Marx and Engels, *Selected Correspondence*, p. 516.

[8] *Poverty of Philosophy*, p. 119.

[9] *Critique of Political Economy*, p. 11; *Capital*, I, 94n., 406 (n. 2).

[10] *Theorien über den Mehrwert*, I, 381–382.

of the economic state of society;[11] that production is the determining (*bestimmende*) moment of history, and social institutions are conditioned (*bedingt*) by production;[12] that production and exchange are the "ultimate cause," the "great moving power," the "final causes," in the last instance the "determining (*bestimmende*) element," "the determining basis" of history.[13]

## THE MODE OF PRODUCTION AS THE ONLY CAUSE

It seems reasonable to conclude that our two writers have in mind a causal relation between the mode of production and the superstructure of institutions and ideas. Now we come to a second question. Does Marx hold that the mode of production is the only governing cause in history, or does he allow play to other factors, and if he does, how much? This question is obviously of first importance and it deserves careful exploration.

Three views may be entertained. One possible contention is that Marx regards production as the only controlling factor, while the other aspects of history are nothing but passive resultants. This contention may be dismissed without hesitation. It must be conceded that at times Marx and his friend say things that are consistent with such an interpretation of their position. But, when the whole case is kept in mind, such a view becomes untenable. A second conceivable argument is that Marx considers production as only one among several dominant and autonomous elements that govern the nature and sequence of historical events; that, in his view, the work of the economic forces is consistently modified by the effect of other autonomous forces, and, consequently, there is no reason for attaching primary importance to economic as against noneconomic agencies. This view must be discarded more readily than the first. It is incompatible with every claim of the materialistic conception of history.

---

[11] See W. Liebknecht, *Karl Marx, Biographical Memoirs*, p. 49.

[12] *Origin of the Family*, p. 9. See the original in German.

[13] *Socialism, Utopian and Scientific*, pp. xviii, 45; Marx and Engels, *Selected Correspondence*, pp. 475, 516.

Marx's attitude is somewhere between these extremes, and two variants claim attention. Academic Marxians and learned socialists in general argue that Marx gives *ample* recognition to noneconomic agencies and allows them to modify considerably the economic development — provided two limitations are kept in mind: one, these noneconomic agencies owe their origin to the system of production and are shaped by it, directly or indirectly; two, the combined effectiveness of all the noneconomic forces yields to the sovereign power of the mode of production. The other variant claims that in insisting on these two reservations the learned Marxians themselves deprive noneconomic elements of essential potency. If the mode of production prevails over the aggregate of all institutional forces, the effect of any particular institution is negligible indeed. There is hardly a perceptible difference between the claim that the mode of production is the only determinant of history and the claim that the mode of production overrides all other influences and in the last resort governs institutions and events. Be it as it may, this second variant asserts that Marx accords a place of *minor* importance to institutions and ideas. They may retard or accelerate the workings of a productive system, and they may modify them in some slight degree. But they exert, in themselves, no serious impact on history.

In my opinion, the second variant comes more closely to expressing Marx's idea, and the following four considerations support this conclusion. First, in the different brief and formal statements which epitomize the essentials of Marx's and Engels' theory, production is invariably advanced as the only factor; there is no acknowledgment that noneconomic factors play a formative part, nor is there implicit emphasis on the reciprocal interactions of the many factors, despite their professed recognition of the operation of the dialectic principle in society.[14] Undoubtedly Marx and Engels were writing with the impetus of controversy, and the protagonist of a favorite idea is prone to neglect necessary modifications. Nevertheless, if other factors had been weighing heavily in their minds, it is

[14] What Engels says on this in some of his last letters will be taken up shortly.

difficult to see how they could consistently ignore them and make repeated declarations in which only one element is stressed as the controlling factor in social life.

Second, we recall Marx's treatment of the origin and nature of institutions and ideas. The children of the mode of production, they are powerless to engender basic changes in the economic situation, and they merely carry out, generally, the dictates of the mode of production. We recall that laws may accelerate factory development, that the state may aid in the speedier inauguration of capitalism, or that religion helps, in an instance or two, to establish the republican form of government. In these instance the noneconomic agencies merely collaborate with the economic trend, but do not persistently frustrate this trend. Ideas and institutions reign, they do not govern.

These two considerations find corroboration in the following reflections. A theory of history has to meet severe demands. The forces at work are to be delineated, sequences and uniformities are to be exhibited, and the configuration of the many elements is to be explored. Marx and Engels are aware of this, and indeed they subject one element to such treatment. They demonstrate how it functions, they analyze its effects, they discuss the factors which necessitate changes in it, and they establish its trend of evolution. This element is the mode of production. Had they thought that other elements were prominent, they would have paused to give these elements similar treatment, indicating their power to react against the mode of production. But this our two writers fail to do.

It is not sufficient for Marxians to point out that other forces are important in Marx's scheme because here he mentions race as of significance, there he indicates that tradition is of some account, in one place he drops a word about leadership, and in another about "outside historical influences." Marx should have taken pains to examine the functions of such factors in the general conjuncture of the forces molding social events. It is obvious that to present a list of "factors" which deserve to be taken into account as a theory of history is exceedingly inadequate.

Third, no different light is offered by the historical monographs in which Marx deals with the political struggles of 1848–1851 on the Continent. The analysis of such stirring events compels an historian to reveal his basic conceptions of historical processes. The philosophy informing these essays exhibits, however, no disposition to give prominence to non-economic tendencies. The discourse on these pages reveals the familiar pattern: the conditions of production and trade, in town and country; property distribution and economic interests; the interrelations of classes and groups, and the gradations of their economic and political power; the treachery and cruelty of the upper classes, the vacillating hypocrisy of the middle classes, and the bravery, sincerity, or ignorance, of the working class; the stratagems of leading personalities, their cunning or stupidity, and their rôle in the acceleration or retardation of events. All this is interlarded with pronouncements of doctrine — that people move within conditions created by production, that institutions and sentiments arise from these conditions, and that men cannot overcome the socio-economic environment; with attacks on the exploiting classes, and with sympathy for the underdog, applause for his successes, and apologies for his failures in terms of immature economic conditions. Throughout, the scientist is struggling with the partisan and moralist. Upon a serene account will often burst the fire of indignation over the hypocrisy and shabbiness of a social order that deprives humanity of its dignity.

In these essays Marx's conception of social being is apparent. Men make their history by their policies, choices, and acts, by giving expression to their feelings and ideas. These acts and ideas move within the framework of the mode of production and class interests. The state is the political arm of the ruling class, religion is a hypocritical mask disguising sordid interests, and pious declarations and ideals are the reflections of economic conditions when they are not the cunning devices of the exploiters. Reforms, promised, fulfilled, or betrayed, find their true focus in the established policy of the predatory class to weaken a mounting threat to its privileges. Institutions, ideas, leadership, tradition, race, and stupidity play a part; but their rôle is in marked contrast to the overshadowing power of the prevailing system of production. In these essays the underlying economic context is original, formative, directive, and decisive.

Fourth, Marx's indulgence in prophecy offers illuminating evidence on our problem. The final test of a scientific proposition lies in its power of prediction. When a theory leaves the terra firma of known facts and projects itself into the stratosphere of the unknown, it is likely to disclose its essential character. To foretell the destiny of our society is Marx's ambition. What factors is he examining, and on what reflections is he relying in order to emerge with the prediction that socialism is the goal of the future? Only the capitalistic mode of production and the concomitant class interests. It is striking that other factors receive no consideration in his analysis of such an enormous question.

His other prophecies are similarly grounded, and only two will be mentioned. We recall his prediction of a speedy revolution when he noticed an electric locomotive on exhibition, contending that a political revolution "is only the expression" of the economic revolution. In 1850 he hails the gold discovery in California as an event surpassing in importance even the discovery of America. The California gold, he prophesies, will give world commerce a new direction, and "what Tyre, Carthage, and Alexandria were in antiquity, what Genoa and Venice were in the Middle Ages, what London and Liverpool have been until now," San Francisco and Panama are in the process of becoming. "Then the Pacific Ocean will play the the same rôle as is now taken by the Atlantic . . . and the Atlantic Ocean will sink to the rôle of an inland sea." The only chance, accordingly, that the European countries have to save themselves from declining to the level of Italy and Spain lies in the overthrow of capitalism and in the establishment of socialism, which will multiply the productive forces and make up for the advantageous geographical position of the western Pacific coast.[15]

Engels is not to be outdone by his colleague in the art of prophecy. One example will suffice. In 1888 he writes from Canada during a hurried visit there: ". . . in ten years this sleepy Canada will be ripe for annexation [by the United States] — the farmers of Manitoba, etc. will demand it themselves . . . and they may tug and resist as much as they like; the economic necessity of an infusion of Yankee blood will have its way and abolish this ridiculous boundary line." [16]

It requires extraordinary confidence in the unmitigated power of the economic element and a remarkable forgetfulness of the many other elements to inspire enthusiastic readiness to build predictions of such enormous importance on such simple economic facts. Throughout the decades of their collaboration every disorder, bad crop, depression, or rumor of war evoked from them the confident assurance of an imminent revolution. Unchastened by repeated failures, they did not return to a reëxamination of their theorems. In 1863 Marx makes the admission that their optimism over the uprisings of 1848 was occasioned by "comfortable delusions and almost childish enthusiasm," and that "stupidity" and "scoundrels" have a place in revolutions.[17] But this did not prevent them from continuing with optimistic predictions on slight provocation.

### ENGELS' LETTERS

There are, finally, the much-referred-to four letters, written by Engels after Marx's death, in reaction to the criticism which had descended on the theory. Those who contend that the two philosophers give a prominent place to noneconomic factors invariably cite these letters as conclusive proof.

Indeed, these letters contain general pronouncements which fall strangely upon the ears accustomed to Marx's and Engels' declarations. He states that production constitutes in the

[15] *Aus dem literarischen Nachlass von K. Marx, F. Engels*, III, 443.

[16] Letter to Sorge, September, 1888, in "Unpublished Letters of Marx and Engels to Americans," *Science and Society*, II (1938), 364–365.

[17] Letter to Engels, in Marx and Engels, *Selected Correspondence*, p. 144.

last instance "the determining element in history. More than this neither Marx nor I have ever asserted," and to distort this proposition to mean that the economic factor is the only determining factor is to convert it "into a meaningless, abstract, and absurd phrase." There is a reciprocity between the economic factor and all the other factors, in which "the economic movement finally asserts itself as necessary." Were this not the case, the application of the theory to any given historical period "would be easier than the solution of a simple equation of the first degree." "What these gentlemen all lack," he says, "is dialectic. They never see anything but here cause and there effect." They do not see, he continues, that in the real world "such metaphysical polar opposites only exist in the real world in crises. . . Hegel has never existed for them." [18]

If one were to stop with these general declarations the impression that these letters attribute considerable influence to noneconomic factors would be justified. But most of the thunder of these declarations disappears, and we begin to hear familiar tones, as we read the letters to the end. First, we discover that the supremacy of the economic factor over the combined influence of all other factors is not only not repudiated but is consistently underscored. He teaches that the interaction of the cultural elements is one of unequal forces, in which the economic movement is "by far the strongest, the most elemental, and the most decisive"; that this interaction is "on the basis of the economic necessity, which *ultimately* always asserts itself"; and that "the economic relations, however much they may be influenced by the other political and ideological ones, are still ultimately the decisive ones, forming the red thread which runs through them [political and ideological relations] and alone leads to understanding." [19]

Second, when Engels offers particulars to give precision to his ideas, we see that what he has in mind by the influence of noneconomic factors is mere milk and water, and nothing at variance with what we customarily encounter in his and Marx's

---

[18] *Selected Correspondence*, pp. 475, 484, 512.
[19] *Selected Correspondence*, pp. 484, 517–518. Engels' italics.

writings. His declaration that the state, once set up by the economic development, is invested with a movement of its own and reacts upon its progenitor, is accompanied by the revealing assertion that if the state goes against the economic trend, "in every great nation [the state power] will go to pieces in the long run." The Prussian state, he continues, evolved by virtue of economic causes, but "it could scarcely be maintained without pedantry" that no other factors were responsible for Brandenburg's emergence as a great power embodying the economic, linguistic, and religious differences of North and South. It would be ridiculous, he asserts, to explain in terms of economic causation the existence of every petty German state in history, "or the origin of the High German consonant mutations (*Lautverschiebung*)." In the other letters he cites as examples of the reaction of the state upon the economic situation the "influence by tariffs, free trade, good or bad fiscal system"; legislation on the working day, and the rôle of the state in the original accumulation and the rise of the bourgeoisie; and he inquires "why do we fight for the political dictatorship of the proletariat if political power is economically impotent?" [20]

He writes in the same vein about law. Legal propositions are a "direct translation" of economic conditions. Law, however, strives for a consistency of internal structure, whereas economic circumstance continually breeds contradictions. Accordingly the fidelity with which law mirrors economic conditions is violated. The point which he is trying to make is not very clear.[21] As an instance of the capacity of law to modify economics "within certain limits," he mentions the law of inheritance. The foundations of this law are economic. "But it would be difficult to prove" that the testamentary freedom in England and the testamentary restrictions in France are due in all their details to economic causes; yet both systems affect the economy by their influence on the distribution of wealth. He does less for the remoter ideologies, like religion and philosophy. Announcing that they "react back . . . even on its

[20] *Selected Correspondence*, pp. 480–481, 475–476, 517, 484.
[21] *Selected Correspondence*, pp. 481–482.

[society's] economic development," he proceeds to offer examples which demonstrate their subjection to "the dominating influence of economic development"! [22]

All these examples are far from breaking new ground. More than anything else, these letters reveal what has been pointed out on previous pages; namely, that in Marx's conception institutions do not function as inert shadows and apart from human traffic, but live in the attitudes and conduct of men and express themselves in human action. In these letters Engels is contending with critics who held that "we deny any and every reaction of the political, etc., *reflexes* of the economic movement upon the movement itself," and that Marx and he denied that the "various ideological spheres" have "any effect on history." [23] These letters give institutions neither an autonomous nor an outstanding part in human affairs. It is necessary to emphasize, too, that the examples which he cites against critics reveal a confusion of action and reaction. The fact that institutions are active is not to be equated to a contention that they counteract and modify the mode of production. The distinguishing question is, of course, whether the action is in harmony with the system of production or is calculated to obstruct or recast it. For example, Engels inquires why Marxians strive for the dictatorship of the proletariat if the political factor exercises no economic effects. He forgets that the dictatorship of the proletariat, preëminently the product of economic situations, in the Marxian scheme, functions to promote and not to counteract the demands of the economic dialectic. The same is obviously true of inheritance laws, tariffs, taxation, and the other examples which he cites: they are not examples of how noneconomic elements exercise a transforming influence on the economy, in defiance of the productive system and in opposition to the interests of the master class.

---

[22] *Selected Correspondence*, pp. 482, 483. Cf. p. 475.

[23] *Selected Correspondence*, pp. 484, 512. My italics. Engels admits that Marx and he were partly responsible for such an interpretation of their views. "We had to emphasize," he says, the economic factor "in opposition to our adversaries, who denied it, and we had not always the time, the place, or the opportunity" to do justice to other factors (*ibid.*, pp. 477, 510, 512).

In these letters Engels exhorts the correspondents to study Marx's *Eighteenth Brumaire* as a splendid example of his application of the theory, and as a study "which deals almost exclusively with the particular part played by political struggles and events." [24] That this historical essay offers no new emphasis and is a piece of the cloth, Engels himself forgetfully acknowledges. In 1895, only a year after he wrote the last of these letters, he informs us that although, when writing his essays on the unrest of 1848–1851 Marx was too close to the events, subsequent studies did not compel him to revise his opinions. Marx, Engels tells us, traces there the "causes" of the events, which are "in the last resort economic causes," and because Marx was familiar with the economic factor, he did not err, and no changes were necessary in the *Eighteenth Brumaire* which retraces the same period.[25] The general impression which these letters make, in common with all the other evidence bearing on the problem, comes to the familiar formula that while institutions and ideas have a part in history, their influence is of such a subordinate character that social events and changes are explicable mainly in terms of economics.

## The Scope of the Theory

To proceed with the purpose of the chapter, it is hardly necessary to labor the point that the aim of Marx's theory is to explain important events, institutions, and sentiments, and not to account for every minor incident or every detail of an important occurrence. It would be grotesque to insist that the theory has met its doom if it cannot explain on economic grounds why Mr. and Mrs. Jones are seeking a divorce, why the teamster's boy wants to be a doctor, why the members of a school board are non-Darwinian, or why a strike was lost or won.

Indeed, all these minor phenomena occur within the framework of a given system of production, and they are associated with people whose mentality is shaped by class interests, by

---

[24] *Selected Correspondence*, p. 484. Engels' italics.
[25] Introduction to *Class Struggles in France*, pp. 9–13.

institutions, mores, and a general atmosphere expressive of a culture fostered by the productive system. Indeed, Marxians would be inclined to perceive in such happenings more of the economic influence than non-Marxians would. Nevertheless, the validity of the theory does not stand or fall with the success or failure of an economic interpretation of such data. Marx was occupied with a philosophy of history, not of minutiae. Of course when these particulars are generalized, they assume the dimensions of institutions. Then we deal with the family, the occupations among social strata, the educational system, and relations of capital and labor. The *Communist Manifesto* cites several such institutions, deploring their plight under the dominion of the bourgeoisie.

Even when we rise to the scale of institutional phenomena the economic factor is not necessarily responsible for every particular or every departure from the type. The economic patterns of capitalistic countries, for instance, may display differences of detail. Likewise, within the limits of their dependence on the productive order, the other institutions can display specific variations. To Marx latter-day capitalism is associated with democracy, and yet the democracies of England, the United States, and France are not precisely identical. There is a distinction between large categories on the one hand and subclassifications and details on the other. Dictatorship, absolute monarchy, and democracy are categories which, in the Marxian system, ought to correspond to different modes of production. In the field of religion Catholicism, Protestantism, and Judaism exemplify categories, whereas the Methodist, Congregationalist, and Baptist denominations are variants of a category. The coexistence of the same mode of production with divergent categories of government, religion or any other institution would be in defiance of Marx's theory; but not the coexistence with different subvarieties of one category. This latter type of coexistence may be due to a complex of circumstances, some economic, others noneconomic; it expresses the allowance which Marx makes for the play of elements of a noneconomic order. The specific examples, like the petty German states or the consonants in high German, in Engels' letters considered above, do not exceed the limits of such an allowance.

For all these limitations, the panorama of Marx's conception is extensive spatially and temporally, and now some of its features will be epitomized. At a remote stage in its evolution a certain species of ape became endowed, by a mutation of a physiological order, with the capacity to work and to manipulate objects. This is to Marx, or at any rate to Engels, the beginning of man. The exercise of this capacity to produce his livelihood and the problems which it perennially presented to him are the prime movers of his development as a human, that is, of the growth of his dexterity, his power of speech, his intelligence, and his gregariousness. After long ages of slow evolution, traced in part by Engels in the *Origin of the Family, Private Property, and the State,* finally emerges the first historical mode of production, primitive communism, and the era of social history begins.

Throughout, the mode of production is the controlling fact. At a given stage of development a certain set of productive forces are available, some conserved from past experience, others newly acquired. The configuration of the productive forces in a scheme of making a living constitutes the mode of production. Implicit in each productive system beyond primitive communism is the class stratification of the participants in it. The régime of production and the associated class pattern form together the social substructure. Next in the picture is the superstructure. First of all the exploiters must be secure in their position of privilege. Hence the state and the law, the tiers closest to the economic base. Then rises the ideological realm of religion, ethics, philosophy, social science, literature, and art; a realm farther removed from the mode of production in the sense that it is less an immediate instrument of safeguarding the power of the predatory class and more the product of a social milieu compounded alike of the productive order and the resulting class psychology, state organization, and legal systems. When expounding aspects of the dialectic in general, the idea is voiced that there is no linear succession in these processes, but rather a mutually conditioning interaction of men, classes, work, institutions, and sentiments, all in a ceaseless flux. But neither in formal pronouncements of the theory nor in the specific consideration of institutions, ideas, classes, or human nature is there any stress, and in many instances even mention, of such interaction. But interaction or no interaction, everywhere pride of place is given to the economic situation; specifically, to the mode of production and its classes.

Certain factors which constitute the backbone in one or another of the many other philosophies of history are fitted into this scheme of thought, more or less. Some consideration is given to the geographic factor. Nature provides raw materials, sheltered or exposed boundaries, climatic encouragement or difficulties; here it stimulates man to activity, there it lulls him to laxity, everywhere it poses problems. But it functions as an economic datum, it expresses its influence as an inescapable premise in men's ways of gaining a livelihood. When the ape emerges as a working animal, nature confronts him as an overwhelming fact, in his labor, in his individual development, and, later, in his social growth. Science, too, is woven into the concept of production, as an accumulation of knowledge and techniques of manipulation. In their enumeration of institutions and ideas in the "superstructure" the two writers omit science It is subsumed under production as a dominant ingredient of technology.

The element of race receives attention, but very scantily. Like nature and science, it is perceived as an economic force. What is meant is not clarified, but it may not be difficult to guess. It may mean that racial peculiarities are essentially a product of economics. Peoples are compelled to organize their modes of making a living in more or less unique environmental settings. Through long ages, divergencies in location, in the conditions of work, and in the resulting social construction engender distinctive, but not profound, differences of habit, temperament, physical energy, and the like. Tradition and the general disinclination to make a change are mentioned here and there. The play of illusions, ideals, loyalties, and prejudices is recognized to some extent, but, as Marx teaches in *The Eighteenth Brumaire* (pages 48–49), they are the unconscious outgrowth of a scheme of production and are nourished by class interests, although those entertaining them are unaware of these hidden sources. There is equally some recognition of the temporary influence of personalities.[26]

The mode of production, class interest, the dialectic, and Marx's theory of knowledge form the four pillars of his philosophy of society. The body of economic theory identified with his name is principally a tool for depicting the transformation of capitalism into socialism. The dialectic he learned from Hegel's system; the philosophical aspects of his radicalism were derived from the neo-Hegelians, and the social aspects of his radicalism, from the French rebels and utopians like Sismondi, Proudhon, and Fourier; the economic theory has its roots mainly in the British classical school. These components and others were organized by an original mind into a conception to which he and Engels refer as "historical materialism" or the "materialistic conception of history."

This theory of history is expounded with a measure of recklessness of thought and with considerable confusion of expression. The reader who consults as a unit the scattered material dealing with a given question often labors in a labyrinth of parallel, intersecting, circular, and zigzagging passages. Genesis, basis, occasion, necessary condition, cause, and determination "in the last instance" are often used with little discrimination. Conjecture, illustration, evidence, and proof are presented at times as though they were on the same plane. The words dialectic, contradiction, inevitable, immanent, and historical necessity often appear to authenticate an argument and not because they easily fit with the context. There are not many important concepts presented with clarity and finality in one place and consistently adhered to in all subsequent discussions, and there are few important theories which do not appear in divergent and therefore puzzling versions. What plagues the reader most is the harvest of ambiguities, inconsistencies,

[26] E.g., Marx, *Civil War in France*, p. 87.

and contradictions, sowing dragon's teeth wherever they fall.

But there is the other side of the shield. We are dealing here with a powerful mind, original, wide-ranging, with flashes of uncommon penetration, generalizing and synthesizing with extraordinary acumen, reflecting and refracting with unique angles and decomposing into new lights everything that went through its many-sided prismatic medium, now meticulously scrupulous about details (see, e.g., the chapters on rent in *Capital*, volume III), and now carelessly painting on a large canvas. Scanning a facsimile of his undecipherable manuscript pages, mainly in old German script, but at times in French or English, one cannot help sensing a mind teeming with ideas and racing like a motor. That he did not sweat these theories out of books or out of himself, and that he must have come easily by them, may be inferred from the fact that in his comparatively brief span of life (1818–1883) — and he practically ceased writing ten years before his death because of illness — he read unusually extensively, learned several languages, and wrote voluminously: four volumes of polemics against contemporaries in the 1840's, three volumes of *Capital*, three volumes of *Theorien über den Mehrwert*, four volumes of correspondence, over half a dozen smaller volumes, and numerous brief essays.

# CHAPTER XVI

## OBSERVATIONS ON THE ECONOMIC SUBSTRUCTURE

BEFORE proceeding with critical observations on various aspects of Marx's theory of history it may be well to indicate briefly some basic postulates which one way or another inform what follows in this and the succeeding chapters.

The phenomena of social life exhibit totalities complex in their nature, evolution, ramifications, and interconnections. It is difficult, and in most cases it is futile, to seek to unravel their causes. There are no isolated particulars in a linear chain of cause and effect, no simple equations, and no easy answers. Even in natural phenomena the problem of cause and effect is generally not a formal exercise of observing and counting, but a labor demanding profound insight. In this regard history is more baffling than natural phenomena. The search for immediate causes, proximate causes, sufficient causes, and the causes of these causes, is often a hopeless enterprise. As Dr. Charles Beard says, history cannot answer why a certain idea went and another came, nor can it demonstrate that a given occurrence was "inevitable"; it can merely describe favorable conditions that made possible what happened.[1] Combating the contention that we know the causes of the American Revolution, he asserts: "We know that thousands of events took place in time, and that thousands of personalities were engaged in them, but we cannot find chains of causes and effects in them." [2]

---

[1] *The Discussion of Human Affairs*, pp. 118–119. Dr. Morris Cohen states that historical events may well be governed by laws, but the laws are not as simple as in physics. "Let us note, to begin with, that the phenomena of civilization are infinitely more complex, since they include biologic and mental as well as inorganic factors. And when situations depend upon too large a number of factors, or when these factors do not form a linear series, but modify each other in complex ways, we may not ever be able to discover the laws or to formulate manageable equations for dealing with the phenomena" ("Causation and Its Application to History," *Journal of the History of Ideas*, III [1942], 26).

[2] Beard, *Discussion of Human Affairs*, p. 91; see also pp. 90–93. An interesting literature has grown up dealing with the nature of historical knowledge and

In zoölogy it is sufficient to state that Charles I died because he was beheaded, but this will not satisfy the historian. The task becomes enormous indeed when we attempt to formulate the general causes of revolutions and the execution of rulers. A multitude of factors combine in varying configurations to throw light on social phenomena: factors like economics, religion, politics, human ambition, ingenuity, depravity, ignorance, emulation, leadership, desire for power, inventiveness, tradition, and accident. Sometimes some of these factors are paramount, sometimes others. Each case is to be studied carefully and is not to be approached with Procrustean designs to make it fit a preconceived theory. It is preferable to state humbly that we do not know than to be ready with answers after a superficial investigation. Marxians think that they know the causes of the downfall of Rome, of the French Revolution, of the American Revolution, or of the Wars of 1914 and 1939. But eminent historians are not sure. To envisage the mode of production as the Pooh-Bah of all civilization is as naïve as it is untenable.

It does not help matters greatly when Marxians reply that in Marx's scheme other factors are given proper weight; only, first, all these factors originate from economic sources, and second, their combined effectiveness cannot overpower the influence of the productive system. The first reservation can hardly be granted, and the second reservation cuts the limb on which the argument rests. The claim that institutions owe their first beginnings to the primitive mode of production is mere opinion. Treatises on anthropology offer varieties of hypotheses and suggestions. What happened, say, ten thousand years ago cannot be recaptured, and definitive conclusions are out of question. Marx and Engels were no anthropologists, and the researches available in their day were more inconclusive than present-day knowledge on the subject. Marx's idea of the economic genesis of institutions is based primarily on a priori deductions from the simple axiom that man must eat before he

---

the possibilities of historical laws. See, e.g., the summary by M. H. Mandelbaum, *The Problem of Historical Knowledge*, Part I.

can turn to philosophy. This is a true axiom; but to erect a necessary condition into a comprehensive and sufficient cause is hardly a proper way of building the cornerstone of a social philosophy. To write a book, one needs paper, pen, and ink; but paper, pen, and ink do not explain what is in the book. Moreover, as will be indicated in the next chapter, history fails to support the contention that in each instance the more modern variants of old institutions emerged as inevitable products of changed systems of production. In general, the question of exact origins of social institutions, like the question of causation in history, presents intractable problems.[3]

Even if it were established that an institution originated in economic circumstances, it would not follow on this account that the evolution of this institution and its modern phases are alike explainable by economic factors. Once it gained its life in economic soil its career and modern manifestations may be governed by noneconomic circumstances, wholly or largely. The Protestantism of today cannot be regarded as an economic product merely because primitive religion sprang, let us grant for the moment, from an environment and from notions bred by the rudimentary ways in which primitive man gained his livelihood. Anthropological economic origins may stand in causal relation to modern forms of institutions only if it is established that after their birth institutions develop into new forms by one inherent principle of growth completely dependent on the originating economic factor, and accordingly independent of all economic and noneconomic influences which are not implicitly fathered by the originating economic factor. If in their evolution institutions are affected by economic circumstances, but these circumstances do not stem directly from the originating economic factor, then these economic circumstances, and not the original economic factor responsible for the birth of institutions, are in causal relation with the subsequent career of institutions.

In urging the second reservation Marxians seemingly do not suspect that they contend against themselves. If the combina-

[3] Cf. R. M. MacIver, *The Modern State*, p. 25.

tion of all the noneconomic factors cannot prevail in the long run against the autonomy of the mode of production, the influence of one such factor, or even of several of them in coöperation, is negligible indeed when competing with the economic element. This point received consideration in the foregoing chapter. It is this persistent relegation of noneconomic forces to a minor position and this unfailing attribution of ultimate supremacy to the productive system, with the consequent substitution of plausible simplicity for complex totalities, that constitute one of the profound weaknesses of Marx's conception.

Marx affirms at times that no preconceived formulas can be indiscriminately applied to the complexities of historical phenomena, but that each situation must be specifically examined before we can discern the governing elements in it and its possible evolution in the future. Formulas, that is, are not to be arbitrarily projected into phenomena but should rather be distilled out of the facts of the case. The attitude is epitomized by the bromide that Marx was not a Marxian. Such an attitude is admirable, but its applicability to Marx is contingent on his explicit repudiation of all claims to a preconceived philosophy of history and on his readiness to investigate social phenomena without preconceptions, and to rest content with whatever results emerge. But Marx does not labor within such a frame. His aim is to present and illustrate a general philosophy of social organization and history, and only now and then does he mention that allowance is to be made for the modification of his theories by inquiring into the facts special to the occasion. Even the explicit incorporation, however, of the necessity to make allowances in one's general conception is unsatisfactory. We recall J. S. Mill's suggestive warning against such a procedure. Commenting on deductive philosophers like those of the Bentham school, he says:

It is not to be imagined possible . . . that these philosophers regarded the few premises of their theory as including all that is required for explaining social phenomena. . . . These philosophers would have applied, and did apply, their principles with innumerable allowances. But it is not allowances that are wanted. There is little chance of making due amends in the superstructure of a theory for the want of sufficient breadth in its foundations. It is unphilosophical to construct a science out of a few of the agencies by which the phenomena are determined, and leave the rest to the routine of practice or the sagacity of conjecture. We either ought not to pretend to scientific form, or we ought to study all the determining agencies equally, and endeavor, so far as it can be done, to include all of them within the pale of the science; else we shall infallibly bestow a disproportionate attention upon those which our theory takes into account . . .[4]

Some scholars assert that in their investigations of social phenomena they find it helpful to start out with the Marxian hypothesis as a coördinating principle. One wonders, however, whether this one-sided hypothesis does not do much harm along with the good. History presents a multitude of facts intermingled in intricate ways, and the more intensive the study the more numerous and complex the details grow. The historian cannot explore all the facts, and he must make a selection. The selection is based on the relevance and importance of the facts for the description and analysis of the phenomenon. But what is relevant and important is not an objective datum; it depends, largely, on the guidance, and on the bias, of the initial hypothesis. Furthermore, the selected facts are not so concrete and simple that mere awareness of them guarantees comprehension. Implicit in them are the overtones of human relations, emotions, thoughts, and errors; and they do not present themselves in apparent constellations. They have to be evaluated and organized. What pattern one makes of the data, and what relative strength one gives them, depends again, and in no small degree, on the controlling premise of the investigator.

Thus bias may creep in at each stage of the study. Consciously or unconsciously the plastic material may be tailored to fit a preconceived theme congenial to the basic presupposition. Theories are generals, facts are soldiers. The investigator is apt to see in the long history of a great nation the supreme confirmation of his private philosophy. The directive hypothesis may often determine from the beginning a result favorable to it: we may get out of history what we put into it. History has been defined as the art of imparting one's prejudices to

[4] *System of Logic*, Book VI, chap. viii, sect. 3, penultimate paragraph.

others. A natural scientist given to a one-sided conception can discover his error by checking his results against objective phenomena. But the historian moves in a circle; the facts against which the theory is to be tested are themselves perceived and conceived in the light of this theory. Small wonder that the same social phenomena will receive different accounts at the hands of Buckle, Carlyle, Durkheim, Freud, Henry George, Marx, Pareto, Sorokin, Spengler, Tarde, and A. J. Toynbee.[5]

It is better, one may suggest, to abandon simplifying preconceptions and to approach historical data with the general hypothesis that many factors are involved, and that only careful exploration will disclose their unique interplay in each instance. Then there is apt to be less initial bias in the selection, organization, and interpretation of facts. In some cases a pattern akin to Marx's may result, in other cases other patterns may offer more light. The charge that this attitude is eclectic or that it admits plural causation is irrelevant.

### THE MODE OF PRODUCTION

(A) WEAKNESSES OF THE CONCEPT. The mode of production and the related class structure form the substructure on which is erected the superstructure of institutions and ideas. The mode of production is presented by Marx as a single, materialistic (economic) datum, and as the independent variable. However, there is reason to doubt the validity of these three attributes. First, a productive system is hardly to be viewed as a distinct, unitary phenomenon. It is rather a composite. Man with his many-sided attributes, intelligence, and skills, working in a simple or elaborate scheme of division and coöperation of labor; the discovery of new materials and the particular way of utilizing natural resources; the accumulated scientific knowledge and the accumulated equipment, appliances, and tech-

---

[5] Professor E. S. Mason, who has made a careful study of the Paris uprising of 1871, shows that their theory of history has misled Marx and his followers into a faulty selection and evaluation of facts, resulting in a distorted conception of this comparatively simple historical episode (Mason, *The Paris Commune*, chaps. vi and vii).

niques — all these are subsumed in Marx's concept of production. To amalgamate, as Marx does, such a variety of components, to give them a collective designation, and to advance the resultant as a single and presumably irreducible factor governing the course of history is an unwarranted procedure.

Second, it is difficult to see why a productive system is to be regarded purely as a materialistic, economic phenomenon. The central impulse behind it is human intelligence and inventiveness. Marx is in the habit of stating that the productive forces develop and grow, as though the process were a matter of spontaneous generation or internal combustion. He does not stop to analyze who develops the productive forces, and how. All living creatures face the imperative of procuring a living, but only man organizes a system of production. It needs little pause to realize that this difference is accountable by the distinctive human traits among which intelligence occupies a preeminent place. Of course, the erect posture, the prehensile hand, and the power of speech were of incalculable assistance, but perhaps these peculiarities were themselves the gradual resultant of a mode of adaptation and behavior inspired by intelligence. Which came first, these physiological peculiarities or intelligence, remains an unsolved problem of science, but intelligence cannot be left out of account.

What intelligence is and what it does or does not do psychologists and philosophers may well argue, disagree, or confess ignorance about. The incontestable fact remains that man is endowed with an intelligence superior to that of other creatures, and it can hardly be denied that this endowment is of the greatest significance in the origin and nature of a system of production and of civilization in general. What is done with geographical surroundings, what response is made to urgent needs, and whether and how problems are perceived and solved, largely depends on noneconomic traits in the human character, among which intelligence occupies a high rank. Mainly on account of intelligence, man's adaptations are active and not passive. Instead of signifying adaptation of the organism to the natural environment, human evolution began to connote, from primitive days, the development of society, institutions, ideas, and ideals. Subtract intelligence and other human traits, and man will be enslaved to nature as other creatures are, and his methods of producing a living will remain as elementary and as immutable as theirs.

Third, a productive order cannot legitimately be presented as the primary and independent variable to which institutions seek to accommodate themselves. The mode of production is itself charged with institutional connotations without which it can have no content and no existence. It is permeated with attributes of property, inequality of possessions, status, contract, and other arrangements. Religion, superstition, art, and taboos were an integral part of productive activities in early times; property and human relations, sanctioned by law, are in organic relation to such activities in more modern times; always noneconomic institutions, conceptions, and mores are indispensable aspects, if not the very heart, of systems of production. The emphasis is to fall on interrelations and not on polarities.

Such concepts as property, slave, serf, guild, landowner, capitalist, and laborer are cornerstones of modes of production, and they cannot be treated implicitly as the derivatives of anterior modes of production. On the contrary, in some instances they are a precondition to the emergence of a scheme of production. Marx recognizes, for instance, that before capitalism could arise two conditions had to be fulfilled: the peasants had to be dispossessed to supply laborers incapable of earning a livelihood except by recourse to the capital in possession of the capitalist, and wealth had to be amassed by the few for the equipment to exploit the dispossessed laborer.[6] Both phenomena grew out of dispensations not indigenous to feudalism. Both receive the quickening impulse, according to Marx, from such extraneous occurrences as geographical discoveries and the expansion of

---

[6] "We have already shown," he says, "in the first volume that it is precisely the *ownership* of means of production by idlers which converts laborers into wage-workers and idlers into capitalists" (*Capital*, III, 54. My italics).

the market. The status of labor and of capital had to receive a new definition before capitalist production could acquire its meaning. To claim that capitalist production produced the class relations of proletariat and capitalist as well as the new concepts of property is to put the cart before the horse. The new status of the members of society, new property arrangements, and new power relations between men were not only essential as antecedent phenomena, they also remain institutional components of production, as vital in characterizing capitalist production as division of labor or technology. To repeat, however, strictly speaking, we are not dealing with a frame of antecedents and consequents but with mutually interacting conditions.

The case is scarcely different with other productive orders. It is inadequate to hold, for instance, that slave production or feudal production instituted themselves first, and then proceeded to fashion the classes of master and slave, of landed nobility and serf, and the new situations affecting property relations. The mode of production is a complex phenomenon compounded of economic and noneconomic elements. To abstract from this comprehensive composite the so-called derivative institutions is to leave a disarray of uncoördinated entities and a shapeless conception. Perhaps Professor Hook [7] has in mind such difficulties, and perhaps he intends to remove them when he interprets Marx to the effect that not the mode of production but social relations constitute the driving impulse of all culture. Such a construction, however, of Marx's central thesis is inadmissible. It is at unequivocal variance with Marx's teaching which exalts the mode of production as the predominant causality of civilization. Furthermore, asserting as it does that institutions like social relations determine all other phenomena and institutions, economic and noneconomic alike, this interpretation fails to relieve Marx of objections similar to those which beset the received interpretation of him. At once such questions spring up as — what is meant by social relations, what governs the social relations, how and

[7] *Towards the Understanding of Karl Marx*, pp. 133–134.

on what consistent historical evidence do social relations mold social processes and human thought, and the like.

Point is given to these observations when we compare one Marxian mode of production with another. Consider, for example, the slave régime of classical antiquity and the feudal system, two distinct productive organizations, according to Marx. The observer following Marx's teaching would not distinguish a difference between the two. In both societies he would note the same technique, the same use of natural resources, and seemingly the same type of labor. People produced goods in the Middle Ages in much the same way as in antiquity. The distinction between them rests, according to Marx, on the status of the laborer: in one case he was a slave, in the other a serf or a journeyman. But status is a question of law, custom, and other institutions, exactly the particulars which Marx does not weave into the mode of production, because he regards them as details of the derived superstructure. More will be said on this in the last section (Recent evidence) of Chapter XVII.

(B) IRREGULARITIES IN THE SUCCESSION OF MODES OF PRODUCTION. Because of their general disinclination to stress adequately the noneconomic factors clustering about a mode of production, and in any other connection, for that matter, and because of their frequent disposition to see simplicity where there is complexity, despite protestations to the contrary, Marx and Engels falter in their account of the transformations of the modes of production into one another. There is no revelation, for instance, of the reasons for the emergence of incurable contradictions and class strife in a gens society. Why a peaceful communal order is thrown into the turmoil of dissolution, how people living under communism happen to come upon the very concept of private property in the absence of a suggestive socio-economic setting, and why they go to the extreme of slavery, is not cleared up. Marxians attempt to explain the appearance of private property on the ground that, as Marx indicates, the productive forces were too scant for communism to survive.[8] If developed productive forces are indispensable to the

---

[8] Marx, *Theorien über den Mehrwert*, II, no. 2, pp. 482–483.

continuance of communism, one wonders how communism succeeded in gaining a foothold in the first place, and at a time
when the productive forces were still more primitive. The circumstance suggested against the continuance of communism
is an argument a fortiori against its very inception.

Nor is it demonstrated how by indigenous processes a slave
society grows into a feudal society. Marx and Engels introduce
the offices of extraneous events to account for the transition.
Wars and barbarian invasions, they narrate, impoverished
Rome, destroyed the markets, and rendered both the *latifundiae*
and slavery useless; they also forced the small farmer to seek
the protection of his strong neighbor at the price of reducing
himself to a serf. Wars and invasions are not the peculiar fruit
of a slave system. Similarly, capitalism does not appear on the
stage without the aid of fortuitous occurrences. The geographical discoveries, the exploitation of new colonies, and the influx
of metals from new regions are described as playing an indispensable part.[9] It is not shown how a feudal order, without an
impulse from the outside, breeds disintegration and as a matter of course paves the way to a capitalist construction.

A conception in which the form of production functions as
the keystone of civilization ought to exercise the utmost care in
noticing and accounting for any considerable irregularity either
in the career or in the sequence of this all-important factor. But
while they record some of the irregularities, it does not occur to
them that for the adequacy of their theory it is essential to
pause and seek the reasons for them as evidence disturbing to
their viewpoint. We are informed that in some instances the
mode of production is frozen to a standstill. "In Asia . . .
conditions of production . . . are reproduced with the regularity of natural phenomena." In India and in Slavic countries the
"old primitive communities . . . could remain in existence for
thousands of years."[10]  Engels acknowledges that in the Mo-
hammedan world economic systems endure on the same plane,
but in Western Christendom they are subject to progressive

[9] See above, Chap. III; also *Capital*, I, chaps. xxvii and xxxi; III, 391, 911.
[10] Marx, *Capital*, I, 158; Engels, *Anti-Dühring*, p. 165.

transformations. In Islam, he records, religious uprisings spring from the economic soil and are essentially economic movements cloaked in religious garb. But these uprisings, he relates, fail to achieve progress. They do not uproot the old order for a new one, but merely represent periodical episodes on the same level of economic development. It is different, he points out, with the upheavals in the Christian West. There, too, in popular movements religion is merely the mask for assaults on outworn economic systems, but the collisions end in overthrowing the old societies and in introducing new ones, and thus "the world moves onward." [11]

We learn also that the succession of the forms of production may be of indeterminate character. We are led to believe that in Marx's scheme, primitive communism evolves into ancient slavery. But we find in a casual footnote that between the dissolution of the communal order and the full establishment of slavery there is, in antiquity, the interlude of an economy with peasant agriculture and the handicrafts as the "economic foundation." [12] The German tribes which took possession of Rome by-passed slavery and changed directly to feudalism.[13] In India, English commerce dissolves communal arrangements and slowly introduces capitalism.[14] Capitalism is often pronounced as the indispensable preliminary to communism because of its function in preparing the requisite productive forces; [15] but, as was indicated in Chapter II, above, on account of communal habits in her agriculture, Marx was of the opinion that under certain favorable conditions Russia might conceivably "escape" the full course of capitalism and go straightway to communism.

These irregularities in the sequence of economic stages do not affect a small corner of Marx's theory of history, but execute a flanking movement against some of its foremost assertions. In the Marxian construction a given mode of production

[11] *Neue Zeit*, XIII, no. 1 (1894–95), p. 5n.

[12] Marx, *Capital*, I, 367n.

[13] See above, pp. 53, 134.

[14] *Capital*, III, 392–393 and n. 51; *New York Tribune*, June 25 and August 8, 1853.

[15] E.g., Marx, *Theorien über den Mehrwert*, II, no. 2, pp. 482–483.

is supposed to breed definite contradictions culminating in a particular new mode. It is of the essence of the dialectic to give order of sequence in the evolution of social arrangements and not a hop, skip, and jump. In a given society the contending classes derive their ideas, interests, and impulses from the realities within their own midst, out of their own relations of production, and not from alien cultures. We are taught by Marx that a given productive system must run its own course of evolution, and cannot be truncated; that it is preposterous to graft on it the fundamentals of another civilization, especially when we realize that the insertion of an extraneous productive order entails, in Marx's thought, the importation of an aggregate of institutions proper to it; that no new problems arise before their solution, or intimations of it, is born within the given society; and that the productive forces which only capitalism is capable of developing are indispensable to communism if it is not to succumb to the maladies which undermined the tribal economy.

Marxians and writers of broad tolerance generally interpret such irregularities as a demonstration that Marx was not under the spell of his materialistic formula, but recognized the uniqueness of special circumstances and the play of many historical factors. But this commendable tolerance does not resolve the problem. To repeat, there would be no problem only if it can be accepted that Marx had no intention of propounding a philosophy of history. A scientist tests his hypothesis or theory against the facts, and he is more solicitous about the phenomena which do not square with his thesis than he is pleased with those which do. In the light of the unaccommodating facts the scientist recasts his theory, or else he abandons it. It does not seem that Marx ranged far and wide in his effort of collecting facts from which to derive his theorems concerning all the forces that forge the character, transformations, and sequence of productive orders in history, and from which to abstract the generalization that the mode of production impresses a sovereign influence on the other phases of civilization. It does not remove the difficulty if Marx shows awareness of departures from his theory and complains that in view of this awareness there is no justification for charging him as the exponent of comparatively simple formulas applicable to complex situations. Nor is the problem resolved by treating the irregularities with the observation that they are accounted for by special historical circumstances. Historical circumstances we always have with us. We cannot tell which ones are not special circumstances and therefore are expected to develop in accordance with his theory, and which ones are special circumstances and therefore can develop at variance with his theory. We are not told whether these latter circumstances spring forth for uniform or special reasons, or whether they give rise to regular or capricious consequences.

It may be observed in parenthesis that the whole question of the linear succession of gens, slavery, feudalism, and capitalism is open to doubt. Investigations of anthropologists demonstrate that communism is not typical of primitive peoples, and that no one general rule can be laid down respecting primitive social organization. The researches of scholars like Eduard Meyer suggest that ancient Greece had a good deal of free labor, and was by no means the slave-ridden society which she is commonly taken to have been. Many a student maintains likewise that in antiquity some societies, like those in Egypt and China, went through the stages not unlike feudalism and capitalism. According to Marx, capitalism made its first appearance in the sixteenth century, but there is evidence that capitalism existed in the Near East many centuries before then, and that it spread from there to the north of the Mediterranean, and from there to Western Europe.[16]

### THE CLASS STRUGGLE

(A) THE ASSUMPTION OF TWO CLASSES. The human element in Marx's formula is epitomized by the class struggle. Self-interest impels the laborers to strive for a new social order.

---

[16] This thesis is treated well by Professor M. M. Knight in *Economic History of Europe to the End of the Middle Ages*. See A. A. Young's introduction, the author's preface, and *passim*.

The theory of the class struggle is based on a chain of assumptions: one, society is ultimately stratified (disregarding the middle class for the moment) into two well-organized classes; two, the oppressed class perceives its interests and possesses the wisdom necessary to promote them; three, the other classes are bankrupt and cannot resist the working class. These asumptions need to be examined.

As to the first assumption. The question of the class struggle is part of the larger phenomenon of emulation and rivalry, of contacts and collisions, among groups in society. Society always consists of a multitude of groups. There are occupational groups, political parties, religious sects, racial blocks, rich and poor; there are industrial regions and agrarian regions, northern interests and southern interests; and there are the silver bloc, the sugar-beet bloc, the oil bloc. It has been so since the beginning of organized society, and history is full of records of group pressures and group contests. All this is true, the Marxians would say, but the present division of society into capital and labor is the most important, and the strife between the two the most significant.

Most important and most significant for what? The answer will be, very likely, for civilization, for the course of human destinies. If so, many will oppose the emphasis on Marx's type of classes. Some will insist that the middle class is the most important one, for from its midst come most of the thinkers, innovators, leaders, professionals, idealists, and writers; and they will quote from political thinkers since Aristotle that the middle class is the backbone of society. Others will hold that all groups and all contests and pressures are important, constituting as they do the stuff of social life, and sometimes one group and sometimes another is of outstanding moment, depending on the total pattern of conditions. Still others will believe that if two classes are to be selected, it is more valid to divide society into the progressive class and the great class of the indifferent. The first consists of those with wakeful minds and sensitive goodwill, alert and ready to labor for social betterment; its members cut across all social layers, and may wear overalls or a white collar.[17] The other is composed of those devoted to personal pursuits unperturbed by what is going on in the world outside their daily orbit, and in this multitude, too, may be found alike the idle rich, the greedy lawyer, and the masses worried over their daily bread. This class plays a helpful, permissive, or restrictive part in relation to the other class.

Furthermore, the postulate of two single-minded, group-conscious classes ready for a final combat is of precarious validity. There are varieties of enduring interests, passions, and prejudices; there are political, social, racial, and religious barriers, among laborers and among employers, which refuse to be overcome by economic factors, and cast a shadow on the idea of consistent unity of class action. Among the workers in this country, for example, we find more or less definite divisions into the skilled and the unskilled; the organized and the unorganized; the C.I.O. and the A.F. of L.; the white-collar labor and labor in overalls; those who have money in the bank and stock in the "company" and those who live from hand to mouth; the colored and the white; the native and the foreign born; the half-illiterate and the holders of a high school diploma; the socialists, the communists, the conservatives, and the great mass of the indifferent.

The worker has no nationality, pronounces the *Communist Manifesto* (page 27). "Modern industrial labor, modern subjection to capital, the same in England as in France, in America as in Germany, has stripped him of every trace of national character," it says; and it urges the workers of the world to unite.[18] But the potency claimed for the economic factor in this pronouncement is not exemplified by facts. The French laborer

[17] Cf. G. Sarton, *The History of Science and the New Humanism*, p. 46. Sir James Frazer refers to the "impulsive energy of the minority" working for progress against "the dead weight of the majority of mankind" (*The Golden Bough*, p. 56).

[18] "But the proletarians have in all countries one and the same interest, one and the same enemy. . . ; the proletarians are, in the great mass, by nature without national prejudice, and their whole upbringing (*Bildung*) and movement are essentially humanitarian, anti-national. Only the proletarians can destroy nationality" ("Das Fest der Nationen in London," *Gesamtausgabe*, Part I, vol. 4, p. 460).

had his heartburnings over Alsace-Lorraine; the American worker is loudly proud of his country, the English worker, less loudly, of the British empire, and both look down on, say, Mexican laborers; the German wage earner, it seems, will obediently hate every nation which it is told to hate. It is this variety of prejudices that used to provide the American employer with a weapon against labor organization. When possible, he would place in one group workers of different European origins. Instead of uniting in common cause against the "capitalist oppressor," they revived old animosities and spent their lunch hours wrangling over national differences.[19] It can be easily surmised that Marx was familiar with such phenomena. He was aware that the Irish worker hated the English worker.[20] But, as usual, he laid little store by noneconomic facts. He did not wish to consider that workers, like plain people generally, are parochial in their loyalties and vaguely distrustful of the large, the theoretical, and the remote.[21]

Martin is right when he points out that the engineer receiving $150 a month is as far from the Italian section-hand as the president of the railroad is from the engineer; that the capitalist farmer feels more at one with his hired laborer than with the capitalist mine owner; that the white carpenter or bricklayer has more class prejudice against the Negro teamster than the Jewish banker has against the Jewish tailor; that the shop girl deems herself as superior to the servant girl as her mistress feels herself superior to the shop girl; that the retail tobacconists showed as much hostility to the tobacco trust as factory hands have ever shown toward an employer; that independent refiners fought the Standard Oil Company as bitterly as the Homestead strikers fought the Carnegie Steel Company; and that miners deported Negroes and Chinese from the gold camps as readily as mine owners deported strikers.[22]

---

[19] Cf. J. B. Bryce, *Modern Democracies*, I, 136-138.

[20] Letter to Kugelmann, March 28, 1870, in *Neue Zeit*, XX, no. 2, p. 478.

[21] It is interesting to note what Ricardo thinks of the investor's attitude in a kindred situation (*Principles of Political Economy*, chap. vii, p. 83).

[22] "Socialism and the Class War," *Quarterly Journal of Economics*, XXIII, 513-515. Cf. F. H. Knight, *The Ethics of Competition and Other Essays*, p. 351n.

(b) THE ASSUMPTION OF A SOPHISTICATED PROLETARIAT. The second assumption, that the working class is aware of its material interests and knows how to further them, is equally open to question. We may assume that laborers desire to improve their lot; everybody does. But desire is not to be equated to achievement. Even in the private life of an individual the comprehension of one's interests, far from appearing as an isolated elementary task involving the rudimentary use of one's sensibilities, is correlated with the many spheres of one's experience, and calls into exercise one's accumulated wisdom. Often enough it is a difficult task.

The perception and solution of class interests is a problem of more difficult dimensions by far. The fulfillment of the dream of the underprivileged is a problem that baffled the thinkers of the ages. Marx confidently entrusts its solution to the proletarians, and he realizes, apparently, what he demands of them. The proletarians will have to possess some idea of social evolution, some understanding of the foundations of our present order, some diagnosis of its maladies, a conviction as to the remedy, and an unbending will to apply it. External economic facts are insufficient to furnish enlightenment, even though Marx assures us that they render the proletarian sophisticated enough to discern that law, morality, and religion are mere bourgeois prejudices.[23]

He is an exuberant man who expects the wage earners to solve the social problem. Marx writes learnedly on the revolutionary events of 1848, discusses with a deft pen the interests of the factions involved, and indicates with the finger of the expert what tactics they should have pursued. It was all clear to Marx; yet, as he points out, the workers were blind to their genuine interests and were tossed about from pillar to post. Years later Marx acknowledged that he had expected too much, that at the time, owing to the immaturity of the conditions of production, the working class was unenlightened, and that with the progress of capitalism the workers will become better informed. Marx does not tell us how he happened to know what

[23] Marx and Engels, *Communist Manifesto*, p. 27.

economic reality was not ready to teach. With the progress of time problems and issues grow more complex: capitalist society shows no trend toward idyllic simplicity so that he who runs may learn its secrets. When the economist assumes that by and large the buyer is motivated by self-interest, Marx makes the skeptical observation: "In bourgeois societies the economic *fictio juris* prevails that everyone, as a buyer, possesses an encyclopedic knowledge of commodities." [24] If it requires encyclopedic knowledge to buy food and clothing, and if the imputation of such knowledge to the buyer is *fictio juris*, what is required of the proletarian to reconstruct the world, and what epithet is to be given to the imputation of such powers to him?

It is to be noted that this theory of the laborers' mission to solve the social problem does not square with Marx's doctrine of how people gain knowledge. He urges, we recall, that most people do not understand the world in which they live, and that they judge by surface appearance. Only a few superior intellects penetrate beneath the surface and gain insight. Even a man like J. S. Mill is at times denied the honor of a place among these few. It is not clear why Marx ascribes superior qualities of mind to the masses of workers. A man who cares nothing for "so-called public opinion," who admonishes the investigator to seek the causes of social change in material facts and not in the illusory notions filling the heads of the acting agents, can hardly bestow on the vast population of wage earners the qualities demanded by their "historical mission."

Another difficulty comes to mind. In the development of human nature Marx places much emphasis on the effectiveness of the environment. What environment he foresees for the proletariat with the advance of capitalism is well known. The proletariat is plagued by the industrial reserve army, by increasing misery, and by the ravages of ever-deepening depressions. It is difficult to see how the masses so circumstanced can form a militant, intelligent unit. In the eyes of an environmen-

[24] *Capital*, I, 42n.

talist, especially, a race of degraded wage slaves is not a race of world builders.[25]

The worker hardly corresponds to the picture which Marx paints of him. The worker is not a Prometheus. He is swayed by a multiplicity of interests, by prejudice, and by inexplicably wayward notions. The vexing problems connected with our present order he perceives but vaguely, nor do such high matters disturb him much. Marx analyzes in the volumes of *Capital* the enormities of the present order, and he indicates where the workers' interests lie. Few workers are eager to read these volumes. The average worker is concerned with his daily cares, and nearby interests are closer to his heart than the theory of socialism. He is less interested in the equality of men than in the inequality of baseball teams. The immediate prospect of a higher or lower wage evoke within him more emotion or tension than general social ills. A few enthusiasts would be willing to suffer for a dream, but the ordinary person is more prosaic.[26] The great mass of laborers is interested, if at all, in bourgeois trade-unionism; and if a worker has ambition it lies in the direction of rising in his job or of saving money and becoming a small capitalist. In a capitalistically advanced country like ours the growth of trade-unionism has been painfully slow and the number of communists in the ranks of labor conspicuously negligible. The "proletarians" vote perennially for the Republican or Democratic candidates. The fear of the army entertained by revolutionist writers is a tacit admission that the workers are not imbued with Marxian class consciousness. Soldiers are, predominantly, proletarians. To claim a revolutionary orientation among the proletarians, and to regard at the same time the army as a menace and not as an aid to the revolution, is paradoxical.

Some Marxians are aware of this difficulty. Karl Kautsky

[25] Cf. Adam Smith's lament over the debasing effects of division of labor on the working population, in *Wealth of Nations*, II, 264–265.

[26] Marx makes too easy a transition from class interests to revolution. One may say with Professor L. T. Hogben: "A social psychology is pre-Shakespearean if it overlooks the fact that people will rather bear the ills they have than fly to others which they know not of" (*Retreat from Reason*, p. 31).

acknowledges that workers will not embrace communism without benefit of bourgeois intellectuals.[27] Lenin is of the same mind. So is Professor Sidney Hook, who suggests, however, that Marx himself held this position, and refers for documentation to Parts II and IV of the *Communist Manifesto*.[28] It is difficult to agree with Professor Hook on this question. In the first place, his reference does not state that without the aid of intellectuals from the capitalist class the workers will not be informed with a revolutionary or socialist outlook. One paragraph on the first page of Part II (page 30) states that the communists constitute "the most advanced and resolute" segment of the workers' parties and that they possess a theoretical conception of the "proletarian movement" as a whole.

The next paragraph adds that the immediate aim of the communists is identical with that of the other proletarian parties: the building of a proletarian class, the overthrow of the bourgeoisie, and the conquest of power. This suggests that without the tutelage of the communists, the workers' parties develop revolutionary objectives. In Part III of the same *Manifesto* (page 54), Marx talks of "the gradual, *spontaneous* class-organization of the proletariat," and refers (page 55), even respecting the immature stage of the proletarian class, to "the first instinctive yearnings of that class for a *general reconstruction of society*."[29] The same document (page 27) states that economic conditions give the proletarian penetrating insight, so that "law, morality, religion are to him so many bourgeois prejudices" nourished by bourgeois interests — and this already in 1848.

In the second place, even if the *Communist Manifesto* offered a statement in explicit support of Professor Hook, it would be at sharp variance with Marx's typical position on this question, as expounded in this very pamphlet [30] and everywhere else.

[27] "Die Revision des Programms der Sozialdemokratie in Oesterreich," *Neue Zeit*, XX, no. 1, p. 79.
[28] *Towards the Understanding of Karl Marx*, pp. 240–241.
[29] My italics. Nothing of particular significance appears in Part IV.
[30] See, for example, the last pages of Part I, tracing the evolution of the proletariat.

His customary standpoint is that capitalism itself breeds its gravediggers; that maturing conditions united with class interests mold the group consciousness of the workers and point to appropriate class strategy; that members of the middle class sink to the proletarian status and "supply the workers with fresh elements of enlightenment and progress"; that "a portion of the bourgeois ideologists" join "the revolutionary class";[31] and that he, Marx, feels uneasy about the infiltration of these ideologists because they adulterate the proletarian ideas with confused bourgeois notions and sentimentalism.[32] In *Anti-Dühring*, written with Marx's knowledge and partial collaboration, Engels discusses the conflict between the new productive forces and the outworn capitalistic mode of production which no longer can make adequate use of them, and declares: "Modern socialism is nothing but the reflex in thought of this actual conflict, its ideal reflection in the minds, first, of the class which is directly suffering under it — the working class."[33] To make the "inevitable" downfall of capitalism and triumph of communism contingent on the pedagogical services of bourgeois intellectuals is to see in Marx a proposition foreign to his scheme of thought.

(c) THE ASSUMPTION OF AN IMPOTENT UPPER CLASS. It is not necessary to dwell on the third assumption, that the upper classes will be impotent against the workers. Whether or not Marx predicts the disappearance of the "new" middle class is not certain; certain it is that the middle class refuses to disappear. The professions, the business managers, the storekeepers, and brokers are multiplying, and even the "old" middle class (the independent farmer, the artisan, the small manufacturer) is far from extinct. These categories are, furthermore, not becoming mere wage earners and are far from regarding themselves as proletarians.[34] Inasmuch as, in Marx's view, the

---

[31] *Communist Manifesto*, p. 26.

[32] Letter to Bebel, September, 1879, in Marx and Engels, *Selected Correspondence*, pp. 375–376.

[33] Page 293.

[34] Cf. T. M. Sogge, "Industrial Classes in the United States in 1930," *Journal of the American Statistical Association*, June, 1933.

middle class, even if it survives, has no directive function in economic activity, he deprives it of political significance in shaping modern social evolution. The precariousness of this conception is obvious and needs no laboring. In every capitalistic country the middle class has been enormously important politically and intellectually, in the ebb and flow of social experience, and in the conspicuous phases of social dynamics alike.

The nonproletarian classes will have no disposition to wait until the workers gather threatening power. More educated, more prosperous, and more cohesive than the workers, they are more alert, more determined, and more resourceful. According to Marxians the rise of fascism merely reflects the final phase of capitalism. Assuredly at such an advanced economic stage the proletarian class ought to be in full vigor, and assuredly it is inimical to fascism. If Marx's theory of the self-consciousness, the acumen, and the power of this class in advancing its interests is sound, fascism should not have gained dominion in face of such opposition. More than once Marx and Engels praised the German workers for their strong organization and advanced theoretical knowledge respecting social processes and its own mission.[35]  To what estate the German workers had sunk under Hitler is only too well known. The last twenty years have taught us more in these matters than is contemplated in Marx's simple formulas.

## HISTORY AND THE PROLETARIAN MISSION

Another Marxian viewpoint may be noted in closing.  Marx and his friend do not tire asserting that no new social system is born without a class struggle, and history demonstrates that it is now the turn of the proletariat to build a new society.  History seems to be indifferent to these claims.  There is no record of a class struggle marking the dissolution of primitive communism and the arrival of slavery.  The pages of the history of Greece and Rome are full of group contests, but they do not record

---

[35] See, e.g., Engels' letter to A. Bebel, December 11, 1884, Marx and Engels, *Selected Correspondence*, pp. 431–435.

that the downfall of Rome was the result of a struggle between two classes, one insisting on the perpetuation of slavery and the other contending, and victoriously, for the higher synthesis of feudalism. It may be remarked that feudalism, at least in its first few centuries commonly referred to as the Dark Ages, is far from exemplifying a higher order of civilization than ancient Greece or Rome.

Only capitalism may be claimed to have been signaled by a class struggle, and even in this instance there are flies in the ointment. First, the struggle was not between the exploiter and the exploited of the old society, that is, between the serf and the nobility or between the journeyman and the guild-master, but between the landed interests and the rising capitalists. Second, a careful reader of competent historians of the events will appreciate that the Cromwell rebellion or the French Revolution can hardly be epitomized by the simple equation to a struggle between the capitalist class and the feudal gentry.[36] The story is much more complicated. Third, the quest for the class struggle which inaugurated capitalism in Germany fails to bring results. Marxians will point to the wars of 1618–1648. However, Marx saw feudalism in the saddle in Germany up to the nineteenth century. As late as 1848 he expects, on the last page of the *Communist Manifesto*, a "bourgeios revolution" in Germany, comparing it to the revolution in England in the seventeenth century and in France in the eighteenth, and predicting that a proletarian revolution would follow immediately. This "bourgeois revolution" never arrived.[37]

The Russian upheaval is neither fish nor fowl. The October revolution of 1917 obviously was not a contest between a feudal class and a newborn bourgeoisie. Nor can it be depicted as a struggle between a mature proletarian class and an advanced

[36] See, e.g., K. Federn, *The Materialist Conception of History*, chap. iv and the references.

[37] His comments on the abortive uprisings of 1848 in Germany underscore his view of Germany as an economically antiquated country and his appraisal of these uprisings as perpetuating an economic anachronism, in contrast to earlier revolutions in England and France. See, e.g., *Aus dem literarischen Nachlass von K. Marx und F. Engels*, III, 211–213.

capitalist class in an obsolescent capitalistic society laden with the antithesis of new productive forces. Marxians can look for such classes and such a struggle in old capitalistic countries but not in the semi-feudal, agrarian Russia of the czars.

History similarly fails to furnish inductive evidence that it is the mission of the proletarians to build a new order. The ancient slave did not erect the feudal system, nor the serf or journeyman the capitalistic system. History does not demonstrate that the exploited class in one society is the architect of the next social organization. Without the leavening and directive aid of members of the other classes, the revolt of the masses hardly ever sufficed to establish a new order. The uprisings of the slaves in ancient societies failed to bring them liberation; and peasants' revolts in feudal societies, like the Peasants' Revolt in sixteenth-century Germany, commonly ended in suppression. The French Revolution was not the exclusive achievement of the sans-culottes, and the Russian upheaval may have come to a different conclusion without Lenin and his group. In time of unsettlement and crisis the confused anger and the vague fears of the fluid populace can often be channeled by a well-organized group of clever manipulators.[38] It is not easy to foresee the shape of the future social construction. That the coming society will be communist and that it is the "historical" mission of the proletariat to constitute it is a conception born of a priori reasoning and wishful thinking. It is not an idea urging itself as the fruit of a scholarly exploration of history.

[38] R. M. MacIver, *The Modern State*, p. 214.

# CHAPTER XVII

## OBSERVATIONS ON INSTITUTIONS

IT is not the purpose of this and the following chapter to undertake a detailed discussion of the many institutions and fields of thought involved in the far-flung conceptions of Marx; nor is it within the competence of the writer to undertake such a task. The aim is to present sketchy observations on a few institutions, like the state, law, and religion, in this chapter; and on some departments of knowledge, like science and philosophy, in the next chapter. The purpose will be to indicate some of the inadequacies resulting from an overemphasis on the economic element.

### THE STATE

To Marx, the state is an engine employed by the owners of the means of production for the subjection and exploitation of the masses. The state can emerge only where there are private property and a predatory class; it has no existence in the classless society of communism, where sovereignty rests with the mass of the population. A social upheaval assumes the character of a revolution and introduces a new state only if the possession of the means of production shifts to a new class and a new class structure results. Otherwise it is only an upheaval. Bloody violence may overthrow a democracy for fascism, but the Marxians will see in the event neither a revolution nor a new state. To Marxians capitalism is followed by communism, and fascism is merely the spasm of expiring capitalism. Representing neither a realignment of classes nor a shift in economic power, fascism does not stand for a new society.

That there is truth in some of the Marxian contentions about the nature of the state can hardly be denied. Commonly presented ideas of the state describe it as the indispensable basis of individual development, as the expression of the will of the majority, as the foundation of orderly social living, or as a separate entity transcending the personal levels of morality. Such views are valid, at least with proper reservations. But cutting across these conceptions is the perennial prosaic question as to where, really, the locus of state power is, who the privileged beneficiaries of things constituted are, and who, more than others, is concerned with the preservation of a given order within its framework. There is suggestiveness in the idea, insisted on by Marx, that the basic power of the state is associated with a relatively small group in the community. The slave masters of antiquity, the feudal lords, or the landed interests in recent Spain or Hungary, are examples. Even in modern democracy it would be stretching a point to insist that ultimate sovereignty is everywhere and always with the poor and the untutored as much as with the rich and the prominent. At least to one who has not probed deeply into historic record, history seems to teach that running through the fluctuating forms of the state is the common denominator of oligarchy.

But such a truth is not the whole truth by far. First, the fact is inescapable that whatever else the state does it serves as an institution which assures orderly living to the community, and such a function is of surpassing importance wherever people mean to live together. A group, however small, needs organization if it serves a purpose and has a task to perform. It will need a body of rules and a degree of force, agreeable to the majority, in order to cope with recalcitrants. Engels regards the police, judges, and prisons as the hallmarks of class domination. But even in a communist society order must be maintained, and there may be misdemeanors, crimes of passion, abuse of state property, insubordination in emergencies, subversive activity, etc. One has to possess a naïve belief in the simplicity of human nature and in the effectiveness of environment to entertain the conviction that in a communist society scores of millions of individuals will become angels. Furthermore, the intricate architecture of modern economic activity demands elaborate planning, organizing, and a gradation of authority. Marx fully realizes this, and there is no dream among Marxians of a spontaneous collocation of men, materials, and equipment. But all this means that without a recognized supreme authority society will drift into chaos and exploitation. To assert that there is no state but a commonwealth, as long as authority is not class authority but one sanctioned by the classless majority, is, in the main, to play with words. The essence of the state is, it seems, the organized strength of society facing the minority or the individual; it is the authority of the mass confronting the inclinations, the mutations, and the freedom of the individual — and it will hardly be different in a communist society.

Second, the state even as a group instrument represents a broader conception than the one envisaged by Marx. Even if it is granted that the underlying form of state has often been an oligarchy, the oligarchy has not always been, or does not necessarily have to be, one of wealth. Marx sees no state in primitive society. Nevertheless, the power over the primitive community rested in many instances in persons distinguished for valor, experience, cunning, physical strength, or magic.[1] The group in power may be a theocracy, as in ancient Egypt, in Tibet, and elsewhere; or a military clique, as in some instances in the history of South America. The Brahmans do not occupy a top position in India exclusively or mainly by virtue of ownership of the means of production. There is little private property in Russia today, and yet the rule of an oligarchical state is much in evidence. There are no classes owning the means of production, and yet there are aspects of dictatorship firmly entrenched there. Nor was the governing class in Nazi Germany or fascist Italy identical with the capitalist class. The rulers maintained sovereign power by military support and by the acquiescence and support not only of the wealthy few but of the miseducated populace generally. In both these countries the economic power of the new ruling minorities came as a corollary of the antecedent conquest of political power. To rest satisfied with the claim that the *origin* of fascism in these and other countries is due primarily to economic causes, and therefore all noneconomic facts, singly or jointly, are of second-

[1] Cf. MacIver, *The Modern State*, p. 48.

ary consideration, is to put a simplified construction on a phenomenon of complex roots.[2]

Third, Marx regards democracy as the unique adjunct of capitalism and as a rhetorical expression devoid of content inasmuch as the ultimate power is in the hands of the capitalist class. Social legislation and any other privileges for the masses are, in his teachings, only grudging concessions which will be revoked when capitalism comes upon hard times, and which will never be extended to the point of a serious encroachment on the prerogatives of the rulers.

While there is no small grain of realism in such a view, it suffers from one-sidedness. Democracy is hardly a mere derivative of capitalism. It was known in primitive societies and in ancient Greece and Rome. It may be suggested that democracy exemplifies the general leavening impulses of human beings to improve their lot, whenever economic, political, and social circumstances allow; to strive for self-government, and to place themselves on par with their fellowmen. Aristotle noted this human trait in his *Politics*.[3] Far from being a creature of transient capitalism, democracy may point to those elemental and primary attributes of man without which social development and progress would be impossible.

Furthermore, the characterization of social betterment as a concession of the master class is a simplification, even if a plausible one. Why there should be concession is, from the Marxian viewpoint, not clear. Under capitalism the owning class has comprehensive control over the means of livelihood of the masses. If capitalism were to use the school, the press, the radio, the theater, and other agencies to regiment and indoctrinate labor into complete subservience to a ruling party, the Marxians would have a ready explanation. With economic dominion, they would say, is inevitably associated political, intellectual, and social dominion. But when the masses have won free education, suffrage, factory legislation, minimum wage

[2] See, e.g., the suggestive comments on the rise of Nazism in J. Frank, *Fate and Freedom*, pp. 10, 340–343.
[3] Book III, section 9; Book V, section 1.

laws, and social insurance; when laws are passed, imperfectly as they may be administered, to curb monopoly, to regulate banks, public utilities, stock market speculation, the issue of securities, and unfair competition; and when income and inheritance taxes become more and more progressive, the Marxians are satisfied with an explanation in terms of concessions.[4] Such a ready explanation loses sight of the climate of opinion formed by free education and developed means of communication, the power of the somewhat awakened masses, the leadership and efforts of aroused sympathetic personalities, a stimulated social consciousness, and other factors, economic and noneconomic alike.

Finally, Marx's thesis that because of the economic factor the state even in a modern democracy looms as a power superimposed over the downtrodden mass seems stilted. We are asked to believe that if, with free education, with books and journals available in public libraries, with more or less reliable newspapers obtainable at nominal prices alongside of the sensation-seeking sheets, with leisure after work, with votes enough to overcome any political opposition, and with enough soldiers recruited from the proletarian class to render the show of military force its own ally instead of a means of its suppression — we are asked to believe that if, in face of all these advantages the vast laboring population prefers to remain dormant about its interests and advancement, while the relatively small capitalist class stays aggressive and successful in impressing its will on the majority, the overriding reason is to be found in the mode of production. It is difficult to perceive that Marx's reasoning here is comprehensive and searching.

Another integral principal of Marx's conception is that the forms of state and government are the derivatives of the forms of production, and therefore change in nature with a change in production. This contention historical experience fails to bear

---

[4] Marx, it seems at times, does not expect even concessions. In proportion, he says, as the class antagonism widened, the capitalist state became more an instrument of "enslavement" — Marx uses the past tense (*Civil War in France*, section iii, third paragraph).

out. Different systems of production are found to coexist with the same type of state, and the same system of production may be associated with different types of state. Such facts make strong evidence against a theory that the mode of production is of preponderant influence in shaping this institution. Let us look at some of the facts.

The gens society, having, according to Marx, neither private property nor classes, is in no need of a state. However, Engels teaches that where the gens type of society persists, as in the Orient, the state arises, and in the form of a despotism.[5] Professor A. M. Tozzer indicates that primitive tribal communities have governments and of divergent varieties.[6] Despotism ruled in Polynesia and aboriginal Africa; the Iroquois Indians had a democracy; while among the Peruvian Incas monarchy prevailed, and "In the last years of the empire the ruler, called the Inca, was a supreme lord and his government investigated and controlled every activity of every individual in all the dominion."[7] Professor Tozzer comments as follows:

There is thus no definite and constant correlation between scale of culture and form of government. . .[8] The different forms of government thus range all the way from absolute authority vested in one man, through those where leadership is held by one or two persons with powers limited by a council, to communities ruled by a council alone with no central authority, and, finally, to the most informal kind of body made up of the elders or of persons of wealth and position.[9]

In classical antiquity the productive system was based on slavery, but we do not witness the consistent functioning of one particular state to correspond to this mode of production. Ancient Greece saw a variety of forms of state. Says one student of this subject: "The political experience of the Greeks was prodigious. It embraced the origins of most of the forms of government yet devised, many political experiments and pro-

[5] *Anti-Dühring*, p. 200.
[6] *Social Origins and Social Continuities*, pp. 199–211.
[7] *Social Origins and Social Continuities*, pp. 207–208. See also R. H. Lowie, *Primitive Society*, chap. xiii.
[8] *Social Origins and Social Continuities*, p. 200.
[9] *Social Origins and Social Continuities*, p. 211.

grams, many failures and many successes." [10] Says another student of the same subject: "Monarchy, aristocracy, oligarchy, timocracy, plutocracy, tyranny, autocracy, despotism, anarchy, democracy, politics are all Greek words. . . But it is more than a matter of terms. The Hellenes seem to have been the first to develop, if not to invent, most of the forms of government mentioned above." [11] Nearly as varied was the experience of Rome, as can be seen in any textbook. Rome set out with an elective royalty, continued with an aristocratic and then a democratic republic, and ended with the absolute monarchy of the Caesars.

There is confusion in the writings of Marx respecting the form of state in medieval and modern eras, as was seen in Chapter VII, above. At times he and his friend assert that absolute monarchy is a state organization proper to feudalism; at times they make it compatible with centuries of capitalism; and then there is the claim that it is entirely incongruous with capitalism, which finds its political expression preëminently in democracy. On this question history presents a variety of facts in defiance of the pattern which would square with Marx's formula of a one-to-one correspondence between the mode of production and the form of state; the more history one studies the more striking the defiance seems to be. Up to the eighteenth century absolute monarchy endeavored by mercantilist policies to uphold capitalism in France, and up to nearly the middle of the seventeenth century the same was true in England. Then came 1688 in England, and 1789 in France. The state is to Marx an institution closest to the economic substructure, and yet democracy or constitutional monarchy appeared on the scene after centuries of capitalism — much later, in the case of England and Germany, than Protestantism — although religion is, to Marx, an institution farther removed from the economic foundation.

Marx and Engels declare more than once that the revolution of 1688 merely brought to England a compromise be-

[10] A. C. Johnson, and Others, *The Greek Political Experience: Studies in Honor of William Kelly Prentice*, p. 3.
[11] *The Greek Political Experience*, p. 14.

tween the landed power and the bourgeois class, while the French Revolution achieved an obliteration of the feudal nobility and a definitive inauguration of the bourgeoisie.[12] We should, therefore, expect in France a government eminently suitable to the requirements of a well-established capitalist class. But history fails to accommodate us. After the Revolution came the relapse to the monarchies of Napoleon I, the Bourbons, and the Orleanists; then came the Republic, then the monarchy of Napoleon III, and then the Republic again. We witness in France the July revolution of 1830, the February revolution of 1848, the *coup d'état* of 1851. England, however, where the revolution culminating in the arrangements of 1688 was, to Marx, merely a compromise, witnesses no such relapses and no such succession of revolutions or upheavals. It is not sufficient to point to particular economic reasons for the experiences of these countries, even if the economic interpretation is accepted. The point at issue is whether history corroborates the contention that to a given mode of production there corresponds one given state.

Recently we saw the emergence of fascism, which to Marxians represents nothing but capitalism in its dying phase. Even if the claim of predominantly economic causation of this phenomenon were accepted, the important consideration suggests itself that, as the final stage of capitalism, fascism should have come first in the mature capitalistic countries like England or the United States, and not in Germany or in backward countries like Italy and Spain, where, it is to be noticed, democracy was seldom known.

Reflection and consultation of facts indicate alike that in the evolution of the forms of state and in the political sphere generally a great variety of factors collaborate to account for a specific result. It is easy to agree with Bertrand Russell when, for the limited sphere of politics (and not, apparently, the larger sphere of state building), he calls attention to some of them:

[12] E.g., Marx, *Eighteenth Brumaire*, p. 10; Engels, *Socialism, Utopian and Scientific*, pp. xxiv, 8, 13.

These four passions — acquisitiveness, vanity, rivalry, and love of power — are often the basic instincts, the prime movers of almost all that happens in politics. . . I think this is the source of what is erroneous in the Marxian interpretation of history, which tacitly [?] assumes that acquisitiveness is the source of all political actions.[13]

## LAW

Law, like the state, is, in Marx's thought, closely associated with the system of production. Its content is property, its essence is economic relations, and its objective is the preservation of the master class in power. Law is the will of the sovereign class.

Such a conception is a simpflication of a complex institution. To begin with, far from functioning as a mere creature of private property, law originates in the inescapable necessity for rules of conduct, to provide the essentials of peaceful social living. The foundation principle of group life is an orderly relationship among its members. Human beings, as Professor J. Dickinson indicates, have a tendency to get "in one another's way and frustrate one another's expectations." Give full freedom to this tendency, and "the result would be fatal to the existence of any human community." Here is the origin of government and law.[14] Says Professor R. M. MacIver: "In the liberty created by the order of law, between as within states, the genuine forces that animate civilization can alone find their fulfillment. Order is the foundation on which life builds." [15]

With some, the absence of law is equated to freedom, so that the less law the more freedom. But there are mutual interactions in the behavior of individuals in a community, and law, by restraining the liberty of some, increases the liberty of many. Law is not the negation of freedom, it is a positive instrument of freedom. Thus law is not to be conceived as the handmaid of the predatory class but as an institution indispensable to the general good. As Professor Morris Cohen

[13] *Selected Papers*, The Modern Library edition, p. 296.
[14] *My Philosophy of Law*. Credos of Sixteen American Scholars, pp. 91–96. Cf. R. Pound, *ibid*., pp. 259–261.
[15] *The Modern State*, pp. 289–290.

points out, some classes are more powerful than others, but law is more a compromise than the registration of the will of an omnipotent class. "And, in general," he continues, "legal order depends more on respect for the law and even on the need to be ruled than on mere brute force." [16]

In primitive society the rudiments of law can be seen in the customs, folkways, and taboos, no less binding in their inflexibility and no less exacting in their compulsion than the most rigid present-day laws. The punishment by death, banishment, and public reprobation or ridicule is commonly no less severe than punishment in modern society.[17] It is difficult to visualize even a communist order without laws, although private property is absent. Family relations, marriage, and divorce; the functions of officials, their election, and the behavior of people toward them; relations to the state, like military obligations, immigration, treason; fiscal, educational, and sanitation problems; the treatment of public property; the formation of associations; antisocial conduct — these and a great variety of other questions inseparable from the complexities of modern society will need to be comprehended by systematic bodies of rules reinforced by appropriate procedural organization, if social life is not to degenerate into an intolerable chaos. To call such regulations rules, or something else, and not laws, and to point to their unique estate as emanating from society as a whole and not from the Olympus of the entrenched class, or to affirm that where there is no state there is no law, is, again, largely to play with words. The communist rules, like the laws of a capitalist society, are binding upon the individual with the sanctions of the superior force of society.

The studies of eminent judges and jurists and of sociologists and anthropologists open up broad vistas of a multitude of factors which collaborate in shaping the law. It is altogether inadequate to make the complex simple by treating alike the legislative bodies, the interpreting judges, and the philosophizing jurists as mere agencies of fortifying the predatory

[16] *My Philosophy of Law*, p. 43.
[17] R. H. Lowie, *Primitive Society*, chap. xiv.

interests of the ruling class, or as humans whose deliberations are merely economically conditioned reactions.

Among early peoples the rules, customs, and taboos, the forerunners of law in later societies, are not mere property derivations, but are so permeated with religious beliefs that it is hard to tell them apart.[18] This is largely true of Judea, Greece, and Rome where early law is grounded in religious conceptions, even, in some instances, when treating of property phenomena.[19] The first written law of Greece, says Professor MacIver, agreeing with Fustel de Coulanges, was a translation, with appropriate modifications, of older customs, set "deeply in the common matrix of religion, morality, and kinship"; and even her later laws were "a collection of heterogeneous rules, religious, moral, and political." The same is true, he holds, of early Roman law.[20] It is significant that the Greek word for law (*nomos*) also means custom. Of the dominance of religion in the law of the Middle Ages bare mention is sufficient. Ideas of justice were permeated in that period with theological conceptions, and they held sway above the power of kings, often in circumstances of an economic nature.[21] Instances are not wanting in which the religious influence asserts itself in modern times. Dr. Roscoe Pound stresses, for instance, the important part of Puritanism "in the formative period of American law," and he talks of the religious influence in the common law of England.[22]

It is necessary to remember that law is the handiwork of men and that human personality plays a part in its making. The notion easiest to accept is that legislatures alone create the law. But judges and jurists are of great influence, too. At certain points in the evolution of the law a prominent personality may put a directive imprint on its future course, by selection from the available legal material, by combining new and old ele-

[18] *Primitive Society*, p. 398; W. A. Robson, *Civilization and the Growth of Law*, pp. 38, 161, 187, 271.

[19] *Civilization and the Growth of Law*, pp. 82, 165–166.

[20] *The Modern State*, pp. 100, 103, 105.

[21] R. Pound, *Interpretations of Legal History*, p. 102.

[22] *Interpretations of Legal History*, pp. 24, 44.

ments into particular patterns of substance and emphasis, and by recasting traditional modes of thought. Every legal system, says Dr. Pound, bears "the personal stamp of the great lawyer"; and he cites the names of Labeo and Julian in ancient Rome, of Du Moulin and Pothier in France, of Henry II, Coke, and Mansfield in England, and of Marshall, Story, and others in this country.[23]

Another significant consideration in the building of the law is the power of ideas and ideals. Kant's philosophy of ethics, Hegel's conception of the unfolding idea, Comte's theory of positivism, Dewey's idea of pragmatism, the theory of evolution, the conception of relativity, the findings of sociology and psychology, set in motion currents of thought which propagate their effects in the field of law. The same is true of the principles of natural law, natural rights, equality, ideas of justice, the fiction theory of the corporation, and of the general ideas relating to the fundamental goals of all law, whether they be the preservation of order, the defense of the social structure, individualism, or social betterment. Speculations and reflections on all such questions, expounded in legal and other treatises, become part of the education of men in the legal profession, and produce practical results in legislative chambers and court decisions.[24]

Still other factors make their contribution. Judge Jerome Frank, for instance, gives us in his notable *Law and the Modern Mind* a broad view of the ramifying effectiveness of the psychological traits of jurist, judge, and lawyer. Dr. Pound, too, draws attention to considerations of a wider area when he says:

We must give up the quest for the one solving idea. The actual legal order is not a simple rational thing. . . On the one hand, we must take account of the social or cultural needs of the time and place in all their

[23] *Interpretations of Legal History*, pp. 138–40, 128, 134, 136.

[24] *Interpretations of Legal History*, pp. 34–37, 41, 46; Robson, *Civilization and the Growth of Law*, pp. 217, 220, 233; *My Philosophy of Law*, pp. 101–103, 125, 184. Says Professor M. Radin: "In all the senses that equity or justice or 'natural justice' may have the idea operates as a censor or corrective of all the sources from which judges derive their determination" (p. 304 of the work last cited).

possibilities of overlapping and of conflict and in all their phases, economic, political, religious and moral. On the other hand, we must take account of suggestion, imitation, traditional faiths or beliefs, and particularly of the belief in logical necessity or authority expressing the social want or demand for general security.[25]

The foregoing paragraphs do not intend to imply that production and group relations have nothing to do with the formation of law. The purpose is rather to suggest that in this instance, as with other institutions, there is the interplay of many factors as regards both the origin and the subsequent career of the phenomenon, and that in some cases the economic element is important while in other cases it fails to offer an explanation.[26] In general, Marx's conception renders service in underscoring such phenomena as the class bias of a judge, the difficulties of the poor in seeking justice on account, among other things, of the legal expense, the part played by economic group pressures in the framing of legislation, and the rôle of the economic environment in forming the mentality of legislators. But one need not study Marx, still less does one need to be a Marxian, to become aware of or to emphasize such considerations.

### Religion

An elementary consideration of the origin of religion and its place in civilization fails to inspire belief in Marx's view of the mode of production as the incubator and the molder of this institution. With Marx, we recall, religion is born of primitive man's dependence on the mercies of nature, in the far-off days when a rudimentary way of making a living was responsible for man's lack of comprehension of his environment. To formulate the sequence of elementary production, therefore lack of intelligence about the environment, therefore religious beliefs, and to claim, moreover, that such a sequence constitutes economic causation of the genesis of religion, is a procedure of dubious merit. It may be as plausible to hold that primitive production was crude because of

[25] Pound, *Interpretations of Legal History*, pp. 21, 90.
[26] Pound, *Interpretations of Legal History*, pp. 88–90, 100–112, 113–115.

limited intelligence and experience as to contend that limited understanding was the sequel of an undeveloped mode of production. Too, the idea that primitive ignorance of nature was the mainspring of religion is an opinion that may be matched by other theories of the origins of this complex institution. The religious character of primitive man's reaction to the unknown may not express a mere reflex of the mode of production, but may rather point to certain basic aspects of human nature. It hardly contributes to the strength of the theory of economic causation to assert that the shaman, the magician, the priest, or the medicine man, was imposing on the members of the tribe because he was greedy for wealth. This suggestion seems to neglect other elements in the picture, like superstition, ignorance, imitation, curiosity, leadership. It fails to consider how it transpires that greed for wealth arises at all in a primitive community which, in Marx's representation, lacks the fact of private property to produce the greed "picture" in people's minds. It equally ignores the question why the few are greedy and cunning while the many are gullible and stupid.

When we turn to transformations in the religious institutions we come upon the same indisposition of history to support Marx's formula of the overmastering influence of the system of production as was noticed in tracing the forms of state. Throughout the centuries, until comparatively recently, there have been societies with production based, in the main, on slavery; but one will have to close one's eyes to the facts to claim that the religious beliefs of the Greco-Roman slave world are discerned as the basis of the religions of the other slave societies. In the United States before the 1860's, there was no fundamental cleavage between the religion of the South, where slavery prevailed, and the religion of the North, where slavery was unknown. Catholicism is considered by Marx as the religion most proper to feudalism. One should expect, then, this institution to have arisen in response to an established feudal order. But Christianity emerged centuries before feudalism. It will be readily admitted that Christianity was not born in a vacuum, that social conditions in ancient Israel had much to do with its rise, and that the Christianity of the feudal days was not precisely identical with the Christianity of, say, the first three centuries. Nevertheless, the birth of a new religion of such overwhelming significance should have come, in the Marxian scheme, as a sequel to a most dramatic change in the mode of production. History does not record, however, an economic revolution prior to the appearance of the Christian faith. It may be added here that we do not learn of an upheaval in the form of production in Arabia as the antecedent economic base of another major religion, Mohammedanism.

Marx pronounces Protestantism, and principally Calvinism, as the religion most expressive of capitalism. It is therefore reasonable to assume that Protestantism should make its first appearance in capitalistically advanced countries. Instead, the Reformation comes in sixteenth-century Germany, which is, as Marx and Engels well know, strongly feudal at the time and backward in the development of a thoroughgoing capitalistic order even as late as the beginning of the nineteenth century.[27] Venice had her quarrels with the Pope, but Calvinism took root, not in this commercial city, but in capitalistically backward (at the time) Scotland. Nor is there a definite correlation between capitalism and the religious institutions in various countries. France was Catholic in the days of feudalism; she is not Protestant under capitalism. Italy, Belgium, and France are mainly Catholic, while Holland, Sweden, and Norway are mainly Protestant, and yet there is no fundamental difference between the productive systems of these two groups of countries. The United States is capitalistic, but there is no one particular religion to "mirror" this economic reality. The Jews are as capitalistic in England as the British, and as capitalistic in France as the French, but their religion is different. The transformation of Japan or czarist Russia into a capitalistic country does not seem to have been associated with

[27] *Communist Manifesto*, p. 58; *Deutsche Ideologie*, p. 453; Engels, *The Mark*, pp. 109–113, reprinted as an appendix to *Socialism, Utopian and Scientific*; Engels, letter to A. Bebel, February 17, 1892, in *La Revue Marxiste*, June, 1929, no. 5, p. 547.

a corresponding tendency toward Protestantism. The conversion of natives by missionaries to the Catholic or Protestant persuasion does not demand the concurrent introduction of capitalism as the supporting economic base.

A theory which contends that the form of production is the all-powerful agency in molding an institution like religion can hardly stand up if we can see in the history of the past and about us today ample evidence that the same form of production is associated with different types of religion, that the same type of religion is associated with different forms of production, and that a change in religion can occur without benefit of an antecedent change in the productive order. Not only is it too much to claim that religion is the child of production, but at times the motives behind it override economic motives, and not infrequently it vies with economics in governing historical events. The early Christians chose to go to the lions for their faith. The Huguenots and the Puritans preferred exile and privation to the desertion of their convictions. The Jews could have bettered their lot immeasureably throughout the centuries had they relinquished the faith of their fathers. For over a century and a half the Poles suffered disabilities in Russia because of their religion and pride of nationality. The same is true of the Armenians and many other groups, large and small. The followers of peculiar religious practices in the darkest and remotest of villages in czarist Russia chose to uproot themselves from their native soil and cross to the strange life in the unknown lands on the continent of America in order to be left unmolested in their quaint religious cults.

Religion occupies a prominent position in primitive and ancient cultures.[28] The history of Assyria and Babylonia, of the ancient Hebrews and Greeks, of old China and India, will hardly be comprehensible if the rôle of religion is omitted. That Christianity had a transforming influence in history few would care to dispute. In the Middle Ages religion colored every phase of human endeavor, including economics. It spread education, preserved (or checked) learning, and

[28] MacIver, *The Modern State*, p. 169.

nursed (or frustrated) intellectual interests. Art, science, industry, and politics were held together by their common subordination to a spiritual ideal. Marx is, of course, aware of this, only he maintains that medieval production accounts for the conspicuous prominence of religion. However, apart from his general position regarding the potency of production, Marx offers no specific evidence or explanation to enlighten us how production is responsible for this unique result. It is also worth recording that it was religious fanaticism that galvanized the Saracens to an astonishing career of invasions, conquests, and learning, with their enormous historical repercussions.

It is not radically different in modern times. The Protestant Reformation has an outstanding part in the totality of events which for two hundred years and more stirred Europe to its depths, arraying nation against nation, exciting war and secession, persecution and alliances, and leaving no interest, material or spiritual, undisturbed. There may be much in Dr. Shailer Mathews' assertion that had it not been for the religious convictions of the seventeenth-century religious leaders, "history would have taken a very different turn," and there may never have been the Dutch Republic, the Puritan Commonwealth, or the Massachusetts Bay Colony.[29] Protestantism contributed much toward the upbuilding of capitalism, according to Max Weber's well-known thesis.[30] The expulsion of the Huguenots had economic consequences in France. The Spanish Inquisition reacted unfavorably on the economy of Spain. Until a century ago the backwardness of the economic developments in Germany was in no small measure accounted for by the bitter religious wars fought on her soil.

Religion seems to be an enduring force even in present-day communities, and it remains to be seen how successful Russia will be in its determined effort to eradicate it from its midst. Even Professor Haeckel, who sees nothing in the universe and man except matter, with its physics and chemistry, who attacks all faith and mysticism, who disparages all belief in the

---

[29] *Spiritual Interpretation of History*, p. 61.
[30] T. Parsons, *The Structure of Social Action*, pp. 575–578.

dualism of matter and spirit, and derides as delusions and fancies all ideas of a personal God, an immortal soul, a life to come, and other notions "unknown and inadmissible to science," even Haeckel realizes the hard fact that religion is a vital agency in the life of the multitude. He proceeds accordingly to elaborate his "monistic religion," with the "three goddesses," the true, the good, and the beautiful, which he would prefer as a substitute for present religious beliefs.[31]

Under communism, Marx and Engels announce, religion will disappear, because natural and social phenomena will become comprehensible to man, and there will be no unknown areas and no mysteries to incline him to religion. But one may well perceive that according to this very theory religion may possess a long lease of life. As civilization advances the provinces of the unknown scarcely exhibit a tendency to shrink. The more we search, the more problems we solve, the more "laws" we discover, the more we appreciate how boundless is the realm of fundamental secrets yet to be unveiled. The microscope and the spectroscope, calculus and evolution, the quantum theory and the atom smasher have released more unexplained phenomena and have inspired more vexing questions than ever disturbed the wakeful minds in centuries past. "The progress of science," observed Alfred Marshall, "while increasing the stock of knowledge, increases also the area of conscious ignorance."[32] We are also aware of the fact that religion is, if anything, more the heritage of the multitude than it is a necessary datum in the life of the comparatively few workers in the fields of science. We shall have to wait for many years before the wayfaring person will gain such a clear mastery of all the problems relating to man, society, nature, and the universe that any reference to something unknown, infinite, and transcending the reaches of the human mind will seem to him a childish irrelevance.

[31] *The Riddle of the Universe*, chap. xviii, also p. 301.
[32] *Industry and Trade*, p. 657.

## RECENT EVIDENCE

In the last quarter century two social transformations of the highest importance have taken place such as have not been witnessed for centuries before. They are signally instructive for the issue of whether the mode of production is the sovereign determinant of the other phases of civilization. In fact, they may be taken as a laboratory experiment to test Marx's fundamental thesis. We have seen the emergence of communism in Russia and of fascism, short-lived, in Germany and elsewhere. The arresting fact stands out that the modes of production in these two countries, as well as in capitalist America and England, are essentially alike. In all of them there is the same organization of labor on the basis of division and coöperation in field and factory, the same use of natural resources, and the same employment of technology and science. In all of them the machine, the factory, large-scale operations, and the preëminence of science are the symbols of production, and in all of them the methods are alike, except that some of these countries are more advanced than the others.

Marx's fundamental thesis asserts that the same mode of production is correlated with the same institutional constellation. The striking fact is, however, that these three sets of countries exhibit pronounced differences in institutions, ideas, and values. On similar economic substructures we see erected divergent superstructures. In America and England there is one type of government, democracy; in Nazi Germany there is another type, dictatorship or tyranny; and in Russia there is a third type, which may be labeled one way or another but which is different from the other two types. The same is true of law, which, to Marx, is in close union with the economic factor. There is one body of law in the capitalist countries, another body in Russia, while in Nazi Germany we saw the resurgence of Draconian edicts in some spheres and wanton lawlessness in other spheres. Religion has the familiar status in America and England, but is under a cloud both in Russia and Nazi Germany. Philosophy is of the staple varieties in the capitalist countries, of the Marxist cast in Russia, and the mumbo jumbo of the Nazi overlords in Germany. In ideas of human conduct, of relation of man to man, of right and wrong, there are understandable and probably minor differences between Russia and America or England; but an astounding upheaval, humiliating to contemplate, took place in Hitler's Germany. We witnessed there the mass production of the fascist man, irrational, unrestrained, brutish, by processes not unlike the mass production and mass salesmanship of commodities in industrial countries. We saw the explosion on an unbelievable scale of a barbarism unexampled in history.

This test-tube evidence tends to corroborate the suggestion voiced on these pages that facts fail to bear out Marx's generalization of a close correspondence between the method of production and the institutional aggregate, and that Marx assigns to production an importance ill-proportioned to realities. But the corroboration goes further than this. To Marx the mode of production implicitly carries with it the corollary of a determined class alignment. The suggestion made in the previous chapter is that a productive system cannot stand in isolation but is indissolubly integrated with institutions, that the class structure is more an institutional, a property, concept than the specific consequent of the manner of producing goods, and that the same productive scheme may be associated with different institutions and with different classes. Thus we see the ancient master and slave on the one hand and the feudal lord and serf on the other hand, although the methods of making goods were essentially identical in classical antiquity and in the Middle Ages.

The recent social changes under consideration seem to give point to this suggestion. In capitalist countries the familiar classes and groups prevail. In Russia the capitalist classes are extinct, and the classes involved in production are the government officials as the planners and bearers of responsibility and the wage earners who may have a voice in management. In Nazi Germany the high party politicians constitute the supreme class; then come the capitalist employers with less authority and initiative than their counterpart in America or England; and then the laborers with a semi-feudal status, perverted by the intoxicating propaganda ceaselessly spraying at them. The class organization, to Marx one of the two components of the all important economic substructure (the mode of production is the other component), far from functioning as the determinant of institutions, is itself a variable phenomenon adaptive to the institutional background.

One more point arrests attention in this connection. In the light of Marx's theorem that human nature is shaped by work and class position it is not easy to account for the emergence of the fascist man, in Germany and elsewhere. Fascism recruited followers from all classes and from all walks of life. Without a large following from the laboring class, fascism could not have triumphed at home and could not have forged an army for the battlefield. The monstrous excesses of the Nazis were not all committed by recruits from the capitalist or the middle class. Of those who went to the concentration camps because of antagonism to the Nazi ideology and practices one cannot say that they were all proletarians. Some professors, some scientists, some artists, some aristocrats, some storekeepers, and some laborers went to concentration camps, while others in all these categories acquiesced or collaborated, reluctantly or enthusiastically. There is more in these types of behavior, cutting transversely through occupation and class allegiance, than can be explained by the simple formula that work and class account for human character and conduct. The Marxian dictum that human nature is an unfolding process is a fruitful generalization, but it leaves unexplored significant areas. We need to know more than Marx tells us about precisely what is subject to the unfolding process, and what conditions the unfolding process, before we can presume to understand the many-faceted conduct of the multitudes in defiance of Marx's economic determinants.

It is the first requirement of scientific inquiry to seek and to examine the facts. It is likewise a prime tenet of scientific effort to give special consideration to facts which are at odds with the hypothesis, and to recast or abandon the hypothesis in view of unaccommodating facts, or else to specify its limitations. When we turn to facts we find impressive evidence that the mode of production cannot be accepted as the only source of a particular class structure and as the prime generator of a civilization.

# CHAPTER XVIII

## OBSERVATIONS ON IDEAS

### SCIENCE AND MOTIVES

To Marx and his colleague the growth of science is preëminently a derivative of productive requirements. Economic activity creates the needs, provides the motives, and furnishes the techniques and facilities for investigation. The emphasis is on economic needs. Should there arise, says Engels, a "technical need," there will be more impulse to scientific progress than can be generated by ten universities.[1] Subsumed under the technique of production, science is, in their view, essentially an economic datum, and they do not mention science independently when citing examples of institutions and ideas as the superstructure on the economic base. Science is treated as a component of the economic substructure.

That economic problems have much to do with the career of science is scarcely debatable. But the general emphasis on needs is subject to reservations, and the unique stress on economic needs goes too far. A well-recognized need will precipitate investigation and may yield results, as often happens during a war. But the assurance that needs invariably produce scientific advances reflects a disposition to regard science as a mechanistic reaction in simple linear causation. Many a need remains unsatisfied for centuries: for example, the cure of cancer or tuberculosis, or the extermination of mosquitoes. The human race is always beset with needs. Often enough needs are not even perceived, and if perceived they get little attention. Often enough what is a need and what is not a need depends on the complex totality of a social environment, and not infrequently a need is recognized only in retrospect, when new situations develop and new comprehensions.[2]

---

[1] Marx and Engels, *Selected Correspondence*, p. 517.
[2] Cf. A. P. Usher, *History of Mechanical Inventions*, p. 16.

Despite such reservations, it has to be admitted that conscious, persistent needs will generally stimulate scientific effort. Even so, the singular emphasis on economic needs is not comprehensive enough. Human needs range as far as human desires and interests go. Needs may be religious, esthetic, hygienic, intellectual, etc. Even the earliest origins of science suggest that economic needs are not exclusive. Some claim that the overflow of the Nile was responsible for geometry in Egypt, but so was the desire to draw figures to adorn the Egyptian temples. It is asserted that seafaring promoted among ancient peoples, like the Phoenicians, the study of astronomy, but this science also owes much to ancient seers and practitioners of magic, as well as to the necessity of determining the time on which religious festivals fell due. Some will argue that the processes of production led to the study of mathematics and physics, but such studies were also stimulated by the erection of temples and altars, by the building of pyramids and other elaborate tombs.[3] It is stressed that the demand for dyes and paints encouraged the development of chemistry, but this science was enriched still more by the desire to cure the sick, to prolong life, and to embalm the deceased. For long ages physicians and pharmacists were the only chemists and their private dwellings the only laboratories.

Already in early times economic needs were present and yet there was not always a response to them, often for reasons of a noneconomic nature. One may well wonder with Professor George A. Sarton, the eminent historian of the evolution of science, why the early Greeks were not induced by economic necessities to develop plain arithmetic, instead of giving their time to playing with "fanciful ideas on the properties of numbers."[4] The Marxian readily explains the lack of mechanical inventions (it is doubtful whether there was such a lack) among the remarkably inventive ancient Greeks by the absence of need for them in a slave economy. It is to be pointed out, however, that mechanical devices would have made the

[3] Cf. J. Dewey, *Creative Intelligence*, pp. 123, 131–133.
[4] *The Study of the History of Mathematics*, p. 18.

slave much more productive, and one wonders why the desire for greater wealth did not stimulate the Greeks to inventions even as it stimulates the modern capitalist, who is not satisfied with a given level of efficiency but is constantly in search of improvements. It is insufficient to say that the modern capitalist is interested in progressive accumulation in a competitive economy, while the social environment in ancient Greece was different. It is necessary to explain why the Greek was not interested in accumulation, and why he chose to compete in poetry and not in sales. In fact, some competent scholars approach this whole question in noneconomic terms.[5]

In science, as in other fields of human culture, growth and development are accounted for by the collaboration of a variety of circumstances, and in some instances some circumstances and in other instances other circumstances are of preponderant weight. Professor Sarton insists, in the case of science, on a multitude of external elements and human motives, and he calls attention to the capriciousness of inventions, for which it is futile to seek a "rational explanation." Generally, he is inclined to give first place to curiosity and the desire to understand.[6] Dr. O. T. Mason, of the Smithsonian Institution, has made an exhaustive study of the origins of tools and devices for purposes of production among primitive peoples. One would expect that at least in this sphere inventions were the exclusive result of economic needs. But in the conclusions drawn from his study, Dr. Mason states that "invention is stimulated" not only by human wants for 1. food, 2. clothing, 3. shelter, 4. rest, 5. locomotion, but also by the wants for "6. delight of the senses; 7. knowledge, the explanation of things; 8. social enjoyment . . . ; 9. spiritual satisfaction."[7]

Many a scientist who reflects on his motives reveals that he is impelled by the sheer search for uniformities and generalizations, and that he is captivated by the order and unity of

[5] Cf. Usher, *History of Mechanical Inventions*, pp. 49–50.
[6] *The History of Science and the New Humanism*, pp. 13, 14, 34–36; *The Study of the History of Mathematics*, pp. 15–19, 25.
[7] *The Origins of Invention*, p. 410.

the manifestations which he studies. Henri Poincaré, the great mathematician and scientist, says:

The scientist does not study nature because it is useful to do so. He studies it because he takes pleasure in it, and he takes pleasure in it because it is beautiful. . . I am not speaking, of course, of that beauty which strikes the senses. What I mean is that more intimate beauty which comes from the harmonious order of its parts, and which a pure intelligence can grasp. . . Intellectual beauty, on the contrary, is self-sufficing, and it is for it, more perhaps than for the future good of humanity, that the scientist condemns himself to long and painful labors.[8]

Even Professor John Dewey objects to the view that an instrumental theory of knowledge implies "that the value of knowing is instrumental to the knower. This is a matter which is as it may be in particular cases; but certainly in many cases the pursuit of science is sport, carried on like other sports, for its own satisfaction." [9] Archeologists and anthropologists, philologists and philosophers do not find in the problems of production incentives to their work. It is not clear why it is necessary to insist that physicists or biologists always do. These latter are not of a different breed. Utilitarian motives and economic interests cannot be ruled out as causes of scientific growth, nor can other motives and other interests.

It is admitted that the personal motives of the scientist do not dispose of the whole problem of incentives to investigation and of the progress of science. Even if the incentives of all the scientists were to be assumed as exclusively noneconomic, the conclusion would not follow that only noneconomic factors are responsible for the growth of science. Apart from the personalities of the scientists, there is a large external background of social situations which provides problems and challenges, and economic factors are part of the background. The individual scientist, carried away by his enthusiasm for the problems at hand and conscious of his nonutilitarian interests, may stay unaware of the economic elements in the general social setting which has much to do with the origin, purposes,

---

[8] *Science and Method*, p. 22. Cf. pp. 27, 59. See the suggestive pages 15–16, 28–29 in Usher, *History of Mechanical Inventions*.

[9] *Experience and Nature*, p. 151.

and possibilities of his interests. The aim of the foregoing paragraphs is merely to suggest that the motives of the scientist are part of the aggregate of stimulants behind the development of science, and that Marx and Engels are hardly on solid ground in their contention that the army of science, like Napoleon's army, travels on its stomach. It may also be mentioned here that the noneconomic motives of the scientist sometime overcome an environment hostile to his researches and his methods, and induce him to jeopardize his safety, position, and well-being to pursue his work. Roger Bacon in the thirteenth century, and Andreas Vesalius (who had to steal cadavers out of fresh graves for his study of physiology) and Galileo in the sixteenth are examples.

## SCIENCE AND SCIENTISTS

Among the forces responsible for the advance of science mention may be made of the achievements of figures of more than ordinary ability. The formulation of new hypotheses, the projection of new conceptions, the shaping of new emphases and patterns of thought give scientific endeavors quickening impulses, new directions, and accelerated results, which by their timing may have enormous consequences in conjuncture with other historical events. "The true heroes of economic history," says Professor A. P. Usher, "are the scientists, the inventors, and the explorers. To them is due the actual transformation of social life." Professor Usher has in mind here "the cumulative accomplishment of many men of considerable gradations in natural ability." [10] To Marx and Engels, it seems, there are no such things as inventions. When an insistent need for an improvement arises, and when previous stages of scientific development have paved the way for it, the discovery cannot help being made, and if one scientist does not make it another scientist will. To give point to this view, Marxians cite inventions which were made simultaneously and independently by two or three individuals. Such views are not well taken if their burden is that inventions are not at all de-

[10] *History of Mechanical Inventions*, pp. 5–6.

pendent on outstanding qualities of mind which are not possessed by each person whether he be a scientist or not, that anybody working in the field could not help stumbling on the innovation, and that inventions are merely part and parcel of the run-of-the-mine daily work of ordinary scientists. That at times such is the case must be conceded, but it is not always so.

Lists of inventions and discoveries by several scientists working independently of each other do not disprove the necessity of considerable mental capacity. They may suggest that in the wide scientific world every now and then two or three persons are found who are so similar in mental endowments that when focusing their efforts on the same problems they react in much the same manner. When at the same stage of knowledge only one or two Newtons become agitated over the question of why the legendary apple fell down and not up, and frame the law of gravity, while every day many people, scientists and others, notice this behavior of apples but raise no questions about it; when one or two Galileos, observing the oscillations of the possibly apocryphal chandeliers in the chapel, are stimulated to inquiry resulting in the formulation of the principles of the pendulum, while many others see swinging objects countless times without perceiving anything deserving attention, it may be reasonably inferred that important scientific innovations depend not only on reality and experience but also on more than ordinary mental powers. The environment may be full of hints and suggestions — it always is — but not everybody is alive to them, and very few can derive from them new conceptions.

To discern a problem demands uncommon capacity. Says Dr. Albert Einstein: "The formulation of a problem is often more essential than its solution . . . To raise new questions, new possibilities, to regard old problems from a new angle, requires creative imagination and marks real advance in science." [11] The scientific world may be full of problems, the scientific journals may be full of accounts of them, and scientific

[11] A. Einstein and L. Infeld, *The Evolution of Physics*, p. 95.

progress may have prepared constituent ideas here and there which may, if put together, open the gate to a possible solution, but not many readers of the journals, and not many workers in the laboratories, will think the thoughts and will conceive the hypotheses and experiments that will open the gate. Such achievements are not mere matters of ordinary responses to stimuli. A stenographer can turn shorthand into words, and a reader of hieroglyphics can transform the emblems into a story. But not every person acquainted with the distracting mass of scientific experiments, laws, theories, hypotheses, and controversies can select a relevant set of facts and theories and synthesize them into, or deduce from them, new principles and solutions. Unique qualities of mind are indispensable, and such qualities are not shared equally by all scientists.[12]

The contention may be advanced that every field of endeavor has among its devotees at all times personalities of outstanding powers on whom we can count as a matter of course to take full advantage of every new development, that accordingly superior capacity may be considered a constant while the other circumstances are the variable, and that the constant cannot be treated as a causal element in the development of science, or in any other field demanding conspicuous qualities. This view is in the Marxian tradition. Agreeing with Helvetius, Marx observes that every social epoch needs leaders, and if it does not find them it invents them; and, as we saw, Engels says that whenever history needed a great man he did not fail to come, and in proof (!) of this assertion Engels points to Caesar, Augustus, and Cromwell, who appeared on the scene when the need for them arose.

As far as this general contention is concerned, one may question first of all whether exceptional ability, even if always present, can be ruled out as a factor in the growth of science on the ground of its being a constant factor. If all humans were of uniform but only average capacities, science,

[12] Cf. Sarton, *The History of Science and the New Humanism*, pp. 20, 23, 46, 50, 174; *The Study of the History of Mathematics*, p. 25.

and everything else, would advance at a much slower pace. Too, it may be indicated that the so-called variables may also be regarded as a constant factor, inasmuch as hypotheses, problems, needs, and other stimuli are always teeming in the world of reality. But aside from such considerations, the assumption of ever-present abilities of high order can hardly be granted. The assumption means that in each field of science (as well as in any other field), and indeed in each of the many special departments in each field, there is such a multitude of scientists that by the law of probability we can confidently expect that at any given time there will be among them highly endowed individuals to give science continual propulsions.

Such a postulate is hardly borne out by the facts. History seems to demonstrate that individuals of finely wrought capacities are scarce and are not in the habit of appearing in response to ever-present needs. Consider the field of economics, for example. In ancient Greece, celebrated for her brilliant contributions in almost every province of human thought, there were hardly any outstanding thinkers with a persistent interest in economic investigation. Had Plato and Aristotle, or Greek thinkers of lower stature but yet of outstanding capacity, turned much of their effort to an investigation of economic problems, this science would have attained to a more advanced state for centuries to come. Economic problems were not wanting then to challenge exploration: the slave economy, the many branches of manufacturing industry, the free artisans working for a wage, domestic and foreign commerce, banks, money, usury, monopoly, debt, and agrarian troubles, are some of the examples. Similarly, for over fifty years after Ricardo, Europe was full of arresting and distressing problems in every domain of economic activity, and yet, with two exceptions, there was no figure of his powers to give them consideration. A. Cournot and Marx are the exceptions. But Cournot was interested in a limited set of topics, and he presented his distinguished studies in the inaccessible language of mathematics. Marx was more interested in exposing the infirmities of capitalism than in the exploration of such problems as claimed the labors of the economists of his day: value, distribution, money, and the like. We have to recall, too, that before his death in 1883 the world knew only the first volume of *Capital*, and despite its general renown, it did not impress contemporary or later economists. Of this book F. W. Taussig says, and not without reason: "The books on socialism deal largely with controversies which do not proceed to the heart of the matter. This seems to me to hold of K. Marx, *Das Kapital* (English translation, 1891), the most famous and influential of socialist books."[13]

This view is not identical with the great man theory, in science or in history generally, if by great men are meant personalities of extraordinary powers towering above men of considerable endowment, and if by the theory is meant that history is merely a succession of the illustrious achievements of the great, apart from and in disregard of the social setting, and that, in the language of Emerson, "an institution is the lengthened shadow of one man." Such a treatment of history generally bespeaks an indisposition to delve into the many circumstances that unite to produce a result. But the repudiation of this theory should not import justification for embracing the other extreme, which forgets human beings altogether and puts exclusive stress on the environment. History, it claims, is governed by objective laws, historical tendencies will bow to no human design, and the course of events is irresistible. One wonders what is meant by law, tendency, and course, and what sort of entities they are that we must think of them as making history for us. One wonders how much more they are than convenient terms which the mind employs, with or without good reason, in the attempt to unravel social phenomena into a framework of sequence and causality, with or without success. Precisely what creates the laws, directs the tendency, and regulates the course? Historical events and social settings are not phenomena of spontaneous generation, but are the handiwork of men. History is the record of the interaction of many-faceted human nature with the many-sided

[13] *Principles of Economics* (3rd ed., 1921), II, 502.

environment. In this interaction the behavior of man is not tropismic but is informed with intelligence, purpose, and the inclination to change and improve.

The question of progress in science is part of the larger question of change and progress in every phase of civilization. By and large there is discernible in humans the desire to improve what is, to take a step ahead. In some people such stirrings are absent, but in many they are intense. They are noticeable in things trivial and important, they are true of the statesman or the housewife, and they apply to groups and societies. This inclination does not lead to spectacular leaps, but it breeds numerous slow and continual changes. Human life means change, biologically and in the higher sense. "When men or nations originate, they live and grow; when they cease to do that, they decay and die," observes Dr. O. T. Mason.[14] There is no deliberate organized effort, but rather haphazard irregular attempts in many directions. The variations, slight as they may be, are selected, imitated and accumulated into considerable departures from given starting points. In this process intelligence, self-interest, self-regard, emulation, rivalry, and other traits play a part in interaction with an environment that offers direction, content, stimulus, or frustration. The stir for betterment may be canceled by the disposition to yield to habit and tradition, but the stir is there, and it often prevails.[15] Else things would stand still and wait for a natural upheaval to compel a change, or for the contact with the influence of another culture. In oriental countries the conservative force is perseverant, and there are undoubtedly important reasons for this which deserve careful investigation.

Among the multitudes who are prone to change and improve things appear at times individuals capable of serious and important advances. They are substantial innovators. Their powers of observing, imagining, and reasoning, and their abilities to associate facts and ideas and to discern relationships among them rise above the average, so that they see phenomena

[14] *The Origins of Invention*, p. 410.
[15] Cf. Usher, *History of Mechanical Inventions*, pp. 8, 27–28.

in new lights, develop new viewpoints and theories, and point to new ways of doing things. Such powers are in part the expression of a biological variation, of inherited endowments. The innovation is at bottom nothing "new," and it may be only a regrouping of parts, or a shift of emphasis; it demands, however, more than ordinary abilities. The environment is important, but what is done with it measures originality. Shakespeare found ready about him ink, paper, words, themes, and characters, but what he did with these things constitutes Shakespeare. Innovation is construction, not creation. Consistent with other things, it is also supplementary to them.

There is no willful tearing up of the fabric of history and no abrupt injection into it of foreign elements. Nor are the tactics always the noblest and the motives the purest. Many minds, many ideas, schemes, and proposals, coöperate, interact, and clash. There is retreat and progress, and eventually the innovators achieve something. New ground is won, the ground won is consolidated, and a new point of departure is created. In some such manner change and progress generally proceed, in legislation, in religion, in attempts to abolish war, in art and science. It would be difficult to find in the writings of Marx an outstanding idea that was entirely original with him. Yet his selection of ideas and his way of grouping, evaluating, and emphasizing them resulted in a system of power, originality, and influence which his followers would be eager to acknowledge, although in the same breath they would argue against the imputation of special significance to individuals.[16] If we believe in hereditary capacities and in differences in hereditary capacities, no stretch of the imagination is required, and no heroic assumption, to entertain the idea that there are innovators and innovations, in the growth of science or in any other

[16] Engels writes to Liebknecht: "Although I have seen him [Marx] tonight stretched out on his bed, the face rigid in death, I cannot grasp the thought that this genius should have ceased to fertilize with his powerful thoughts the proletarian movement of both worlds. Whatever we all are, we are through him; and whatever the movement of today is, it is through his theoretical and practical work; without him we should still be stuck in the mire of confusion." Quoted in Liebknecht, *Karl Marx, Biographical Memoirs*, p. 46. Cf. Marx and Engels, *Selected Correspondence*, pp. 415–416.

department of human knowledge and activity. "The fact," says Bryce, "that the progress of mankind in arts and sciences and letters and every form of thought has been due to the efforts of a comparatively small number of highly gifted minds rising out of the common mass speaks for itself." [17]

## SCIENCE AND CAPITALISM

As was suggested before, when an examination is made of a social phenomenon without a preconceived frame of reference, one will find that the coöperation of many factors is commonly responsible for the result, and among them in some cases non-economic factors and in other cases economic factors loom as of particular moment. It is no different when we consider the remarkable growth of science in recent centuries. Many needs, motives, and other forces are determinative of this phenomenon, including the contributions of eminent scientists. But among these factors a prominent place must be assigned to capitalism. The development of industry made possible the scientific instruments, from the microscope to the cyclotron, without which much experimentation would be unthinkable,[18] and the growth of wealth made possible the support of scientific activity alike in industrial plants and institutions of learning. Of course, one cannot treat capitalism as an exclusively economic fact. The concept of capitalism, and capitalism is a concept and not a palpable object, embraces a complex aggregate compounded of many related institutions, ideas, and attitudes. Yet it seems reasonable to stress that in the career

[17] *Modern Democracies*, I, 62. Says Dr. A. N. Whitehead: "A brief, and sufficiently accurate, description of the intellectual life of the European races during the succeeding two centuries and a quarter up to our own times is that they have been living upon the accumulated capital of ideas provided for them by the genius of the seventeenth century . . ." "The issue of the combined labors of these four men [Galileo, Newton, Descartes, and Huyghens] has some right to be considered as the greatest single intellectual success which mankind has achieved" (*Science and the Modern World*, pp. 57, 67). "The problem of social action," says Professor F. H. Knight, "is almost wholly a problem of leadership . . . Leadership on a religious-emotional basis is an infinitely more natural, and easier, and less costly system of order than any other" (*The Ethics of Competition and Other Essays*, pp. 349–352).

[18] Whitehead, *Science and the Modern World*, pp. 166–167. Cf. Usher, *History of Mechanical Inventions*, pp. 21, 61–62.

of modern science the economic component of capitalism can claim considerable influence.

One is tempted to say that the economic factor has been not only of considerable moment but of preponderant effect on science in the modern era. But we are given pause by two important considerations. Capitalism is preëminently dependent on science. Remove the science of the last few centuries, and production goes back to the medieval ways. Science, however, cannot be treated as a purely economic phenomenon; nor is it legitimate to assert simply that economic facts appear first and science follows as a matter of course. As usual, there is reciprocal interplay between the two. Then there is another important consideration. The seventeenth century laid the foundations of the scientific world of the recent centuries and thus made modern capitalism possible.[19] Scholarly studies bring to light the fact that in the phenomenal growth of science in this age of Newton noneconomic circumstances occupy a conspicuous position.

Professor G. N. Clark indicates that the stimulus to science in the Newtonian age came, in addition to economics, from five sources: medicine, the fine arts (the chemistry of pigments, acoustics, organ making), war, religion (e.g., Newton's search into the ways of God's world), and love of truth.[20] Professor R. K. Merton investigated the career of science in the same period. His cautious summary states that "from forty to seventy per cent" of the research projects of the Royal Society "occurred in the category of pure science; and, conversely, that from thirty to sixty per cent were influenced by practical requirements," in which he includes noneconomic requirements as well.[21] In another study he develops the thesis that in seventeenth-century England puritanism exercised a considerable influence on the growth of science. "The deep-rooted religious *interests* of the day demanded in their forceful implica-

[19] Whitehead, *Science and the Modern World*, chap. iii; Usher, *History of Mechanical Inventions*, pp. 21–22, 58–65, and chap. vii.

[20] *Science and Social Welfare in the Age of Newton*, chap. iii.

[21] "Science and the Economy of Seventeenth-Century England," *Science and Society*, III, no. 1 (1939), 26.

tions the systematic, rational, and empirical study of Nature for the glorification of God in His works and the control of the corrupt world." [22]

## PHILOSOPHY

(A) THE DERIVATION OF IDEAS. Marx pictures philosophy as a domain akin to theology, a serious term of opprobrium in his ideology. Philosophy thrives on fantasy and mystification, and not on experience and reason. One wonders, then, why Marx is so often preoccupied with philosophical questions and saturates his organon with philosophical doctrines. It is sufficient to refer, for example, to his theories of human nature, the derivation of ideas, necessity and freedom, the doctrine of conflict, and the dialectic.

To Marx philosophy flourishes only as long as man is without an understanding of himself and his world, only as long as he fails to see the interrelations of the many branches of knowledge in a unified scheme. It follows from such a view that philosophy ought to flourish in economically backward countries, where understanding is meager, and ought to languish in economically advanced countries where greater knowledge reigns. But this is hardly the case. Rome, according to Marx and his friend, was not so well developed in enterprise as Greece was, and yet Rome could not match Greece in philosophy. The backward Balkans, or Spain or Turkey, did not flood the market with philosophical output, whereas in the comparatively advanced countries, like America, England, France, or Germany, philosophic speculation has hardly diminished with the passage of time.

To pursue every philosophical thesis of Marx's would demand a book in itself and a writer well trained in the field. The intention here is only to touch lightly on two problems, the derivation of ideas and the dialectic. Marx's theory of knowledge assigns a crucial place to material reality. Whether ideas are pictures formed in the mind by external objects, or are the

---

[22] "Puritanism, Pietism and Science," *Sociological Review*, XXVIII, no. 1 (January, 1936), pp. 1–2. See also pp. 13ff., 29. Italics not mine.

result of scientific analysis, his distaste for imponderables inclines him to the view of external materiality as the mother of ideas. In the social realm, Marx affirms, even the problem itself will emerge only when the material conditions of its solution are already in evidence.

Such a view has a solid substratum of validity, but it does not go far enough. Engels tells us that we must have seen rectangles revolve about an axis before we could reach the idea of a cylinder. He does not wonder what objects mathematicians had to see before they developed the determinant, differential equations, or the theory of the function of a complex variable. Henri Poincaré says: "The genesis of mathematical discovery is a problem which must inspire the psychologist with the keenest interest. For this is the process in which the human mind seems to borrow least from the external world." [23] The latest developments in the physical sciences have widened the gap between sense-perception and the ideas of the physical world. Professor A. S. Eddington asserts that "the physicist used to borrow the raw material of his world from the familiar world, but he does so no longer. His raw materials are aether, electrons, quanta, potentials, Hamiltonian functions, etc., and he is nowadays scrupulously careful to guard these from contamination by conceptions borrowed from the other world." [24] The quantum theory, the theory of relativity, and the newer principles of thermodynamics have wrought strange and profound changes in the ideas of "reality," removed from the world of consciousness; have given a new eminence to the rôle of the "alchemist Mind" in the search for what transcends sense-perception; and, instead of diminishing the scope of philosophy, as Marx expected, have provided new material for its widening meditations. [25] In fact, even simple scientific processes rest on

[23] *Science and Method*, pp. 46, 36. Professor Albert Einstein states that "in so far as the theorems of mathematics are about reality they are not certain; and in so far as they are certain they are not about reality" (*Geometrie und Erfahrung*, p. 3).

[24] *The Nature of the Physical World*, p. xiii.

[25] Professor A. S. Eddington states that "the mind has by its selective power fitted the processes of Nature into a frame of law of a pattern largely of its own choosing; and in the discovery of this system of law the mind may be regarded

philosophic foundations. "Induction," says Whitehead, "pre-supposes metaphysics. In other words, it rests upon an antecedent rationalism." [26]

In Marx's theory every form of knowledge and every form of expression are governed mainly by the productive organization. Science, philosophy, political ideas, literature, and art are correlated, by and large, with the economic order as their incubator. History fails to substantiate such a correlation. Readers of Plato and Aristotle, of Euripides and Sophocles, fail to see in their works the unique fruits of a slave economy. The far-flung empire of ideas built by Plato and Aristotle had close counterparts — imitations would be more correct — under the different economies throughout the centuries. The validity of Marx's thesis demands that the intellectual, literary, and artistic productions of ancient Greece should be as irrelevant to our modern society as Greek slavery is foreign and irrelevant to modern production. Yet in all intellectual and esthetic spheres the achievements of the Greek genius, far from appearing to us as something rudimentary, parallel with the rudimentary mode of Greek production, are preëminent for their penetrating instructiveness and rich suggestiveness, and stand before us as models to emulate.

Marx does not probe into this anomaly, except for art. He asserts, we recall,[27] that Greek art and poetry were based on Greek mythology, and we cannot produce art like that of the Greeks, because, he says, her "unripe social conditions" do not prevail among us, and mythology has been banished by our mastery over nature. In an age, he asserts, of machinery, the telegraph, and locomotives, Vulcan, Jupiter, Hermes, and the *Iliad* are unthinkable. It is obvious that Marx is far from touching on the vital issue. When we admire or discuss Greek

---

as regaining from Nature that which the Mind has put into Nature" (*The Nature of the Physical World*, p. 244). Consider the philosophical literature inspired by the latest developments in physics; e.g., Whitehead, *Science and the Modern World;* H. Reichenbach, *Philosophic Foundations of Quantum Mechanics;* C. E. M. Joad, *Philosophical Aspects of Modern Science.*

[26] *Science and the Modern World*, p. 65.

[27] Chapter VIII, section on Art, above.

art we think of its surpassing excellence, which we can only imitate or equal but hardly excel, and not the particular content, themes, or techniques that Marx is talking about.

Marx proceeds then to inquire why Greek art has still a great appeal to us and gives us so much enjoyment. He explains that we enjoy the artless ways of the child, and the Greeks were normal children with "the most beautiful development" of childhood. We are not informed why Sparta, Egypt, Syria, or ancient India did not display a similarly beautiful childhood, and why we do not hold their works in equal esteem. Marx's suggestion is far from explaining why Greek art ranks as classic, and in more than one sense. Equally far is it from explaining why Plato and Aristotle stand high among the few greatest thinkers the human race has produced, why Plato's *Republic* is one of the few timeless and thought-provoking books, why Aristotle's political discussions are so strikingly modern in their relevance to the problems and thinking of our age, whereas the Greek mode of production can be of no interest whatever to the modern capitalist. It is also noteworthy that the material realities of no other slave economy, ancient, medieval, or modern, ever generated thoughts so prolific and profound, a literature so remarkable in quality, and an art so magnificent in its beauty as to qualify even for a remote comparison with the Greek or Roman achievement.

The situation is hardly different beyond the classical age, and a few stray examples will suffice. To the reader who keeps in mind medieval economic theory it will seem farfetched to insist that the ideas of Thomas Aquinas are the specific reflex of feudalism, and Marxians ought to wonder why the Catholic savants of today find the teachings of the Doctor eminently acceptable seven centuries later when the economic foundations are immensely different. One wonders why feudal Europe produced Aquinas, Roger Bacon, and copious patristic writings of penetrating insight, while feudalism in other lands fell far short in such accomplishments. That Hegel's philosophy was charged with revolutionary implications was demonstrated by the neo-Hegelians and was appreciated by Marx and his colleague. Socialism, they point out, is a German product. But it is strange, from the Marxian perspective, that revolutionary doctrines and revolutionaries like Marx and Engels should come from semi-feudal Germany and not exclusively from capitalistically mature countries. Backward feudal or semi-feudal Russia produced out of a mere handful of educated people during the nineteenth century a literature that could stand more than favorable comparison with the literature of economically more forward countries. It is necessary to explain how it is that we, the children of a new economic world, can read the Bible, Homer, Dante, Shakespeare, and Tolstoy with emotion, understanding, and enrichment.

When we notice the dispersion of ideas ruling in a given country at a given time new questions arise. According to Marx, there are the ideas of the upper class, of the exploited class, and of the genuine scientist. First, in Marx's view, the ideas of the master class are distorted by their class interests which do not permit a detached consideration of social phenomena.

Second, in estimating the ideas of the proletariat, to use capitalist society as an example, Marx and Engels are on both sides of the fence.[28] If the proletarian is to build a new world, he must be clear-eyed about the aberrations of the capitalist order and must view capitalist institutions in a knowing and critical temper. It is not clear how this superior wisdom comes to him. Stressing the influence of work in shaping our character and mentality, Marx elaborates on the demoralizing effect of the excessive toil of the worker who functions as a mere lackey to the machine. From this, it is a sudden transition to come upon pronouncements that the proletarian is intellectually acute enough to penetrate to the sham of the bourgeois state, law, morality, and religion, and to be qualified to transform the social foundations. By Marx's emphasis on labor and class environment in molding man's nature, attitudes, and ideas we are not prepared to expect persons of the nonproletarian class to take a prominent part in the movement for factory

---

[28] See above, Chapter VIII, section on Illusionism.

legislation, and for social betterment generally, in England, in America, and in every other country. Always about us we see people of the nonproletarian orientation taking a leading part in behalf of the workers, and rare is the case when social improvement is achieved without an effort of some members of the upper classes, often more virile and more perseverant than the effort of the underdog.

Third, we are similarly unprepared to understand the phenomenon of the genuine scholar. A thesis which stresses work and class position above other factors has to demonstrate how such factors tend to develop impartial nonclass investigation and thinking. We want to know what produced Marx, originally a member of the bourgeois class, and his ideas, in the light of Marx's frame. It seems that Marx exempts himself, Engels, and a few others of nonproletarian status, from the distorting influence of class environment.

This exemption, it may be observed, does not stand alone. On Marx's view, the theorems which he himself developed are ultimately grounded in material facts, and as facts change the theorems ought to change with them. His own theories presumably fall victim to relativity and occupy a temporary place in the eternal flux of facts and ideas. Marx's theory of relativity thus devours his own theories, the theory of relativity included. There is no assertion, however, in Marx that he expected as a matter of course such a fate for his ideas. It is conceivable, but we cannot be sure, that there is room in his organon for certain principles which transcend time and space, unyielding, like the multiplication table, to the law of relativity, impervious to the dialectic "hostility" with which everything is impressed, and impregnable to the dialectic contradictions which transform everything into new syntheses. Among such truths he may place overarching disciplines or principles like logic, the dialectic, and the materialistic conception of history. If so, questions arise regarding the final sources from which the time and space defying absolutes are derived, regarding the processes by which the scientist derives them, and regarding the criterion by which they lay claim to exemption from the reign of relativity and the corrosive action of dialectic contradictions.

The dispersion of ideas is not confined to the different strata of society, but rules as well within a given group of social thinkers and even among natural scientists. In any period of time, long or short, there is a great variety of views among scholars in a given field, and the pages of learned journals record divergent theories, many shades of opinion, and unceasing controversies. Marx and Marxians repeat the formula that ideas "mirror" socio-economic realities. It is probably safe to say that ideas deal with realities, by and large. But the proposition that ideas deal with realities is different from the proposition that ideas mirror realities. It is not clear which ideas mirror realities and which do not when we confront the whole spectrum of ideas on a given problem. To consider one of the multitudes of examples, take the period 1750–1820 in England, marking the beginnings of the Industrial Revolution. In the field of economics, dealing with the same aspects of realities, were the ideas of Cantillon (1750), Hume (1752), Adam Smith (1776), Thornton (1803), Lauderdale (1804), Ricardo (1817), Malthus (1821), and others, differing on one or more essential questions of economic analysis.[29]

In the same period in industrially less advanced Italy and France, Bernouilli (1738), Galiani (1750), Turgot (1766), and Condillac (1776), foreshadow, as does Cantillon, the marginal utility theory of value which came into prominence in the 1870's, in a more advanced economic setting. It is curious to note that, according to Marx, Quesnay (1758) was in some important respects ahead of Adam Smith and even Ricardo; or that J. B. Say (1803) was more sound than Adam Smith or Ricardo in stressing the cost of capital in the determination of value, and that he induced Ricardo to change his mind on this point by 1820.[30] It is also interesting to note that a Swiss, Sismondi (1819), was in advance of British radical writers in

---

[29] The dates refer to important publications.

[30] Cf. F. A. Fetter, Review of W. Stark, *The History of Economics in Its Relation to Social Development*, in *American Economic Review*, XXXV (December, 1945), 945.

stressing the enormities of capitalism and in fathering a theory of crises and other theories from which Marx learned so much.[31] In anthropology, economics, philosophy, psychology, sociology, and other fields, we see a wide diversity of ideas at any given time, and it is anticlimactic for Marx to pronounce that ideas are born of material and social conditions.

(B) THE DIALECTIC. As a protean problem in philosophy, the dialectic no doubt has clustering about it profound and fruitful propositions. However, even one uninitiated in its technicalities may venture observations on some aspects of this problem as it is depicted by Marx and Engels. First, while it is true that components, phases, and facts generally are interrelated, the claim of all-embracing interrelations merging into one great totality is, for many purposes, barren. It serves little purpose to talk of interconnections between cabbages and kings, even if it is true that, as with Tennyson's "flower in the crannied wall," if we knew all about cabbages we would know much more about humans. Too, the idea of the unity of opposites may not always apply. Many facts, for many purposes, are either one thing or another and not both at the same time, or else embody a union of several attributes, but the attributes are not "opposites." It is not fruitful, in economics, to assert that a farm both does and does not yield economic rent in a given period. Nor is it significant to regard the interest and the rent aspects of quasi-rent as opposites.

Second, the theory of the negation of the negation is often farfetched. It postulates progress by opposites and by negation, whereas change or progress proceeds by variation, differentiation, redistribution of emphasis, and in many other ways. In the evolution of the theory of value it is not enlightening to classify as a negation of the negation each theory in the series of the labor theory, the cost of production theory, the utility theory, the equilibrium theory, the monopolistic competition theory, and the mathematical variants from Cournot through Walras and down to presentations in mathematical journals

---

[31] Marx and Engels pay tribute to Sismondi in *Communist Manifesto*, p. 46.

today. The assertion, further, that the negation of the negation yields a synthesis of a higher order is not always valid. If we do not steer the examples to the desired result, a higher synthesis may not materialize. The product $-a$ times $-a$ gives $a^2$, but subtract $-a$ from $-a$ and we get zero. The one procedure is as much a negation as the other, and as legitimate and useful. It may be noted that it is grandiose and to no purpose to read the dialectic into multiplication and subtraction. It is like breaking the butterfly on the wheel. Engels excludes from consideration the act of grinding barley into flour, because it does not give the result which he seeks: more barley. But making flour out of barley is as important and as customary an enterprise as planting it (else what is the purpose of planting it?), and it is equally a negation of negation.

Third, the assertion that cumulative changes of a quantitative character effect, at a critical point, a sudden transition to a new quality is subject to question. The change is not always a sudden "leap"; e.g., the change from spring to summer, from middle age to old age, or from feudalism to capitalism. The idea of the leap is in contradiction to Marx's doctrine of gradual change and to his repudiation of sharp lines of demarcation. Doubtful, too, is the thesis that a new quality is merely the summation of certain quantitative cumulations, and that qualitative differences can be equated to quantitative differences. Such a concept is mere speculation. It has not been demonstrated that the difference between Raphael and the sign painter is a quantitative concept, and that Isaac Newton is merely a multiplied dull boy who agonizes over an algebraic equation. Equally questionable is the idea that quantitative changes always precipitate a new quality. More books in the library are more books, more flowers in the field are just more flowers, and weight or length multiplied by any constant are still weight and length.

The dialectic may be regarded as a game of classifying and putting into pigeonholes aspects of phenomena after the event. Before the event it does not enable us to predict the pattern of the process of development. Often enough there is no dialectic at all, and frequently an aspect of the dialectic triad is missing. The succession of the seasons follows a cyclical routine instead of a dialectical progression. It is of no particular enlightenment to seek the negation of negation in marriage because it results in children, in the manner of Engels who sees the dialectic in barley and more barley. If death is a negation of life, it does not follow from the dialectic as such that the higher synthesis of a life hereafter must follow. In this instance Engels expressly denies the synthesis by repudiating the idea of life after death.[32] The same irregularities appear in history. The destruction of the pre-Homeric Mycenean civilization, the fall of ancient Greece, the barbarian invasions of Rome, or the expulsion of the Moors from Spain did not mark the achievement of a higher civilization. Only centuries later did societies even of the same level arise. Nor did higher social organizations follow upon the decline of ancient Egypt, Babylonia, Palestine, or upon the fall of the Hittites or the Incas. There was conflict in Asia through the centuries but, as Engels acknowledges, no progress resulted. The path of history is strewn with examples of cyclical development, stagnation, retrogression, or the extinction of civilizations, instead of a progressive dialectic march.

Despite its commendable stress on observation and investigation of facts, and despite the elementary truth that the dialectic is a concept and man, not the dialectic, is the active agent in history, the impression can scarcely be escaped that there dwells in Marx's and Engels' dialectic an element of mysticism. Their dialectic teaches that everything is impressed with a hostility against itself, and that contradictions are invested with the motive power of evolution, and it postulates an all-pervading purpose in history and an exalted predestined end toward which society moves. Matter, plants, and animals are represented as constrained to behave in contradictions by an attribute implicit in their texture. In social evolution, disregarding comparatively brief fluctuations, there is in the historical perspective, according to Marx, a rectilinear sweep upward

[32] *Dialectics of Nature*, p. 164.

in the attainment of human freedom, and the communist society takes its place in the dialectic framework as a synthesis of enhanced proportions in the reflected light of the first thesis of tribal communism and by an inherent thesis-synthesis kinship with this humble estate of primitive man.

In the hands of Marx and Engels, moreover, both before and after the event, the dialectic is often a pliable means of arriving at formulas pleasing at the moment. "The nebulous hybrids of Marx's conceptions," says E. Dühring, "will however surprise no one who realizes what phantasies can be built up with the Hegelian dialectics as the scientific basis." [33] Whether Marx intended it to be so or not, the dialectic often serves as a respectable authentication of propositions insufficiently demonstrated. To Marxians the theorem that communism is the child of the near future is invested with a compelling sanction when they can repeat that the future society is the certain outcome of the inevitable synthesis towards which the inexorable dialectic moves irresistibly in its relentless historical processes.

Marx and Engels, as we saw, present two variants of such a dialectic. Primitive communism represents the thesis; the private property of slavery, feudalism, and capitalism is the antithesis; and the communism of the future will reëstablish the communal property of archaic days, but as a synthesis of a higher dimension.[34] In *Capital* Marx depicts a dialectic formula on a reduced scale. The thesis is embodied in the latter Middle Ages, when the means of production were the private possession of the direct producers, the peasant who owned the land and the artisan who owned the tools. The negation of this thesis is charged to capitalism, which separated both peasant and laborer from the means of production. The negation of this negation will emerge when communism restores the productive property to the coöperative association of the workers.[35]

As is to be expected, the two philosophers can read the dialectic into phenomena after they had occurred, but are not

[33] Quoted in Engels, *Anti-Dühring*, p. 142.
[34] *Anti-Dühring*, pp. 151–152.
[35] *Capital*, I, 835–837.

successful in predicting the result before the event. Their difficulty finds ample exemplification in the attempts to foretell the place and the time of the coming revolution. According to Marx, France will "proclaim" the problem of the proletariat by precipitating the class struggle, which will spread the conflagration to all nations, while the definitive solution of the problem will take place in England, where the proletariat will win supreme power.[36] According to Engels, the workers will first triumph over capitalism in Germany, and other countries will follow.[37] The *Communist Manifesto* (page 58) states in 1848 that Germany is on the eve of a bourgeois revolution which would be "the prelude to an immediately following proletarian revolution. . ." In 1853 Marx sees an imminent cataclysm in France: "Workers from all over France will be attracted to Paris by the low price of bread, and thus the revolutionary army will be recruited." [38] In 1881 he writes about Henry George's *Progress and Poverty*: "I consider it as a last attempt to save the capitalist régime. Of course this is not the meaning of the author." [39] In another letter in the same year he sees the capitalist countries on the verge of dissolution into communism.[40] We saw in Chapter XIII, above,[41] that revolutions were expected in the first crisis after 1850, then during the crises of 1857 and 1873. After Marx's death in 1883 Engels expects the final struggle soon after 1886, and in 1891 he writes to Bebel that "we have the almost absolute certainty of coming to power within ten years." [42]

Marx and Engels seem to have been obsessed with expectations of swift dialectic upturns, and saw "signs" on every occasion. Marx was sure of a speedy revolution when he noticed the electric locomotive on exhibition in London. He hailed the

[36] *Klassenkämpfe in Frankreich*, p. 85.

[37] *Socialism, Utopian and Scientific*, p. xxxviii.

[38] Letter to Engels, October 12, 1853, in Marx and Engels, *Gesamtausgabe*, Part III, vol. I, p. 509.

[39] Letter to Swinton, June, 1881, in "Unpublished Letters of Karl Marx and Friedrich Engels to Americans," *Science and Society*, II, 227.

[40] D. Rjazanov, ed., *Marx-Engels, Archiv*, I, 319–320, 324, 326, 331.

[41] Section on The "Breakdown" of Capitalism.

[42] Marx and Engels, *Selected Correspondence*, p. 491.

Chartist movement as the promise of a new day. He greeted (before he became disappointed) the English trade-unions as the nursery of the class struggle destined to bring a new era. He saw promise of a social transformation in the coöperative movement. He treated the Paris Commune as a phenomenon of immense historical proportions and (before he changed his mind) as a model to follow in the revolution of the future. Engels, too, saw the "eve of revolution" every now and then, was sure of victory in the "near future," and always heard the successor of capitalism knocking at the door.[43] Immersed in their revolutionary speculations, Marx and his friend indulged, as other humans would in the circumstances, in wishful thinking, and the dialectic proved an eminently accommodating tool.

[43] *Anti-Dühring*, pp. 129, 180, 183.

# CHAPTER XIX

### THE SIGNIFICANCE OF THE THEORY

IT is not easy to evaluate in brief compass a figure like Marx and an empire of ideas such as he built. It may be mentioned at the outset that the evaluation of Marx in the 1940's is apt to be more lenient than the same attempt in the 1920's. At least three circumstances may account for the difference. First, in the 1920's, after a catastrophic war, the capitalist world rebounded with astounding vigor and launched into a period of expansion and prosperity. In prosperity even the coolheaded student, under the spell of infectious optimism, is apt to discount more heavily the jeremiads of the critics of the present order. Second, in the 1920's there was lacking the upsurge of interest in the business cycle which we witness today, and it is in this field that Marx made a striking impression. Third, in the 1920's economic analysis was moving in the traditional manner in the grooves of value, distribution, money, and the like, and viewed with customary disdain the theorems of Marx as vague, discordant, and strange.

The scene has changed in the 1940's. Since 1929 the modern world has seen the longest period of depression and unemployment, and now, after World War II, it faces disorganization and uncertainty. Even in prosperity the ghost of 1929 will not be far from the banquet table, beside the palpable presence of socialism in various countries and communism on more than one sixth of the earth's surface. Second, the exploration of the business cycle has received in recent years extraordinary emphasis, and the recurring breakdowns have begun to engrave themselves on our consciousness as a threat to the established order. Marx, who never ceased to point accusingly to depressions, seems now more relevant. Third, recent developments in economic theory have tended to give standing to Marx. J. M. Keynes's *General Theory*, with its penetrating effect on economic thought, has raised the underconsumption approach to the level of respectability, and has brought into vogue an analytical framework in some respects a first cousin to the synthesis which Marx labored to build. Of some influence, too, has been, very likely, the Chamberlin–Robinson emphasis that our economy, far from being the citadel of competition, is riddled with varying degrees of monopoly power, with an equilibrium, if any, marked by maldistribution of resources, by nonmaximization of satisfactions, by prices away from the competitive norm, and by incessant advertising and salesmanship as the partly wasteful adjunct, if not matrix, of economic processes. We are not living in the best of all possible worlds. Marx's prediction of chronic unemployment and of ever-increasing monopoly, although not the offspring of analysis identical with the modern conceptual apparatus, cannot help pursuing the economist with disturbing echoes.

In 1926 Keynes wrote of Marx as follows:

The principles of *laissez-faire* . . . have been reinforced by the poor quality of the opponent proposals — Protectionism on one hand, and Marxian Socialism on the other. . . Both are examples of poor thinking, of inability to analyze a process and follow it out to its conclusion. . . Of these two, Protectionism is at least plausible. . . But Marxian Socialism must always remain a portent to the historians of Opinion — how a doctrine so illogical and so dull can have exercised so powerful and enduring an influence over the minds of men, and through them, the events of history. . .[1]

How can I accept a doctrine [Russian communism] which sets up as its bible, above and beyond criticism, an obsolete economic textbook [Marx's *Capital*] which I know to be not only scientifically erroneous but without interest or application for the modern world?[2]

But in the *General Theory*, while still entertaining a none too flattering opinion of Marx's socialism, he acknowledges that after Malthus it was Marx who kept alive the concept of effective demand.[3] No doubt other economists, although adverse to Marxism, would take more kindly to Marx for his relevance to the present intellectual climate in economics.

[1] *Laissez-Faire and Communism*, pp. 47–48.
[2] *Laissez-Faire and Communism*, p. 99.
[3] Pages 355, 32.

## THE PRAGMATIC TEST

(A) MARX'S POPULARITY. We often come upon the claim that Marx's significance in the field of social thought can be proved convincingly by the pragmatic test. The fact, it is asserted, that he exercised a lasting influence on social movements demonstrates that his ideas possess a vitality with which only powerful truths are endowed. And indeed it is admitted everywhere that he has been an enormous stimulus in social creeds and social agitations. Radicals have been known since time out of mind. Each society has had its critics who thought that they could do better; without Marx there would have been no want of schemes for social regeneration. Nonetheless, the socialist and communist movements, the hardiest and most formidable of all social movements, owe him a great debt. He gave them a vigor unknown to them before, and he set them out on a career more instructed, more solemn, and more persevering. He equipped them with methods of attack on the existing orders and with theories on the destinies of societies. He invested them with the dignity of scientific stature, relieving them of the previous status as symbols of utopias, hopes, and exhortations; and he electrified them with the assurance of ultimate triumph. Not only socialism and communism but other radical constructions as well draw nourishment from his principles. Fabianism, syndicalism, anarchism, and reformism of many a hue draw ammunition from the abundant arsenal which he built.

However, the popularity of a doctrine is no guarantee of its validity. People may be devoted to a body of ideas and may be inspired by them to notable deeds, not because the ideas represent vital truths, but because they appeal to the emotions; and the appeal to the emotions is not a test of truth. History is full of examples of how wrong conceptions and emotional schemes have taken possession of the multitudes for long spans of time. It is equally unconvincing to point to Russia as proof of the validity of Marx's theorems. As was pointed out previously,[4] the appearance of communism in Russia is not an exemplification of Marx's analysis or of his successful predictions. To many the mere fact that Russia adopted communism confers a unique sanction on Marx's ideas. They do not suspect that by the same pragmatic token they would have to judge as valid truths ancient mythologies and polytheisms, shintoism, dictatorship, the divine right of kings, and the protective tariff. "What is is right" cannot be accepted as a maxim in ethics or social science.

(B) MARX'S PREDICTIONS. Many are impressed by Marx's predictions come true. Without looking into the analyses on which they rest and without examining the ratio of predictions fulfilled to those unfulfilled, they seem to be of the opinion that successful forecasts are an indication of solid scientific procedure, that they establish the superiority of Marx's economics over orthodox economics.[5] Since much store is laid, in various quarters, by Marx's forecasts, is it of moment to look into them. It is insufficiently realized, first of all, that many of his predictions failed to materialize. As was partly indicated above,[6] and as can be seen from his correspondence, he expected a revolution with each crisis and each war after 1848. Esteeming the German working class as almost qualified for the revolution already in his day, he expected of it greater deeds than the wholesale submission, where it was not enthusiastic loyalty, to Hitler. In 1848 he predicted crises of progressive severity, whereas, despite the prolonged depression of the 1930's, there was no such trend for the past century as a whole. He predicted the final crystallization of only two — or three — contending classes, but everywhere we see varieties of groups, some torn from within by divisive emotions and interests. Whether or not he predicted the disappearance of the middle class is not altogether clear, but certain it is that he predicted for it a minor rôle in society. Yet everywhere this class, if there is such a thing as a class at all, occupies a promi-

[4] Chapter II, section Marx on Russia.
[5] See, for example, J. F. Brown, *Psychology and the Social Order*, p. 458.
[6] Pages 267, 387.

nent position in industry, in commerce, in the professions, and in science, literature, and art.

He predicted a mounting revolutionary ardor in the proletariat, but instead we see the perennial striving of the workers after the fruit of capitalism. The American or English worker wants a larger slice of the capitalist, or state capitalist, melon; he is not yearning for the fleshpots of Russia. Marx predicted the unceasing displacement of men by the machines and the growth of the idle reserve of labor, but, so far, with the industrial revolution have come a growing working population and greater employment. He predicted increasing poverty of the masses, whereas the masses are better off in every capitalist country than they were decades ago. He predicted poorer working conditions induced by the greed of the capitalist and by his zeal to counteract the falling tendency of the rate of profit; but the trend of improvement in working conditions shows no sign of faltering. He predicted a rising oppressiveness of the capitalist state over the masses, but everywhere we witness the rising power, leadership, and dignity of the workers. He predicted the gradual extinction of philosophy, in the wake of the widening conquests of science and the broadening understanding of our environment; while everywhere philosophy pursues its inquiries without conspicuous mitigation. He predicted [7] that the Pacific Coast of America would overshadow alike the Atlantic Coast and the Mediterranean Sea in economic and strategic importance, but such a contingency is hardly developing.

Among the forecasts commonly accepted as having seen fulfillment are the rising tide of monopoly, the increasing mechanization of industry, the steady enlargement of the scale of production, the declining of rate of profit, and the growth of fortunes. But even here reservations are pertinent, at least with respect to some of these prognostications. Consider the rise of monopoly, the forecast most widely circulated. Everywhere, it seems, we come upon monopoly, in corroboration of Marx's thesis. But this closet is not without a skeleton or two.

[7] See above, p. 305.

First, it must be emphasized against a very popular conception to the contrary that the whole idea of the decline of competition and its replacement by monopoly has by no means been established, and it awaits a fresh and careful exploration. There was more monopoly in the past, and there is more competition today, than is commonly recognized. The forms of monopoly power have changed. In the past, because of limited means of communication, there was much spatial monopoly, and much oligopoly in isolated communities. These days, differentiation of product and regional or national oligopoly are prevalent forms. It is not easy to measure monopoly power, and it is not easy to trace its trend over a long period of time. Since the beginnings of our modern economy, say, since the eighteenth century, there have been fluctuating blends of competition and different types of monopoly; the reference generally made to our economy as competitive before 1870 and as monopolistic since then is without foundation in fact or analysis. It may well be that the economy of a bygone day, marked by the oligopolies of manufacturers, storekeepers, and artisans in the numerous isolated localities, and coupled with a somewhat monopolistic agriculture (now, in various aspects, the classic example of pure competition) catering to local markets, exercised as much of an impact on the derangement from the optimum allocation of resources for the country as a whole and on the redistribution of wealth as can be charged to our present economy, with its more spectacular and more talked-about forms of monopoly.[8]

Second, the analysis on which Marx based his prediction will hardly stand examination. To Marx, the economies of size tend to rise indefinitely. But such economies emerge only up to a certain point. Beyond this point an extension of operations entails net diseconomies and rising average unit costs. We are dealing with the familiar U-shaped curve describing the cost behavior of the firm as its scale of production is enlarged. On

[8] Cf. E. S. Mason, "Industrial Concentration and the Decline of Competition," in *Explorations in Economics: Notes and Essays Contributed in Honor of F. W. Taussig.*

the basis of cost and efficiency alone many an industry cannot be expected to fall under the sway of one or even a few huge concerns. If some industries are monopolized, it is often not on account of the superior efficiency of concentration and centralization, as Marx would have it, but for other reasons: promotional profits, the quest for power, etc. When accordingly Marx contends, as we recall, that monopolization will progress to the point of bringing each industry, and eventually agricultural enterprise, too, under the control of one colossal management, he indulges in a prediction for which his analytical support is precarious. Nor is there factual evidence for such extreme tendencies today.

Third, it is not unimportant to note that Marx often talks of the monopoly of the single proprietor who renders himself open to easy expropriation by the state on its way to socialism. Modern industry, however, is corporate industry, especially in the big concerns, as Marx well knows, so that even in a monopolized industry ownership is vested in a multitude of stockholders, some of them proletarians. In the instance of most of the stockholders, the ownership is modest indeed, but a few shares of stock bear the same significance to the average small stockholder as do the large holdings to the wealthy *rentier*; and the small owner may be relied on to resist "subversive" encroachments on property rights with nearly the same zeal as the big capitalist, with whom he may be proud to parade a financial kinship.

To take another forecast, the increasing mechanization of industry. Profit is derived, according to Marx, exclusively from unpaid labor. It follows that, to maintain the rate of profit and to save the economy from the fatal consequences of a falling rate of profit, entrepreneurs ought to favor the employment of labor as against the use of labor-saving machinery, and thus prevent $c$ from rising faster than $v$ in $\dfrac{s}{c+v}$. True, Marx teaches that in the atomism of competition the business man, acting singly and without concern for ultimate general results, is in search of improvements which would give him a temporary cost advantage over his rivals. But what Marx envisages for capitalism is not the reign of competition but a rising tide of monopoly. It is easy for the monopolist, or the oligopolists, in each industry to refuse to invite the mischief of a low rate of profit, by avoiding undue mechanization as a matter of course and by aiming at the utilization of the available labor force, the seedbed of surplus-value.

In monopolized industry, be it added, mechanical innovations are not needed as a device to displace labor in order to depress wages and keep them from eating into surplus-value, for the reason that monopolists, as monopsonists of labor power, can be counted on to maintain wages at desired levels. With a diminished tendency toward the mechanization of industry there will be a weaker trend to large scale production, a slower displacement of labor by the machine, and a much smaller industrial reserve army. Several of Marx's predictions thus stand and fall together. Progressive monopolization of industry may also be calculated to mitigate the anarchy of competition, to introduce planning and order into our economy, to moderate the cyclical fluctuations, and to usher in the eclipse of the fetishism of commodities. In proportion as monopoly gains headway, a corrective is introduced for most of the ills which Marx predicts for capitalism. Marx's predictions are at odds with each other, and his theoretical structure is a house divided against itself.[9]

Marx's forecasts do not grow as the logical fruit of consistent economic theory. In economic prediction, as in arithmetic, correct answers are not proof of correct analysis. His successful predictions are rather the pronouncements of an observer with a penetrating eye and an intuitive judgment for the failings of modern capitalism. There is much truth in Professor Leontief's remark that the success of Marx's forecasts does not rest on a masterful analysis of the capitalist processes but rather on his realistic acquaintance with the ways of our present order. "Marx was the great character reader of the capitalist system.

[9] The weaknesses of his prediction regarding the falling rate of profit have been indicated in Chapter XI, above.

As many individuals of his type, Marx had also his rational theories, but these theories in general do not hold water." [10]

Confronting the classical economists with arrays of Marx's predictions in proof of his superiority is neither relevant nor convincing. Marx was preëminently a revolutionary philosopher of history. Interested in the dissolution of present society and the establishment of communism, he could hardly avoid prognostication. The classical economists were principally students of the everyday workings of our economy and not interpreters of history bent on building a case for a definite trend in social evolution. Thorough and modest scholars, they perceived that economics was not advanced enough in any case to render prophecy a rewarding enterprise. The reader is reminded, e.g., of many statements to this effect in J. S. Mill's *Logic*. Their labors were centered on the outstanding economic problems within the framework of the society in which they lived.

Nevertheless, one may venture the opinion that had the classical economists attempted as many predictions as did Marx the proportion of their successes would have compared favorably with Marx's. Even so, their analyses involved at times opinions of future developments within the capitalist frame, and the record is far from indifferent. They forecast a rising accumulation of capital and a decline in the rate of profit; a more elaborate division of labor and the attendant rise in the scale of production, with the widening of the market; and mounting economic rents with the progress of society. Adam Smith recognized the persistent monopolizing urge of tradesmen, and he pours his criticism on them as the disrupters of the competitive system: this is not a far cry from the view of a steady tendency toward monopoly. The prediction of overpopulation can scarcely be laughed out of court in the face of India, China, Japan, and other countries. Those who perceive a mature economy about us will recall the classical idea of the

---

[10] W. Leontief, "The Significance of Marxian Economics for Present Day Economic Theory," *American Economic Review*, XXVIII (March, 1938), Supplement, p. 8.

stationary state, and those who believe that the machine displaces the worker will recall that Ricardo argued their view, and that on this point Marx only follows Ricardo.

## REASONS FOR MARX'S APPEAL

In the next two sections concluding opinions will be offered of Marx's standing as an economic theorist and as a philosopher of social evolution. Here general reasons will be sketched which may account for his widespread popularity. There is, first, the great prestige of the natural sciences and their signal achievements in recent decades. The social scientist casts an envious eye toward the laboratory, where concrete objects are handled, observed, and made to yield generalizations. He increasingly recoils from imponderables and speculations which lengthen the distance between his work and the work of the physicist and bring it closely to the province of the philosopher and theologian. Preoccupation with figures, charts, and graphs, with measuring, counting, and lines of regression, and generally with earthly and prosaic phenomena, makes him feel that he walks in the way of modern science and not in the path of medieval logicians; that he deals with the evidence of the senses and external realities and not with opinion and the resources of subjective rationalization. Too, the appeal to facts seems to satisfy the quest for certainty in an uncertain age bewildered by the jungle growth of questions, complexity, and distress.

Marx's emphasis on the prosaic fact of making a living, on earth-bound self-interest instead of noble ideals, on the struggle for self-betterment in the clash of opposing class interest, and on terrestrial materialities as the basis of institutions and ideas, bears the stamp of the modern, the scientific, and the sophisticated. It points to the man with his feet on the ground and his head level with the facts. Spinoza's position that moral evils are to be investigated on the same plane as thunderstorms has been extended to all the planes of social inquiry. Marx introduces the reign of law into the affairs of men comparable to the reign of law in nature. He detests explanations by the intangible, the spiritual, and the subjective. The final appeal is to things.[11] One may be permitted the paraphrase, but in language which he would spurn, that in this connection Marx believed in the divine right of things.

A second reason for Marx's influence lies in his message to the perennial well-wishers of humanity, the contingents of sincere and enthusiastic reformers. That society is plagued with ugliness and maladies, on every continent, is axiomatic. There is no want of individuals who, unhappy over social ills and in search of a clarification and a program, are impressed by what Marx has to offer. Even to the milk and water reformer the fervor of Marx's analysis, the vehemence of his indictments, and the apocalyptic grandeur of his large-dimensioned constructions, combined with the legendary overtones clustering about his revolutionary name, have a compelling attraction; he will refer to Marx's ideas with admiration although not often with much understanding.

Marx was the master critic of capitalist society. No weakness of our modern order has escaped his sharp eye. Not only the reformer but many others brought up in the Western tradition are strongly impressed by his indictments of the concentration on pecuniary values, of the exploitation of man by man, and of the preoccupation with private interests. The measurement of behavior by money is of incalculable service to economics as a discipline with the claim to a science, but the implications of the pecuniary motive have irked many an economist. J. S. Mill had his socialist leanings; so had Marshall at one time, before he took to economics. A seemingly stoical economist like F. W. Taussig is irritated by the "sullied growth" of the early railroads and the "blatant advertising" pouring at the consumer. J. M. Keynes is not happy over "the habitual appeal to the money motive in nine-tenths of the activities of life" and over "the social approbation of money as the measure of constructive success. . . Perhaps, therefore, Russian Communism does represent the first confused stirrings of a great religion." [12]

---

[11] "We are just beginning to catch up with Marx now, a hundred years later," a promising young sociologist said to me, in this connection, in the summer of 1940.     [12] *Laissez-Faire and Communism*, pp. 134–135.

Examples can be multiplied. Marx's stress of higher human values makes an enduring impression.

It is his many-sided appeal that has established him as the standard bearer of reformers, malcontents, and revolutionaries. Not his concept of history or his economic theories, nor yet his voluminous philosophical polemics and extended historical and political dissertations, keep his name in prominence, but his prophetic message to the ever-present circles and organizations that are distressed by the evils of the day. It is this "religious" appeal and the political following which his work inspires that promise to keep Marx's name alive.[13]

It may be added that the fact that Marx labored so much in the vineyard of dissent and protest makes his contributions stand out in a field not marked, in our age, by minds of enormous capacity. One who has made a comparable contribution in the accepted areas of learning, where many minds of great caliber made many increments to knowledge, would not tower to the stature which Marx attained. He would be at best one hill among many, and not a hill in the valley. Strip his writings of the crusading appeals to the emotions and the revolutionary spirit, remove the philippics against capitalism, and leave only the dispassionate discourse on philosophy, history, the philosophy of history, and economic theory, and he will take his place among the ranks, and not necessarily always the upper ranks, of the scholars known in these fields. His renown would be less extravagant, and his name no longer a byword.

Third, a strong foundation for Marx's prominence comes to view when we turn away from the particular claims and unique technical formulations which compose his specific system, and wander over the wide areas of his own suggestions and observations, as well as of implications and ramifications, to the contemplation of which one is stimulated even by those utterances which may not be acceptable as they stand. Then we find ourselves in a large realm of fruitful possibilities.

[13] F. H. Knight, "Some Notes on the Economic Interpretation of History," *Studies in the History of Culture* (February, 1942), p. 217; J. A. Schumpeter, *Capitalism, Socialism and Democracy*, pp. 5–6.

Consider, for example, the mode of production. It is one thing to urge it as the incubator of institutions and ideas and as the impulse of historical evolution. It is a different thing to be carried to the suggestion that the way in which people gain a livelihood has much to do with their outlook and behavior. A farming community, a fishing settlement, a mining camp, a lumber region, a factory town, are characteristically stamped in numerous respects. The ways of pursuing the daily economic tasks largely define people's needs, appetites, and wants, enlarge or limit their horizons, and mold their habits of thought; they may mean the ways of isolated villages or the ways of noisy cities with the imperative of the watch and clock in the punctualities of the daily traffic. The farmer, the factory hand, the speculator, the professor are in many ways different personalities because of the differences imprinted on them by their work. We are reminded of the treatment of this theme by Veblen, in whom Marx's influence is unmistakable. All this was recognized in novels, essays, and even political writings before Marx was born, but his writings gave it the pointedness and suggestiveness of focus and generalization.

Similarly with classes. One must question the doctrine that throughout history social transformations are the exclusive achievement of the struggle of the exploited against the exploiters, invariably eventuating in a superior order in which the formerly subjected class becomes the master class; and that it is now the turn of the proletariat to build the next civilization. We seek in vain for inductive evidence that the design of history is to prepare the way for the proletariat as the architect of the future. History does not seem to demonstrate that the world belongs to the rabbits; it rather forces the unfortunate conclusion that, so far, the rabbits have belonged to the foxes. But there is value in the suggestions that society is not a homogeneous unit but is composed of groups defined in numerous ways, by creed, race, politics, geographical position, income, ancestry, and the like; that history is full of abuse of man by man, of group by group, and of a people by a people — for imperialism, far from being distinctly a phenomenon of capitalism, has been known since antiquity — with the corollaries of internal strife, mass movements, and wars; that antagonism, division, pressure, and coöperation among groups form much of the content of social conduct, and account in part for legislation, reforms, political maneuvers, and social mores. The assertion, too, that man is principally a creature of his class goes too far, but there is force in it when it is toned down in scale. Often the group or class is a profound although a subterranean factor in shaping the conceptions and values of the individual. Only we have to keep in mind that this is not by any means a complete account of what shapes human conduct, as was indicated above, in Chapter IV, last section. All in all, the idea can hardly be repudiated that the immediate determinants of the average wayfaring individual are largely to be found in such variables as his work, his associates, and his neighborhood. That such ideas had been known before Marx does not subtract from the concentrated impact of Marx's expositions on the question.

One more example. It may be presumptuous to teach that ideas are primarily reflections of conditions fostered by the mode of production; that the fundamental orientation of all thinking is to be sought in the socio-economic realities; that, being merely adaptive to the causal economic medium, ideas have no independent history; that the ruling ideas in any period are the ideas of the ruling class; that investigation in the natural sciences is little more than the adjunct of the needs of production; and that the center of gravity of all social studies is justification of the interests of the predatory class. The inadequacy of such views is stressed in the preceding chapter as well as in the next section. However, on another plane, some implications of these teachings deserve underscoring. All scientific inquiry proceeds within an established framework of knowledge, problems, techniques, and intellectual interests. These contexts are of immense importance in equipping the inquirer with an apparatus of directive concepts and categories of thought, and in governing the spirit in which problems are selected, formulated, and attacked. The scientist is limited by the intellectual climate, and only if there is greatness in him will he rise above it and change it, creating a new mental environment for those who follow.

Such considerations apply more strikingly in the social sciences. The general cultural conditions, the class origins of the investigator, the training of respected teachers, the large principles in the air, like the survival of the fittest, natural rights, *laissez faire*, and full employment — these and other social facts envelop him and unconsciously shape his convictions and values. Often even the trained social thinker feels first, believes next, and then looks for reasons. The social scientist, the judge, the preacher, the publicist cannot always dissociate himself from the imperatives of the cultural medium in which he is immersed. Such conceptions are in common circulation now, but not in Marx's day.

Volumes can be written on the proliferations of the possible implications of Marx's theories, apart from the unique formulations constituting his particular interpretation of society, which alone is the subject of this book. Wherever one turns, the mind is stirred to the consideration of basic issues in the broad fields of social study and philosophy. Everywhere he challenges the reader to ask fundamental questions, to forsake phraseology and hypocrisy, and to reëxamine his premises. Of course, this is true of any thinker who wrote abundantly and dealt with important problems. There have been many writers, from Plato to A. J. Toynbee, whose ideas one need not accept, but who offer tremendous stimulus to self-searching over a large area of fundamentals. True, but this does not diminish Marx's stature. Not every prolific writer touching on many problems produced a profound impression on many people in the relevant fields of learning. There has to be richness, suggestiveness, and stimulation in their work. They have to be Platos and A. J. Toynbees. Gustav Schmoller's writings are voluminous and varied enough. But they lack in force for a lasting impact.

MARX THE ECONOMIST

(A) ECONOMIC THEORY. That Marx's economics is an organic part, and a part of first importance, of his conception of history is evident when the structure of his system is viewed as a whole. We may divide his economics into two departments, economic theory and economic methodology. We shall omit his writings on economic history. The economic theory of Marx's day dealt principally with value, distribution, money, international trade, and the incidence of taxes. They are the standard problems today, too, but others have been added. On these problems, which embody most economic principles, Marx's contribution must be judged as of minor importance. His labor theory of value is invalid, despite the extraneous virtues claimed for it: e.g., that it puts the focus on exploitation, that it fathers the celebrated concept of surplus-value, and that it stresses the division of income into earned and nonearned categories. A false theory cannot claim acceptance because it serves certain purposes no matter how worthy. It may be noted in passing that the question of exploitation or of nonearned income can be analyzed without benefit of this faulty theory of value. His price of production theory is superior, but, like all cost of production theories, it is deficient for its neglect of demand. In general, his theory of value, like his theory of distribution, suffers from the absence of the marginal analysis, and those of his followers who make play with the "futility of marginal utility" miss the point. On the problem of value Marx is inferior to such contemporaries as Cournot, Gossen, Jevons, Walras, Menger, and possibly even J. S. Mill. In relation to modern theory, it is rudimentary indeed. There is no hint of monopolistic competition in Marx: he talks of monopoly in the sense of one seller, of collusion, or of schemes of amalgamation.

His theory of distribution is equally inadequate. He does not go beyond the classical cost of production theory, better known as the subsistence theory, of wages, adding to the idea of market fluctuations of wages the idea of cyclical fluctuations. Like the classical economists, he relies on overpopulation to keep wages down, but unlike them, he finds the explanation of a redundant population not in malthusianism but in the displacement of men by mechanical processes. There is no concept of marginal productivity, and a rise in wages is perceived as the accompaniment of a mounting demand for labor power, and the concomitant shrinking of the industrial reserve army, during the transient periods of prosperity. Profit, interest, and rent are the three elements of surplus-value, representing categories of income without a basis of corresponding functions in production. Thus the entrepreneur receives a profit only because, as owner of the means of production, he is in a position to force a tribute. There is no determinant indicated of the scale of profit. Together with interest it is treated as a residual after the deduction of rent. There is no inquiry into risk, uncertainty, innovations, dynamics, and the like, in relation to enterprise and profit. The business man's alleged functions of management are performed, Marx teaches, by hired managers, for a wage. He does not analyze how this wage compares with the wage of ordinary labor. There is only mention that in time supervisors sink to the level of proletarians.

The many pages devoted to money, capital, and interest [14] reveal no new ideas on the theory of interest. Interest is treated conspicuously as a category of ownership. Senior's abstinence is derided; so is the idea of the time element. The owner of money levies an arbitrary fee on the business man, the borrower. He robs the business man just as the business man robs the laborer, with this difference, that while the amount which the business man can wrest from the laborer is limited by the minimum that must be left to the laborer, the level of interest has no comparable upper limit, except that it cannot for any length of time absorb the whole of profit on which the business man thrives. It is evident that his theory of profit and interest is hardly on par even with the gropings of his contemporaries. On rent he follows Ricardo, and, while the long discourse shows great ability to play the many angles of a problem, little that is of significance to theory is added. Hardly more can be said of

[14] Marx, *Capital*, III, 397–719.

his treatment of money. The strained and somewhat dialectical discussion in the first volume of *Capital*, as well as the extended exposition in the third volume, raise few of the outstanding theoretical issues stirred up before and during his day, and resolve none. As with earlier economists, money is not considered an element inwrought into economic processes, capable of independently setting in motion chains of development, but is treated as a surface phenomenon masking underlying fundamentals. Credit can, in certain circumstances, accelerate economic processes, but basically it remains external to them. As was seen in the chapter on crises, Marx brands as superficial the idea that credit may be causally contributory to depressions. Finally, there is nothing in Marx of theoretical moment in the field of international trade or public finance.

It is different with the problem of the business cycle. There Marx easily deserves the palm of distinction. The economists of his day refused to be impressed by the recurring economic breakdowns, regarding them as extraneous and self-corrective disturbances from the normal state of prosperity. The totality of economic processses was viewed in the perspective of J. B. Say's law. Even later economists did not turn to business cycle theory. Marshall and the Austrian and Lausanne Schools centered their interest on equilibrium economics. Of all men the least inclined to slur the maladies of capitalism, Marx stressed crises as a phenomenon inborn in capitalism and fatal to it. He did much in exposing the defects of the law of markets. More important, while his treatment of crises is sketchy, embodied as it is in stray posthumous notes, it ranks as a noteworthy chapter in the literature on cycle theory. Having emerged from under a cloud through the brilliance of J. M. Keynes, the many-lived underconsumption theory will always be linked with Marx's name, although Malthus and Sismondi, if not others as well, paved the way. Other strands of cycle theory found in him, like the falling rate of profit and the concept of disproportionalities, are of more than marginal significance.

Scattered and incomplete are discussions and observations on other points of theoretical interest. Among these, prominent mention must be made of the last two chapters in the second volume of *Capital*, where the formulation is attempted of the relation between the capital goods and the consumption goods departments of production. This exploration, striking for its originality, is in line with his customary emphasis on the importance of a theory of circulation such as received its first impulse from Quesnay, but was, according to Marx's charge, abandoned by English economists. Indeed, the whole of this volume of *Capital* is devoted to the circulation of goods and contains many suggestive ideas on the problem. It may be mentioned in passing that this charge by Marx is not fully valid. What Quesnay was apparently groping for was an equilibrium analysis for the total economy. This is essentially Adam Smith's objective; and the full fruit of this approach came with the Lausanne School.[15]

The foregoing paragraphs have in mind definite contributions in advance of the thought of the day. There is no attempt to deny that Marx's fertile brain has filled the numerous pages given to economic questions with pregnant theoretic remarks, hints, and criticisms, especially in the posthumous two volumes of *Capital* and *Theorien über den Mehrwert*. The judgments expressed above must strike a discordant and irritating note to the ears of those who are inclined to anoint each syllable of Marx's with oracular implications, to magnify a casual and vague observation of his into a full-blown theory — after the theory had been enunciated by a modern writer — and to believe that in the six decades since his death little has happened in economics except the vindication and expansion of ideas sprung from Marx's brain. The inclination to claim for Marx retroactive paternity when a new idea, never before discerned in him, emerges on the horizon is a less certain way of establishing Marx as the forerunner of modern economic theories than the attempt to discover in Marx new analyses before a

---

[15] L. Robbins, *An Essay on the Nature and Significance of Economic Science*, p. 68.

Harrod, Hawtrey, Hayek, Hicks, or Robertson gives them to us.

(B) MARX AND KEYNES. The preceding section attempts an evaluation of Marx the theorist from the viewpoint of orthodox economics, the economics which held the field before J. M. Keynes's *General Theory* introduced the stormy changes that laid the foundation of the "New Economics." To an economist of this new persuasion what is significant is not that Marx failed to add to the old themes of production, value, and distribution, but that his analytical framework reveals striking similarities to Keynes's system.

Indeed, it seems that as a precursor of Keynes Marx fared better than as a cultivator in the classical vineyard. Running through the expositions of the adherents of underconsumption theories is a common denominator of similarities. Not only in Marx but already in Malthus and Sismondi, with whose teachings Marx was eminently familiar, we come upon conceptions which remind us of the basic attitudes and elements in Keynes's analysis.

We find in them a macroscopic approach; that is, an emphasis on aggregative economics and not so much the microscopic view of partial analysis. They put much more stress on short-run developments, on trade fluctuations, and, with the exception of Marx, on policy considerations. The idea of effective demand appears in all three, perhaps more sharply in Malthus than in Marx. They all reject J. B. Say's law, the foundation stone of many, but by no means all, pre-Keynesian economists; and they maintain accordingly that a general glut is possible because of an inadequate demand, and that breakdowns, far from being the fruit of outside forces, are inherent in capitalism as periodic afflictions. As another corollary of the repudiation of Say's law, it is already asserted by Malthus [16] that savings do not necessarily rise at the expense of consumption, but that in a condition of unemployment both can rise. This idea is also entertained by Marx.

[16] T. R. Malthus, *Principles of Political Economy*, pp. 353ff., 419–420.

The novel idea emerges in these three writers (Malthus, Sismondi, and Marx) alike that capitalism is not a well-working, self-adjusting mechanism, but an organization suffering from the disorders of oversaving, overinvestment, and underconsumption. To Malthus and Sismondi, as to Keynes, these maladies are aggravated by the maldistribution of income, while to Marx these evils are inseparable companions of our present order, and a better distribution would fail to resolve them. There is no implication in Marx of a policy of public works in a depression, inasmuch as the mitigation of the infirmities of capitalism was a concern foreign to his revolutionary temper. But there is recognition of the expedient of public expenditures in both Malthus and Sismondi, and we recall Malthus' defense of unproductive consumption as a partial offset to a deficient demand. It is very doubtful that Keynes was familiar enough with Sismondi and Marx to learn from them, but, as his biography of Malthus demonstrates, he was impressed by Malthus' non-Ricardian economics at least by 1933; [17] however, this in itself is far from establishing that Keynes borrowed from Malthus.

Marx's analytical apparatus also contains a number of conceptions similar to Keynes's which are not noticed in Malthus or Sismondi. Modern writers see, for example, a close kinship between Marx's falling rate of profit and Keynes's marginal efficiency of capital. It may be observed that this idea is in the tradition of Smith, Ricardo, and Mill, who for different reasons foresaw a declining rate of profit on accumulated capital. Again, Marx's rising industrial reserve army suggests, as does the falling rate of profit, chronic unemployment and stagnation. Here, too, Marx walks in the way of the classicists. Smith, Ricardo, and Mill talked of the stationary state: Smith concerned with the consequences to labor, Ricardo vexed by the serious difficulties to the entrepreneur, and Mill consoling himself with the cultural compensations.[18] Further, in the fragmentary discussion of the interrelations between the depart-

---

[17] J. M. Keynes, *Essays in Biography*.
[18] Mill, *Principles of Political Economy*, Book IV, chapter vi.

ments of capital and consumption goods in the last chapter of the second volume of *Capital*, Marx seems to touch on connections between saving and investment that may bear resemblance to Keynes's formulations. Finally, the peculiarly Marxian concepts, like surplus-value, rate of exploitation, constant and variable capital, the organic composition of capital, and simple and extended reproduction of capital, are flexible to manipulation, and he who is skilled with equations and models may put them into forms of a Keynesian complexion.

A comparison of Marx and Keynes demands as well at least a brief indication of some of the constructions integral to Keynes's line of thought but not noticeable in Marx. In Keynes's scheme the rate of interest is an outstanding determinant; without it, among other things, the concept of the marginal efficiency of capital would lack content. Marx considers the rate of interest as of negligible moment. He recognizes no unique determinant of its level, and he does not counterpose the declining rate of profit to the rate of interest: as was already pointed out, his falling rate of profit includes interest. The consumption function is a dominant principle in Keynes; and one of its various services is to explain the turning points in the business cycle. In the Marxian exposition the consumption function is hardly farther advanced than the idea generally held by economists of all schools that the well-to-do save and the poor do not. Marx explains the revival after a depression without reference to consumption. In fact, as was seen in the chapter on crises, he voices in this connection the theory that lower money wages induce employment and the business upswing, a thesis charged with skepticism and controversy among the Keynesians. Of course, his underconsumption theory stresses lack of consumption as accounting for the breakdown of prosperity; in this, it may be observed, Malthus is more consistent than Marx.[19]

In Keynes's thought overinvestment "only occurs through mistakes of foresight," while to Marx overinvestment is consistently associated with oversaving; whatever is saved is in-

[19] Malthus, *Principles of Political Economy*, pp. 351–375, 511–512.

vested, and accumulated errors are periodically corrected by crises. Apart from equating savings and investment by definition, Keynes conceives the achievement of this equality through income adjustments via the propensity to consume.[20] Such an approach to this equality is hardly evident in Marx, although he clearly does not accept the classical principle that the rate of interest brings savings and investment into equilibrium. In Keynes's analysis a high level of savings, if it is offset by investment, will not induce unemployment. To Keynes the root-trouble of our economy lies in the twin phenomena of a high inclination to save and a low motivation to invest. In Marx's presentation, savings are invested as a matter of course (except for such imbalances as are considered in his disproportionality theory of crises), and yet unemployment is not only cyclical but perennial as well. Like the more elementary of underconsumption theorists before and after his day, Marx perceived oversaving not as saving unmatched by investment, but as excessive saving in the sense that too much is invested and consequently too much produced for a market with limited consumption.

When we turn from the building blocks to the larger aspects of the structure — and no hard line can be drawn between the two — we face a difficult problem of evaluation. The five strategic components (the propensity to consume, the marginal efficiency of capital, liquidity preference, the wage-unit, and the quantity of money,[21] and their unique analytical integration) constitute the heart of Keynes's contribution. There are points of resemblance between some of these components and some of Marx's formulations, but it would be going too far to claim that out of the welter of Marx's finished and unfinished chapters and notes arises a total synthesis essentially similar. Furthermore, the matrix of Keynes's analysis is lodged in the income-savings-investment complex, in contradistinction to the traditional themes of the allocation of resources, supply and demand, production and distribution. It is difficult to locate

[20] *General Theory*, p. 184.
[21] *General Theory*, pp. 246–247.

the focus of Marx's structure. Perhaps it is surplus-value and the exploitation of class by class. The center of gravity of his system shifts from one point of intersection to another. Here he stresses surplus-value and underconsumption, there he seems to underline saving and investment; now he shifts to the falling rate of profit, and then he strikes out for the connection between consumption goods and capital goods with the inevitable imbalances. Then Keynes presents a synthesis in which full employment is a special case of equilibrium admitting the application of the theories of the classical economists; [22] while Marx's analysis can hardly find its ultimate description as an organon in which the central classical postulate fits as a special case. It is, finally, of relevance to note that money and interest are so prominent in Keynes's scheme that he takes them up as "the first chapter of the argument" in his first attempt to "re-express" the thesis of his *General Theory*.[23] These two topics are in the title of his book. The cornerstone to Keynes, they are the least significant to Marx.

To summarize, Marx's conceptions come to us as stray pictures, often blurred, often incomplete, and without coherence into unity. More important, these pictures assume a Keynesian aspect primarily when examined in the Keynesian perspective, when the proper adjustments are made in the background assumptions and when the angle of vision is conveniently slanted. What is uniquely Keynesian was not discovered in Marx before Marx was discovered in Keynes. There is, however, the other side of the shield. It is evident that now and then Marx broke away from the traditional paths and turned his efforts to problems which Keynesians (and non-Keynesians) regard as of enormous urgency in our age. To recognize such problems so long ago, and in an environment in which their recognition was under suspicion as revealing a lack of mastery of economic fundamentals, bespeaks a mind independent and penetrating. Moreover, despite exceptions and qualifications,

[22] *General Theory*, pp. 377ff.

[23] Keynes, "The General Theory of Employment," *Quarterly Journal of Economics*, LI (February, 1937), 209-223.

it is equally evident that the treatment of some of these problems is informed with a temper implicit in Keynes. It is accordingly not strange if a follower of Keynes, even if he is as conservative in his social attitudes as is Keynes himself, takes kindly to Marx and regards him as a path-breaking, ill-treated, and legendary co-worker.

(c) METHODOLOGY. The formal *Methodenstreit* in economics is at least a century old, having probably begun with the rise of the German historical school. The controversy ramifies into many troublesome questions. Here only a few points will be taken up briefly.

Foremost is the issue raised by Marx concerning the plane of economic inquiry. Are the subject matter and the underlying causality in economic theory to be sought in the changing social relations fostered by changing modes of production, or in the alleged eternal properties of things? In a few notable pages [24] Marx registers a protest against the disposition of economists, especially vulgar economists, to center their efforts on the analysis of things, categories, and forms, instead of on the analysis of origins and realities of class relations; to treat economic phenomena as derivatives of alleged permanent qualities of goods, capital, land, and labor, and to pervert the social character of the phenomena into an alleged natural character; to stress supply, price, and market, but to leave human beings to implication or to the function as vehicles by which impersonal processes reveal themselves; to exalt value and the shares of income as categories expressive of the immutable properties of things, thus "proclaiming the natural necessity and eternal justification" of the unearned revenues, and sanctioning the interests of the predatory class (page 967); and to present economic laws as absolute in time and space, while ignoring the historical context, the class medium, and the surrounding institutions.

Economics, Marx insists, cannot occupy itself with exchange relations in abstraction from human relations. Value is not the

[24] *Capital*, III, 947–968; I, 83–96.

expression of physical or chemical attributes of goods; it is the expression of the historical relations governing men. The relations of men in production define the value relations of labor power, of commodities, and of the unearned wealth. Profit, interest, and rent are not explainable by the functions of the capitalist and the revenue-producing character of capital or land. These revenues are pried away from the toiling proletarians by the lever of class domination and the fulcrum of property power. The ownership of capital forces the tribute of surplus-value to the employer; of loanable funds to the lender; and of land to the landed gentry. Capital, says Marx, is a "perennial pumping machine" of surplus-value, and monopoly of land is a "perennial magnet" attracting part of surplus-value (page 957). The trinitarian formula (capital, land, labor) is incongruous and out of relation to social realities (pages 947–949). The theory of income springs from the fiat of class relations, and as class relations change the theory changes. Back of the impersonal processes of "free" markets, Marx insists, are force and robbery sanctioned by institutions (pages 952–954). The orthodox economist sees force and robbery in monopoly, the protective tariff, and the like; Marx sees it in all incomes save wages. To the orthodox economist the touchstone is the free market, to Marx class power.

The habits of thought of the economists are to Marx an exemplification of illusionism — of the cult of appearances and of the failure to penetrate to the internal connections in a mode of production and its social relations. It is the cult of things, the fetishism of commodities.[25] Impersonal objects, mystifying categories, and inexorable processes are perceived as the essence of realities and as the terrain of learned economic inquiry. Society is treated as the adjunct of the market mechanism, classes as incidental illustration, and the human being as the instrumentality of the price process. The result is that the commodity dominates men's mentality, and that for the failure to reveal the substratum of human relations men live in the twi-

---

[25] The celebrated concept of the fetishism of commodities is specifically presented in *Capital*, I, 83–96.

light, facing economic phenomena as incomprehensible explosive natural forces that "rule them irresistibly and enforce their rule over them as blind necessities." [26]

At this point it is necessary to digress. The charge of reification of social processes does not apply with full force to the classical economists. Back of their conceptual framework the early economists recognized the large classes as special to basic aspects of economic processes. They, moreover, treated one class or another as harmful or as the recipient of an unearned income. Adam Smith assailed the monopolizing spirit of tradesmen, who threatened the "obvious and simple system of natural liberty," who favored protection, insisted on mercantilistic practices at home and in the colonies, and plotted against the "laboring poor" and the consumer. Ricardo made it clear that, in Adam Smith's phraseology, the landlord reaped where he never sowed, that with the passage of time the landlord alone would gain in income, and that the incomes of the entrepreneur and the worker were reciprocal to each other, with the concomitant struggle between the two. In Parliament, Ricardo, the landlord, voted against the landed interests. Socialists can quote with satisfaction from these two economists, more from Adam Smith than from Ricardo. Malthus' defense of the landlords as the spending class contributing to effective demand underlines the emphasis on social groups in early economic thinking. Following Ricardo in the main, J. S. Mill, too, gives attention to economic classes, and against his support of Senior's abstinence theory of interest can be set his assertion that the distribution of income is a matter of institutional convention. With Marshall and his followers, and especially with the Austrian and Lausanne Schools, the idea of classes as bearers of economic processes begins to fade. Contributing at least in small part to this turn is the appearance of the marginal analysis. The idea of marginal utility and marginal productivity have driven another nail in the coffin of the labor theory of value and the neat formulation of surplus-value, and the Ricardian implication of a conflict between employer and em-

[26] *Capital*, III, 968.

ployee has been lifted by the demonstration that the shares of both can rise without encroaching on each other.

It is also necessary to emphasize that the *laissez faire* concept, whether of the classical school or of any later economists, has hardly ever been intended as an apology for privilege. On the contrary, in the minds of the early economists it epitomizes the assault on the regulations and repressions of an autocratic state and on the privileges of aristocracy or shopkeepers. The product of the eighteenth-century emphasis on the individual, this concept or policy was fashioned as a weapon of economic freedom. Profound observers of human conduct, these economists were impressed by the seemingly ineradicable inclination of men to exert arbitrary power over their fellows. These economists contemplated with uneasy suspicion the exercise of state authority, be it capitalistic or communistic, and they trusted to competition to remove the tyranny of man over man in economic dealings. They were convinced that the arbitrament of the competitive market would assure economic liberty and plenty, while monopoly or the interference of the state would restrict freedom and diminish well-being. Freedom and well-being were the primary goals of these economists no less than they were Marx's. The difference lay only in the means. To Marx, competition stood for irrationality, chaos, and oppression, and only collective action informed by social intelligence was the gateway to the rational disposition by men of their own destinies: either we plan or we suffer from the fetishism of commodities.

The fashionable notion that the classical economists were heartless thinkers under the sway of empty norms and interested in a successful operation even though the patient died is largely a myth.[27] What is true of the classical economists in this respect applies, generally, to economists of all persuasions and at any time since. Even when the entrepreneur is openly favored, the reason commonly is that he is regarded as the means of promoting the community's well-being. Well-being

---

[27] Even a man of the stature of John Dewey succumbs to this fashion. See his *Logic*, pp. 505–506.

is the only reason why economists are nearly unanimous against monopoly, unearned privilege, unfair business practices, protection, and undue state interference. Professor A. C. Pigou, the eminent British economist, speaks for economists of all ranks when he says: "It is not wonder, but rather the social enthusiasm which revolts from the sordidness of mean streets and the joylessness of withered lives, that is the beginning of economic science." [28]

Marx recognizes the truth of the foregoing, but only with regard to some of the classical economists, and even then only partially. After 1830, as was noticed above (page 160), he sees the ascendancy of vulgar economics. Even the earlier economists do not receive a clean bill of health because they did not go far enough. They failed to penetrate to the profounder implications of the relations of production. They took the segmentation of society into classes as part of the natural order, as a reasonable arrangement in the great scheme of division of labor and specialization of function. They did not recognize the class structure of their day as a temporary historical situation. More important, they failed to realize that the changing classes and relations of production are the soil out of which grow the changing economic processes and the correspondingly changing theories and laws which they studied so diligently. And this returns us to our theme.

The issue is clear. In his attack on the reification of economic processes Marx does not have in mind the failure of giving institutional description, like the class structure, prominent space alongside theoretical discussion; nor would he be content even with the exposition of class dominance as the explanation of certain categories of income. He insists that the prevailing form of property and class relations generates the unique sequences and configurations of economic data, shapes the causes of the essential economic processes, and accordingly constitutes the final frame of reference to the specific direction, content, and tonality of economic analysis. In sum,

---

[28] *Economics of Welfare*, chapter i, section 1.

economic theory is relative to the class relations engendered by the modes of production.

At the opposite pole is the position of traditional economics. Social relations and other institutions are perceived as not necessarily associated in a strict causal connection with the basic aspects of those phenomena which constitute the material for standard theoretical inquiry. Integrating and characterizing this material is the following set of ideas. Among the varieties of ends pursued by men a prominent place is occupied by the pursuit of satisfactions from goods and services. The resources for the achievement of this set of ends are scarce, and they have alternate uses. The problem is to maximize the satisfactions with the given resources in a given medium of institutions and knowledge. Of coördinate importance are two principles independent of the institutional surroundings, one natural and the other psychological; one, the law of nonproportional returns, and the other, the law of diminishing marginal utility. Added is the idea of the time element: we value the enjoyment of present goods differently from the enjoyment of future goods. Self-interest has a prominent place. It is not the exclusive motive in the valuations involved in buying and selling goods and services, but it is the outstanding motive although modified in varying degrees by other considerations.

These ideas crystallize certain constants in human nature and refer to aspects of human behavior which transcend, more or less, the evolutionary variations in the large social settings. These constants, in other words, express themselves in a uniformity of causal sequences and interconnections largely independent of the institutional context. On these ideas, derived from general observation and the record of human conduct in the past, is built a body of economic theory dealing with the relations of means to ends in a system of valuations and preferences. The analysis is abstract, as analysis generally is, and is easily given to mathematical formulation. New institutions may change the scale of valuation, the standards of preference, and the magnitude of calculation; they may induce new practices and remove old ones, shifting the emphasis of theory from one set of problems to another. But whenever the phenomena are essentially similar, the structure of reactions and therefore the theoretical approach will remain similar.[29]

This does not argue that throughout the ages the economic behavior of the race has always been the same. The social organization may be so elementary that certain economic phenomena, familiar to us, do not exist; and in the succession of social orders certain economic arrangements are excluded or modified. In such instances the pertinent phases of economic theory are suspended or modified. A Robinson Crusoe is not a landlord or an employer of labor, and the theory of rent or wages does not apply. But even he, be it noted, has to choose between more and less fertile, more and less accessible, plots of ground; has to consider the alternative uses of the plots; and has to weigh the desirability of applying successive hours of labor on each plot.[30] Up to a century or two ago advertising was in scant practice, and the theory of advertising was not conceived. But when, in recent decades, this means of attempting to influence the demand for a product became a staple, the theory of advertising could sooner or later be formulated and incorporated in the theory of monopolistic competition, an achievement with which the name of Professor E. H. Chamberlin is prominently associated.[31] If Marx's injunction "from each according to his capacity, to each according to his need" is adopted by a communist society, distribution of income on the basis of marginal productivity gives way to distribution on the basis of some political, psychological, ethical, or other criterion. However, if the communist order preserves the traditional attempt at the optimum allocation of resources, orthodox economics provides a more adequate set of principles of economic calculus than can be built out of Marx's economics.

When, to repeat, similar basic economic circumstances obtain, similar human reactions will be associated with them, and similar results will follow; the same categories of explanation

[29] J. A. Schumpeter, *Theory of Economic Development*, pp. 11, 80, 138–147.
[30] Cf. Marx, *Capital*, I, 88.
[31] See his *Theory of Monopolistic Competition*.

and the same tools of analysis will apply. In ancient Judea, Greece, or China a bumper crop of wheat meant a reduced price per unit, unless there was an increased demand. There was monopoly in ancient and medieval times, and the monopolists acted much like those of today. Whenever, throughout the centuries, goods sold in markets, they sold under conditions of supply and demand, of blends of competition and monopoly not unlike those of today, and with the same explanations, whether or not the relevant economic theory was known at the time. The wide-awake Greek slave owner or his counterpart in the South before the Civil War would not employ so many slaves in the mine or on the plantation that they failed to earn their keep. Marginal productivity applied then as now in some respects. Similarly under serfdom. Despite disapproval by philosophers and condemnation by the Church, interest on loans was known in medieval times, very likely with determinants of scale similar to those at present. It is striking that as early as the sixteenth and seventeenth centuries there were scholastic writings on interest of extraordinary penetration and in anticipation of modern views on the problem.[32] The Egyptian kings, it may well be assumed, did not undertake the building of pyramids, to which J. M. Keynes playfully refers, for the purpose of solving an unemployment problem. Nor did they use much of any but forced labor. But it is hardly stretching a point to conceive that if times were slack and if the expenditures on pyramids added to aggregate expenditures as they would have otherwise been, pyramid building, like our public works, raised employment — and with the multiplier effect. A modern economist finding himself in ancient Greece or fourteenth-century China would explain the economic processes about him with the tools of modern economics. He would hardly see the wisdom of the assertion that Greek economic theory was valid for the Greek times, and Chinese theory for Chinese circumstances, while our theories apply only to our times. He could teach relevant parts of modern economic theory to Greek or Chinese scholars with benefit to the pupils.

[32] See B. W. Dempsey, *Interest and Usury*.

It is regrettable that Marx's writings do not reveal specific examples of changing economic laws as derived from changing social relations. He talks of debt and usury and the upheavals which they bred in antiquity, of usury in feudal society,[33] and of interest on merchant's, industrial, and finance capital. But there is no exhibit of the succession of theories analyzing the underlying considerations which govern the rate of interest. The scale of interest, in his view, seems *always* to be subject to the arbitrary determination of custom and bargaining and of the necessitous condition of the borrower and the exploitative power of the lender. There is ample institutional description of the personalities of the borrowers and lenders, but no exposition of the relativity of economic theories of interest. The income of the slave, the serf, the journeyman, or the modern wage earner is consistently equated to subsistence; there is no delineation of the different wage theories for the different class relations. Concomitantly, while he recognizes that surplus labor power is extracted from the slave, the serf, the journeyman, and the modern proletarian, he does not present the special principles governing this surplus in each age. On the contrary, he applies to this surplus the same quantitative determinant — what is left over and above the subsistence of the exploited agent. He sees rent in medieval days [34] and under capitalism, but he does not offer varying principles of rent to suit each period. He designates the labor theory of value as eminently applicable to a society in which small independent producers, owning their scant equipment, provide for a competitive market, but he urges this theory as the cornerstone of exchange in modern capitalistic conditions as well, not only in the first volume but even in the third volume of *Capital*. He tells us that each era has its own economic law of population, but we do not learn about these laws for any but capitalistic society.

On two other important aspects of methodology Marx's position is interesting and suggestive. The first relates to the idea

[33] See especially *Capital*, III, chapter xxxvi.
[34] *Capital*, III, 917–925.

of weaving economic analysis with description of economic institutions, to give the discourse a sense of reality and movement. It is primarily the idea of combining economic theory with digressions on economic history, sociology, and reflections on institutional structure and social synthesis. Adam Smith was the leader among orthodox economists in this practice, and Alfred Marshall occasionally made the attempt. The master of them of all was Marx. Institutions, striking illustration, unique episode, not to mention emotional comment, relieve with impressive skill the chapters of abstract analysis. That this procedure gives color and effect to the exposition there is no doubt. But it is by no means certain that it is much more than an expository device. It is a matter of taste. There is reason for the preference for the type of austere and abstract discussion exemplified by Ricardo. The analysis is unbroken and moves with the vigor and impressiveness of its own logic and architecture. Economic analysis and economic history are, furthermore, disciplines demanding different casts of mentality, and either discipline is a master that wants exclusive attention. Often enough the theorist is not a good historian, or has little time or patience for historical investigation, and the little history which he includes with theoretical presentation is apt to be borrowed and precarious. There is no want of authentic treatises on economic institutions by scholars in the field, and to these the reader can repair with greater benefit.

Of greater significance is the problem of incorporating the analysis of the dynamics of our society as part of economic theory. Traditional economics, the economics of the classical, Marshallian, Austrian, and Lausanne Schools, is static. It is occupied with exchange phenomena, in the frame of capitalism, as an equilibrium of prices, the prices of goods and the prices of services used to produce the goods. There is consideration of such circumstances as occasion a deviation from equilibrium, in order to examine the process of redressing the equilibrium; e.g., the effects of an excise tax or of a tariff. But an examination of the factors responsible for orderly or revolutionary steps toward new economic and social constructions is regarded as lying outside the boundaries of economic analysis. Besides, such inquiry appears to them as traffic with disarrays of data too wayward and complex to admit logical procedure and manageable formulation.

But this was meat and drink to Marx's exuberant mind. The transitory character of social orders and the eventual replacement of capitalism by communism were pivotal theorems in his thought, and the study of social evolution seemed to him an indispensable component of economic investigation. His analysis of the dynamic developments of capitalism takes two approaches. First, proceeding from such premises as private property, the class cleavage of society into exploiters and exploited, competition, and the drive for profit regardless of the human cost, he arrives, as was seen above in the chapters on his economics, at instances of dynamism like the mechanization of industry, increasing misery, concentration and centralization, and the falling rate of profit, all culminating in progressively aggravated crises which finally bring the capitalist system to a standstill. The second approach is the heavy-structured materialistic interpretation of history, pointing, likewise, to the inevitable downfall of capitalism.

It is of importance to record that, in the opinion of some, even in the first approach the frame of capitalist developments is not deduced implicitly from economic theory but primarily from the underlying institutional data, so that without the importation of institutional premises the economic theory approach would not necessarily lead to results which Marx specifies. Says Dr. O. R. Lange: "A theory of economic evolution can be established only on very definite assumptions concerning the institutional framework in which the economic process goes on. The instability of the technique of production which is the basis of the Marxian theory of economic evolution can be shown to be inevitable only under very specific institutional data." [35] It may be observed, however, that any body of eco-

---

[35] "Marxian Economics and Modern Economic Theory," *Review of Economic Studies* (June, 1935), p. 198. See also pp. 200–201. Dr. Lange stresses "the instability of the technique of production" as the matrix of the dynamics of capi-

nomic theory is built on a set of assumptions which may be termed institutional or psychological, and that Marx is not peculiar in this respect. More significant is the circumstance that, as was noted on various pages above, his dynamic phases of capitalism are not self-consistent, and that the economic theory which sustains them will not stand the strain of examination.

That static analysis is indispensable and legitimately constitutes a major element in the structure of economic theory, if economic theory is to illuminate the everyday economic processes, few would care to dispute. But the neglect of the kinetics of our economic order is regrettable as a conspicuous gap in the structure. An exploration of the evolutionary trends would be valuable in itself and would alike enrich the static analysis. Superior to Marx's economics in explaining the capitalist world about us, traditional economics has been inattentive to its evolutionary possibilities. There is a literature accumulating on business cycle theory; a certain amount of work has been done in tracing monopoly through the decades; the evolution of one movement or another has been outlined; and much has been done in economic history. But much of all this is informed with an empirical orientation. What is lacking is the integration of these and other dynamic trends with a consistent body of economic theory, treating them as the necessary fruit of fundamentals inherent in our economic order. That this attempt must be apart from the speculative field of philosophy of history needs hardly to be stressed. Perhaps economic theory is not ready for the task, but Marx's dynamic approach casts in sharper focus the importance of such an attempt.

### Conclusion

The last few chapters, if not the whole book, are an attempt at an evaluation of Marx's theory of history. But a few con-

---

talism according to Marx — in the sense that the urge to mechanization is nourished primarily by the desire to create an idle reserve of labor in order to keep wages down. Marx did not quite see mechanization in this manner. To him mechanization was rather a correlative of competition, as was seen on previous pages; Dr. Lange is aware of this, as he indicates on p. 199n.

cluding opinions may be expressed now. The supreme aim of a social science is to order facts into a coherent sequence, to seek integrating principles which place phenomena into meaningful patterns, and to reveal causal relations which enable us to foresee the tendencies and consequences of social processes. The task is difficult, and only in few social fields can it be even partially undertaken. It is close to the impossible to achieve it when the vast panorama of history and the immense realm of social developments at once become the object of inquiry. The philosopher of history undertakes a synthesis of overpowering dimensions and defying complexity. "Analysis leads to the elimination of errors; synthesis — meaning generalizations — accumulates them," says Augustin Cournot.[36] Errors in a synthesis of history are unavoidable. Professor R. J. Hoffman observes that Marx's conception is "a transcendental search for the causation and end of the historical process: a search, that is, for what the human mind, from its very nature and constitution, is unable to discover." [37]

Once the formidable task has been assumed, it will of necessity be reduced in scale and simplified in conception; one or two factors will be shouldered with the burden of explaining inaccessible complexities; deceptive plausibilities will be treated as objective certainties; and opaque generalizations, sustained by little more than vague intuitions, will follow one another. Marx does not escape this fate although he probed more deeply than nearly all of those who made similar attempts. He makes institutions, ideas, and values little more than the tail of the economic dog; he leaves out of account complicated and baffling phases of human nature; and he abstracts from the many-sided factors which come into play in historical processes. He substitutes alluring simplicity for exacting complexity, and reduces three-dimensional solids to thin linearities.

It is late in the season to stress the place of the multiple non-economic elements involved in the social scene, but there is

---

[36] *Essai sur le fondement de nos connaissances*, II, 95.

[37] "The Marxian Philosophy of History," *The American Review* (October, 1936), pp. 508–509.

temptation to offer the following observation by Professor A. P. Usher. Referring to George Unwin, another eminent economic historian, and in evident agreement with him, Professor Usher says:

> The true outcome of history is to be found not in particular institutions [like outward forms of government and type of church], but in the "inward possessions and experiences of mankind — religion, art, literature, science, music, philosophy — but, above all, the ever-widening and deepening communion of human minds and souls with each other." The chief creators of this result are to be found in the whole body of the people; in the reformers, the artists, the scientists, the scholars, the inventors.
>
> Such a view carries us close to the deeper realities of history, and opens up new judgments of men and events which will make it easier for the historian to achieve the ultimate ideal of all historical writing — the presentation of a record in which we shall "see life without rearrangement." [38]

Presenting a ready precept, Marx's simplification tends to keep one from pursuing a question more diligently and more objectively. It sacrifices slow inquiry for easygoing, quick answers. It barters prosaic truth or honest doubt for beguiling plausibility. It induces truncated research, misplaced and unbalanced emphasis, and unwarranted assuredness. It fosters a disposition, often unconscious, not to examine facts but to give them the third degree for the purpose of gouging out of them a pattern congenial to the preconceived framework. Inhibiting a fresh approach, it breeds an almost automatic inclination to turn to the economic factor as the master principle at the bottom of everything. See for example Engels' own explanation of anti-Semitism.[39] He sees only the economic element in this hydra-headed phenomenon.

Some earnest scholars, even of the non-Marxian persuasion, assert that Marx's theory of history serves them as a working hypothesis. When they consider a civilization, a complicated event, or even a simple episode, this hypothesis, they say, puts them on the track, and gives direction and proportion to their investigation. It keeps them from riding off in all directions. It makes them sophisticated, sure-footed, and hardheaded. They know where they are.

[38] *History of Mechanical Inventions*, p. 7.
[39] Marx and Engels, *Selected Correspondence*, pp. 469–471.

If by a working hypothesis they mean that the system of production and the class structure explain the phenomenon under consideration, they accept a precarious guide. Fruitful in some instances, it may be misleading in others. Enough was probably said on this in previous chapters. If by this hypothesis is meant that valuable light is gained on the problem if one turns to production and class relations for orientation, it stops too soon. Still more light and a surer orientation may be won if there is an exploration as well of such areas as politics, religion, science, literature, dominant ideas, and leading personalities.

But with all its weaknesses, it remains true that Marx's interpretation of history towers as a signal contribution to social science. First of all, it served as a powerful antidote to older and more one-sided theories. In his time some regarded history as the special creation of great men; others treated it from the angle of dynastic ambitions, political maneuverings, and state strategy; and still others saw in the social drama nothing but the clashes of races and the marches and countermarches of peoples. There were some who gave disproportionate emphasis to the geographical environment, to ethical consciousness, or to the *Zeitgeist*; and there were those who clothed history with one variety or another of mystical idealism. Marx's conception dealt a body blow to such emphases. He called the historians from their lofty imaginings down to the earth of humble daily facts, of simple busy people, and of classes motivated by questions of bread and butter or wealth and power.

Too, Marx's theory stimulated new investigations of the past, encouraged inquiries into human cultures, and provoked questions and posed problems that had not previously been noticed. It gave new dimensions, proportions, and coloration to old and new facts, to old and new ideas. It forced thinkers to restate their values and reshape their frame of reference. It projected a catalytic agent into all social study, and new variables into deliberations on social phenomena. Today, at the distance of nearly seven decades, during which many of his ideas became outgrown or commonplace, it is easy to overlook the startling effects of his manifold constructions. We are dealing with a mentality which transformed everything it touched, to better or poorer results. Marx's mind, says Professor Hoffman, is superior not only to the eighteenth-century rationalist mind but also to the nineteenth-century positivist mind. "It asks more questions, searches for more relationships, and it demands analysis of much which Ranke and his disciples simply ignored." [40] It demands analysis of much which many a social scientist besides Ranke simply ignored.

However, eminent though it may be among the various attempts at the formulation of a philosophy of society, Marx's conception falls heir to the fate of all one-sided theories. His interpretation is not a master key to history. It is a key that fits many locks but opens few doors.

[40] "The Marxian Philosophy of History," *The American Review* (October, 1936), pp. 509–510.

# BIBLIOGRAPHY

*Only works cited in the text are included in this bibliography. As the manuscript left my hands in November 1946, this book contains no reference to publications reasonably prior to, and beyond, that date.*

## I. WORKS OF KARL MARX AND FRIEDRICH ENGELS

### KARL MARX

"On Feuerbach." Eleven "theses" reprinted as an appendix to Engels' *Feuerbach*, pp. 129ff.; also in *Gesamtausgabe*, Part I, Vol. 5, pp. 533–535.

*Die Heilige Familie*, in *Gesamtausgabe*, Part I, Vol. 3.

*The Poverty of Philosophy.* Translated by H. Quelch. Chicago, 1910.

*Wage-Labor and Capital.* Translated by J. L. Joynes. Chicago: Charles H. Kerr, no date.

*Die Klassenkämpfe in Frankreich, 1848 bis 1850.* Berlin, 1911.
  In English: *The Class Struggles in France (1848–1850)*. New York, 1934.

*The Eighteenth Brumaire of Louis Bonaparte.* Translated by Daniel de Leon. Chicago, 1914.

*A Contribution to the Critique of Political Economy.* Translated by N. I. Stone. Chicago, 1907.

*Value, Price and Profit.* Edited by Eleanor Marx Aveling. Chicago, 1908.

*The Eastern Question.* Edited by Eleanor Marx Aveling and Edward Aveling. London, 1897.

*Capital, A Critique of Political Economy.* Edited by Friedrich Engels.
  Vol. I. The Process of Capitalist Production. Translated by S. Moore and Edward Aveling. Chicago, London, 1909.
  Vol. II. The Process of Circulation of Capital. Translated by Ernest Untermann. Chicago, London, 1907.
  Vol. III. The Process of Capitalist Production as a Whole. Translated by Ernest Untermann. Chicago, 1909.

*The Civil War in France.* Appears under the title of *The Paris Commune*. New York, 1919.

*Free Trade.* Reprinted in *Poverty of Philosophy* as Appendix III, pp. 208–227.

"Einleitung zu einer Kritik der politischen Oekonomie," *Die Neue Zeit*, XXI, No. 1 (1902–1903), 710–718, 741–745, 772–781. Appears in English as an appendix to *Critique of Political Economy*, pp. 266–312.

*Critique of the Gotha Programme.* New York, 1933.

*Theorien über den Mehrwert.* Edited by Karl Kautsky. Three volumes. Stuttgart, 1905–1910.

Letters to Dr. Kugelmann, in *Die Neue Zeit*, XX (1901–1902), No. 1, pp. 708–710; No. 2, pp. 222–223, 477–478.

*Letters to Dr. Kugelmann.* New York, 1934.

*Die Inauguraladresse der internationalen Arbeiter-Association.* Edited by Karl Kautsky. Berlin, 1922.

"Lettre sur le développement économique de la Russie," *Le mouvement socialiste*, VII, No. 93 (1902), 968–972.

"Der politische Indifferentismus," *Die Neue Zeit*, XXXII (1913–1914), No. 1, pp. 40–44.

### KARL MARX AND FRIEDRICH ENGELS

*Historisch-kritische Gesamtausgabe.* Edited by D. Rjazanov. Part (*Abteilung*) I, 7 volumes; Part III, 4 volumes. Berlin, 1927–1932. Referred to in the text and in this bibliography as *Gesamtausgabe*.

*Die Deutsche Ideologie*, in *Gesamtausgabe*, Part I, Vol. 5.

*Aus dem literarischen Nachlass von Karl Marx, Friedrich Engels.* Edited by Franz Mehring. Three volumes. Stuttgart, 1902.

*The Communist Manifesto.* Chicago, 1915.

*Der Briefwechsel zwischen Friedrich Engels und Karl Marx, 1844 bis 1883.* Edited by August Bebel and Eduard Bernstein. Four volumes. Stuttgart, 1913.

*Selected Correspondence, 1846–1895.* Translated by Dona Torr. New York, 1942.

"Unpublished Letters of Karl Marx and Friedrich Engels to Americans," *Science and Society*, II, Nos. 2 and 3 (1938). Translated and edited by Leonard E. Mins.

### FRIEDRICH ENGELS

*The Condition of the Working Class in England in 1844.* Translated by F. K. Wischnewetzky. London, 1892.

*Herr Eugen Dühring's Revolution in Science (Anti-Dühring).* Translated by Emile Burns. New York, 1939.

*Revolution and Counter-Revolution, or Germany in 1848.* Edited by Eleanor Marx Aveling. Chicago, 1907.

*Socialism, Utopian and Scientific.* Translated by Edward Aveling. New York, 1892.

*Feuerbach, the Roots of Socialist Philosophy.* Translated by Austin Lewis. Chicago, 1908. In German: *Ludwig Feuerbach und der Ausgang der klassischen deutschen Philosophie.* Stuttgart, 1919.

*The Origin of the Family, Private Property, and the State.* Translated by Ernest Untermann. Chicago, 1902.

*Grundsätze des Kommunismus.* Edited by Eduard Bernstein. Berlin, 1914.

*The Mark.* Reprinted in *Socialism, Utopian and Scientific*, Appendix, pp. 89–117.

*Dialectics of Nature.* New York, 1940.

"Zur Geschichte des Urchristentums," *Die Neue Zeit,* XIII, No. 1 (1894–1895), 4–13, 36–43.

"Die Bauernfrage in Frankreich und Deutschland," *Die Neue Zeit,* XIII, No. 1 (1894–1895), 292–306.

"Der Anteil der Arbeit an der Menschwerdung der Affen," *Die Neue Zeit,* XIV, No. 2 (1895–1896), 545–554. Reprinted as Chapter IX in *Dialectics of Nature.*

"Zur Kritik des sozialdemokratischen Programmentwurfes 1891," *Die Neue Zeit,* XX, No. 1 (1901–1902), 5–13.

"Über das Autoritätsprinzip," *Die Neue Zeit,* XXXII, No. 1 (1913–1914), 37–39.

"Die Bewegungen von 1847," *Der Kampf,* VI (1912–1913), 207–213.

"Der Anfang des Endes in Oesterreich," *Der Kampf,* VI (1912–1913), 393–397.

"Socialisme de juristes," *Le mouvement socialiste,* XII, No. 132 (1904), 96–120. Translated into French by L. Remy.

## II. OTHER WORKS

ARISTOTLE. *Politics.* Translated by Benjamin Jowett. Oxford, 1916.

BARTH, PAUL. *Die Philosophie der Geschichte als Soziologie.* Leipzig, 1915.

BEARD, C. A. *The Discussion of Human Affairs.* New York, 1936.

BEBEL, AUGUST. *Aus meinem Leben.* Vol. II. Berlin, 1922.

BÖHM-BAWERK, EUGEN. *Karl Marx and the Close of His System.* Translated by A. M. Macdonald. London, 1898.

BROWN, J. F. *Psychology and the Social Order.* New York, 1936.

BRYCE, J. B. *Modern Democracies.* New York, 1921.

CHAMBERLIN, E. H. *The Theory of Monopolistic Competition.* Cambridge, Massachusetts, 1933.

CLARK, G. N. *Science and Social Welfare in the Age of Newton.* Oxford, 1937.

COHEN, MORRIS. "Causation and Its Application to History," *Journal of the History of Ideas,* III (1942), 12–29.

—— AND J. DICKINSON, R. POUND, M. RADIN, AND OTHERS. *My Philosophy Of Law.* Credos of Sixteen American Scholars. Boston, 1941.

COURNOT, AUGUSTIN. *Essai sur les fondements de nos connaissances.* Vol. II. Paris, 1851.

CROCE, BENEDETTO. *Historical Materialism and the Economics of Karl Marx.* Translated by C. M. Meredith. New York, 1914.

CUNOW, HEINRICH. "Technik und Kultur," *Die Neue Zeit,* XXIX, No. 2 (1911), 855–859, 894–902.

DEMPSEY, B. W. *Interest and Usury*. Washington, D. C., 1943.

DEWEY, JOHN. *Creative Intelligence*. New York, 1917.

—— *Human Nature and Conduct*. New York, 1922.

—— *Experience and Nature*. Chicago, 1925.

—— *Logic*. New York, 1938.

DICKINSON, J., AND OTHERS. *My Philosophy of Law*. Boston, 1941.

DUNAYEVSKAYA, RAYA. "A New Revision of Marxian Economics," *American Economic Review*, XXXIV, No. 3 (September 1944), 531–537.

EASTMAN, MAX. *Marxism: Is It Science?* New York, 1940.

EDDINGTON, A. S. *The Nature of the Physical World*. New York, 1929.

EINSTEIN, ALBERT. *Geometrie und Erfahrung*. Berlin, 1921.

—— AND INFELD, L. *The Evolution of Physics*. New York, 1938.

FEDERN, KARL. *The Materialist Conception of History*. London, 1939.

FETTER, F. A. Review of W. Stark, *The History of Economics in Its Relation to Social Development*, in *American Economic Review*, XXXV (1945), 945–946.

FRANK, JEROME. *Law and the Modern Mind*. New York, 1935.

—— *Fate and Freedom*. New York, 1945.

FRAZER, JAMES. *The Golden Bough*. One-volume edition. New York, 1927.

HAECKEL, ERNST H. *The Riddle of the Universe*. New York, 1900.

HANSEN, A. H. "The Technological Interpretation of History," *Quarterly Journal of Economics*, XXXVI (1921–1922), 72–83.

HOFFMAN, R. J. "The Marxian Philosophy of History," *The American Review* (1936), pp. 507–515.

HOGBEN, L. T. *Retreat from Reason*. New York, 1938.

HOLLANDER, J. H., editor. *Letters of David Ricardo to J. R. McCulloch*. Publications of the American Economic Association, X, Nos. 5–6 (1895).

HOOK, SIDNEY. *Towards the Understanding of Karl Marx*. New York, 1933.

—— *From Hegel to Marx*. New York, 1936.

JOAD, C. E. M. *Philosophical Aspects of Modern Science*. New York, 1932.

JOHNSON, A. C., AND OTHERS. *The Greek Political Experience*; *Studies in Honor of William Kelly Prentice*. Princeton, 1941.

KAUTSKY, KARL. "Was will und kann die materialistische Geschichtsauffassung leisten?" *Die Neue Zeit*, XV, No. 1 (1896–1897), 213–218, 228–238, 260–271.

—— "Verelendung und Zusammenbruch," *Die Neue Zeit*, XXVI, No. 2 (1908), 540–551, 607–612.

—— "Die Revision des Programms der Sozialdemokratie in Oesterreich," *Die Neue Zeit*, XX, No. 1 (1901–1902), 68–82.

—— *The Dictatorship of the Proletariat.* Translated by J. H. Stenning. London, 1919.

KEYNES, J. M. *Laissez–Faire and Communism.* New Republic edition. New York, 1926.

—— *Essays in Biography.* New York, 1933.

—— *General Theory of Employment, Interest and Money.* New York, 1936.

—— "The General Theory of Employment," *Quarterly Journal of Economics*, LI (February 1937), 209–223.

KNIGHT, F. H. *The Ethics of Competition and Other Essays.* New York, 1935.

—— "Some Notes on the Economic Interpretation of History." *Studies in the History of Culture* (1942), pp. 217–231.

KNIGHT, M. M. *Economic History of Europe to the End of the Middle Ages.* Boston, 1926.

LANGE, O. R. "The Rate of Interest and the Optimum Propensity to Consume," *Readings in Business Cycle Theory.* Selected by a Committee of the American Economic Association. Philadelphia, 1944.

—— "Marxian Economics and Modern Economic Theory," *Review of Economic Studies*, II, No. 3, pp. 189–201.

—— "Marxian Economics in the Soviet Union," *American Economic Review*, XXXV, No. 1 (March 1945), 127–133.

LENIN, V. I. *Staat und Revolution.* Berlin-Wilmersdorf, 1918.

LEONTIEF, WASSILY W. "The Significance of Marxian Economics for Present Day Economic Theory," *American Economic Review*, XXVIII, Supplement (1938), 1–9.

LIEBKNECHT, WILHELM. *Karl Marx, Biographical Memoirs.* Translated by Ernest Untermann. Chicago, 1908.

LOWIE, R. H. *Primitive Society.* New York, 1925.

MACIVER, R. M. *The Modern State.* London, 1926.

MALTHUS, T. R. *Principles of Political Economy.* London, 1820.

MANDELBAUM, M. H. *The Problem of Historical Knowledge.* New York, 1938.

MARSHALL, ALFRED. *Industry and Trade.* London, 1919.

—— *Principles of Economics.* Eighth edition. London, 1922.

MARTIN, J. "Socialism and the Class War," *Quarterly Journal of Economics*, XXIII (1908–1909), 512–517.

MASON, E. S. *The Paris Commune.* New York, 1930.

—— "Industrial Concentration and the Decline of Competition," in *Explorations in Economics: Notes and Essays Contributed in Honor of F. W. Taussig.* New York, 1936.

MASON, O. T. *The Origins of Invention.* London, 1895.

MATHEWS, SHAILER. *The Spiritual Interpretation of History*. Cambridge, Massachusetts, 1916.

MAUTNER, WILHELM. *Der Bolschewismus*. Berlin, 1920.

MENGER, ANTON. *The Right to the Whole Produce of Labor*. Translated by M. E. Tanner. New York, 1899.

MERTON, R. K. "Science and the Economy of Seventeenth-Century England," *Science and Society*, III, No. 1 (1939).

—— "Puritanism, Pietism and Science," *Sociological Review*, XXVIII, No. 1 (1936).

MILL, JOHN STUART. *Principles of Political Economy*. Ashley's edition. London, 1923.

—— *System of Logic*. Two volumes. London, 1851.

PARETO, VILFREDO. *Systèmes socialistes*. Vol II. Paris, 1902.

PARSONS, TALCOTT. *The Structure of Social Action*. New York, 1937.

PIGOU, A. C. *Economics of Welfare*. Second edition. London, 1924.

POINCARÉ, HENRI. *Science and Method*. Translated by F. Maitland. New York, 1914.

POUND, ROSCOE. *Interpretations of Legal History*. New York, 1923.

REICHENBACH, HANS. *Philosophic Foundations of Quantum Mechanics*. Berkeley, California, 1944.

RICARDO, DAVID. *The Principles of Political Economy and Taxation*. Everyman edition, 1917.

RJAZANOV, DAVID, editor. *Marx-Engels, Archiv*. Vol. I. Frankfurt, 1927.

ROBBINS, LIONEL. *An Essay on the Nature and Significance of Economic Science*. New York, 1937.

ROBINSON, MRS. JOAN. *Essay on Marxian Economics*. London, 1942.

—— "Marx on Unemployment," *Economic Journal*, LI (June–September 1941), 234–248.

ROBSON, W. A. *Civilization and the Growth of Law*. New York, 1935.

RUSSELL, BERTRAND. *Selected Papers*. New York: The Modern Library, 1927.

SARTON, GEORGE. *The Study of the History of Mathematics*. Cambridge, Massachusetts, 1936.

—— The History of Science and the New Humanism. Cambridge, Massachusetts, 1937.

SCHUMPETER, J. A. *The Theory of Economic Development*. Cambridge, Massachusetts, 1934.

—— *Capitalism, Socialism and Democracy*. New York, 1942.

SHOVE, G. F. "Mrs. Robinson on Marxian Economics," *Economic Journal*, LIV (April 1944), 47–61.

SMITH, ADAM. *Theory of Moral Sentiments*. Vol. I of *Works of Adam Smith*. London, 1812.

—— *Wealth of Nations*. Everyman edition, 1917.

SOGGE, T. M. "Industrial Classes in the United States in 1930," *Journal of the American Statistical Association*, June 1933.

SOMBART, WERNER. "Technik und Kultur," *Archiv für Sozialwissenschaft und Sozialpolitik*, XXXIII (1911), 305–347.

—— *Grundlagen und Kritik des Sozialismus*. Vol. I. Berlin, 1919.

STEKLOFF, G. M. *History of the First International*. Translated by Eden and Cedar Paul. New York, 1928.

SWEEZY, P. M. *The Theory of Capitalist Development*. New York, 1942.

TAUSSIG, F. W. *Principles of Economics*. Third edition, Vol. II. New York, 1921.

TOZZER, A. M. *Social Origins and Social Continuities*. New York, 1925.

TUGAN-BARANOWSKY, M. I. *Theoretische Grundlagen des Marxismus*. Leipzig, 1905.

USHER, A. P. *History of Mechanical Inventions*. New York, 1929.

VEBLEN, THORSTEIN. *The Place of Science in Modern Civilization*. New York, 1919.

WHITEHEAD, A. N. *Science and the Modern World*. New York, 1926.

YOUNG, A. A. "The Trend of Economics," *Quarterly Journal of Economics*, XXXIX (1924–1925), 155–183.

# INDEX